Urban Transport Economics

Urban Transport Economics

EDITED BY

DAVID A. HENSHER
Commonwealth Bureau of Roads, Australia,
and Macquarie University

CAMBRIDGE UNIVERSITY PRESS
CAMBRIDGE
LONDON · NEW YORK · MELBOURNE

Published by the Syndics of the Cambridge University Press
The Pitt Building, Trumpington Street, Cambridge CB2 1RP
Bentley House, 200 Euston Road, London NW1 2DB
32 East 57th Street, New York, NY 10022, USA
296 Beaconsfield Parade, Middle Park, Melbourne 3206, Australia

First published 1977

Photoset and Printed in Malta by Interprint (Malta) Ltd

Library of Congress Cataloguing in Publication Data

Main entry under title:
Urban transport economics.

Includes index.
1. Urban transportation – Addresses, essays, lectures.
I. Hensher, David A., 1947–
HE305.U69 388.4′042 76-11061
ISBN 0 521 21128 X hard covers
ISBN 0 521 29140 2 paperback

Contents

Contributors

John Beggs	Queensland Department of Main Roads and Department of Economics, University of Queensland
George Docwra	Department of Economics, University of Queensland
Alan Duhs	Department of Economics, University of Queensland
Peter Forsyth	School of Economics, University of New South Wales
Stein Hansen	Institute for International Development, Harvard University
Patrick Healey	Royal Commission on Human Relationships, New South Wales
David Hensher	Commonwealth Bureau of Roads, Australia and Macquarie University
Stuart Hicks	School of Economics, University of New South Wales
William Hotchkiss	School of Economics, University of New South Wales
Helmut Kolsen	Department of Economics, University of Queensland
Christopher Nash	Institute for Transport Studies, University of Leeds
John Paterson	John Paterson Urban Systems Pty Ltd, Melbourne
Peter Rimmer	Department of Human Geography, Research School of Pacific Studies, The Australian National University
John Stanley	Commonwealth Bureau of Roads, Australia

Acknowledgements

During the course of writing this book, many individuals have devoted considerable time in commenting on the basic outline of the document and on individual chapters. The contributors must be thanked for their enthusiastic support. We are indebted to others, in particular Ambi Ambirajan (University of New South Wales), Clem Tisdell (Newcastle University), John Flemming (Nuffield College, University of Oxford), Tony Harrison (UK Department of the Environment), Phil Goodwin (Greater London Council), David Pearce (Leicester University), Max Neutze and John Black (Australian National University), Ian Heggie (University of Oxford) and Tony Shaw (Bureau of Transport Economics, Canberra).

Unless otherwise specified, Australian dollars have been used throughout.

I

Introduction

D. A. Hensher

Transport economics has developed into an important specialisation, drawing on the theoretical base of microeconomics and a variety of interdisciplinary concepts. The writing of a book in the area of urban transport economics is a challenging and rewarding task, drawing on the talents of a group of individuals from a variety of backgrounds. The chapters in this book have been written with a common objective of providing a much needed textbook in urban transport economics.

While a book on urban transport economics draws heavily on economic concepts, in recent years there has been an extensive interdisciplinary effort in the search for an understanding of urban transport issues, and for this reason the economics emphasis has become part of a more diversified approach to issues having an economic theme. This has been mellowed by social, political and institutional constraints of sufficient magnitude to require their explicit consideration as major influencing forces in an economic exposition of transport requirements and policy prescription. This book on urban transport economics would not be contributing to the field of transportation methods and practice if these other issues were not discussed.

A basic theme emerging from the entire book is the allocation of scarce resources between alternative ends, these ends defined according to the particular context, but often within the limits of the transport sector of the economy and its relationship to location and urban structure. The price mechanism is an active central mechanism in resource allocation, but its presumed simple relevance is soon clouded by the complexity of the urban transport market, which precludes the derivation of simple rules of thumb for pricing. The use of price policy in achieving objectives, its limitations and the possible need for non-price methods (regulation) are discussed in detail by Kolsen and Dowcra (ch. 2) and Forsyth (ch. 3). The interdependence between transport and land use (chs. 8, 9) requires the application of regulation and planning. However, this must accord with principles which achieve objectives concerned with the welfare of urban dwellers. Chapters 2 and 3 describe how prices and costs provide a basic mechanism which puts a constraint on how far it is possible to adopt other principles. Issues of location, transport and other relevant matters should be systematically related to each other and modifications made to any unconstrained outcome associated with the basic pricing principle when there is a clear argument for, and community acceptance of, the direct or implied subsidy or tax which deviation from this systematic price–cost relationship implies.

Forsyth develops pricing arguments in the context of constraints, such as the commitment of government to cover its costs, and its ability to use prices and taxes to influence income distribution. If everything was optimally arranged throughout the economy, prices should be equal to marginal cost. Distortions in the economy and governmental policies may lead to suboptimality: taxation is one such example, unless it can be made non-marginal as in the case of lump-sum taxes. These will be socially regressive, so the problem for the government is to find some pattern of taxation (subsidy) which minimises the cost of distortions to consumption patterns or work/leisure choices. Multiple objectives and constraints create a necessity to modify simple pricing rules.

Efficient and equitable allocation of resources requires a set of rules to identify alternatives and the content of relevant issues and items to consider. While the pricing methodology and application provides a basic underlying rationale for the rules of allocation, it does not fulfil the need for a framework in which the alternatives can be evaluated. The use of cost–benefit analysis for the evaluation of urban transport improvements is now widely accepted as being superior to any rules of thumb. Two chapters dicuss a number of important issues in cost–benefit analysis in a general context (ch. 4 – Hotchkiss) and then in the urban transport context (ch. 5 – Stanley and Nash). In simple terms, cost–benefit analysis is a framework for careful consideration of the costs and benefits of alternative courses of action, quantified in money terms wherever possible, as a rational method of social decision-taking. Despite the popular appeal of this method, it has many shortcomings, in particular its adoption of the assumption of a constant marginal utility of income, and the limitation of the user benefit variable set to easily quantifiable influences. Stanley and Nash group the shortcomings under the headings of the philosophical basis of cost–benefit analysis, the applicability of the prices attached to those effects of transport improvements typically considered (e.g. time savings, accident reductions), and the wide range of effects that are typically not considered at all in formal cost–benefit analysis. The criticism of the technique should not be taken as a rejection of its usefulness, but rather as a warning that the technique can be (and often is) misused because of a lack of detailed knowledge as to how the numerical results are typically derived, and because of the assumptions governing the modelling procedures. The overemphasis on quantification has provided open ammunition for a criticism of its ability to account for social implications associated with alternatives. While social evaluation methods (e.g. public participation to establish views of different groups on project consequences) are briefly referred to in chapter 5, they are developed in greater detail in a later chapter (ch. 11 – Healey) where the scope of evaluation as a guide to decision-makers is broadened by shifting the emphasis from technique to process.

Underlying any evaluation of alternatives and the determination of the future patterns of movement of people and goods within urban areas is required knowledge of the demand for movement. This requires us to investigate the influencing factors behind the decision processes leading to acts of choice, the existing choices providing an initial basis for determining expected usage of a facility. Hensher (ch. 6) and Hicks (ch. 7) outline respectively the passenger and freight considerations which need to be investigated in order to gain an understanding of what the basic influences of the demand for travel are. The state of the art is more advanced on the passenger side, and so more rigour is possible in modelling. This does not, however, dispel a belief that the passenger transport problem is less complex than the freight problem. It simply reflects a conscious commitment in the past to a belief that the urban passenger problem was more important, to the relative neglect of the urban freight problem. Hicks provides a thorough discussion of the nature of urban freight, the costs of urban freight movement, the cost of urban structure, and some potential solutions to achieving movement and terminal efficiency.

An important consideration in chapters 6 and 7 is the identification of the basic unit of analysis, because the approach to modelling and evaluation is highly influenced by the assumption of the investigation unit. In passenger travel studies, until recently, the basic unit has been the geographical zone, comprising a heterogeneous mixture of traveller types (in terms of socio-economic characteristics and other choice influences), which has the associated restriction of within-zone variance often exceeding between-zone variance on relevant determinants of travel choice. While more behavioural based models using the individual traveller as the basic unit of analysis, and drawing on utility theory, are now available, data limitations have still heavily constrained the opportunity to apply improved models in operational contexts. These matters are developed in detail by Hensher. Rimmer (ch. 10) devotes a considerable amount of space to the identification of the roles of various actors in the transport decision-making process. This helps to decide on the appropriate unit of analysis in passenger and freight demand analysis. For example, is the consignment or the vehicle the operational unit? This is related to the aspect of level of analysis aggregation. Does information loss increase as the level of aggregation increases? Hensher investigates this matter for passenger movement, while Rimmer outlines the aggregation implications associated with various assumptions on the roles of actors as the conceptual units in the transport decision-making process.

Since the urban transport problem is an integral part of the urban problem, it is necessary to examine the dependency between urban structure and transport networks. In an operational context the allowance for this mutual interdependence is complex, with the result that the majority of transport investigations have been limited in usefulness by the assumption that land use is given and is at best modified according to transport adjustments, rather than any dual-directional effects. Hansen (ch. 8) and Paterson (ch. 9) relate the transport problem to locational considerations as part of the determination of urban structure. Hansen identifies the typical characteristics of the development of urban structures, and focuses attention on some major theoretical findings from equilibrium models that have to be seriously considered by those working as practising urban planners. The chapter concludes with attention drawn to model frameworks for integrated land-use transport planning that explicitly try to recognise those desirable model characteristics identified at the beginning of the chapter, such as indivisibility, interdependency, welfare criteria, uncertainty, spatial and sectorial disaggregation, and foundations in behavioural theories. Paterson complements Hansen's chapter, beginning with the centrally dominated general equilibrium models of Wingo, Muth, Alonso, and Mills as the point of departure, and investigating the key relationship between accessibility and location premiums in the context of this class of conceptual models. Visualisation of the city in terms of a multitude of overlapping fields of accessibility is shown to permit a more flexible approach to the modelling of transport-land-use interactions than is possible within the context of the centralised general equilibrium models. Both chapters cite empirical evidence to support their argument.

Since the basic requirement in cost–benefit analysis is aggregating and trading off various effects which have relatively 'easily' identifiable market values, this raises serious problems with many social costs and benefits which cannot easily be expressed in this way. Chapter 11 outlines the development and role of sociological input into transport issues, which were at first in the past handled more or less as engineering matters and only subsequently as economic problems. Initially, when sociologists entered transport planning to provide social impact statements of road projects, what was often required of them was that they should express social factors in a monetary form in order to introduce them into an overall cost–benefit analysis. Many freeway opposition groups currently consider that a comprehensive evaluation of this kind is desirable in road planning and demand that cost–benefit analysis should be carried out before road plans are finalised. What is generally not understood is that in cost–benefit analysis evaluation the broad range of social factors expressed in monetary terms will always be relatively less significant than a small number of other costs and benefits in the calculation. The attempt by the Commonwealth Bureau of Roads (Australia) in its cost–benefit analysis calculations of urban roads projects to incorporate social costs by doubling housing acquisition costs demonstrated this. Even with this doubling, the social costs in dollar terms had less overall influence in determining warranted projects than other factors. Situations arise therefore, in which the transport planner is dealing with a wide range of fundamental social factors, and yet he cannot in any sense adequately allow for this through the economic weighting of these factors in cost–benefit analysis.

The assumptions and the requirements of cost–benefit evaluation will inevitably mean that many social objectives, whether generally supported or sympathetic only to the interests of particular factions, will be excluded. Cost–benefit analysis in transport planning is consistent with the pursuit of only a very select number of objectives, and is incompatible with the broad range of social and political goals articulated by diverse interests in society. These matters are developed further by Healey as a basis for suggesting that social and environmental evaluation in planning may mean that in the future conflicts will concern explicit choices between goals of a more general significance than those implicit in engineering, economic or narrow impact evaluation.

Much of the operational expression of transportation planning in urban areas is exemplified by transportation studies. The concluding chapter is designed principally to illustrate the general attitudes in planning to the utilisation of economic concepts, and to provide a critical appraisal of the extent to which such studies are satisfactory methods of representing the urban transport problem from an economic and social perspective. Chapter 12 (Duhs and Beggs) examines the methodology of the urban transportation plan in terms of data collection, analytical models and evaluation. A particular concern is the evaluation of alternative plans reflecting alternative town plans and modal split (the relative use of different modes of transport) possibilities, and varying assumptions on the valuation of time saving, the selection of discount rate(s) and summary criteria, the treatment of uncertainty, the analysis of major plan components, and institutional constraints.

The entire book is written as a comprehensive frame of reference for identifying the key issues in urban transport economics, with an additional emphasis on the relationship between economics and other disciplinary implications of the urban transport problem.

2

Resource allocation, price theory and policy

H. M. Kolsen and G. Docwra

Introduction

There is a well established body of knowledge in the classical tradition which carefully ties together the price, output, and investment policies of entities pursuing economic activities on the production side with the choices exercised by users or consumers on the consumption side.

In such a system, with perfect competition between production entities, and perfect knowledge and availability of alternatives for consumers, communication between producers and consumers was achieved through prices. If consumer demand declined for a commodity, its price would fall in the short run, its production would become unprofitable at the existing output level, and its output would be reduced. If consumer demand increased for a commodity, its price would rise in the short run, its production would become more profitable at the existing output level, and its output would be increased in the long run. When everything had settled down, the new pattern of outputs would again reflect consumer demand. Prices would be related to costs in a systematic way, because if they did not, producers would increase those outputs which were more profitable, i.e. for which price exceeded costs more than was the case for other possible outputs.

Some of the mechanisms of this automatic system of adjusting output to user demand do not adequately perform the functions assumed for them in the perfect system. There are many reasons for this, but they can conveniently be grouped into two categories. One is that the community, through its governments, provides an institutional framework which, in many cases, provides alternative solutions to those which would have been produced by the automatic system. The system then works under what Mishan has called the 'Virtual Constitution'.[1] This group includes all the reasons which governments have accepted in regulating the system to achieve results different from those which would have been achieved under the automatic system. These reasons have priority over the 'reasons' of the invisible hand.

The second group includes reasons which indicate that even without government regulation the system would not have been able to achieve its avowed objective, the highest level of satisfaction for consumers under given constraints of scarcity and technical knowledge. One of the most important of these is to be found in the deficiencies of the adjustment mechanism when there is interdependence between the price, output, and investment decisions of otherwise unconnected production entities, and particularly when each produces outputs which are very expensive and last a long time. This rather technical description deserves an example to show that it describes a very real problem. In the urban context, a decision by a road supplier to build a road from *A* to *B* has an effect on the uses to which the land at, around, and between *A* and *B* can be put. It will have this effect for as long as the road is kept in existence. The value of land at and between *A* and *B* changes. Furthermore, the increased use made by people of this land, whether for residential, industrial or commercial purposes, will change demand for transport in other parts of the region. The same arguments apply to rail suppliers, and to independently determined changes in existing land uses.

The consumer is still trying to maximise his satisfaction in this system, but has very imperfect knowledge. He will still try to make the best of any situation with which he is confronted, but it will no longer be possible to say that this represents the best of all possible economic worlds. If the road had been constructed from *A* to *C*, or a railway instead of the road, would he have been better off or worse off? The point is simply that land usage and transport and different transport modes are interdependent, and decisions about one taken without reference to the others will put the consumer in the best possible position only by an unlikely and very lucky accident. The interdependence must be recognised at the outset and the decision to change anything (e.g. land use or transport), must be made by reference to all the interdependent factors.

No one would argue this to be an easy exercise. The discussion here was only intended to show that policy objectives, broadly defined as making the consumer as well off as he can possibly be under given economic, institutional, and technical constraints, cannot be achieved effectively by an unaided automatic system – the invisible hand – in the urban transport field.

In the first section we take up the question of resource allocation in the urban transport sector. The broad policy objective is examined in the second section, with a discussion of the uses of price policy in achieving objectives, and their limitations and the possible need for non-price methods (regulation) in the third section; the fourth section examines actual price policies pursued by transport suppliers; finally there is a brief conclusion which attempts to place the discussion of urban transport policies in an appropriate time perspective.

Economic efficiency and resource allocation in urban transport

Resource allocation problems arise at a number of levels. There is the problem of efficient allocation: this refers to the value of benefits which flow from a marginal unit of expenditure. If all expenditure decisions are made 'efficiently', the value of the benefits will be equal for all conceivable marginal types of expenditure. This will theoretically apply in all sectors (urban and non-urban) of transport expenditure. Though this utopian principle is quite universal in application, it should be pointed out that the actual pattern of outputs would depend on the way in which income and wealth are distributed. The point here is to establish the principle; discussion of what are and are not 'good' distributions of income and wealth are beyond the scope of this chapter (see chs. 4, 5).

It is difficult to apply the principle of economic efficiency in practice to the more general problems in resource allocation, such as the problem of determining optimum city size. Though there is much discussion to the contrary, there is no standard city. Each location has particular advantages and disadvantages with respect to economies and diseconomies in providing services, including transport. Furthermore, the benefits from larger population concentrations, such as wider ranges of job and education opportunities, recreation and entertainment, and variety of environment, are not easily quantified. Transport is but one of the many aspects of city development, and few people would want to build a city which has as its sole objective the minimisation of transport costs.

Within the urban area, the application of the principle still faces major obstacles. A major problem is the obvious interdependence of land use and transport. Decisions about what are regarded as desirable land-use patterns must be made prior to decisions about modal choice, but cannot be made efficiently without information about the effects of alternative land-use patterns on transport costs and qualities. Land use, as such, is not our concern in this chapter (see chs. 8, 9).

What is our concern, however, is that the appropriate information about transport costs is available to those making land-use decisions, and that the transport modes supplied satisfy broadly the requirements of economic efficiency. This requires that land-use patterns, no matter what they are, are serviced by transport modes in such a way that a marginal unit of expenditure on transport will roughly return the same value of benefit, no matter where in the transport system it is spent.

Apart from the problem of interdependence, there are many other reasons why the market cannot be expected to supply transport services which would be regarded as efficient in terms of relative quantities and qualities. Thus road space is not sold in the usual way, nor is it supplied whenever and wherever it makes a profit. Public transport systems follow price and supply policies which are a far cry from what would result in the absence of severe regulation of any alternative suppliers. Many of the market's inabilities are the result of intervention by various institutions to control, regulate, encourage and, more often, discourage various transport activities. Thus hire-and-reward operation by owners of private cars not holding a taxi licence is not permitted, for reasons which were generated in the 1920s when few people owned cars, but which may no longer have much relevance to the circumstances of today. For all these and other reasons, evaluations of alternatives must take this non-market generated information into consideration, and a cost–benefit methodology for doing so can be used.

Because road space is not sold in the usual way, high-demand road space has a 'price' similar to low demand road space. Hence high demand road space is not rationed by price, but by congestion and overcrowding of transport services. In the absence of an increased supply of road space where demand is high, failure to ration it by price or other means has caused increases in the use of the private motor vehicle and reduced public transport patronage during the off-peak periods. It has become increasingly difficult, and in most cases impossible, for the suppliers of public transport services to operate without subsidy. This in turn has affected the quantity or capacity they are prepared to provide for peak-hour purposes. A substantial part of the increase in peak-hour traffic has thus been met by overcrowding and infrequent services.

It is clear that the problems we have described above are capable of being solved. It is possible both in a technical and economic sense to provide better quality urban transport services and facilities. The question which requires an answer is: What form of urban transportation is likely to be most efficient? What is efficient and what is best frequently means different things to different people. In the case of urban transportation, what people view as the ingredients of an efficient transport system is frequently no more than a reflection of their likes and dislikes for the various transport modes and/or alternative land-use patterns. In what follows we attempt a brief outline of the meaning of the concept of efficiency to the economist and examine the implications for urban transport policies.

To the economist the answer to the question of whether one policy is more efficient than another or, alternatively whether one configuration of community resource use is more efficient than another depends on the relationship between the value of outputs (benefits) and the value of inputs (costs) associated with each alternative. In a fully employed economy the economic or opportunity cost of producing more of one output, say road space, is the value of the output of some other good or service (the best alternative) which has to be forgone. As far as conventional economic theory is concerned the value of output is, subject to various qualifications, measured by what consumers or users are prepared to pay, while the value of inputs, again subject to qualifications, is measured by the price paid by producers.[2] The qualifications include, *inter alia*, that the appropriate adjustments for externalities are made, and that input prices reflect their real resource cost. Thus an efficient allocation of resources is achieved (for a particular distribution of income) when it is not possible to produce by a reallocation of resources a combination of outputs which is more highly valued by the community. A crude example will serve to illustrate this point. Let us suppose that two equal cost outputs X and Y are produced and that the prices paid for each output at the margin are respectively \$1.20 and \$1.30. Under these circumstances the price–cost ratios for each output differ and consequently it is possible by shifting resources from X to Y to increase the total value of output until such time as the price–cost ratios are equal. As has been argued elsewhere, it is more important from the standpoint of efficiency to ensure that price–cost ratios (more formally, price–long-run marginal cost ratios) are similar for substitutes than it is for commodities which are not close substitutes.[3]

The same kind of methodology forms the basis of what is known in the literature as cost–benefit analysis (see ch. 4).[4] This technique is frequently used to assess the relative worthwhileness of alternative uses of resources (given a budgetary constraint) in those circumstances where for one reason or another, the price system does not work effectively. In this situation the economist attempts to estimate by various means the amounts consumers would pay for outputs if it were possible to charge them, i.e. an attempt is made to ascertain by substitute methods an estimate of benefits. In this way the net benefits of alternative projects or plans (given the distribution of income) are determined. It follows that in determining whether one set of proposals aimed at improving the quantity/quality of urban transportation is more efficient than another requires an appraisal of both the value placed by consumers on the various outputs and the resource costs involved.

There is, however, another aspect of the concept of efficiency which needs to be mentioned. There is obviously a range of efficient solutions to the urban transport problem, each of which is related to the number and kind of constraints which are accepted by those who are responsible for controlling and regulating the urban transport market. Thus, for example, if a decision is made to preclude the possibility of increasing the supply of road space in city areas, the modal mix of an efficient urban transport system will be different from that which would result if such a constraint were not accepted. Thus there will be different, but 'efficient' outcomes according to what is accepted regarding price and investment policies for road space, patterns of land use, regulation of private vehicles for hire during peak periods, institutional arrangements and so on.

Policy objectives

To state that the objective of pricing and/or regulatory policy in urban transport is to make the user or consumer as well off as it is possible to make him requires a large number of interpretations of possible meanings. Thus there is the question of the user's judgement. Is it to be final, without any paternalistic questioning of the level of the user's wisdom? The answer is no, but it is a constrained no. There is here, as everywhere, the institutional framework within which he makes his choice. There will be choices which the community will disallow, whether for good reason or bad. Where his choices affect the welfare of others, again there is need for intervention. Where there is lack of knowledge about alternatives, there is a need to increase that knowledge. But having intervened where necessary to ensure that the community's will is defined, and to ensure that harmful effects on others are adequately controlled, and presented him with adequate information on alternatives, then there is no further point in directing him towards one alternative rather than another. If he chooses to wear his clothes longer and eat cheaper foods in order to have a block of land further from the city centre than some others do, or a better car, then this is hardly irrational behaviour.

It is also true that the institutional framework within which he makes his choices must be questioned, and adjusted at regular intervals since reasons which were good a century ago may not be (and usually are not) good today. The method for changing many institutional details is through the political mechanism, and we can hardly discuss this in detail in a chapter on price theory and policy, even if we knew much about it. We will restrict ourselves to discussions of changes in the institutional framework only where these are highly relevant to the workings of some part of urban transport systems, and where they are alternatives to pricing policies.

Another aspect of the freedom-of-user-choice-within-constraints discussion in achieving the maximum-satisfaction-within-constraints objective is the question of what are the accepted constraints. The technical constraints are clear. If we cannot costlessly dematerialise a person at *A* and costlessly rematerialise him at *B*, then this is a sad but very real constraint on our ability to shift him from *A* to *B*. The known means of transport are all we have to work with. The economic constraints are not quite so clear-cut. If prices are given, different income levels and preferences will produce different demands for price–quality bundles of transport outputs. Strap-hanging on a bus when a chauffeur-driven Rolls Royce is available can be explained by differences in incomes, differences in preferences, or perhaps by extreme idiosyncracy.

Economists find themselves in real difficulties here. On the one hand it can be easily shown that a given sum of money transferred from the Rolls Royce occupant to the strap-hanger will produce more additional economic welfare for the strap-hanger than an equivalent expenditure on giving the strap-hanger a higher quality transport service or the same quality at a lower price. This is because the strap-hanger can make a choice about how he spends the sum of money given to him, and spending it on better transport is but one of many possibilities. It will depend on his tastes. But if his transport means are subsidised, he is forced to spend the income transfer on transport even if he would otherwise have a choice to buy more steak, a larger or better house, or spend it on his own or his children's education.

The last example is thrown in to show that many objectives more laudable than better transport might result from a cash transfer. Unless the transfer is for a purpose considered meritorious for reasons thought to be beyond the immediate comprehension of the user, e.g. for the education of his children or for some acceptable paternalist reason, it makes the recipient better off to give him cash than to fiddle with the relative prices at which he buys his transport services.

On the other hand, it is frequently very difficult to make adequate cash transfers, and the relative inefficiency with which it is done through transport services may be argued to be worth putting up with if there is no alternative. We cannot accept this argument. This is because the income transfer, through the transport system, is still trying to achieve an equity objective, namely, a more equal distribution of real income than is possible without it. No one would argue that such transfers were desirable if the strap-hanger was richer than the motorist. The problem is to ensure that the benefits from such subsidies do indeed flow to the poorest sections of the community with a minimum of side effects for the rich. Transport subsidies are a very blunt and inaccurate instrument by which to achieve that objective, especially since few poor people own central business district real estate and subsidised public transport certainly increases its value.

Our own conclusion need not be yours. But unless it can be shown that subsidising transport prices has more beneficial effects on income distribution than subsidising anything else (food, clothing, electricity, housing etc.) and that it is impossible to achieve the income distribution results by any other means, it is clear that transport prices are an inefficient way of achieving income distribution objectives. Finally, we might mention that transport authorities are hardly qualified to make decisions about income redistribution[5] and would have to be subjected to very close control in carrying out this function as a deliberate policy objective.[6]

Price policy and regulation

Various methods exist for achieving any particular result in the urban transport context. Price policy can be used as an 'inducement' to guide users onto particular transport modes at particular times. Other methods of a prescriptive or proscriptive type are also available. For example, a high parking charge at certain places and at certain times may be an alternative to a complete ban on parking. In many cases, a combination of both is used. Parking may be entirely prohibited in certain roads during peak hours, permitted subject to a charge between peaks, and permitted free at night.

The general attitude of urban authorities on which methods are most approrpriate seems to be remarkably homogeneous. We hasten to add that this is largely the result of common ignorance rather than common knowledge. There have been few discussions of the relative merits of alternative policies until recent times, though related matters such as the inability to use one or some methods and the effects of this on a particular problem have received considerable airing as part of the general problem of second best in the urban transport area.[7]

What are the major non-price policies, and what effects are they thought to have? There is, in nearly all cities, a restriction on what transport may be supplied for hire-and-reward. The number and types of vehicles permitted to take fare-paying passengers are determined by various authorities. It is against the law to accept fare-paying passengers in a private motorcar other than a duly licensed taxi or hire car. Similarly, regular bus services are provided either by a public authority undertaking, or by licensed and controlled private operators. Privately supplied rail services are not available. This is, then, a major area in which private supply is not permitted at all, or permitted subject to rigorous regulation.

It is difficult to find reasons for some of these restrictions unless some reference is made to their historical background. At the time when most of these regulations were formulated, circumstances were very different from what they are now. With the possible exception of the USA, car ownership was not very widespread in the 1920s and early 1930s. The private car was not a viable alternative urban transport mode. Bus operation was dominated by the thought that it must be on regular routes and according to published timetables, and buses 'snatching' passengers were referred to as 'pirates' in England, and their operations phased out. The virtues of the effective monopoly achieved by the public authority supplier were the ability to provide an integrated network of services at regulated prices, permitting internal cross-subsidisation to provide some services regarded to be desirable in the public interest even if they could not be justified by the revenue they produced.

The extent to which such regulations are still necessary in the 1970s to achieve the objectives of regularity and coordination is worth a short but necessarily inadequate discussion. The missing links in most discussions of this subject are the efficiency and adequacy of the resulting system of transport services. Merely requiring regular and coordinated services does not ensure that the regulation and coordination achieve the results expected of them. And it is the effects of a policy which must concern us.

The regulated public authority transport services face competition from privately supplied ancillary personal transport which is usually less directly regulated (so long as it remains ancillary), but subject to some other constraints such as inability to park, or high cost of parking. This competition is provided by a very wide range of cost–quality bundles running from the motor scooter to the chauffeur-driven Rolls. Given the constraints on the destination end, the user compares the cost–quality bundle he can supply with those supplied by the public transport authorities, and selects that which he regards as best for his purpose. The refusal, in the past, to provide any variety in the cost–quality bundles offered by public transport authorities means that many passengers which could have been retained on the public transport system by a different cost–quality mix to the one actually supplied are lost to the privately supplied alternative.[8]

The point is that public transport suppliers have not responded to the widening range of privately supplied cost–quality transport bundles. Very little experimentation with mini-buses, express buses, reserved seat buses, or reserved seat trains, etc. has taken place. The coordinated system of regular services does not attempt to match the variety privately available, but contents itself with running standard vehicles on standard routes. Though the vehicles have improved since the 1930s, variety has not.

Whether a coordinated system running to regular timetables produces an effective and efficient transport network thus depends on the quality of the services produced, and how effectively they compete with those produced under the restrictions imposed on private suppliers. In the absence of effective response by public transport suppliers, one might ask whether fewer restrictions on private supply might not have desirable effects. The mini-bus services in Hong Kong, originally supplied illegally, were eventually permitted to operate under licences which did not require them to work fixed routes at stated times.[9] Nor does it bend the mind too much to explore the possibilities of permitting private cars, insured and licensed for this purpose, to pick up fare-paying passengers if they so wish. This would usually take place on their way to and from work. Indeed, since it is the journey to and from work which creates most of the problems, the operation of private cars as hire-and-reward carriers could be restricted to the hours during which most work journeys take place.

It will have become clear that price policies which have objectives of influencing modal choices have not been used with great vigour. It is true that public transport suppliers usually operate at a loss, but until recently this was not claimed to be the result of deliberate policy to induce more people to use public transport. It has long been argued by many economists that a congestion tax could be levied on these using city roads during the peak, by a variety of readily available methods.[10]

Although price policies aimed at influencing modal choice are not much used, this does not mean that the price 'policies' which are used do not have any effect. Thus prices are charged for public and private transport services, but they are charged within a general framework thought to be dominated by non-price influences and directions. While this may be thought to be the case, transport users continue to make their choices within the constraints imposed upon them and costs, prices and qualities are a very important part of the information on the basis of which they ultimately make their decisions. Users can thus be nudged into making what is regarded as the 'right' decision by a judicious combination of price and non-price inducements.

One of the most important factors under the control of transport authorities is the supply of urban and city road space. No adequate discussion is possible here, but ultimately the major decisions faced by transport authorities include decisions about where and when additional road space should be supplied. This takes us far afield, and includes the question of the nature of future central business districts in which communication technology requires less eyeball contact and for which highly concentrated activity centres may well be less important.

Actual price policies pursued by transport suppliers

Major concern here is with hire-and-reward transport suppliers, and particularly public transport suppliers. It is interesting to note that public transport suppliers in urban areas follow fairly similar basic price policies, whether it be in London, Sydney or New York. As mentioned earlier, this is not necessarily, or perhaps even possibly, the result of careful analyses of the alternatives. The selection of price policies is usually made on the bases of administrative convenience, and apparent equity, as seen through the eyes of those who made decisions in the 1920s and 1930s.

The normal price policy is a basic structure of prices which are a function of distance travelled. In many cases there is a distance taper, so that the price per mile falls as the number of miles travelled rises. The rough objective is to recover costs, or as much of them as possible, from a fare structure based on distance. If the gap between total costs and total revenues becomes too wide, and if it is not possible to write off some bygone capital costs, fares are increased, usually uniformly by some standard multiple, or a subsidy is given to cover the deficit. Thus fares might change, but the structure remains largely unaltered.

It should be said at once that the above paragraph is a very wide generalisation, to which there are a host of exceptions. Off-peak or shoppers' tickets are offered in many places at lower fares, and experiments with other variations have taken place. But these variations have been the exception to the price-based-on-distance policy.

In some cities there is coordination between the different modes of public transport, providing tickets which permit transfer from one mode to another and charging a fare for the whole journey. Whether this is so depends largely on whether the public transport system is regulated by one authority, or whether separate authorities supply rail and bus services.

Such simple price policies may well be convenient from an administrative point of view, and have the superficial appearance of being 'fair'. Closer examination reveals a number of reasons for arguing that a more complex structure of fares based more closely on cost of supply and on other economic considerations would be more effective in achieving the objectives of efficiency, even in the distorted urban transport scene. It is particularly obvious that equity objectives are not necessarily achieved by such a simple fare structure, since it provides wide scope for internal cross-subsidisation between different routes and at different times of the day. For example, in areas settled by the relatively richer transport users, car ownership will be more widespread, and off-peak use of public transport less than elsewhere. Much depends on the characteristics of the people who inhabit the suburbs through which a service passes. Other things being equal, the cost of operating a service where there is little off-peak demand will be higher than the cost of operating a service with considerable off-peak demand.

A major characteristic of interest is the peakedness of demand or, to borrow a term from the electricity industry, the load factor of the service. Another characteristic is density. It is more expensive to collect people from less densely populated areas, which are usually further from the main activity centres, yet the distance-taper policy tends to charge them less per mile of travel. Peakedness and density can be taken into consideration in price policy. It is, of course, also important that they be taken into consideration so far as supply of services is concerned. The usual practice is to supply the quantity of transport services needed by interpreting 'needs' as the number of people wishing to travel at particular times with the given price policy and with all the other constraints taken as given, and by making a rough guess at the quality of service to be maintained.

The other for-hire passenger transport suppliers deserve a short mention. In Australia, taxis are operated under licence. Their number is strictly controlled. Although there are some licences which restrict area of operation, generally taxis are free to seek customers wherever they think they might be. Fares are subject to control by the licensing authority, and usually consist of a hiring charge (flag-fall) plus a charge which is a direct function of distance travelled. There is a waiting or time charge and, for longer journeys with little chance of back-haul, there is provision for an additional charge. While taxis are an important segment of off-peak transport supply, they do not provide a significant proportion of peak services.[11]

An important area of price policy – or perhaps lack of it – is the road space used by private and public vehicles. As in previous examples, it is hardly appropriate to speak of a price policy when in effect we are discussing prices which are charged in the pursuit of unknown policy objectives. However, motorists are influenced by such prices or charges, and respond to them. These charges would include, depending on the journey destination, the parking fees paid. It is important to note that it is the costs which the motorist actually takes into consideration which determine his choices, and not the costs which a sophisticated economic evaluation would show him to be actually incurring (see chs. 5, 6). It is worth noting that this is also the case so far as his use of public transport modes is concerned. His decisions are based on the prices and charges he has to pay, and his estimate of some other variables, e.g. his time and comfort.

The motorist faces an annual charge for registration, licence, and compulsory insurance. This is relevant to a decision about acquiring a vehicle, but not relevant to whether, when, and how to use it. He pays for fuels, which include taxes which are partly charges for road space, and about whose cost per mile he will have some fairly good information. Wear and tear items, especially tyres, are probably not seriously taken into consideration. Any other cash outlay – parking charge, bridge toll – will be included. A rough estimate of the value of time to him (to be considered in ch. 6) and comfort and convenience will also appear in his calculations. Some of the prices charged for some services to some motorists can be manipulated to influence his choice of mode, but usually at the cost of considerable distortion. Thus parking charges are not effective for those who have parking places provided for them; higher bridge tolls in isolation lead to route distortion. The fuels tax cannot differentiate between peak and off-peak use, at least not sufficiently, though it is true that more fuel is used in covering congested mileage.

Authorities have shown no willingness to impose a congestion charge, which would be able to exert a powerful influence on decisions concerned with modal choice. Motorists at present are charged prices which are not directly related to their use of high demand road space. This means that the value of time, comfort, convenience, and the availability of a parking space play the major roles in modal decision making.

An important part is played by road space supply authorities. In many ways their supply response is similar to that of the public transport suppliers. Given the existing prices and charges and the unwillingness to make significant changes, rough guesses are made about the appropriate quality of service to be maintained over the periods of heavy demand. Supply is increased by various means including cheap methods like one-way streets, coordinated signalling at intersections, or by more expensive methods which actually increase road space. It should be noted again that demand is taken as vehicle quantities under the existing framework, and that practically no thought at all is given to much less costly methods such as allowing fare-paying passengers to be taken by car transport other than taxis and/or a charge on the use of high demand road space.

Conclusion: urban transport policies in perspective

It is an unfortunate fact of life that towns and cities grow up over a long period of time, and man's knowledge about almost everything, including transport, changes a great deal during such long periods. If we assume the average length of useful life of a building to be 40 years then, given some rate of growth, a large proportion of all buildings at any moment of time will be more than 20 years old. This means they were located according to the technical and institutional framework which existed 20 or more years ago. In actual life, this period is considerably longer. Railways are built, and affect location so long as they continue to exist. The point simply is that much of the urban location and transport policies must serve a wide time spectrum, and it is never possible to get everything optimal with respect to a particular state of knowledge. So the problem is to provide flexibility in transport policy to enable it to cope with the ancient as well as with the not yet known, without too much friction.

Because of the interdependence between some factors in the urban sector, especially transport and land use, there is no doubt that regulation and planning must play an important part. But the regulation and planning must be according to some principles which achieve objectives concerned with the welfare of the urban dwellers. The basic principle should be that the price mechanism be followed unless there are clear reasons on social grounds or on grounds of distortions to efficiency for using taxes or subsidies. This sounds very much like a utopian principle, until it is remembered that all this takes place within an institutional framework and is subjected to various overriding considerations. It is also subject to a correct interpretation of costs. Although the 'bygones are bygones' argument has been widely misinterpreted, it represents an interpretation which permits older modes with heavy investment in long-lived and specific assets to survive long periods of shrinking demand by appropriate downward valuations of such assets.[12] Written in long-hand, all that is required is that no decisions are made which, other things being equal, result in a transport use which consumes more scarce resources than another, or which induces users, either by regulation or misguided price policy, to substitute a price–quality bundle of lower quality and higher cost for another of higher quality and lower cost, or to locate in an area supplied by high cost but low priced transport, or result in any of the more obviously bad allocations of scarce resources which can be shown to be inefficient because there are others available which are unambiguously more efficient.

This may also be the place to point out that the presence of certain constraints does not seriously affect the argument that price–cost ratios for substitutes should be similar, but that this may require a subsidy for public transport if other modes cannot or are not made to pay the full costs of the inputs they use and/or cannot be made to reflect these costs in the prices they charge.[13] But even at the level of second best, so long as substitutability is the dominant relationship between the modes, a similar price–cost relationship across the modes (strictly speaking, a similar price–marginal resource cost ratio) is necessary. This is also required within modes, to put limits on the extent on internal cross-subsidisation which is permitted.

The most obvious shortcoming of existing price and regulatory policies is the failure to reflect differences in peak and off-peak demand and supply. This applies to public transport systems, and to city road space. For the former, some increase in fares for the peak periods (say 7.30–8.30 a.m. and 4.30–6.00 p.m. though this may differ between cities) together with a significant reduction in off-peak fares, is required. The argument here is on the relative prices of peak and off-peak services, and not necessarily the absolute prices. Similar arguments apply to road space, although here it is only possible to increase the price for or ration the use of, road space during the peak.

Finally, it must be pointed out that regulation and control by direct means must be reviewed at regular intervals. It may come as a shock to many readers to learn that the objectives which many of our transport prescriptions and proscriptions try to achieve are either lost in antiquity, or have long since been overtaken by a new conventional wisdom (which, though better than the old, will face the same fate in a few years time).

3

The pricing of urban transport: some implications of recent theory

P. J. Forsyth

Introduction

The object of this chapter is to examine recent theory in the field of taxation and public sector pricing in relation to urban transport. Broadly, the problems to be dealt with are as follows. If everything is optimally organised throughout the economy, and lump-sum transfers are possible, prices in a sector such as urban transport ought to be set equal to marginal cost. The type of restriction on the achievement of optimality we consider lies in the necessity of the government to raise finance, for one reason or another, and its inability to do this by a means, such as lump-sum taxation, which will have no impact on the efficiency of the economy. Typically, a government will use commodity and income taxes, which distort consumption and/or work/leisure choices. The problem for the government is to find some pattern of taxation which minimises the costs of these distortions. In general, there is no reason why urban transport should be excluded from the tax base. At a more concrete level the transport operator, be it the state railway or city bus service, or an overall urban transport authority, may be, wisely or unwisely, required to earn a target profit (or at least cover its costs). The question then arises of how to minimise the costs of distortions imposed by this constraint.

Along with this theory there has been the explicit consideration of the distributional aspects of pricing. Different prices have different impacts on income distribution, and these may be regarded as relevant to the setting of prices. The justification of the inclusion of these matters is discussed in the next section. It does seem appropriate to discuss this problem together with the other, as both stem from the inability of the price maker in a particular sector (be it the government or not) to arrange matters elsewhere in the economy exactly to his liking. Thus, the two basic issues considered here are (a) that of the revenue effects of urban transport pricing, when governments cannot raise revenue without distortions, and (b) the distributional aspects.

It should be mentioned here that second-best theory is not dealt with in this chapter since the chapter is intended to concentrate on the issues mentioned above. This does not mean second-best theory is unimportant in transport economics: for example, the inability to charge private car users the marginal cost of their use of the road and at the same time recoup the cost of road building by non-distorting methods (e.g. lump-sum taxes) will have important implications for public transport pricing.

An outline of the issues

One particular way in which the urban transport pricing problem can be looked at is as part of the overall government taxing and pricing problem. Viewed this way, the government will put taxes on private sector outputs, and choose public sector prices such that an optimum is reached; this optimum will reflect the necessity of the government to provide public goods, redistribute income in the ways it wishes and cover any losses made by public sector outputs. The appropriate prices would reflect the conditions under which the urban transport market operates, and would be determined as part of the overall optimisation exercise. Urban transport pricing is just one aspect of the optimum taxation problem, which was examined by Ramsey[1] as early as 1927, and in greatest detail recently by Diamond and Mirrlees.[2] An overall optimisation approach can be useful to find out the likely nature of the solution, the variables relevant to it, and how they enter it. On the other hand, it is probably not the easiest way to conceptualise the problem, and provide some practical guidelines for pricing.

The moral of such analyses is much more important than the details. Whatever pricing policy is followed, it will have implications for the revenue received by the government. It is incorrect to suppose, as much literature on pricing does, that the profits or losses of following a particular policy can be treated at face value, or covered by taxation raised costlessly. To raise an extra $1.00 in taxation may involve losses elsewhere in the economy of $1.15, because of the distortions caused by imposing the tax (and also because of administrative costs). If this is so, this fact must be taken into account in determining the pricing and investment policies of those outputs which could influence government finances, that is, the set of priced government outputs. This shadow price of government revenues reflects its existing pricing and tax policies, which may or may not be sensible, but which will not be changed by the policies followed by any urban transport authority. The pricing problem becomes a technical one for the analyst once he is informed of the appropriate shadow price. As with most applied welfare economics, problems start creeping in and some of these will be considered later.

This approach to the problem does provide an answer to the question of what to do when marginal cost pricing implies a loss. How should this be covered – by imposing distortions by taxes elsewhere in the economy? The answer is essentially to balance the distortions caused by extra taxes in one place, and those of raising prices above marginal costs in another, in such a way as to minimise the overall loss. Leaving aside any other considerations, such as the effects on managerial efficiency of making losses, this would be the best instruction from a government to a public enterprise.

Other considerations do enter, and more direct instructions will often be given to controllers of public outputs. Very often, they are instructed not to make a loss (as in the case with many transport authorities in the UK), or to achieve a target rate of profit. It is possible that this constraint will, approximately, reflect the shadow price of funds and the circumstances of the industry, but more often it will be quite arbitrary. The industry, be it a public transport authority for a city, or an operator of a particular transport service, will then have to meet this constraint by choosing some pricing structure. One which will meet it is that of average cost pricing – in the case where it controls one output in one market, this will be the only policy that satisfies the constraint (if multi-part tariffs are ruled out). Where there are many outputs in differentiated markets, as with most urban transport undertakings, there are a variety of possible pricing policies; there is no presumption that an average cost pricing policy will be the optimal one – indeed, the very definition of average cost is usually quite arbitrary under these conditions. The problem is one of finding a pricing policy which meets the constraint at least cost to efficiency. This question was first considered in detail by Boiteux,[3] though it has been analysed in various contexts, such as road pricing, in simpler form, by various authors.[4]

There are a variety of ways by which a public sector industry might raise revenue in excess of that obtained by setting prices equal to marginal cost. If it produces a range of outputs, it may set prices above marginal cost for these outputs, according to some rule. If price discrimination (charging different prices in different markets for the same output, but the same price to all users in any one market) is feasible, then it should be used. In a perfect economy, where a first-best optimum is feasible then it should not be, but where there is a budget constraint, it may yield a second-best solution in the Pareto efficiency sense. Another method open to many operators is that of the two-part tariff, including a block charge for use at all, and a charge per unit of use. This technique is also inefficient if lump-sum taxation is possible, but if it is not, the inefficiencies of using such a system (in excluding some users who would be prepared to pay the marginal costs of use) may be less than those of raising funds in other ways. This is a method of pricing frequently used by government authorities though there has been little rigorous discussion of its use in an optimal pricing policy. Such discussion of it as there has been is either general,[5] or has not concentrated on the trade-off between the fixed and variable charges to achieve an optimal combination of them,[6] though the place of the two-part tariff in the profit maximisation for the private producer has been examined in some depth.[7] Since the purpose of this chapter is to discuss the relevance of existing contributions to the pricing problems, the two part tariff solution, which ideally should be included as part of an overall pricing solution which takes account of the issues raised here, is not specifically discussed, though this is not to suggest that it should not play its part.

It will be assumed here that the profits constraint is a minimum rather than a maximum. This would be the more likely constraint for most urban transport authorities. It is conceivable that a maximum profit constraint might be imposed on some bodies, say an authority charged with pricing congested urban roads. Setting prices at marginal social cost might result in embarrassingly large profits, and the government might not like to be seen to be 'profiteering' from congested roads. If government revenue commands a premium, as has been suggested, this constraint would operate perversely, and lower efficiency more than would marginal cost pricing. The analysis need not be considered specifically, as it would be the reverse of the minimum profits case.

The problem of taking into account the distributional consequences of pricing policies may seem to be of a different type from that of handling a revenue or profits constraint. Yet both will arise from the same overriding limitation; that the tax system must work via the price mechanism, and that raising revenue to provide public sector goods or to redistribute incomes will have implications for efficiency. The government may be assumed *not* to have the means at its disposal to raise revenue in non-distorting ways for these purposes, such as lump-sum taxes or subsidies. Limitations on the tax system imply limitations on the ability to redistribute, and it is relevant to ask what are the distributional consequences of particular pricing policies, and also how they might be used to further the government's distributional objectives.

The scope for using public sector and private sector prices to redistribute real income lies in different output combinations that different income groups purchase and, sometimes, the different markets in which they purchase the goods. A good might be characterised by the income groups, and size of these groups, that purchase it, at various prices. By and large, it is not possible to practice overt price discrimination and charge a specific price according to the circumstances of each buyer; this would be the ideal method of affecting distribution via prices. Theoretically the aim is to appropriate consumers' surplus, though in practice one can only approximate to this objective and a single price will have to be charged to all users in any one market. It will still be possible to incorporate income distribution and other objectives. If the size distribution of incomes, expressed as a density function, and the propensity to consume a good at different income levels are known a distributional characteristic of goods, depending on the average of the income groups who consume it, weighted by their propensity to consume, can be determined.[8] This will give a measure of the distributional impact of prices, which can then be chosen to have the most favourable impact. If a social welfare function is specified, then the prices (and taxes) which should be charged for all goods can be determined. (It is assumed in this chapter that the decision-maker has a social welfare function, which puts weights on the benefits or incomes of each income group or it may be specified over more characteristics than income, such as household size.) A commonly used form is that where individual utilities are aggregated and where the elasticity of marginal utility with respect to income is constant. This is a social welfare function which may be held by the government or decision-maker, which respects individual preferences.

Even if setting prices at marginal cost would ensure exact budget balance, it would be improbable that such prices would be desirable. In general, goods consumed mainly by lower income groups should have prices less than marginal cost, and those consumed by higher income groups greater than marginal cost. The social welfare function, in a sense, represents the integration of 'equity' and 'efficiency' considerations (not that these can strictly be separated), and the pricing policy will reflect this trade off. Alternatively, it could be regarded that the marginal social benefits of outputs – willingness to pay weighted according to who is paying – are set equal to the marginal social costs of supplying the outputs. When there is the problem of ensuring budget balance, the two considerations, of influencing distribution and balancing the budget, must be reflected in the pricing and taxation policy, which has the simultaneous objective of minimising the social cost of the distortions entered by ensuring budget balance, and of ensuring that prices are arranged so that social welfare, as described by the social welfare function, is maximised. Ideally, the pricing of urban transport should achieve these objectives, and it is instructive to examine how far it might have bearing on them in the practical context.

Historical precedents and practical importance

When seeking an understanding of a principle, or a solution to a problem, it is often useful to look at what has been done in the past. While, apart from neglected contributions in the past, the issues set out in the previous section have only recently attracted theoretical attention, analogous issues have faced producers in public and private sectors, and their pricing policies have reflected them. A similar case of an analogy in public sector pricing is peak-load pricing. This was hardly a theory thought up by writers on public sector pricing; different prices for peak and off peak have been charged by profit maximising enterprises producing services with fluctuating demand for centuries. Similarly, with the problems discussed in this chapter, the private sector has used pricing policies to solve analogous problems, though too much should not be read into past practices. Also governments may often have taken into account distributional aspects of indirect tax and public sector output prices.

A good example of the similarity of past pricing policies to the solutions proposed to the problems discussed here concerns what is sometimes called the 'inverse elasticity rule'.[9] In a simplified model, as will be discussed in the next section, it can be shown that the costs of a budget constraint can be minimised by charging prices which exceed marginal cost in inverse proportion to the elasticity of demand; this will result in minimal reduction of demand overall. This is very similar to the pricing policies advocated by many practical writers, and actually adopted by many railways. There are a variety of versions of this, but it may take the form of 'value of service pricing', or of setting prices tailored for the contract.[10] This may be done to maximise profits, or it may be done to enable the railway to cover its costs in a way that does least harm to its customers. Similarly, airports invariably charge prices which are related to the size of the aircraft, which bears little relation to costs of providing the service; but size of aircraft is likely to be inversely related to the elasticity of demand. This is hardly surprising; the simplest of economic theories would indicate that, for a multi-product firm maximising its profits, prices would tend to be proportionately more above marginal cost where the elasticity of demand is lower than where it is high. It is also intuitively obvious that when net revenue becomes important as a variable in its own right, as in the constrained optimal pricing problem, elasticity of demand for the different outputs is also relevant.

It should be emphasized, however, that the objectives of public sector industry do not lead it to adopt the same pricing policy as profit maximising firms; it should do this only when the profit constraint is the maximum profit constraint, i.e. where it has no freedom of pricing policy at all. In the simple, revenue constrained, model it is a question of trading off potential benefits to satisfy the constraint, rather than maximisation of profits alone. The analogy arises in that the variables that affect net revenue are the same. Furthermore, especially in the urban transport context, the situation may be more complex than one of simply satisfying a constraint. The variables used, i.e. the prices, to achieve the solution may have secondary effects, e.g. on work/leisure choices, which the government or transport authority may also wish to consider. Cross elasticities, as well as own price elasticities, will be large, and must be allowed for. Following simple inverse elasticity rules may achieve budget balance, yet it may fail to minimise the social costs of doing so. A further reason for introducing distributional considerations lies in the fact that these will often be related to demand elasticities – in either direction. It may be the poor who have no cars, have inelastic demand for off-peak public transport, or it may be the well off who have inelastic demand for car parks. By ignoring the distributional aspects, following a simple rule could have perverse effects.

Turning from the matter of historical and practical analogies, it is necessary to establish whether budget constraints are of any importance generally, and whether they are likely to be of much significance for the pricing of urban transport. It is certainly not a problem that has attracted the attention of many writers on transport pricing theory[11] but this is no reason for assuming that it is insignificant as other problems which are frequently of critical importance, such as that of the handling of uncertainty, are quite nelgected also. But discussion of the financial aspects of transport does usually turn up in applied analyses though the recommendation is often to adopt some muddled form of average cost pricing.[12] There is a clash between the interests of theorists, who ignore revenue implications and recommend marginal cost pricing sometimes modified to allow for second-best considerations, and applied economists, who pay a good deal of attention to revenue implications.[13] If this attention is justified, it must be resolve in a theoretically satisfactory way. Certainly the impression is that governments do regard the financial aspects as important and, rightly or wrongly, impose financial targets which will influence overall efficiency.

At the most general level, the answer to the question of whether the central government operates on a budget constraint must be yes. The possibility of debt finance does complicate the scene, but essentially the government must raise taxes to cover expenditure. This expenditure may be on public goods, transfers, or on meeting deficits of public undertakings, and it will usually raise taxation on incomes, goods, and various other minor sources, and will receive profits of public undertakings. In the absence of lump-sum taxes, and assuming that the profits of government undertakings, pricing at marginal cost, are insufficient to finance all government spending (hardly an unrealistic assumption), taxes which make the distortions throughout the economy will be used. The shadow price of government revenue will exceed its nominal value, and ideally this shadow price would be used in assessing all spending, and in the determination of all price structures. An overall, constrained optimum could be achieved. Thus, at the most fundamental level, the central government is subject to a budget balancing constraint (over time), and the theoretical problem has a clear practical context – the difficulty is to find out, for an economy, what the implied shadow price might be, so that it can be used.

The situation is rarely as simple as this, as there is in most countries some decentralisation of functions, and urban transport is usually the responsibility of a subordinate authority. Not only this, but usually it is under the control not of one authority, but of several, as well as there being a substantial private sector. Thus, in Australia, the state government may be responsible for railways and main roads, the city council (which may cover only a small part of the urban area) may control buses, and car parks, statutory authorities responsible to the state government may also have control over some transport, some modes (taxis, certain buses, ferries) may be privately operated, and cars are privately driven, though they are subject to control by other bodies. The financial position of a state government may be quite different from that of a central government (though it is conceivable that its shadow price for funds is *less* than that of the central government, if the latter is generous, or the state has access to more types of taxation than the central government). Similarly, the financial positions of the other authorities are different from, though linked to, those of the parent government. Given the limited room for manoeuvre of a city council, its shadow price for funds could be quite high. Authorities, such as public transport authorities, may be set budget balance, or profit target, constraints. The complexity of the financial structure, as well as the presence of a substantial private sector, makes it dubious to talk of any single shadow price for funds, or budget constraint for urban transport, at least for Australian cities. However, in this chapter, the implications of an overall constraint are examined to illustrate the basic results; it is not possible to make a general analysis of a variety of complex structures.

In the United Kingdom structures are simpler, though still quite complicated. For the major cities, reorganisation has resulted in passenger transport authorities, charged with responsibility over public transport generally; however they do not have responsibility for all the railways in their area, but may influence railway policy. They are responsible to city councils, which in turn receive grants from central government, and have control over roads and their use. Between them, these authorities have control over the operation, and to a lesser extent the pricing, of most of the urban transport in their area – the main gaps being railway and private transport. The financial position of the authorities is closely linked to their parents, though a council may impose arbitrary budgetary constraints on transport authorities. Also the central government may make specific grants for certain modes – e.g. road improvements, though these grants are becoming much less specific. In these circumstances, it makes much more sense to speak of the shadow price of funds of an urban transport authority, and to work out the implications of it for pricing of all modes. Outside the major cities, such as London, Birmingham and Manchester, urban transport is the responsibility of many more (conflicting) authorities, and the position is even more complex than it is in Australia – what is significant is that some of the cities subject to these arrangements are large ones, such as Bristol.[14]

A brief glance at the organisation of urban transport in Australia and the UK is sufficient to indicate, *a posteriori*, that the issue raised in this chapter is an important practical one. Urban transport, in most major cities, is operated by a variety of authorities, for whom financial arrangements are important and may differ. For some, the constraints that are put on them may be quite arbitrary, or they may closely reflect the financial position of the parent body. If anything, in major cities, the trend seems to be towards greater unification and thus makes for a simpler analytical task. For the analyst, who takes the organisation and social welfare function as given, the task would be substantial in the more complex cases and the matters discussed in this chapter are only one aspect of the pricing problem, even if it is for one mode or authority. To derive reliable recommendations it is necessary to specify the structure and constraints over the whole system and solve for the price structure which maximises social welfare under these conditions. The material in this chapter would be an essential input for the determination of this solution.

The incorporation of financial considerations into the pricing problem is one matter; that of distributional considerations is less easy to justify to a conventionally thinking economist. The purist argument, that equity and efficiency can and should be separated and that prices should be determined to ensure efficiency and not tampered with for distributional reasons, is supported by many applied welfare economists. Usually such economists do not examine the reverse side of their recommendations, and they assume that finance, if needed, is raised by lump-sum taxation, and that any distributional objective can be achieved by taxation elsewhere in the economy. This type of assumption makes analysis simpler, but if the view expressed earlier is accepted it is incorrect, as equity and efficiency, in economies such as we operate, cannot be separated either analytically or in practice.

It may be maintained that commodity taxes, such as on public sector output prices, are inefficient instruments with which to affect income distribution.[15] This argument has some strength; the instruments in the governments' control all have defects, though some may be better for some purposes than others. On the other side of the coin, governments or transport authorities are faced with making decisions about public and private sector output prices which have distributional consequences and the possibility of compensating for adverse effects may be very limited. Hence the structure of indirect taxation reflects not only efficiency considerations, but also distributional ones; foods are rarely taxed and often subsidised, whereas luxuries are frequently taxed highly, even if demand for them is fairly elastic. On pure efficiency grounds, perhaps food should be very highly taxed.[16]

For the same reasons, the undoubted distributional consequences of urban transport pricing should be included in the analysis. Some policies might be regressive; theoretically the losers might be compensated, but this would be a difficult business, and almost certainly it will not happen. Sometimes an authority may make specific prices for specific groups; the best example is concessionary or free fares for pensioners – if anything, pure 'efficiency' arguments would indicate that pensioners should be charged more than the richer traveller, who is more likely to switch from public transport to the car! Generally, distinct groups cannot be identified for special prices, so prices will have to reflect the mix of groups using the service. The authority will set prices over the range of services that it operates, in accordance with its social welfare function. In the assessment of investment projects, distributional judgements also are imposed, for example, in UK urban transport projects which must be evaluated at a particular value of time-saving set by the Department of the Environment, no matter to whom it accrues. This prevents a bias in favour of projects which improve transport for richer persons only, who can afford to pay more to save time. (see ch. 5).

Little has been said about the nature of the social welfare function. It is simply a systematic expression of the social preferences about income or benefits accruing to one group or individual relative to those accruing to others. It may reflect preferences of the central government, the city council, or the transport authority, or individuals, etc. – each is entitled to its objectives. A lower tier authority, such as a state government in Australia, or a city council in the UK, may have a different social welfare function from that of the parent government. It will be within its rights to redistribute income via the prices of its outputs and inputs as it believes is appropriate. As the opportunities are restricted, it may only be through such outputs that it can influence distribution. It will be seeking to maximise social welfare, as it sees it, by operation of the variables in its control, and urban transport prices are usually some of these.

Optimal taxation theory and urban transport

It would be convenient if it were possible to draw upon some extensive summary of the literature of the past few years to choose which propositions seem applicable to urban transport and to then investigate their significance. This is not possible, as no such summary has been produced – those which exist[17] are too elementary and do not examine some propositions which, as will be argued, are of substantial relevance in this field. A less easy approach, for reader as well as writer, must be taken, one of selecting those propositions from the original literature which seem important for the field and discussing them, even though the original statements may not have been elaborated upon much, nor intended for the uses to which they are to be put here. It is a matter of viewing the field, picking out items of interest and putting them to the test of relevance. As some of these propositions are complex to prove, they will merely be quoted with some heuristic justification.

The pattern of this section will be to take a simple model and to introduce successive complications, many of which have been analysed in general terms in the literature. In effect, these complications are likely to be of such importance that they constitute major objections to the simple model, but that is no particular disadvantage. The destruction of simplistic models is useful, as it indicates that simple rules of thumb do not necessarily lead us to what we seek. It is less easy to substitute substantial rules, however complex, to determine adjustments that may need to be made to urban transport prices and in some cases even the qualitative nature of the results may not be very clear. Nevertheless, they establish the data requirements, which for urban transport are not prohibitive, and give the general direction to which recent theory leads in this field.

The urban transport authority is assumed to have effective control over the urban transport market. This may be through direct control over all modes, which is unlikely, or indirect control via traffic management and taxation powers – e.g. cars may be operated privately, but road pricing is possible. Where surpluses are earned by entities other than the authority, such as private bus companies, the simple formulations would not apply but it would be a straightforward matter to correct for them. The authority may be subject to a budget constraint or be informed of the shadow price of government funds and it is assumed to maximise social benefits according to some social welfare function. Urban transport may be viewed as a variety of different modes operating at different speeds; the better or faster the mode the more expensive it will generally be; a bus, tram, car hierarchy could be envisaged. Various periods in the day may be distinguished but for analytical purposes it will be assumed that there will be peak period journeys, associated with work travel mainly, week day off-peak, associated with shopping and some work travel (e.g. between the morning and afternoon peak), and off-peak travel, mainly at night and weekends, associated mainly with recreational travel. This is roughly the pattern for many cities; others could equally well be assumed.

A simple model

It is convenient to start with a model which illustrates the basis of an approach to the problems. Its limitations can be analysed later. Even the simplest of models is difficult to show diagrammatically, however an attempt is made in this section. For some other elementary discussions of the pricing rules which follow, readers should refer to Walters[18] or Baumol and Bradford.[19]

The 'goods' in the model are taken to be journeys by different modes, in different time categories. The number of each type of journey i, undertaken in a period, within a city or district is taken as q_i, and there are n different types of journey ($q_i = q_1, q_2, \ldots, q_n$); corresponding to each journey type i there is a price, p_i. We may assume that the urban transport authority fixes all prices and chooses them to maximise net benefits. In practice, it may not be able to fix all prices nor receive all revenues from the fares but this could be written into the model as an additional constraint, e.g. it may not be able to influence car travel prices or receive revenues from car travel. This will make a difference to the solution, as the fewer constraints there are the higher will be the total net benefits.

The first question arises in determining how to express benefits to the user. For each individual user, benefits will depend on his use of different modes, or they could be expressed as a function of the prices of each mode. The model could be expressed rigorously in terms of utility functions, or less so in terms of consumer's surplus. It is aggregate benefits that we are concerned with, and aggregation usually presents difficulties. Given a weighting system, a set of prices will imply a set of benefits to individuals which can be uniquely aggregated – thus we may write total benefits B as a function $\overline{B}(\ )$ of prices:

$$B = \overline{B}(p_1, p_2, \ldots, p_n) \tag{1}$$

Writing benefits as a function of outputs, such as

$$B = B(q_1, q_2, \ldots, q_n) \tag{2}$$

is less acceptable, as benefits depend on who uses the services, and one can be less sure that benefits are a unique function of each quantity. We may assume aggregate demand functions of the form

$$q_i = q_i(p_1, p_2, \ldots, p_n) \tag{3}$$

and regard (2) as nevertheless a good enough approximation to the total benefit function.

The authority will vary prices to change quantities, so it is more natural as well as more rigorous to use prices as the instrumental variables. It is, on the other hand, more convenient to use quantities since these lead more quickly to results. Thus we write total benefits as a function of quantities, and assume that the authority varies prices to achieve the requisite demand patterns. Total benefits V may be written as the sum of net benefits to consumers and net revenues to the authority, weighted by their shadow price, s. Much the same results would follow if a net revenue constraint were assumed on the authority, but it is more general to assume a shadow price for funds. Thus:

$$V = B(q_1, q_2, \ldots, q_n) - \sum_j p_j(q_1, q_2, \ldots, q_n)q_j$$
$$+ s\Big[\sum_j p_j(q_1, q_2, \ldots, q_n)q_j - \sum_j c_j(q_1, q_2, \ldots, q_n)\Big] \tag{4}$$

where $c_j(q_1, q_2, \ldots, q_n)$ is the total cost function. To obtain the optimum pricing policy for a service i, we differentiate V with respect to i and set the equation to zero. Assuming $\partial c_j/\partial q_i = 0$ for $i \neq j$, and changing prices to keep $q_{j\neq i}$ constant, we get:

$$\frac{\partial V}{\partial q_i} = \frac{\partial B}{\partial q_i} - \sum_j \frac{\partial p_j}{\partial q_i} q_j - p_i + s\ \sum_j \frac{\partial p_j}{\partial q_i} q_j + p_i - \frac{\partial c_i}{\partial q_i} = 0 \tag{5}$$

Given that $\epsilon_{ij} = p_j \partial q_i / q_i \partial p_j$, (where ϵ_{ij} is the elasticity of demand for i with respect to a change in the price of j) and on recognising that $\partial B / \partial q_i = p_i$, and with rearranging and cancelling terms, we get:

$$sp_i - s(mc)_i - (1 - s)\left[\sum_{j \neq 1} \frac{1}{\epsilon_{ij}} \frac{q_j}{q_i} p_j + (1 - s) \frac{1}{\epsilon_{ii}} p_i\right] \tag{6}$$

where $(mc) = \partial c / \partial q$. With further rearranging a solution for p_i may be obtained:

$$p_i = \frac{1}{[s - (1 - s)(1/\epsilon_{ii})]} (1 - s) \sum_{j \neq 1} \frac{1}{\epsilon_{ij}} \frac{q_j}{q_i} p_j + s(mc)_i \tag{7}$$

If all cross elasticities are zero, ($\epsilon_{ij} = 0$ for $\forall i \neq j, \forall j$) the equation can be expressed as:

$$p_i = \frac{s(mc)_i}{[s - (1 - s)(1/\epsilon_{ij})]} \tag{8}$$

If $s > 1$ and the absolute value of ϵ_{ii} exceeds $[(s - 1)/s]$ the ratio of $p/mc > 1$. If ϵ_{ii} were less than $s - 1/s$, strictly speaking infinite prices would be called for. But this case can be discounted, since it is impossible that demand could be so inelastic at all possible prices. If cross elasticities are ignored, as the absolute value of ϵ_{ii} rises, the ratio of price to marginal cost becomes closer to unity. Another aspect of this result is that the reduction in output, as compared to the unconstrained, price equals marginal cost, output, in the simple case is proportionately constant regardless of the elasticity of demand.

To show this proposition diagrammatically, assume a consumers' plus producers' surplus maximand. To maximise net benefits, marginal consumers' surplus gain should equal marginal profit loss, i.e. marginal revenue minus marginal cost. When there is a shadow price for revenue, it is marginal profit loss, evaluated at its shadow price, which should be equated to marginal consumers' surplus loss. Figure 1 shows the maximum for the unadjusted case.

In this, marginal cost is shown by *GH*, demand by *AB*, marginal revenue by *AC*, and marginal profit by *JD*. A marginal consumers' surplus curve *OF* can be derived from the demand curve (given *M*, where *M* = consumers' surplus and differentiating with respect to $p: dM/dp = -q$) and it intersects the marginal loss curve *DE* at output *X*, i.e. where price *OG* equals marginal cost.

For Figures 2a and 2b assume, without loss of generality, that marginal costs are zero. Optimal outputs would be *OD*. If $s > 1$ then the marginal loss curve BC' is proportionately steeper; suppose $s = 1.5$, so that BC' has 1.5 times the slope of *BC* – this is shown in 2a and 2b. The optimal outputs OX_a and OX_b imply a higher price, p_a, for the inelastic demand case than for the elastic demand case, p_b. In fact, this representation conflicts with

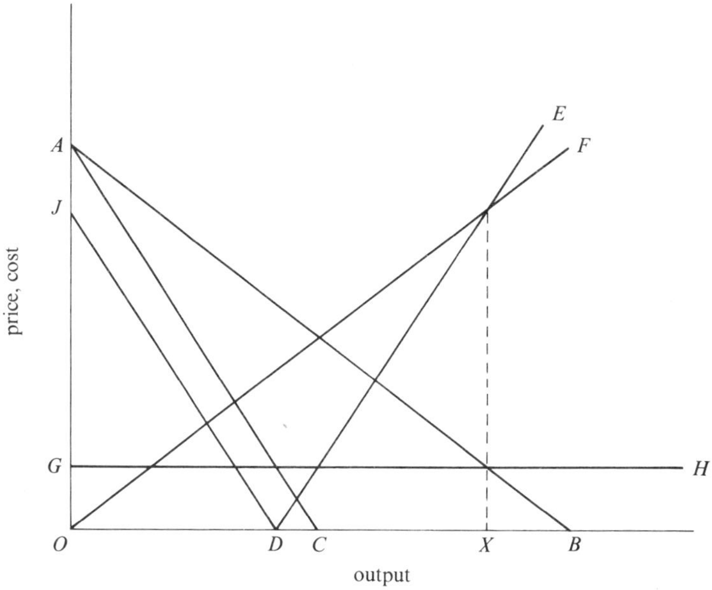

Fig. 1. Simple optimisation.

equations (7) and (8), where price is expressed as a multiple of marginal cost, here assumed to be zero. But this is because the basic condition (5) was expressed in this way. The relationship $\epsilon = -(s - 1)/s$ is the correct relationship when $mc = 0$. It may not always be possible to make it hold; in such cases a unique optimum will not exist. This implies that the ϵ_{ii} must be the same in both cases; price must be raised more in case (a) than in (b) to equate elasticities. Demand in case (b) is more elastic than in case (a), for any given price–quantity ratio.

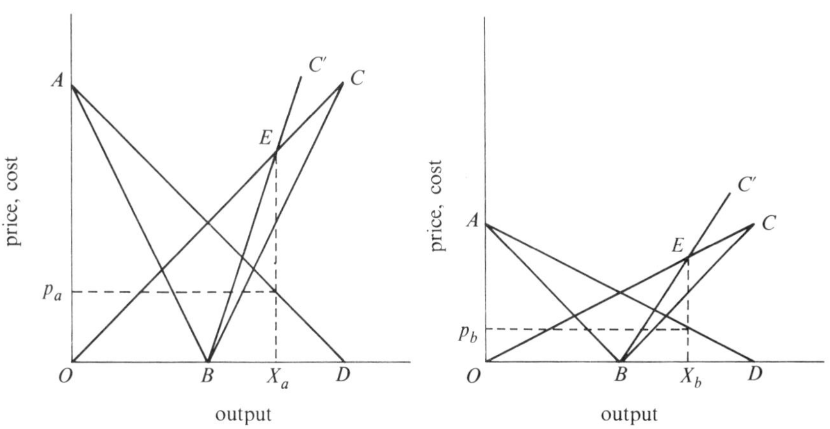

Fig. 2. Adjusted optimisation (a). Adjusted optimisation (b).

This result is analogous to the results of a variety of optimal tax problems, though its simplicity arises from the simplicity of its assumptions. Supply elasticities do not enter into the first order condition, though they will be relevant in determining where the solution lies in a particular case – i.e. how far from the price-equals-marginal-cost output the new output should be. In more general models they will enter explicitly, though such considerations can usually be dispensed with by assumption of constant costs. In this chapter they will not be brought in directly except where crucial to an argument. This model gives a general argument against uniform tax rates, or price to marginal cost ratios, which is reflected throughout the literature (though, under certain highly restrictive cases, uniform taxes are optimal). The information that the authority needs to know to solve its optimisation problem concerns the elasticities (including cross elasticities) of demand for the outputs. The simplification to the own price elasticity rule is unlikely to operate in urban transport, because cross elasticities are likely to be of the same order of importance as own elasticities (increased train fares make travel on buses and cars increase). This should prove no burden, as the object of modal choice studies is to provide that information which can be used to calculate these elasticities.

Certain services are inelastically demanded – for example, peak hour services where there are few substitutes. These should be charged a high price relative to marginal cost. Off peak bus services, for example, may be inelastically demanded when alternatives are few, and thus they should be heavily taxed. Demand for other services in the off peak may be elastic and these should be charged prices only slightly above marginal cost. Urban transport, especially work trips, may be relatively inelastically demanded (at least in the short run, when location is a poor substitute) as people have to get to work, and overall this would indicate a high price–marginal cost ratio. The initial impression that there are few good substitutes for it in general leads to the implication that it is a good tax base, like alcohol and tobacco, and that little distortion will be created by charging high prices. This conclusion may not be acceptable, and in fact it is arrived at only by ignoring several significant features of urban transport, and neglecting the income distribution effects of such a policy.

This pricing pattern has been arrived at from a partial equilibrium analysis, which is correct in its own terms. The assumptions for such an analysis to be valid are quite stringent and are, in this case, likely to be violated. It has been assumed that the market is entirely isolated with no interrelation with the rest of the economy, either through substitution or income effects. While demand may be fairly inelastic, income effects as do exist may prove important. Also, no effects have been assumed on production and this is unlikely to be the case, especially in the long run. The effect of bringing in these extra considerations is to substantially weaken these improbable conclusions.

Implications of a general equilibrium analysis

It is not within the scope of this chapter to set up a general equilibrium model and include urban transport to draw implications about the prices that ought to be charged for it. It is, however, possible to imagine a subset of outputs (urban transport), which may be related in some ways to other outputs, or inputs. They would be treated, like other outputs, as final goods. Apart from substitution effects income effects would be taken into account, as the more that is spent on transport the less on other goods which will affect the solution. The rest of the economy might be more or less subject to control; if it were not subject to complete control via the tax system a second best solution, taking account of the constraints in order to achieve the desired price–output policies, would be sought. The precise conditions desired depend on the specification of the general equilibrium problem and there may be many of these, as many as we care to think of.

Apart from the matters that will be dealt with later in this section, it is unlikely that a general equilibrium model would produce results very different from those indicated in the model above, as the additional linkages specified would not be all that important. For example, an application of a general equilibrium optimal tax model to some broad commodity groups[20] (albeit using fairly restrictive utility functions) indicated that some groups in inelastic demand, such as food, should be taxed heavily. If transport were included in such a model, it is likely that it would also have a high tax rate. Such income effects as would be allowed for would not produce much difference in the likely tax pattern.

Putting urban transport into a general equilibrium framework is, of itself, unlikely to lead to substantially different pricing rules, if a simple general equilibrium model is used. The conclusion may be different for a more complex model. Distributional aspects of the pricing policies may, for example, have a significant effect. In the following sections certain considerations, which are dealt with in some general analyses, are examined in the urban transport context, where it is argued that they prove important qualifications to the basic model.

Urban transport as an intermediate good

In all the discussion above, urban transport has been treated as a final, consumer, good which consumers purchase for its own sake. To some extent it is; it may be purchased to facilitate consumption of other goods (e.g. shopping and recreation trips). But with work trips, travel is not undertaken for its own sake; it is undertaken to enable income to be earned. Under most forms of urban transport travel is paid for directly by the traveller but this need not be the case. It could be provided by the employer in which case it would constitute part of the productive process; and in some cases this is what happens. The precise form of organisation should not influence the way a good is taxed; yet the journey to work could be regarded as either an intermediate or a final good.

If the literature suggested that all kinds of 'good', final or not, should be treated similarly, such a category problem would be irrelevant. But this is not so. It has been shown that, in general, in a constrained optimum, production efficiency is desirable[21] (contrary to the suggestions of some second best theories[22]). This means that the distortions that are to be made to balance the government's budget should be via variations in the price–marginal cost ratios, but allowing for efficient production of the chosen outputs and not in the production process itself. This implies equal marginal rates of substitution between factors (and intermediate goods) for all producers. To achieve this it would be necessary to have no *differential* taxes on intermediate goods and if a realistic economy is assumed, in which a producer may have a choice of using direct production or an intermediate good, strictly there should be no tax at all on the intermediate good. This suggests that if urban transport is an intermediate good, then it should be left untaxed – contrary to what has been suggested before.

This conclusion is weakened in a variety of ways. Firstly, there is no presumption that productive efficiency does exist elsewhere, or that there is an optimal tax structure elsewhere in the economy. Thus, the strong preference for productive efficiency is not necessarily called for in a real, imperfect economy. Secondly, this desirability of productive efficiency does depend upon the ability of the government to tax. Essentially what is assumed is that it can achieve all it needs via commodity taxes. This may not be possible and it may be desirable to impose taxes on intermediate goods, as differential taxes on factors, as a way to get around the inability to tax certain goods, as has been suggested by Feldstein,[23] and Stiglitz and Das Gupta.[24] Loosely speaking, productive efficiency is a good thing, but it can be abandoned if there is something to be achieved in resource allocation elsewhere by doing so. The question is whether taxing urban transport does achieve any particular desirable effects that could not be achieved by other means.

It is clear that putting taxes on urban transport or charging prices above marginal cost can distort productive patterns. Where the transport is part of the productive process it may lead to other, less efficient, methods of communication being used. In general though, it will lead to different location patterns of firms, or firms with particular locational characteristics, e.g. those near their work force obtaining an advantage over competitors even though this will have no desirable effect on resource allocation. In the long term, it could lead to more concentrated and congested cities (though it is not presumed here that residential and industrial location is or is not optimal). It is possible that this effect could be good. It might be advisable to charge a lot for transport in a city which is producing an untaxed good, thereby taxing it indirectly. This is not a very likely situation, though. More plausible is the case where transport prices are used to correct location patterns. If it is considered that a city is too spread out, or that certain industries should be located more centrally, taxes on urban transport may correct for the production inefficiency already present; though again, it would seem better to tackle the problem directly, say through land taxes. Thus the validity of these propositions may be accepted, but it is unlikely that taxing urban transport will prove a good way of using 'back door' methods to tax otherwise untaxable goods. It is difficult to escape the conclusion that, if we treat urban transport as an intermediate good, there is no clear case for taxing it.

But it is misleading to treat it strictly as either a consumer or an intermediate good; really it is a little of both, and the essential difficulty lies in determining to what extent it is one rather than the other. Electricity may be both, but it is possible to distinguish its uses, whether it goes into a factory (intermediate) or a home (final), and price accordingly; optimal pricing requires different prices, in general, to be charged for each use.[25] The peculiarity of urban transport is that it is both an intermediate and a final good *at the same time*. There is certainly an element of final good in the work journey, as the worker can choose to use more or less resources in exchange for different travel characteristics, and this can be regarded as part of his choice as a consumer. In the short run, transport prices may influence his choice of work, which is an aspect of his choice between consumption goods and negative consumption (work).

This situation, where it is not possible to unscramble the different characteristics of the good, is analogous to that where a single price must be charged to consumers and producers, even though it is desirable to differentiate.[26] The overall price–marginal cost ratio that should be used will be some weighted average of the ratios relevant to each case. If it is felt that a work travel service functions primarily as an intermediate good, or that the consumption aspects of the travel can be approached in other ways, e.g. by taxes/subsidies on residential locations and areas of work, then it will be correct to treat the service as if it is an intermediate good charging a price equal to, or approaching, marginal cost. If it is considered that it is largely a consumption good, which cannot be taxed in other ways, it ought to be taxed as such and, as indicated before, perhaps quite highly.

This has implications for pricing in different periods of the week. Peak-hour journeys, dominated by work travel, are perhaps close to intermediate goods, and thus should be taxed lightly. Journeys in off-peak times which are not good substitutes for peak times contain a mixture of work journeys and consumption (e.g. shopping) journeys; probably they are dominated by the latter. The prices charged for these might be relatively high in relation to marginal costs (though they might still be less than peak prices, as marginal costs may be much lower). Then there are those off-peak journeys, at night and weekend, which are primarily consumption orientated, and have little intermediate good element, and thus should be charged the highest price–marginal cost ratios of all. It is less easy to make generalisations about the prices for different modes. Leaving aside time considerations (discussed in the next section) it can be argued that extra costs are incurred by car users to obtain extra comfort and that this is for consumption reasons and has little to do with production. On these grounds car travel ought to be taxed more heavily at the peak than public transport, since some of it represents increased consumption expenditure. There is probably not much, theoretically or empirically, in this argument. In general, regarding urban transport, especially for the work journey, as partly an intermediate good does make a substantial difference to the pricing/taxing policies that ought to be applied.

Relationship to untaxed sectors: work and leisure implications

Little mention has been made so far of substitution and complementarity relationships between transport and other goods, or the notion that some sectors may be untaxed or overtaxed, and that corrections might be applied via other goods. Probably the major interrelationship between transport and other consumption choices is in the work/leisure choice, which happens to be rather distorted. An argument for differential taxes, for taxing an untaxed good, leisure, via taxing a good complementary to it, was put forward in 1953[27] by Corlett and Hague, and has been reinforced by recent optimal taxation literature.[28] Not only is leisure as such, untaxed, but work is also discouraged (at the margin, often heavily) by taxation. The implications of transport upon the work done and leisure enjoyed could be quite substantial. Following the general argument, those services which encourage work, or discourage leisure, ought to be taxed little (or perhaps subsidised) and those complementary to leisure should be taxed heavily. Thus, it is important to check what effects urban transport pricing could have on work/leisure choices.

Firstly consider transport at different times in the week. Overall prices at the peak are not likely to have a clear influence either way on the work/leisure choice. This will be especially true if employees need to make a journey at peak times each work day to earn a living. High prices may induce some to give up work altogether but they may also induce others to travel off peak, have quicker journeys, and work more. Day-time-off-peak journeys include a number of work trips by those, particularly working women, who are likely to be most sensitive to fares in their work/leisure choices – high fares may make it not worth their while to travel to work. The extent to which such people travel at these times, their sensitivity to fares, and the social costs of inducing them to stop work, should provide reasons for prices in such periods to be reduced. The direction of the effect is clear, but whether it is important or not is doubtful. So far as the third time category is concerned, it is difficult to see the effect on work/leisure choices being profound.

Secondly, consider the different modes of transport. When considering transport, one of the assumptions of the models mentioned above is violated; there is no longer a fixed quota of time to be spent on work or leisure – there is now a quota to be spent on work, leisure, and transport. By lowering journey time it is possible to increase leisure and work simultaneously; leisure is no longer work not done. Thus, while travel time-savings increase leisure they may also increase work; speedy travel can be regarded for analytical purposes as a complement to work, and this is the important characteristic; while it is, in a sense, also a 'complement to leisure', it is not so in the sense of being a substitute for work as implied by the models, e.g. the Corlett and Hague model mentioned above, and this effect is not of primary importance.

If journey speed is regarded as a complement to work, and work should be encouraged, those modes which are quick should be encouraged relative to those which are slow. The degree of complementarity depends on the time period; peak-hour savings may readily be converted into work, day-time off-peak less readily, and night or weekend time-savings perhaps only in rare cases. Thus, at the peak, emphasis should be put on fast modes and, on the face of it, this would suggest that the price–marginal cost ratio for car travel be low, probably less than unity, and that for buses high. Perhaps car travel ought to be subsidised. This blunt approach is misleading as important factors are ignored. Interactions between different modes' speeds (e.g. car and bus) are ignored, yet they are critical, and supply elasticities have not been mentioned. It would be difficult and costly to make possible much more travel by car in cities. Given the supply interactions, total time may be saved by taxing cars heavily, and allowing substantial speed improvements to more heavily occupied buses.

Another way of making this proposition is to state that the social value of time may be high, and indicate changes in existing modes to improve speeds, and that it may be higher than the individual's own valuation of it. This is because the time they save is partly converted into extra work and goods, yielding taxation which provides goods for others in the economy – if employees receive less than their social marginal product (which is what the work/leisure distortion is about) they will value their travel time less than its social value. Most likely the travel time and quality mix of existing modes is far from optimal, and especially for the lower quality low speed modes improvements would be worth while. These are possible through technical changes, greater control over competing road users (cars), and through bus priority or busway schemes.

In general, the implication of this section is that prices should be arranged to induce users to save time, if individuals undervalue their own time, especially on work journeys. This does not mean simple minded biases in favour of those modes *at present* quickest; it may mean a structure of prices which discriminates against them, so that total time saved is increased, as is work time. This would most likely be reinforced if distributional aspects were brought in. Also, modes should not be seen purely in terms of their present time characteristics; they may be changed rapidly by certain measures, and more slowly by others; and many of these processes are probably worth while. In peak periods, if savings in travel time are converted into work time to some extent, the returns to such improvements are likely to be large, though this effect is likely to be of little importance in the off peak, where savings are not converted into extra work. The optimal price structure depends on what changes are made, and is not easy to forecast; it is difficult even if nothing is done, but because of supply interactions, it could well involve a relatively high price–marginal cost ratio for the mode (the car), which takes least time, per passenger, at present.

Income distribution and pricing

The matters raised in the previous two subsections have a variety of implications, not all of which are clear cut. It is possible to suggest ways of application. If it is accepted that income distribution is a relevant factor in pricing it would seem likely that those goods (modes) consumed in the main by the worse off would tend to be subsidised, and those consumed by the rich taxed. Here some suggestions of Feldstein[29] are examined for present purposes, and ways of estimating their impact are proposed. The likely effect on the structure of urban transport prices is commented upon.

The primary difficulty in incorporating distribution into pricing rules lies in finding a way to summarise the distributional effects of different prices. These must be somehow specified and evaluated. To find a pricing rule it is necessary to specify how total social benefits change with price and also how social costs vary. To estimate social benefits we need to know the amounts consumed by different income groups, as given by the demand functions for those groups, the proportion of each income group in the total, as given by a relative density function of incomes, and the social weightings. It is then possible to estimate the socially weighted valuation of a particular level of output. It is the ratio of this social valuation to output that Feldstein terms the 'distribution characteristic', R_i. If the relative proportions of each income group's consumption stay constant, such a parameter does not change with prices and outputs – though, strictly, this is unlikely for transport modes. Pricing rules can then be expressed in terms of this distributional characteristic and other parameters, such as elasticity of demand and marginal cost.[30]

An important component of any pricing solution is the social welfare function. The economist may not be able to specify this himself, but he can suggest analytically simple forms to the authority which makes the decisions and ask it to make the choice of parameters. A convenient form is the constant elasticity of marginal utility function, with aggregate utility being the measure of social welfare. This a fairly plausible form which can be used to yield simple results. Only one parameter needs to be specified; essentially how egalitarian it is to be. With information about use of modes at various times by different income groups, and a social welfare function, it would be possible to summarise distributional aspects in the 'distribution characteristic'.

As with many problems in the urban field, the most important limitation of this approach in urban transport would be the presence of significant cross elasticities. Feldstein's formulation assumes independent goods. Nevertheless, it would be possible to take the basic ideas of the approach and develop them to allow for interdependence. Pricing rules could not then be set out usefully in terms of a distribution characteristic as the latter would change as prices changed. For example, bus travel would become a luxury if it became significantly more expensive than car travel, and its users (if any) would, on average, be richer. However, it may be useful to summarise the characteristics of a good in a 'distribution characteristic', partly for static comparisons, and for judging the impact of price changes that make little difference to the proportions of income groups that use the mode.

A problem which arises no matter how distribution is handled is how to value costs socially. The users of a service may be easily identified but the distributional impacts of the inputs, which make up the cost side of the equation, are usually diverse and would be difficult to determine. In the absence of information to the contrary, it is probably best to use the unadjusted financial cost of the inputs.

As mentioned before in an urban context, the pattern of the R_i will depend substantially on the absolute price of the mode; the mode chosen will have a price which is positively correlated with the person's income. Thus, it is possible, *ceteris paribus*, that a price–marginal cost ratio less than one may be required for buses, and greater than one for car users. The R_i corresponding to a mode will vary according to the time of day. It could well be that the R_i for bus and train rise during the off peak, and for cars fall further. This would be because well-off persons may tend to use buses or trains at peak periods, but cars in the evening. Only the captive users may use public transport in the evening and weekend. This would tend to modify the suggestion made above (pp. 38–9), that off-peak travel should, in general, be expensive relative to marginal cost. This conclusion would now only apply to cars. Demand for public transport off peak may be inelastic primarily because those who use it are generally not sufficiently well off to afford alternatives – thus there is a cancelling of arguments.

If prices are to reflect distributional considerations, the urban transport market should prove a fairly easy one to put this into effect. The information requirements are, to a moderate degree of accuracy, frequently met. It is also easy to check the implications of different income weightings by sensitivity analysis. The main problem is one of weighting urban transport users relative to the rest of the community. That is, of finding a weighting factor for the costs.

Conclusion

A good deal of ground has been covered, but only for the simplest of cases have pricing rules been determined. To obtain efficient price structures, it is necessary to go fairly deeply into the nature of the urban transport market. It is easy to suggest that, because of revenue requirements, unadjusted marginal cost pricing should be adopted. But it is dangerous to go from here to suggest a simple inverse elasticity rule for pricing, for either part or the whole of the market. Such a rule can be derived from a basic model, but one which leaves out the more important features of urban transport. As suggested in the previous sections, significant cross elasticities of demand (with the existence of non-taxed or non-taxable sectors of the market), the 'intermediateness' of the service being supplied, the implications for work/leisure choices, and the distinct distributional effects, all complicate the task of determining optimal prices. They can all, in theory, be handled, though they may lead to complex price structures, and such structures could be determined in practice given the data and simplifications appropriate to a given situation. It is difficult to develop unambiguous recommendations from the theory alone.

Granted that there are constraints on revenue raising and income distribution, it no longer follows that there is a general presumption in favour of setting prices equal to marginal costs. Distributional questions aside, the argument above (pp. 29–34) at least indicates that urban transport, like other goods and services, ought to be taxed, or alternatively prices should be set above marginal cost. If there were suitable, fairly 'pure', general equilibrium models, prices–marginal cost ratios might be expressed in terms of own, and cross elasticities of demand and supply, as well as tax rates elsewhere, and the general shadow price of government funds. Certainly there seems some support for the simpler versions of optimal taxation rules[31] and in less complex markets this might be justified.

The dangers of using these rules too readily are pointed out in (c), (d) and (e). Urban transport, at the peak especially, is something of an intermediate good, and one should be careful to justify substantial taxation of such a good when final goods can be, and are, taxed. This argument does not extend to off-peak periods, and it does not have any clear implications for different types of modes. Consideration of the work/leisure choice is also important for the peak and daytime off-peak pricing problems. This operates mainly through the different travel time characteristics of modes, and their possible characteristics once allowance is made for this effect of transport. The implications may be differently expressed by stating that the value of travel time, which can be converted into equivalent work time, will be underestimated by those who experience it. It is difficult, without investigation in depth of the cost functions of different modes, and their interdependence, to suggest the price structure that might follow from this consideration; the simple, obvious, one might be far from the correct solution. Introduction of equity into pricing is straightforward, and it is possible to indicate ways of estimating its impact. It is also relatively easy to indicate implications for the pricing structure for different modes, routes and periods. It would contradict the impression gained earlier that off-peak public transport should have high price–marginal cost ratios.

The exact price–marginal cost ratios in the urban transport sector will depend on the structure of that sector, its impact on others, and the government's need for funds. By and large, the implications of a simple view of the problem, that it constitutes a good tax base, that little distortion would result from taxing it heavily, and that the ratios should be high, do not stand up. In certain times for certain modes, e.g. car travel off peak, there seems some justification for high marginal taxes, but otherwise not. The broad outlines of the optimal pricing approach have been sketched here – they can be filled in only with the actual data for a specific context, and information about its structure, though this discussion should have indicated the nature of the optimising problem faced by the authority.

4

Cost–benefit analysis

W. E. Hotchkiss

Introduction

Cost–benefit analysis (CBA) is a term used to cover a wide range of techniques which have as their ultimate aim the improvement of decision-making in economic planning. It is, therefore, a branch of welfare economics, which has been described as 'the theory of how and by what criteria economists and policy-makers make or ought to make their choices between alternative policies and between good and bad institutions'.[1] Founded on this theory, CBA is a method for appraising a project from the viewpoint of the community and taking account of costs and benefits whether or not they pass through the market. It originated as a technique for guiding resource allocation in a number of different fields, and after being used in the appraisal of water resource projects, gradually spread to transport, health, education and other areas.

In this chapter we shall discuss some of the issues concerning the valuation of costs and benefits. The general logic of CBA is well documented in many books,[2] and thus it seems appropriate here only to outline a number of important points so as to remind the reader of the problems inherent in the technique. This will provide a useful introduction to the next chapter, which is concerned with the application of CBA in the transport context.

The social discount rate and evaluation criteria

Investment decisions in transport are very often dependent on the public sector, and almost universally so for major investments. Hence, although the principles discussed would be equally applicable in the context of private investment projects, this section discusses cost–benefit analysis in the public sector context.

The discount rate

Public investment projects do not appear, fulfil their purpose and disappear overnight. Large projects, in particular, not only have considerable gestation periods but usually continue to produce benefits far into the future. Time distribution is thus particularly important for government investment. There is also a second consideration: the proposed investment might take resources that would otherwise be used for private investment. Each of these two problems requires discounting by use of an appropriate interest rate to determine whether it is worth investing to obtain those future benefits.

There are two major conceptual approaches to the discount rate. The first relates to society's valuation of future benefits, including those which will be enjoyed by future generations, as compared with benefits available now. The second approach is concerned with the possibility that the resources required will be drawn out of alternative uses in the private sector of the economy. The first case is known as 'social time preference' and the second as 'social opportunity cost'. In a world which was perfectly competitive these two would coincide, but in our less-than-perfect world they will inevitably differ. Considering the first case, 'The social time preference (STP) rate is a normative measure of the relative value of present and future consumption'.[3] Two major reasons often advanced in favour of a positive STP rate are, firstly, that society does prefer consumption now to consumption in the future, and, secondly, that income and consumption levels are likely to be higher in the future and that if the principle of diminishing marginal utility applies, any given increment of consumption will be less highly valued in the future than it would be valued now. As against this, some writers take the view that the government is the custodian of future generations as well as of the present. Further, an individual might be prepared to give up a certain amount of consumption for the sake of the future providing he was assured that others would do the same, so that his willingness to make the sacrifice would depend upon the certainty that a similar sacrifice would be made by others. So a public decision to set the resources aside is required, which means that the guideline STP rate used in investment appraisal should be low in order to ensure sufficient investment, for if the STP is high this will bring rejection of many projects whose benefits will only accrue in the future. The resources will be used instead for projects producing benefits in the present.[4]

The second fundamental issue in choosing a discount rate relates to social opportunity cost (SOC). Here the point is made that assuming a full employment economy, use of the resources for the project under consideration will prevent them being used on some alternative project and that one must allow for the extent to which private investment will be displaced. The rate at which the government can borrow funds is one measure of costs, because it is a financial cost, and also it can be said to be in a sense the 'risk-free rate of interest'. But the government bond rate is not simply a reflection of supply and demand in the capital market, it is varied by the government as a normal part of its armoury of monetary controls in the economy. Further, there is no evidence that the bond rate does equal the return on private investment at the margin after adjustment of the latter for risk. The average rate of return on private investment may differ considerably from that on the project displaced by the government investment and, also, the private investor takes account of the effects of taxes so that he demands a gross return which may be much higher than the net figure he expects. Thus neither the bond rate nor the average rate of return on private funds tells us what the SOC rate should be.

Baumol[5] claimed that private corporations expect a rate of return of, say, r after paying tax at rate T. In addition, firms include in their expected rate of return r a premium for risk-bearing. So the gap between r and the bond rate b (abstracting from government manipulation of the latter) will be correspondingly greater. The market values the firm's output at $r + T$ so a public investment producing a yield equal to b will be drawing resources into a lower-valued use.

Riskiness again becomes a central item in the discussion with the raising of the point that public investment includes the assumption of social risk by taxpayers. Arrow & Lind[6] introduced the issue, stating that the government distributes the risk of investment over many people, so that the risk for each person is small (except where particular individuals receive benefits or pay costs). So a public investment with an expected return below that of a private investment might still be the better proposition.

Mishan[7] then made the point that if public investment is financed wholly from current consumption, society will still gain from it, even if it has a lower return than private investment, as long as the return rate on the former is greater than society's time preference rate.

The STP and SOC rates will only coincide under the conditions of a perfectly competitive economy; the theoretical issues underlying the two rates have not yet been settled. In any case the use of a social discount rate requires a number of value judgements and a 'synthetic' rate using what amounts to a weighted average of STP and SOC rates has been advocated by Marglin.[8] It is generally held that there is a situation of under-investment even in advanced economies, which implies that insufficient resources are being devoted to the future, so that the STP rate will be below the SOC rate. While the gap exists, use of the SOC rate will mean that no investment will be undertaken in the public sector which will yield less than the alternative open in the private sector. One way in which the efficiency criterion could be complied with and at the same time the socially desired amount of investment more closely approached would be through the financing of projects by taxation designed to reduce consumption, rather than financing by the issue of bonds which would be likely to compete with private investment for funds.[9]

The discount rate reflects society's trade-off between present and future benefits. Efficiency must also be taken into account, and this requires that the discount rate be modified or that a 'shadow price' be used when costing the resource inputs needed for the project. In practice, use of a range of discount rates, which at the upper level takes account of the market rates prevailing for projects of a similar degree of risk and at the lower level takes account of social time preferences, provides information as to the degree of sensitivity of the project to varying rates of discount. Decisions about the total amount of investment are ultimately political, even where there are well-developed capital markets, and use of a range of rates does provide the decision-maker with information about both the efficiency and the social criteria concerning the project.

Evaluation criteria

There are a number of commonly used methods for evaluating an investment project. Among these is the net present value (NPV) method: consider first a single increment of income. How much would it be worth paying to be certain of receiving \$100 in a year's time? If the \$100 were received now it could be invested to earn interest so that one year hence it would be worth \$(100 + r) where r is the amount of interest earned. At the beginning of next year the amount available for investment would be \$(100 + r) and so on each year. This gives us the formula we need

$$V = \frac{x}{(1 + r)^t}$$

where V = present value
x = sum to be discounted
r = interest (discount) rate
t = time in years

With this formula we can provide for both outlays (or costs) and receipts (or benefits) over time, reducing them to present values so that we can see whether the benefits justify incurring the costs, assuming that both can be valued in money terms.

Example:
Discount rate 10%
Initial outlay \$2000 = C_0
C_1 = cost in year 1, B_1 = benefit in year 1
Net present value =

$$= C_0 + \frac{B_1 - C_1}{1 + r} + \frac{B_2 - C_2}{(1 + r)^2} + \frac{B_3 - C_3}{(1 + r)^3} + \frac{B_4 - C_4}{(1 + r)^4}$$

$$= -2000 + \frac{0 - 4000}{1.1} + \frac{2000 - 1000}{(1.1)^2} + \frac{3500 - 500}{(1.1)^3} + \frac{4100 - 100}{(1.1)^4}$$

$$= -2000 - 3636 + 826 + 2253 + 2732$$

NPV = \$175

Here we have discounted future costs and benefits to get the net present value (NPV) of the project. In the example, the initial outlays are high, as could be expected during the period of construction, and then taper off until in Year 4 only running costs are incurred. Benefits do not commence until Year 2 and then rise as full production is reached. This project is worth carrying out because its present value is positive. However, because the bulk of the costs are incurred early and the benefits accrue later, as is typically the case, it is the benefits upon which the discounting falls most heavily. An interest rate of 10 per cent was used in the example but the project would have been rejected under a discount rate of 12 per cent. So the choice of discount rate can be a crucial factor in determining whether the present value of the project is such as to make it appear worthwhile. Further, a low discount rate will favour projects with high capital costs and low running costs as against projects with low capital costs and high running costs, thus affecting the choice between two ways of producing the same output, e.g. as between nuclear and coal-fired power stations.

Other methods of investment appraisal of interest here are:

1. Internal rate of return (IRR) and,
2. Rate of return (engineers') (RRE).

Taking the second method first, RRE is a method commonly used by engineers to evaluate road projects. Briefly, the procedure is to calculate the annual rate of return in the first year, i.e. to express the benefits in that year as a percentage of the capital cost.[10] Given three conditions, this annual net benefit as a percentage of capital cost will equal the IRR. The conditions are that

i. the capital costs are incurred in the first year of operation (or they are properly discounted to that year).
ii. net benefits are a constant annual amount.
iii. the project has an infinite life.

These are extremely restrictive conditions not likely to be met in the real world. The method might seem suitable for comparing similar projects such as two road proposals, but even here the construction periods may differ or the estimated economic lives may differ, and then the method fails to take account of the differences between the project which might be just as important as the similarities.[11]

The RRE method avoids the complexities which were referred to when discussing NPV and this may be the reason why it has appealed to engineers. However, simplicity at the cost of correctness is not something to be encouraged. Public investment projects have wide effects upon society and to ignore them because it is not easy to assess them is no way to improve the lives of the people. Ultimately the justification for undertaking any investment must be that with it the society will be better off than without it. To take the easy way out each time a difficulty of assessment arises is to ensure that we shall fail to get full value for expenditure.

The IRR does not encounter the need for a special set of conditions in the way the REE does. The time profile of a project is allowed for by discounting the annual net benefits over the life of the investment as with the NPV method. The internal rate of return is that discount rate which makes the net present value zero.[12]

The NPV method uses the same formula as IRR, but as the discount rate is known, it avoids the successive approximations needed to obtain the result in the IRR case.[13] However Dawson sees the fact that the internal rate of return makes incorrect comparisons between the values of future and present benefits as the major reason for preferring NPV.[14]

Mishan has put forward a normalisation procedure[15] under which either NPV or IRR will produce the same order of ranking for investment streams being compared. His procedure assumes five conditions; i. full employment of resources, implying that new government investment will displace an equivalent amount of activity in the private sector; ii. no uncertainty as to the returns; iii. society's time preference rate is represented by a single interest rate, r; iv. there is a single rate of return, r_p, to all private investment; v. r is less than r_p.

The procedure itself is as follows:

1. All costs and benefits of each project are compounded forward to the same terminal date to give the terminal value (TV). The maximum investment potential is realised for each revenue stream. If reinvested, the appropriate interest rate for compounding is r_p but if, perhaps due to political constraints, some part of the benefits is not collected by the government, this part should be regarded as consumed at the time and so r becomes the appropriate compounding rate for it.
2. The terminal date must be common to all projects, so that any projects ending before it are extended simply by reinvesting the proceeds until that terminal date.

The decision rule for IRR is 'select all projects with an internal rate of return not less than some specified interest rate'. For NPV the interest rate was selected in advance so the rule is 'select all projects with a present value greater than a certain figure. Under capital rationing, projects should be chosen in order of their NPV per unit of constrained cost until the capital amount is exhausted.

The planning balance sheet

No matter which of the mathematical evaluation criteria is used, it will fail to bring out the incidence of costs and benefits. It will not show which groups are the gainers and which the losers. Little's requirement for a policy, 'that the income redistribution not be "bad"', may or may not be met by a project that is acceptable under the above evaluation criterion formulae.

To overcome this weakness, Lichfield[16] developed the planning balance sheet, using the methods of social accounting. Tables are prepared showing the magnitude of the various items that the project involves, e.g. a dam affects future flood levels; it also permanently covers some land. The advantages to be sought, or the disadvantages to be avoided, are specified. These are the 'instrumental objectives'. All projects involve and affect, directly or indirectly, organisations or individuals, each of whom is either a 'producer' of the effect or a 'consumer' of it, and an entry is made in the appropriate column in the planning table. Thus, an expressway is built by a highway department which displaces tenants from buildings demolished and increases noise for residents remaining in the area. The department would appear as producer of the need to relocate and of the noise. The displaced tenants and the remaining residents would appear as consumers of relocation and of noise respectively. The owners of the demolished buildings would appear as consumers of the loss of the buildings. Any compensation paid to a consumer would be entered as an offset to the first entry, the net balance indicating the gain or loss to that consumer. The motorists using the expressway would also be consumers, of course.

The significant advance which use of the planning balance sheet can make possible is the identification of the size of gains and losses and of the groups to whom they accrue.[17] It is then possible to obtain contributions from gainers or provide adequate compensation to losers, so that the decision maker can meet Little's requirement.[18] It should be stressed, however, that the move toward optimality remains merely potential. The decision-maker may not take the necessary steps to implement it. The matter then becomes a political rather than an economic issue.

Externalities

Nature and effects of externalities

When we speak of the 'external effects' (or 'externalities') of some action we are referring to the costs and benefits generated by one person but accruing to someone not a party to the activity. Externalities can arise from production or from consumption. An example of the latter is the pollution of streams and waterways from the use of detergents in homes. An example of the former is the pollution from the smokestacks of a steelworks. James Meade's[19] example of the apple-growers and the beekeepers, in which expansion of apple-growing provides more nectar for the bees so that honey output increases as a result of the increase in factors used in apple-growing, is a type of externality which he calls 'unpaid factors of production'. It arises because of the difficulty the farmer would encounter in trying to charge for the bees' food.

There is another case which Meade calls 'creation of atmosphere'. This type of externality is involved in much of the discussion over the case for government intervention to establish new cities. The existence of a number of industries in an area makes it easier for newcomers to obtain the specialised labour and inputs they require, so that an industrialist will establish in a new area once he is assured that other industries will do the same. No one firm is prepared to face the costs involved in bringing the labour from elsewhere but these costs will not arise if the actions of the firms can be co-ordinated because acting together they will provide sufficient inducement for the labour to move, without special payment for doing so. In a system where complete information was available to all parties and they could negotiate with one another, no cost being involved, then by payments between them the use of real resources would be adjusted so as to bring about an optimum allocation. Such a system simply does not exist normally.

Dasgupta & Pearce[20] point out that the existing distribution of income will affect the result of any attempt to use CBA to take account of the failure of the market where externalities exist. There is an asymmetry in the valuation of costs and benefits. Coase[21] deals with a system in which full property rights are introduced to cover all non-market outcomes, e.g. where one would have a saleable right to clean air. If a poor man enjoying clean air were given that right then he might require, say, $150 as compensation for forgoing his clean air and accepting polluted air. But if instead his air was polluted and he was merely given the right to buy a certain degree of cleanliness in his air, the amount he would be willing to pay for it could well be less than $150 because he would be limited by his income. If a cost–benefit study valued the cost of air pollution on the basis of willingness-to-pay rather than compensation-for-deprivation the price used could be well below the amount required under the latter principle (see ch. 6 for examples of the effect of such an approach).

As Mishan[22] points out, many externalities cannot be incorporated in the pricing mechanism due to the nature of things. The existence of these externalities brings a divergence between social and private costs and benefits, which requires cost–benefit methods for evaluation. There are goods which are non-marketable because of their intrinsic nature, in that their provision is in the nature of a joint supply to many users. Two features in combination will determine whether such a jointly supplied good is a private or a public one. If (a) supply to one person necessarily means supply to others because of the impossibility of excluding them (at least without prohibitive cost) and (b) consumption by one person does not lessen the amount available for consumption by those others, the good is 'public'. A lighthouse illustrates the case of the public good and air pollution the case of the public 'bad'.

Externalities prevent the market from operating to bring about optimal solutions and CBA usually attempts to value external costs and benefits separately. In the special case of public goods there is an added complication in that there is no market indicator which would serve as an adequate guide in valuation. Willingness-to-pay based on a consumer survey will not necessarily be any indication of the value consumers place on such items because, as has often been said,[23] the respondents would have an incentive to understate the value unless they were certain that the supply would be financed by some method requiring no contribution from them.

Intangibles

External effects may come about directly, as part of the process of production or consumption, e.g. the smoke and detergent pollution examples, or they may be indirect, e.g. a child education programme reduces thefts and thus a smaller police force is required. They may also be tangible or intangible. The washing dirtied by smoke is certainly tangible, but the loss of a beautiful view as a result of mining in a national park is intangible.

One's choices in the market may reveal something about one's utility function, but welfare goes beyond those items purchasable in the market. Public goods are elements in the welfare function and the fact that many of them are intangible does not alter this. It follows that CBA must take account of intangible as well as tangible items. But there is no clear-cut procedure for their correct valuation. Much work is being done at present to design valuation systems for various non-marketed items, both tangible and intangible. In the meantime, where an item cannot be valued it must still appear in the CBA so that the decision-maker can allow for it, even though his allowance must necessarily be subjective.

Internalisation

Take the case of a congested road as an example of the way in which a producer of an externality may be induced to allow for it. Every new vehicle entering the traffic stream forces added time and convenience losses onto every vehicle already in it. Suppose a congestion charge is imposed, just equal to the value of time and convenience loss caused by the vehicle paying it. Then anyone who does not value the trip as highly as the charge will not pay it. He or she will stay at home, travel at a different time, take a different route or travel by a different method.

There is no *a priori* presumption that a 'bad' externality should be totally removed. In some situations imposition of a tax would entirely stop the externality-creating activity. In others it would merely change the scale of the activity. The actual outcome in either case would reflect the net value placed upon the activity, and if that value was positive the activity would continue, although its scale might be changed. If the value was not positive the activity would cease altogether.

Compensation – actual or potential?

When evaluating a project it is often assumed in practice that the project is desirable if the benefits exceed the costs, irrespective of the persons to whom the costs or benefits accrue. Thus Knowles, discussing railway closures, said, 'In CBA, consumers make their own decisions, and are assumed to maximise the benefit they can obtain from their incomes.'[24] Kaldor[25] argued that, providing there was an increase in aggregate real income as a result of adoption of some proposal, any losers *could* be compensated for their losses and the community would be better off. Whether the losers were *actually* compensated was simply a matter of income distribution, which was rightly a political decision. These two approaches are quite compatible with making the rich richer and the poor poorer as a result of accepting the CBA of a particular proposal, which seems hardly to be in line with general views in the community.[26] In practice, many projects are carried out without compensation being paid to the losers, who are given no choice in the matter. In such a context it is highly questionable whether the simple assumption, as put forward by Knowles, should be accepted. The use of market prices for valuing costs and benefits provides a weighting in favour of the higher income groups as against the lower, for the greater purchasing power of the former leads the market to give preference to their wants. Thus there is likely to be a positive weighting in favour of projects desired by the higher income groups, which would be carried out at the cost of those on lower incomes (ch. 6 considers a number of aspects of the unevenness of the distribution of costs and benefits).

One justification for ignoring income effects when considering specific projects has been that the community undertakes a large number of projects, whose effects are likely to be randomly distributed, so that *in toto* the resulting income redistribution effects would be small. However, as recent examples have shown, many transport projects tend to impose external costs upon the lower-income groups in inner urban areas and their benefits accrue particularly to middle- and upper-income groups.[27] The very fact that their income is low makes it difficult for the poorer classes to use part of it to mitigate the adverse effect of spillovers from new developments. So it would seem that unless allowance is made for the income effects upon the disadvantaged groups, the direction of movement towards an optimum allocation of resources pointed out by Little's two propositions is being ignored.

It is not merely externalities that have their impact upon individuals. Many public projects involve compulsory acquisition of property from individuals and here, too, market prices do not provide an adequate guide to the amounts needed to restore these individuals to their former level of welfare.[28]

Looking at the question in terms of simple refusal to make interpersonal comparisons, welfare economists could take the view that as long as compensation could potentially be paid out of increased income the community would be made better off by a particular course of action. However, once the two value judgements proposed by Little are accepted, the failure to actually pay compensation makes it very doubtful whether that course of action has advanced the welfare of the community. Experience has shown that the failure is likely to mean that a number of individuals are shifted away from their chosen position. They are forced to bear the burden for others' gains. Ultimately, the judgement is an ethical one, but many would refuse to accept as desirable a course of action which added to the wealth of the wealthy and to the poverty of the poor at the same time.

Conclusion

In CBA we have a means of helping decision-makers to take account of the effects of economic activities on individuals not directly involved and also to allow for failures of the market place, whether they be due to monopolistic practices, government actions or the simple fact that the effects are untraded and untradeable under our present laws or property rights.

Society is composed of individuals upon whom various activities impinge in different ways and their ability to minimise any adverse effects upon themselves varies with their level of income. Once this is recognised, CBA can be used to help trace the incidence of costs and benefits upon individuals and determine their magnitude.

CBA also enables analysis of an investment proposal to allow for the time pattern of costs and benefits. In general, it can be said that CBA goes well beyond the methods conventionally used for evaluating investment proposals in the private sector and attempts to take account of externalities in addition to those items considered by the private decision-maker. It must be stressed, however, that it is merely an aid to decision-making and no more. There is nothing sacred about a positive net present value. Like the planning balance sheet the NPV is just one item (although an important item) in the total information an investment decision-maker must take into account.

5

The evaluation of urban transport improvements

J. K. Stanley and C. A. Nash

Introduction

Effects of urban transport projects can conveniently be classified according to whether they are:

i. direct market impacts (e.g. construction costs)
ii. physically quantifiable non-market impacts (e.g. private time savings)
iii. 'intangible' effects having no obvious physical or monetary dimension (e.g. emotional effects of compulsory property acquisition)

Attempts have been made to assign monetary values to some project effects in categories (ii) and (iii), including the examples given in them. For purposes of this chapter we use the term cost–benefit analysis to refer to consideration of project consequences measured in monetary terms, whether this is based on imputing monetary values based on individual behaviour (e.g. value of private travel time savings) or on some 'postulated' price,[1] for example. It thus includes category (i) effects and those category (ii) and (iii) effects where some effort has been made to assign monetary values to effects. We concentrate on this method of analysis initially then move on to consider project evaluation in a wider sense, encompassing both monetary and non-monetary effects.

The use of cost–benefit analysis for the evaluation of urban transport improvements is now so widely accepted that it is scarcely necessary to argue its superiority over the various rules of thumb it has largely replaced. Admittedly, indices such as traffic flow per lane are still widely used in the generation and initial screening of projects and economic evaluation tends to be used less in determining the overall size of the transport budget than in its composition. But for the most part it is accepted that a careful consideration of the costs and benefits of alternative courses of action, quantified in money terms wherever possible, is the rational method of social decision-taking.

Indeed, it is the authors' belief that the pendulum may have swung too far in the opposite direction and that too much faith may now be placed in cost–benefit studies, particularly by those who lack detailed knowledge as to how the numerical results are typically derived. For this reason, we intend in this chapter to concentrate on the shortcomings of cost–benefit analysis as it is currently applied to transport improvements. Broadly, these shortcomings may be grouped under three headings: first, those concerning the philosophical basis of cost–benefit analysis itself; second, the applicability of the prices attached to those effects of transport improvements typically considered; and third, the very wide range of effects that are typically not considered at all in the formal analysis. While cost–benefit analysts usually concede that non-monetary effects should form part of their analysis, practice usually leads to monetary effects dominating.

The philosophical basis of cost–benefit analysis[2]

Books on cost–benefit analysis have explained how it is conventionally regarded as the application of the Kaldor–Hicks compensation test for potential Pareto improvements in welfare. The applicability of this test in circumstances in which the distribution of income is not ideal and in which compensation is not normally paid has already been questioned. The importance of this issue in evaluation of transport improvements is particularly great, since the transport and housing patterns of different socio-economic groups are so distinct that transport improvements frequently benefit particular groups systematically at the expense of others.

But it is not always appreciated that the compensation test approach is not the only way of carrying out cost–benefit analysis. Indeed, there are as many different forms of cost–benefit analysis as there are ways of measuring and valuing costs and benefits.

Which method is actually chosen depends on the value judgements of the evaluator and on the practicability of the approach. The Kaldor–Hicks approach seeks to value effects in accordance with individual's preferences as reflected in their 'willingness to pay' for them. This approach gives a person more influence in social decisions the higher his income. We personally regard this as unjust, and would wish to neutralise the effect of variations in market power, for instance by adopting the 'willingness to pay' of a consumer of mean income rather than that of the individual actually affected. Furthermore, we would still wish on equity grounds to give more weight to the preferences of those who are disadvantaged in other areas of the economy until such time as a more efficient way of aiding them is devised and implemented. Fortunately, whichever attitude is taken to the distributional issue, the method of analysing costs and benefits set out below remains a necessary input into the evaluation procedure.

Differences in the value judgements as to which set of preferences should be adopted are a bigger problem. In the first place, there may well be effects with respect to which it is felt that individuals do not know what is best for them. While in general we would deplore the substitution of planners' preferences for the preferences of those affected by schemes, there may be specific cases – for instance with regard to medical and psychological effects of noise and air pollution, which may be little known to the public at large – where we would wish to disregard revealed individual preferences. But even where individual preferences are to count, it is not necessarily the case that the values revealed by individuals in their market transactions are the values that they themselves would wish to see used in social decision-taking. In other words, cost–benefit analysis based on individual market preferences may form a very undemocratic method of advising on decision-taking and it is not easy to reconcile its use with the growing demands for public participation in transport planning. We return to this question on page 67.

Much of the force is taken from these criticisms if cost–benefit analysis is seen as a way of gathering and presenting information on who is affected by transport improvements and to what extent, rather than as a decision-rule in itself. This approach is predicated on our belief that, because of the value judgements involved, evaluation is ultimately a political, not a technical, exercise. The remainder of this chapter will attempt to assess how well cost–benefit analysis performs this less ambitious role in the case of transport improvements.

The measurement and evaluation of the effects of urban transport improvements

User Benefits

The usual approach to the evaluation of user benefits regards all users, whether they are firms or households, as producers of a commodity, transport, for which they use a number of inputs. Some of these inputs – vehicles, fuel, parking space, etc. – they buy or hire on the market, while others – primarily the users' time – they supply themselves. The total cost of this bundle of inputs is known as the 'generalised' cost of a trip and it is the reduction in this generalised cost that is regarded as the benefit to the user. One difficulty arises with respect to trips that are diverted from another route or mode, or generated completely afresh, as a result of such a cost reduction. The usual approach is to value the benefits to these at one half of the figure for existing users, on the assumption of a linear demand curve.[3]

A major problem of practicability will be immediately apparent. While there are many different types of vehicle in use, each with different capital and running costs, as a practical matter traffic forecasts can only be prepared for broad vehicle groups. More seriously, the value placed on inputs such as users' time will vary from person to person in accordance with a host of factors, such as time of day, length of trip, weather and comfort of the transport mode used. But research on the values placed on time spent travelling has not yet reached the stage where these factors can be adequately taken into account (ch. 6).

In practice, only a very limited number of categories of such inputs – e.g. work time and leisure time – can be separately valued; for the rest, common prices are attached to all units of the input in question. This is equivalent to assuming that all trips are homogeneous with respect to trip characteristics, tastes of the user and vehicle used. Already, a considerable degree of approximation through averaging will be seen to exist,[4] and biases may be introduced in the case of projects which do not affect all categories of user and trip in the same proportions.

When it comes to the placing of money values on vehicle capital and operating costs a number of issues arise. In the first place, there is the perennial problem of whether market imperfections and externalities prevent market prices from being appropriate measures of the opportunity cost of resources used at all. The transport industry is a major user of inputs of oil, coal and steel, all of which are major polluting and resource depleting industries. Moreover, future prices of these items throughout the life of the project also need to be known. In the light of recent events in the oil industry, the importance of this statement needs hardly to be stressed.[5] Secondly, certain items, particularly motor fuel, bear heavy taxation. It is now standard practice to omit the tax element of market prices in calculating generalised costs for purposes of evaluation, with the justification that these are transfer payments rather than net costs. Thirdly, there is a problem of how to treat the capital costs of vehicles. Strictly, the effect of the transport improvement on the size of the vehicle stock and frequency of replacement should be forecast and added in as a cost of the scheme. In practice, normal procedure is to treat part of the cost of the vehicle as a running cost spread over an assumed lifetime mileage run and the remainder, together with interest charges, as an invariant overhead. The assumptions about vehicle stock implicit in this are not only implausible but inconsistent too, as the latter part assumes a constant vehicle stock whilst the former assumes that the vehicle stock changes with mileage run.[6]

Conventionally, it is assumed that the costs perceived by the user are those which best explain his behaviour (i.e. perceived cost equals behavioural cost). Hence values of travel time derived from behavioural studies are usually used in evaluations. That this might not be the case has been suggested by Hensher's studies of mode choice and the value of time.[7] Moreover, studies such as these indicate that people frequently misperceive travel times and money cost of trips. In such circumstances the usual procedure is to estimate the 'true' value of the cost but it is not clear that this is a more appropriate measure for evaluation purposes than the perceived cost, which is what the individual believes that the trip is costing him. The issue hangs on whether he would perceive the benefits of a change in true costs in terms of the time or money available for other goods, although he does not know where the extra resources have come from.[8]

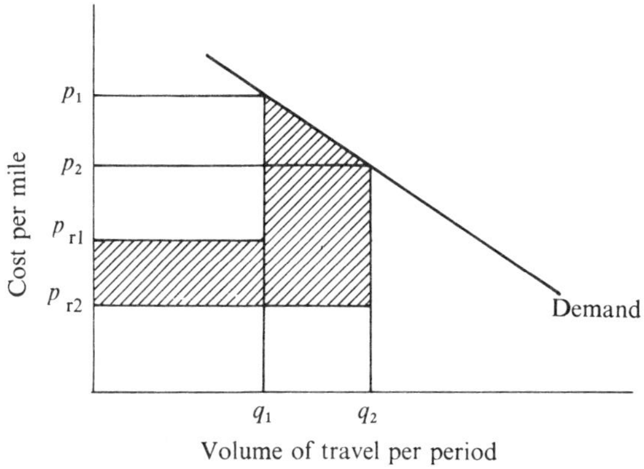

Fig. 1. Measurement of user benefits.

The measure of user benefit so far described is illustrated by the shaded area in figure. 1. It will be seen to comprise the resource cost saving on existing trips, plus the difference between the measures of willingness to pay for diverted and/or generated trips and the resource cost incurred in providing these trips. It will be noticed that this measure is partial in nature, looking solely at one market. This approach is reasonable only if price is equal to marginal social cost in all other markets affected by the improvement, since then surplus gains and losses due to non-marginal changes elsewhere will exactly cancel each other out.[9]

Unfortunately, the urban transport sector is notorious for price–marginal social cost divergences, and many closely related markets will incur losses or gains of surpluses unbalanced by changes elsewhere. In the first place, without a system for charging local users for the congestion and pollution they cause, marginal social cost will typically exceed price on other roads in the area. Thus if traffic is diverted from these roads there will be benefits to remaining users of them and inhabitants of the area, while if use of a road as a feeder to a new project increases traffic the converse applies. It is therefore necessary to model and evaluate whole networks of roads rather than individual improvements and this is, of course, standard practice in urban transport planning. The public transport sector is less often included in the evaluation, unless improvements to it are specifically under review.

But here again, the presence of high overheads and a severe peak-load problem, together with financial and administrative constraints, frequently requiring the undertaking to break even and to charge the same fares in peak and off-peak periods, lead to price distortions (ch. 4). For instance, suppose that a road improvement diverts off-peak users away from a public transport service operating with excess capacity. Public transport loses revenue (i.e. producer's surplus). The typical response, to comply with financial constraints, will be to raise price and/or reduce service levels and

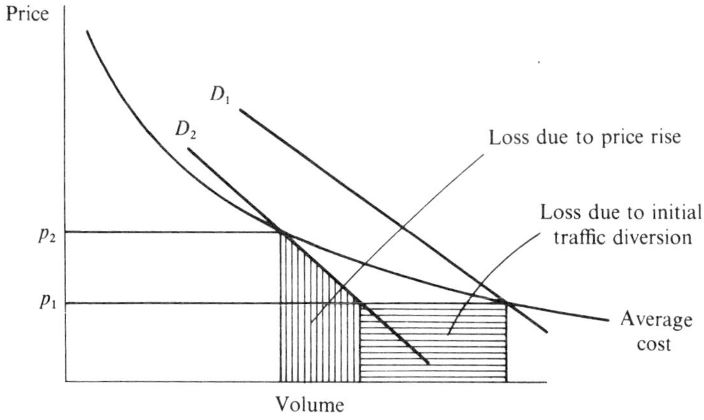

Fig. 2. Effect of a road improvement on public transport.

make matters worse, as is illustrated in figure 2. For simplicity, it is assumed in this diagram that the total cost of the public transport service is constant and that this must always be covered by fare revenue. In practice, any offsetting cost savings in these circumstances are likely to be slight.

We have now reached the stage of arguing in favour of a comprehensive transport sector evaluation, in which changes in surplus on all routes and modes are aggregated to give a measure of user benefit. It should be appreciated that this aggregation itself introduces a further problem, as it involves evaluation of a line integral of the form

$$\sum_{i=1}^{n} \int_{p_{i2}}^{p_{i2}} f_i(p_i)dp_i$$

where $f_i(p_i)$ = demand curve on route/mode i after improvement

p_{i1}, p_{i2} = prices before and after improvement.

Hotelling[10] has shown that for this measure to be independent of the path of integration chosen (if several prices change) requires equality of cross price derivatives between all goods whose prices change, i.e. $\partial x_i/\partial p_j = \partial x_j/\partial p_i$. This will only hold if the income elasticities of the goods in question are equal.[11] Otherwise, the exact measure of benefit derived will vary with the order in which one integrates measures of benefit under the relevant demand curves. In practice, the choice of path of integration has been arbitrary, or based on ease of computation; for instance, the London Transportation Study used a straight-line path.

Of course, market imperfections abound elsewhere in the economy as well and it is strictly not enough to model and evaluate interactions within the transport sector alone. One case in which allowance for this has been attempted is that of the so-called taxation adjustment.[12] Suppose that a road improvement diverts expenditure from other forms of consumption to motoring. There will be a surplus accruing initially to the government in the form of increased motor tax revenue. On the other hand, there will be a loss of surplus on the goods from which expenditure is diverted, equal to $T \triangle M_{tr}/(1 + T)$.

where $\triangle M_{tr}$ = change in money spending on transport by users
T = mean rate of taxation (as a proportion of supply prices excluding taxes) on goods from which expenditure is diverted to transport

If it is assumed that spending is diverted proportionately from all other goods, then T may be taken as the mean rate of indirect taxation in the economy, and the above 'tax loss' deducted from the benefits of the project.

Further difficulties arise in forecasting the incidence of benefits and costs. In a recent set of Sydney urban project evaluations carried out by the Commonwealth Bureau of Roads, two thirds of total expected benefits accrued to commercial vehicle usage. Within the Kaldor–Hicks framework for cost–benefit analysis this would not raise any particular problems, since benefits can be measured at any point in the economic system if one uses that approach. However, if one does care about distributional consequences this poses a major problem, since knowledge of the ultimate incidence of benefits which accrue initially to commercial vehicle usage is virtually nil. They may accrue to road hauliers, producers or consumer in the form of lower prices. Such considerations tend to make the past concentration on private vehicle travel and on the value of private travel time savings appear excessive.

It is hoped that the discussion in this section has been sufficient to show that the evaluation of user benefits from a transport improvement is by no means straightforward. As a parting shot, it is worth making the point that inaccuracies from all these sources may well pale into insignificance alongside those arising from faulty traffic forecasting. The problems of this stage in the procedure and the inadequacies of the usual techniques are dealt with elsewhere (chs. 6, 12) and we shall here confine ourselves to a brief comment on their significance for evaluation. What is needed are forecasts with and without the proposed transport improvement – i.e. for two different cost situations. But methods of forecasting based on projection of past trends assume implicitly that previous trends in transport costs will continue to prevail, and are unable to produce a demand relationship between traffic volume and cost. This may lead to inaccuracies in the forecasts as well as difficulties in identifying that part of the forecast which is properly regarded as 'generated' traffic due to the improvement.[13]

Costs of construction

The major part of the costs usually entered under this category comprise the market prices of acquiring the necessary property, labour and other inputs necessary for the construction of the new facilities. Now it is quite possible that market prices may be inappropriate in all these cases. For instance, there may be unemployment among road construction workers, so the opportunity cost of labour is below the wage rate (although this is not likely in urban evaluations in developed economies); also, the supply of road-building materials such as gravel and cement is a considerable externality-creating activity implying prices less than marginal social cost. However, in this section we wish to concentrate on the particular problems involved in valuing property acquired for transport improvements. In Australia, for example, property acquisition costs typically comprise about 40 per cent of urban road project capital costs.

Suppose, initially, that all land required for transport improvements were currently vacant. The opportunity cost of using it would then comprise the present value of the stream of benefits which could have been derived from applying the land to the best non-transport use. This would be provided by the current free market value of the land only if the alternative use provided no externalities (e.g. industrial pollution), and if the market rate of discount coincided with the social rate. However, precisely because of these external effects, the use of land is subject to development control. Thus market price represents the value of the land in the most profitable use to which planners will permit it to be put. In other words, in addition to the above conditions, it is also necessary for the planners' decisions to be regarded as optimal if the market price is to be taken as an appropriate valuation. In practice, a common mistake is to take the historical cost of acquiring the land, which may be well below market value.[14]

Worse follows when it is remembered that most land required for urban transport projects is currently in residential or other use and frequently has property built on it.[15] For instance, following Downs[16] we may identify the following costs imposed upon owner-occupiers whose houses are acquired for transport schemes:

i. Loss of property (i.e. house and land at the market price which would have prevailed in the absence of blight).
ii. Removal costs.
iii. Costs of seeking alternative housing (i.e. search costs, agents' fees, etc.).
iv. Higher housing costs imposed by the non-availability of equivalent housing at the same price as that acquired.[17]
v. Loss of advantages peculiar to the site, such as low travel costs. In part these will be reflected in market prices, but to the extent that the advantages are individual-specific, they may not be.
vi. Disruption of established personal and environmental relationships ('psychic' costs).[18]

It should be noted that costs (ii) to (vi) will also be relevant to tenants of rented accomodation. Also, some of the costs (iv) to (vi) may turn out to be benefits in particular cases.

Costs (ii) to (vi) are over and above market prices, and represent the 'householders' surplus' enjoyed by the majority of house-occupiers. These costs will vary greatly with the social composition of the affected population, and taking them into account may have significant implications for route-planning. For instance, being guided solely by market prices, it will usually be cheaper to acquire areas of older low-income housing. However, such areas will often comprise close-knit immobile communities with an above average age composition. Thus, costs such as (iv), (v) and (vi) may be much higher than for new estates populated by more mobile younger persons.

Two main approaches to measuring the surplus in monetary terms for evaluation purposes have been used. Firstly, the Roskill Commission research team, investigating the siting of the third London airport, attempted to ascertain the mean size of the surplus by use of a questionnaire survey among owners not affected by any proposed development.[19] The principal difficulties here relate to specification of an appropriate set of conditions under which the householder would be forced to move,[20] and to the treatment of the valuation of householders' surplus of the substantial number of respondents who declared that no amount of money would compensate them for the move.

An alternative approach is to try to measure directly those items of cost for which market prices exist; this is the approach adopted by the Commonwealth Bureau of Roads in Australia. Clearly, it will not identify category (vi), the 'psychic' costs, but it may at least provide a reliable lower limit. In any case, it is not clear that it is possible to measure these 'psychic' elements in terms of compensating variations; where people's whole way of life is affected by the move, it is not surprising that they find it difficult to translate such effects into a money figure. Furthermore, their tastes may also be changed by the move, in which case *ex ante* and *ex post* valuations will differ. Although *ex ante* valuations are normally used in practice, it is not clear that these are more appropriate than *ex post*.

A similar list of effects may be spelt out for non-residential property. Indeed, these may be more extensive, involving losses to former customers and employees as well as owners. The attention which has been given to factors such as these in cost–benefit studies to date is miniscule.

There are other external costs resulting from the construction of new transport facilities: for instance, delays to road users due to construction works and noise, dust and fumes imposed upon residents and workers in the area. The conceptual difficulties involved in analysing these costs are identical to those considered in the previous (pp. 57–61) and following sections.

Externalities in operation

Of the effects of transport improvements considered under this heading, the only one that is typically quantified in money terms is accident cost. Moreover, a considerable portion of accident cost is more correctly regarded as a part of user cost, Thus if users are perfectly informed about accident risks, they will take into account average expected accident cost to road users as a part of generalised user cost in taking transport decision, and it will only be the excess of marginal over average cost to users that will be an externality.[21] However, many of the costs of road accidents (provision of emergency services, part of loss of output, damage to property, etc,) are borne by non-users, and it seems appropriate to discuss accident costs in general in this section, concentrating on fatality costs.

Reynolds[22] divided accident costs into cold- and warm-blooded costs, The most important and most controversial item in the cold-blooded category is the loss of output due to injury or death. This is usually valued according to the wage rate of the victim, on the (dubious) assumption that this equals the marginal value product of labour. The difficulties this presents in the case of labour for which there is no market price, of which the largest category is the services of housewives, are obvious. But in the case of death, the surviving population does not suffer a net loss of this volume of output, since whatever would have been spent on providing goods and services to the victim is saved. Thus it has been normal practice to deduct the consumption of the victim from the resulting figure for loss of output.[23] But presumably a part of government and investment spending is saved by the reduction in population and should also be deducted. The real issue is the effect on the mean standard of living of a reduction in population size. It is unlikely that the current procedure in the treatment of accident costs sheds any light on this.

Some commentators (e.g. Mishan[24]) have been disturbed by the fact that the above procedure implies that there are net benefits from the death of persons (e.g. pensioners) who consume but do not produce. This is not surprising, since we have so far ignored all the warm-blooded costs of pain, grief and any intrinstic value of a human life to itself and others. A recent trend has been to add back the consumption of the victim as a cost to him of his death.[25] But it is not clear what relation this bears to anyone's willingness-to-pay to avoid death! Schelling[26] argues that the latter can be measured when it is realised that the relevant choice is not between certain life and certain death, but between different probabilities of life or death. Thus for instance, consumers might be permitted to choose between cheap unsafe means of transport and expensive safe ones. In any case, no workable method of measuring such preferences has yet been put into practice, although work is proceeding.[27] Moreover, the warm-blooded costs imposed on relatives and friends remain unmeasured.

Finally, it should be mentioned that economists have frequently turned to governments for valuations of these effects, either expressed directly[28] or implicit in past decisions.[29] For instance expenditure on pensioners is taken to yield no cold-blooded benefits, and thus to be a pure measure of warm-blooded benefits of life. The first approach involves the value judgement that the government's preferences should decide the issue; the second adds the assumption that the government has optimised in terms of its own objectives in the past. We do not accept either of these propositions.[30] But for those (e.g. government decision-takers?) who do, the problem is solved.

There may be many who will object to the whole tone of this section and argue on moral grounds that all have a right to live, and that transport planners should do everything in their power to preserve that right. If they still hold this view when its implications (that all resources of the community will be diverted to the preservation of life, and that mobility and material welfare will be entirely sacrificed to this end) are explained, then for them the solution is clear; they will want transport plans to be evaluated solely in terms of number of lives lost in accidents, and most of the content of this chapter will cease to be relevant.

We have devoted some space to criticising existing practice in valuing accident costs, not out of vindictiveness towards those who have shown great skill and ingenuity in devising these techniques, but rather because we consider it important to show that even here, where established measures do exist, they may be totally unreliable. With respect to the other externalities caused by transport systems in use, the situation is even worse. In the case of traffic noise, well-established techniques exist for physical measurement and forecasting, and considerable progress has been made in developing similar methods in the case of air pollution, visual intrusion and vibration.[31] Market prices may exist for some of the costs imposed on affected persons by these externalities: for instance, air pollution may lead to extra spending on building repairs and cleaning and replacement of clothing,[32] while noise may lead to a decision to install double-glazing.[33] But clearly none of this ameliorative expenditure wholly undoes the harm of a worsened environment. While some kinds of relationships of these costs to transport system changes may be derived, they can at best only indicate lower bounds on cost.

A favourite approach to valuing such items arises from the hypothesis that many of the effects will be capitalised in the value of affected houses. For instance, empirical work has tried to find the relationship between noise level and house prices. However, doubts about the reliability of this approach arise, both at the theoretical level if a perfect market is assumed[34] (where the fall in house-price represents the value of noise nuisance to the marginal occupier of a noisy house, and this may represent a lower limit to the mean compensating variation), and because of the all-pervasive nature of imperfections in the housing market,[35] which would generally bias the measure in the opposite direction. In any event, empirical work so far has generally failed to throw up the expected relationship.[36] Again, any such results would provide minimum values only, since noise is also experienced at places of work, entertainment and shopping.

Perhaps the most surprising, and indefensible, omission from most transport project evaluations to date is any consideration of effects on pedestrian movement, especially given the finding of some studies that time-saving on the walked section of a public transport trip are valued much more highly than those savings made in-vehicle (ch. 6). However, many difficulties remain in modelling and forecasting pedestrian movements, which needs to be done to a much finer scale (although usually over a much narrower area) than for vehicles, and in valuing pedestrian time savings. (Finding suitable conditions for behavioural studies, except in the case of the walked section of a longer trip, is difficult.) Moreover, formerly attractive walks may become noisy, dirty and frightening or even dangerous, whether the pedestrian route crosses facilities at ground-level, by footbridge or by subways. The social implications of placing physical barriers (e.g. new roads or rail lines) through existing communities extend, of course, much wider than this (Chapter 12).

Our conclusion in this section must be that very little progress has been made to date in obtaining monetary values to be placed on several important externalities of urban transport improvements (e.g. 'psychic' costs of compulsory residential acquisition; fatality costs; noise and air pollution costs). Furthermore, the value basis of the compensating variation approach to evaluation in these (and many other) situations is also extremely questionable.[37]

We noted in Section 2 that even where one believes individual preferences should be normative for social choice questions, it is not necessarily the case that the values revealed in market behaviour are the values individuals would wish to see used to guide social decision-taking. The promise of a unique evaluation result if all computations are carried out in monetary terms has tended to obscure this issue. The value judgment that social choice questions should generally be decided with reference to individual preferences leads one just as naturally to a participation program to reveal such preferences as it does to market behaviour. Given the arguable value basis of the compensating variation approach with regard to many urban transport project impacts, the case for participation seems particularly strong.

In many situations the motivation behind public involvement in planning has been pragmatic, in particular to increase the legitimacy of the planning process in a bid to avoid the delays and cost caused by citizen opposition at plan implementation stage. However, we see participation procedures as an appropriate way of revealing the value positions of various groups on public projects. Participation programmes are perhaps the most promising way of deriving comprehensive data on 'ethical' preferences, such data as we believe should be used for guiding social choice questions.[38] This does not mean that no 'market' preference data should be used, but it does mean

market data on particular effects would not be used if one had any reason to suspect a divergence of 'ethical' and 'subjective' preferences on particular effects

one would not necessarily attempt to impute monetary prices to non-market effects, measurement of these being carried out in physical units where possible or otherwise described as fully as possible.

Aggregating the results

Evaluation is essentially concerned with assessing

i. qualitatively different effects on
ii. different groups of people over
iii. time.

Aggregation to produce a unique evaluation result thus involves considerations of benefits and costs on different types of effects, groups of persons and time. The cost–benefit approach to evaluation handles monetary effects, sometimes differentiates affected groups and allows for timing of effects through choice of analysis period and discounting. Aggregation of monetary benefits and costs is discussed in relation to these issues by Nash, Pearce and Stanley,[39] and Nash,[40] so we do not dwell on them here. We are concerned here with consideration of non-monetary effects and their integration with monetary measures of impact.

Recent developments in public participation processes have shown that it is quite possible to develop direct non-monetary assessments of how various groups see particular effects of projects. So long as evaluation is thought to be about individual preferences, basic evaluation data need not relate only to monetary effects. Participation processes can thus fulfil evaluative functions, both for non-monetary consequences and as between various monetary and non-monetary effects. Chapter 11 provides a more detailed discussion of participation and its role in planning and evaluation.

Given that participation can be used for evaluative purposes in planning, the next question to consider is whether such participation should be directed to achieve a unique evaluation result. Since preferences of different groups for project effects will generally diverge, should participation be directed solely to revealing these divergences or should it be intended to reconcile them to produce a unique evaluation result as well?

There is no doubt that the Kaldor–Hicks approach to cost–benefit analysis purports to be a conflict resolving rule for social choice decisions. Probably under the influence of systems analysis, cost–benefit studies tend to be presented as a 'rational' process from which the choice to be made emerges clearly. However, if one moves the emphasis to the value judgements involved the outcome becomes less clear. While it would be ideal if consensus could emerge from a participatory process, this cannot generally be expected. Resolution between conflicting value judgements then will remain as a task for the decision-maker. Since the ultimate choice does lie with the decision-maker, the participation process should identify the relevant issues and value positions thereon as seen by each group. Planners may seek to reach a unique decision based on such data and we can see advantages in this if the sensitivity of the evaluation results to varying value judgements is examined. Such an exercise can provide the decision maker with useful additional information.

However, in the course of this process, data on the views of the various groups should not become submerged in a single reported criterion. What is important is that all value judgements be made clear, that the value positions of all interested groups be eleborated, and that the decision maker be in a position to make his own judgements on all relevant issues. We thus envisage a process which informs the decision-maker on monetary and non-monetary consequences on various groups, and of the views of these respective groups towards such effects. This situation is well summarised by Bellomo and Lockwood[41] with reference to the Boston Transportation Planning Review (BTPR):

> a participatory approach to planning as developed by the BTPR recognised that the questions under review are related to resource allocation and trade-offs among costs and benefits. These are basically political questions not technical ones. Only elected officials have the mandate to make the required decision. The role of the planning process is to assure that for each alternative under consideration, all those affected by such a decision are aware of the true consequence and that the decision maker is aware of the range and magnitude of the public reaction.

The comprehensiveness of evaluation studies

Previous sections have raised the question of comprehensiveness of transport project evaluation. Participation processes have been suggested as a practical and ethically attractive method of generally extending the scope of evaluation considerations. We move on now to consider a number of particular issues we believe have received inadequate attention in past transport project evaluations.[42]

In the first place, do cost–benefit studies measure all the benefits of improved accessibility? The transport project analyst typically ascribes benefits only to those who actually travel. But might not inhabitants of a city benefit simply from the availability of transport services; i.e. the knowledge that should they wish to travel (in an emergency, or simply on the spur of the moment), their journey would be readily accomplished? This type of benefit has been labelled 'option demand',[43] and is perhaps most significant when considering provision of a basic minimum level of service. Similarly, non-travellers may benefit from increased travel on the part of the rest of the population; the lonely, sick and aged may, for instance, receive more visitors.

One long-standing controversy on the comprehensiveness of cost–benefit analysis relates to blight. To the extent that blight simply reflects the uncompensated losses imposed on those whose property is affected by transport improvements, it lies within the framework of costs discussed above. Any further allowance for falls in property values would amount to double-counting.[44] But blight often imposes costs on those whose property is not ultimately affected, or who have moved before work on the project commences. Such costs may or may not wholly be transfers. To a considerable extent they are the result of uncertainty as to the outcome of the planning process. For instance, if a motoring route is announced and then scrapped it cannot seriously be argued that there has been no cost to holders of affected property even if they kept their property and its value was fully restored. That blight is relevant to the choice of transport schemes is proved by the realisation that different schemes cause different degrees of blight; holding firmly to a 'do-nothing' option, for instance, causes none.

Another serious implication of transport improvements for the urban environment arises from the fact that transport improvements influence patterns of location and land use (see chs. 8, 9). For instance, transport improvements may encourage workers to live further from their place of work in order to enjoy a higher standard of residential amenity.[45] The extra traffic resulting will be assigned the usual benefits accruing to generated traffic. These benefits will be a proxy for the benefits of an improved residential environment, and to consider the latter separately as well would be double-counting.

However, local authorities also greatly influence patterns of land use by means of planning decisions. Thus in considering alternative transport plans they should, logically, at the same time consider alternative patterns of land use. Suppose such a package of transport and land use plans increases the number and/or length of car-trips to work. It is no longer clear that such extra journeys provide any benefits to those making them. The usual approach in evaluating land use plans is to treat these extra journeys as a cost, and to examine environmental improvements separately. But how can extra journeys generated by planning constraints be distinguished from those generated by transport improvements?

Perhaps the greatest failure in terms of comprehensiveness of transport project evaluation to date has been the failure adequately to relate transport planning and land use planning. This has been associated with a tendency to look at only a small proportion of the options available. Transport improvements are highly interdependent and just because a particular scheme, formulated typically to deal with a specific existing or forecast traffic problem, yields benefits over a do-nothing alternative, does not mean that it is a good scheme. There may be numerous better schemes which have never been considered and evaluated. It may be thought that this is a criticism of the transport planning process, rather than of evaluation per se. To the extent that this is true, it is a reflection on the limited conception of evaluation held by transport planners, who see it as no more than a method of assessing impacts of projects selected initially on other criteria. Evaluation criteria in this system have no influence on project selection. A properly functioning evaluation procedure, however, will iterate back to project selection so that the criteria used in assessing projects are also an integral part of project selection. In this system the planning and evaluation processes become indistinguishable. Public involvement from the initial goal formulation stage may be directed towards achieving this end. The extension of this process to what may be called social evaluation is discussed in chapter 11.

A final point may be added on the question of uncertainty. Traffic forecasting, shadow price forecasting and public opinion forecasting are all hazardous procedures. Of the many techniques that have been proposed for dealing with uncertainty in investment appraisal,[46] sensitivity analysis (i.e. an examination of the sensitivity of the final results to alternative forecasts of the exogenous variables and alternative estimates of the structural parameters of the model) is the most readily and most widely used. But this is solely a method of obtaining and presenting information, rather than a way of actually taking the decision. In view of the degree of uncertainty surrounding transport forecasts, it may be thought that there is great merit in formulating transport plans containing a high degree of flexibility. Again, this is a factor not directly measured in a project evaluation.

These are difficult problems, and we realise that we have here done nothing to help solve them. But it is essential that they should be recognised in any discussion of the state of the art of evaluating transport improvements.

Conclusion

It has become fashionable when seeking to define cost–benefit analysis to quote from the classic article by Prest and Turvey:[47] 'Cost–Benefit Analysis is a practical way of assessing the desirability of projects, where it is important to take a long view (in the sense of looking at repercussions in the further as well as the nearer future) and a wide view (in the sense of allowing for side effects of many kinds on many persons, industries, regions, etc.)'.

Unfortunately, it is the conclusion of this chapter that cost–benefit analysis as applied to the evaluation of transport improvements has fallen a very long way short of this ideal.[48] The ready availability of market prices for many items has led to a failure to trace through the effects of schemes on the economy as a whole, and to appreciate fully the all-pervasiveness of externalities in such interactions. Items for which money values are not readily available have, with the major exception of time savings, been subjected to far too little scrutiny. Evaluation has been used as a hurdle which a scheme prepared on other grounds must negotiate before implementation, rather than as an integral part of the planning process.[49] Results have often been presented in such a way that little light is shed on the incidence and magnitude of the effects of the scheme, and public discussion and participation is obstructed rather than facilitated by the analysis. When it is remembered that this whole process is applied to a set of traffic forecasts which is itself of doubtful reliability, the question may reasonably be asked whether the whole procedure has any value at all.

We believe that cost–benefit analysis is of value, but that it needs to be applied rather differently from current normal practice. In particular, it needs to be integrated into the general consideration of alternative approaches to future development of the area in question and used in examining a wide range of alternative plans, even if this means that modelling and forecasting for each plan has to be much more limited than at present.[50]

Emphasis should become rather less on *technique* and much more on the development and use of open planning processes. The latter should not be seen only as responding to plans and ideas generated by planners, but should be expected to produce ideas and plans. In other words, we see project evaluation becoming much more synonymous with participation in planning. The technical issues we have raised in this chapter have to be seen in this light. They form important questions related to project acceptability, but the broader evaluation framework within which they are located must emphasise participation and the role of cost–benefit analysis as a supplier of information to a much greater extent if evaluation is to remain useful. We reject the idea that project evaluation results can be meaningfully conveyed in terms of cost–benefit ratios or net present value terms alone. These only serve to hide the essentially political nature of evaluation.

6

Demand for urban passenger transport

D. A. Hensher

Introduction: emphasis and scope

Responsible policy recommendations related to any activity require a consideration of the likely effects associated with the implementation of proposed policies. This commitment involves an assessment of the desire of a specified behavioural set (e.g. the community) to obtain the advantages which can result from an activity (e.g. travel); that is, a knowledge of the demand for an activity is required. Underlying any analysis relating to the explanation, prediction and evaluation of any project or system study of travel-related matters is a consideration (in varying degrees of rigour) of the demand aspects. While there are difficulties associated with the identification and measurement of usage and demand for travel facilities, a considerable amount of conceptual and empirical work has been undertaken, even though only a small proportion has been successfully integrated into analytical transport planning.[1] While demand aspects go wider than the identification of the consumer's expected usage of a facility, they do encompass usage and hence a basic starting point has commonly been an investigation of present travel patterns and the set of influencing conditions. Chapters 4 and 5 have discussed the problem of selecting the behavioural set in terms of the distributional consequences associated with the variational impact of the demand for travel between behavioural sets; for example, the commuter versus the resident adjacent to a radial expressway; or the low income versus the high income commuter. This chapter concentrates on more direct demand matters.

Developments in transport planning have taken two directions, with an emphasis on the trade-off between underlying theoretical requirements and operational necessity. The first approach commonly incorporated in the traditional urban transport modelling system (discussed in ch. 12) emphasises the aggregate movement patterns of mode-specific trips within a travel network, expressed in terms of origin and destination attractive and generative influences (such as population and employment) and the trip characteristics (e.g. distance or time involved). In contrast, the less operationally developed behavioural approaches have emphasised the need to investigate individual traveller behaviour and values as a basis for more realistic measurement of the demand for urban travel facilities (concomitant to the demand for travel); and then subsequently to integrate this knowledge of the theoretical and conceptual basis of travel demand (which has to date only been empirically tested and applied to specific projects) into the spatially designed modelling system. This behavioural approach has stemmed largely from the application of basic principles of consumer choice theory, in contrast to the theoretical underpinnings of the urban transport modelling system stemming from Newtonian mechanics, where a law analogous to the Newtonian Gravity law 'governs' the level of interaction between groups in spatially separated areas, the interaction level being dependent upon some conveniently defined impedance term and some state variables referring to the local potentials generating and attracting trips.[2]

The economic rationale orientates this chapter towards a consideration of conceptual procedures that are based on individual choice behaviour, although we must not ignore the constraints associated with the need to plan with improved insights; and so it is crucial to attempt cross-fertilisation by adopting relatively simple behavioural assumptions concerning the underlying decision process leading to acts of choice and reactions to policy adjustments. Diminishing returns in sophisticated modelling quickly set in when the objective of identifying the demand for trip making is realised. The emphasis of this chapter is on the demand function itself rather than the analysis of the interactions among demand, cost and pricing policies.[3] It is argued that identifying the underlying bases of travel demand is necessary to any subsequent utilisation of a 'demand function', and that the most neglected issue in the prolific amount of pricing and investment planning research which relates trip price to volume of trips is the identification of the empirical demand determinants as a basis for identifying the sensitivity of expected usage to changes in the transport system.

The chapter is divided into three sections. In the first section we are concerned with theoretical and methodological matters, with the emphasis on modelling techniques as a mechanism for relating, under various strong and weak assumptions, the theoretical argument to the empirical identification and measurement of various component choice acts of the overall travel demand. Consideration is also given to the usefulness of choice functions which underly demand for obtaining various evaluation parameters such as the value of travel time savings. The next section outlines two empirical studies as a means of illustrating the application of various choice theories in order to identify demand together with a discussion of their usefulness in a policy context. The final section broadly outlines a number of issues related to demand which have not been adequately investigated, but rather identified with the areas for future research.

Theory and method

The 'demand' for urban passenger transport[4] is a commonly used notion having little identifiable content, because of its relatively unobservable nature and the general existence of empirical evidence for only one point in the demand hypersurface for any one single individual. The other points are hypothetical extrapolations around the consumers' present usage by the use of various sensitivity measures (for example, direct and cross elasticities; and direct probability estimates associated with variations in one travel influence, ceteris paribus),[5] and evidence from other individuals located at different points in the demand hypersurface. Given this situation, there is an even greater need to investigate the sets of possible theories developed in the behavioural sciences as a means of improving our knowledge of the individual (and group) traveller's choice behaviour as related to urban passenger transport demand decisions. In this way we are able to at least theoretically justify the underlying basis of travel demand, which is a more manageable objective, postulate relationships between the taxonomy of choice acts influencing demand, and then finally impose necessary restrictions on the demand function that will aid in the empirical estimation of the models' parameters. The major weakness of the traditional urban transport modelling system has been the absence of an underlying behavioural theory.[6]

The theory of rational individual consumer behaviour assumes a situation in which an individual who has complete knowledge of all alternatives facing him, irrespective of the degree of substitutability or complementarity, will always choose that alternative which maximises his welfare function. This broad approach has to be modified because the situation often facing the individual is one of incomplete knowledge, due, among other considerations, to the resources (time, cost, effort etc.) required to acquire full knowledge, and to the feeling that complete knowledge is not required. The consumer also deems some commodities as non-relevant, even though they may influence his welfare experience at certain times, because he is not able to consider an infinite or even large set of characteristics simultaneously. This apparent refutation of the classical rule of rationality can be justified in the context of an action space containing close substitute and complement choice mechanisms, such as travel choice considerations, including location influences. In this set of circumstances we refer to the 'rational irrationality'[7] of an individual who acts in a rational manner within a 'relevant set'. The relevant commodity space is assumed to be the constraining bound within which an individual chooses whether or not to travel, where to travel and how to travel. Since some travel activity decision processes are mellowed somewhat by habit (for example, the journey to work) and most are subject to the psychological phenomena of learning and perception errors, in addition to adjustments over time in the relevant set, the deterministic flavour of economic consumer theory must be modified explicitly to allow for probabilistic behaviour in the choice theory itself. There is a basic difference between a deterministic theory in which the parameters of the model are estimated by techniques which have random unobserved disturbance assumed to account for all the factors not explicitly included in the model, and a theory in which explicit consideration is given of the probabilistic human behaviour in the choice theory itself.[8] Utilities of alternatives are not certain but rather random variables determined by a specific distribution. In addition to errors in determining the individual's optimal commodity bundle, his preferences are also subject to random shocks.[9]

In the context of urban passenger transport demand, there are good *a priori* and empirical reasons for restricting the substitute goods to alternative transport modes, times of day, destinations and daily trip frequencies; and the complementary goods to the prices and availability of goods that are selected in connection with a given trip, and the prices of other trips that are taken in connection with a given trip. The next consideration becomes the procedure by which these substitute and complement goods are viewed in the context of arriving at a decision. That is, what is the logical structure and interaction of the various choices which lead to travel?

The logical operation of the decision-process within the relevant set is as important as the identification of the relevant set. The traditional approach to identifying usage expresses the production of trips, the spatial allocation (distribution) of trips between origins and destinations, mode and route choice, as a series of sequential independent processes, implying for example that the decision as to whether or not to travel bears no relationship to the factors influencing the selection of a method of transport for that trip. The absence of any circular flow or feedback is a major weakness of these earlier models, despite any subsequent structural improvement to each of the separate demand sub-models (see ch. 12). Errors in sub-models were compounded in any forward linkage. Trip production is described as a process relating the number of trips commencing or terminating in a particular location (usually a geographically defined area) to the existing land-use and socio-economic characteristics of that location. Since the price of the activity for which travel is undertaken is not considered, nor the supply price of travel itself, trip production generates only potential usage. This independently derived area number of trips (usage) is then allocated between possible destinations, and available modes of transport. The magnitude of total trips is completely unresponsive to the costs of modes and activities performed at destinations, these costs only affecting the allocation of the fixed stock of trips. The final mechanism in the forward linkage process involves the allocation to specific routes of a pre-determined number of trips between an origin and a destination by a particular mode. The actual level of traffic between an origin and a destination is at this stage assumed completely inelastic.

This sequential recursive[10] (independence) procedure is largely the result of historical accident and computational convenience, where the logic associated with consumer decision-processes was totally ignored. A fixed stock of trips is not in reality allocated among modes; rather, total trip demand is elastic and will respond to changes in time, cost and other relevant influences. Neuburger[11] produced evidence to indicate an elasticity of trip production with respect to car travel time of 0.73 with a standard error of 0.19. As such, this sequential process also assumes no relationship between production/distribution and the quality of the travel network. The level of area activity is assumed independent of its accessibility and even if this level remains constant, the propensity of people to travel is also assumed unaffected by accessibility. While this hypothesis of fixed trip ends is difficult to defend, it has been an assumption of subsequent, more behavioural, investigations of travel choice. The development of urban areas along transport routes, the decline of residential development with distance from the centre of cities, and the response of industrial location to transport investment, provide contrary evidence to the hypothesis of fixed trip ends. The reasonable assumption that travel choice patterns in urban areas for the major journey purposes (to and from work and to and from the shops, together forming the greater percentage of all urban passenger travel) emanate from relatively fixed origins to a limited number of alternative destinations (one destination only for work trips) in terms of present usage, does add a constraint on any possible identification of travel demand, the latter including unmet or latent demand.

The economic inconsistencies inherent in this particular sequential process stem largely from the almost complete independence between each model sequence, making each subsequent sub-model stage an addition to a pre-determined and earlier sub-model. For example, because the modal choice function is added after the largely mechanical production, attraction and distribution functions are determined, the policy variables included in the modal split function are only able to change the split between modes. The total number of trips and the distribution between zones is already predetermined, largely without regard to the transportation system. This existence of these procedures is essentially the result of a failure of critics to provide an operationally acceptable alternative methodology, despite the developments in transport research.

Alternative efforts to identify improved urban travel demand models that are consistent with the individual traveller's decision processes have been made in a number of directions. Initially repeated dissatisfaction with the traditional urban transport modelling system lead to a significant research effort in matters related to particular choice acts with the individual traveller as the behavioural unit (e.g. modal choice or trip distribution), but very few attempts to relate all the isolated developments back into a total travel demand framework. Much of the research into the simultaneous representation of travel demand (the combination of the production, attraction, distribution and mode choice components) developed out of studies on inter-urban travel, such as the North East Corridor Study in the USA. These studies, however, because of data deficiencies, were restricted to attempting to apply consumer choice theories at a level of aggregation of data ('the physical zone') which prevented any real behavioural assessment of the true demand.[12] Another possible reason why the simultaneous aggregate procedure did not perform very well is that the decision-process is too complex for a single simultaneous modelling approach. At the level of individual traveller behaviour there have been two orientations, the first emphasising the continuous sequencing of various travel choice acts, but in a way that ensures interaction through the explicit incorporation of relationships from other decision functions.[13] A number of simplifying assumptions are made in order to derive a workable framework. The second emphasises the simultaneous consideration of the various travel choice acts through the inclusion of joint and conditional choice probabilities for individual traveller behaviour.[14]

The new sequential process emanated from an initial consideration of simultaneous procedures. That is, a number of simplifying assumptions were made so as to contain the large number of simultaneous combinations of dimensions of the various choice acts. Even when restricting the analysis to relevant substitutes or complements and the range of attributes characterising alternatives within and between choice acts, there is a compounding number of potential variables. With two modes, two times of the day (peak/off peak), three destinations per traveller, two trip frequencies and four modal and trip characteristics per option, 96 variables would have to be considered. Hence by factoring the overall demand function into its destination and frequency of travel, the estimation procedure is considerably simplified. In economic terminology, we are assuming the additivity of the choice functions. The important distinction between this procedure and the UTMS is the explicit recognition of a travel demand function comprising simultaneous choice acts, which is simplified only for empirical analysis. Since theories of individual choice behaviour relate to the order of preferences through utility functions, it is appropriate to refer to the assumption of the additivity of the utility function. The class of utility functions adopted are (functional) separable utility functions.[15]

Separability is concerned with the possibility of dividing up the commodity bundle into a number of sub-bundles in such a way that the level of utility afforded by a particular commodity bundle depends only on levels of utility yielded by various sub-collections of the given commodity bundle and on a uniform relationship between goods in different sub-collections. Commodities within a sub-group may bear any relationship with another, but commodities from different sub-collections must bear a similar relationship to one another. The additive decision rule has been postulated for the way in which various types of utility are aggregated together to produce an overall utility level. That is, the marginal rates of substitution between attributes within a particular choice set (e.g. mode choice) are the same regardless of any variations in the attributes contained within other separable choice sets (such as frequency of travel).

The separate choice acts can be interrelated through the characteristics of the trip, such as travel times and costs, producing a demand model that is responsive to changes in instrumental variables, and consistent with the assumption of restricted marginal rates of substitution between attributes within a choice act. If a one-direction sequence of choice acts is to be used, then the particular sequencing must be justified. Despite the improvement of the separable additive model over the traditional transport modelling system, there are still difficulties in identifying the most behaviourally valid sequencing of choices. If separability is a realistic assumption, then is there a logical or natural ordering of travel decisions? The separable sequential travel choice assumption can be supported by a number of hypotheses. Within the relevant set, 'bounded rationality', defined in terms of a restricted (perceived) satisfactory set of evaluation criteria operates to create sequential choice. A search and learning process, mellowed by experience, selects alternatives sequentially, which are then compared to a reduced set of criteria until an alternative is found which satisfies the decision-maker.[16] Adaptability combined with uncertainty (in a constant time period) could also be added in the form of a regret function (i.e. a decision tree approach) to theoretically justify a particular sequence. Another weaker hypothesis is that decision-making proceeds from the latest to the earliest decisions; and so, for example, an individual may be assumed to have some view on the modal and route alternatives when selecting his destination. Akiva showed empirically[17] that different values of the trip characteristics, time and cost, were obtained when mode choice was assumed prior and subsequent to destination choice, and when the two travel choices were considered jointly. Brand[18] discussed a number of behavioural hypotheses and concluded that there may be few clear-cut travel choice orderings that can be assumed from the standpoint of travel behaviour; and hence combined choices should be estimated simultaneously: 'Fewer sequence *assumptions* can lead to improved use of the separability *property* for combining the separately modelled choices into a demand model'.[19] Akiva also indicated that 'The problem with travel decisions is that we cannot find a unique "natural" sequence of partitions that will be generally applicable. Therefore a simultaneous structure is superior to a recursive structure.'[20]

The simultaneous consideration of travel decisions at the level of the individual has a very recent history, with little empirical evidence to support the advantage of one model with many alternatives (given the feasibility of estimating joint probabilities) over four sequential models with a smaller number of alternatives. The strength of the simultaneous approach is at present drawn from its intuitively plausible assumptions. Simultaneity refers to the non-singular directional interdependency relationship between travel choices, in contrast to the recursive (or uni-directional) assumption. A simultaneous model requires the estimation of either a marginal probability or the direct estimate of joint probability, in contrast to the recursive structure which predicts the joint probability by multiplying the conditional probabilities. The joint probability can be illustrated (for an arbitrary order) as the probability that an individual will undertake a trip with frequency (f) to destination (d) during time of day (h) using mode (m) and via route (r) out of a choice set comprising all possible combinations of frequencies, destinations, times of day, modes and routes available to an individual within his relevant set. For example:

$$P(f, d, h, m, r,) = P(f)P(d/f)P(h/f, d)P(m/f, d, h,)P(r/f, d, h, m).$$

The simultaneous model also requires a separability assumption in order to make the analysis manageable. Whereas the sequential approach assumed functional separability (i.e. the marginal rate of substitution among a set of variables is independent of other variables), the simultaneous approach assumes separability of choices, which implies that the conditional probability for a given choice depends only on a part of the total utility function. The latter is a weaker assumption. An example would be (in the case of two choices) with respect to mode choice, that the conditional probabilities of choosing a mode giving a frequency of travel (for example) is a function of the variables for all modes, but for only one specific level of travel frequency.

The complexity of the simultaneous model must require a pruning of the alternatives within and between travel choices, just like the factoring assumption of the separable recursive model. Decomposition of a total simultaneous system would result in a system of structural probabilities which comprises simultaneous and recursive choices. For example, if we are concerned with the journey to and from work, then we can usefully eliminate the time of day choice since it is effectively constrained; and also the frequency of work journeys, which is relatively constant over a given time period for an individual. The following structural probabilities would appear to be relatively realistic representations of the travel decision process: $P(d, m)$; $P(r/d, m)$. The choices of mode and destination are simultaneous, and the choice of route is recursive with respect to choice of mode and destination.

The previous discussion has investigated the desirable approach to assessing travel demand, in accordance with theoretical requirements. However the procedures adopted to date have not opted for the probabilistic approach to traveller behaviour, but rather a deterministic orientation in which the basic behavioural unit was not the individual traveller or his household, but rather the physical zone, defined by geographical area. The reason for this was largely due to the inability to handle large data sets at the level of the individual traveller, and to the very broad macro-planning objectives of earlier studies. Even though transportation studies collected data at the level of the single household, they did not gather the sort of information required to estimate probabilities of various travel choices at the level of the individual, and hence emphasised broad movement patterns by frequency, mode and destination, with no consideration of alternatives within a particular travel choice act. The physical zone was regarded as a useful tool in forecasting the patterns of movement between urban locations, because the emphasis was on spatial patterns of movement and not on the strict requirements of travellers and non-travellers (i.e. observable and latent demand). Traditional levels of service and land-use variables, defined as zonal means, were used to forecast travel 'demand' (see ch. 12). Modelling procedures were developed along recursive and simultaneous lines but, given the aggregate nature of the data, were completely deterministic and unrelated to realistic behavioural theories of choice. There have been many criticisms of the aggregate models, most of the comment relating to data deficiencies rather than the models themselves, which are in many ways an artifact of data limitations. An example of an aggregate recursive model where trips are aggregated by the origin zone, exemplified by the urban transportation study approaches, is:

Number of Trips:

Production: $V_o = g_1(S_o, T_o)$

Attraction: $V_d = g_2(A_d)$

Trip Allocation:

$$\frac{V_{od}}{V_o} = g_3(\tilde{V}_d, L_{od}), \forall_d, \text{ subject to the constraint } \Sigma_o V_{od} = V_d.$$

Modal Split:

$$\frac{V_{odm}}{V_{od}} = g_4[S_o, A_d(L_{odm})]\forall_m,$$

where S = socioeconomic variables

A = spatial opportunities variables (demand constraints)

T = aggregation variables, such as the resident population of the origin zone, which is the set of all potential trip makers in origin o (supply constraints)

L = level of service characteristics (perceived price)

V = volume of trips

o = origin zone

d = destination zone

m = mode of travel

We have already discussed the major inadequacies of the aggregate recursive procedure of the urban transport modelling system, and much more detail is presented in chapter 12. The aggregate simultaneous models are being widely used to predict the volume of trips by various modes between an origin and a destination. The general form of such models is:

$$V_{odm} = g_5[T_o, S_o, A_d(L_{odm})]\forall_m,$$

These models, referred to as direct demand models, typically employ data observations on geographical aggregates. A number of these models have been applied to urban travel demand.[21] Such models express the number of trips between any zonal pair for a given purpose and modes as a function of the number of individuals or households in the origin zone and their socio-economic characteristics, the appropriate measure of level of activity and other relevant socio-economic and land-use characteristics in the destination zone, together with the travel times and costs of the usual and alternative modes. The advantage of this approach over the traditional modelling system is that both the total number of trips and the allocations to modes are responsive to policy variables. Since these models do not consider alternative destinations only the choices of frequency and mode of travel have been modelled simultaneously. The assumption of no competing destinations may be acceptable for long-distance intercity travel, but not really for intra-urban travel. Since all aggregate models define the (continuous) dependent variable as the number of trips, they cannot adequately represent frequency choice for each individual traveller: 'They implicitly assume a choice between 0 and 1 alternative daily frequencies, or independent frequency choice.'[22]

All the present aggregate models, because of data constraints, embody the critical assumption that individuals or households within a given spatial zone are reasonably homogeneous and that variations in zonal averages for the selected variables accurately reflect the variations between individuals. Empirical evidence has disproved this hypothesis. For example, Fleet and Robertson[23] showed for Madison, Wisconsin, that aggregation of trips data to the zonal level reduced the variation in the number of trips between observations to only 20 per cent of the household level value. This criticism should not be made of the aggregate model structure for losing information it never had; rather we should be critical of the use of a geographical zone as the unit of analysis. Watson has recently demonstrated, using a recursive disaggregate model of mode choice[24] and a single data set, that the probabilistic assessment of mode choice at the level of the individual traveller gives a much lower predictive error than the deterministic assessment of mode choice at the level of the spatial zone (using a common set of variables). He concluded that: 'the data aggregation process conceals the behavioral basis of the mode choice decision, while the disaggregate approach yields models which are both behaviorally and statistically sound'[25]

The disaggregate travel choice models have several conceptual and practical advantages over aggregate models:

1. They provide a more natural setting for the development of causal relationships among their components, based on non-complex assumptions about the behaviour patterns of individuals rather than on statistically derived correlations in aggregate analysis.

2. They avoid ecological fallacies of inference whereby characteristics which coincidentally dominate the behaviour of arbitrary groups on an aggregate analysis are interpreted to affect the behaviour of individuals.
3. Being structured in terms of more plausible theories of consumer choice, disaggregate approaches provide useful guidance for an appropriate procedure for aggregating data and relationships in the development of more efficient and operational aggregate models.
4. They provide more efficient estimates of parameters at a smaller computational cost.
5. There is a greater degree of transferability potential of *models* from one data area to another, and the possibility of using the same set of models for multi-level planning is high.
6. Disaggregate models provide a basis for inferring the values that individuals put on various characteristics of the transportation system, such as the value of travel time savings.
7. The dependent variable is probabilistic (e.g. probability of choosing the mode m for travel from the origin o) in comparison to the deterministic dependent variable used in aggregate (zonal) models (e.g. number of trips by mode m from origin o).

The disaggregate travel demand models are concerned with discrete choices of an individual (e.g. no trip, one trip, two trips), whereas the aggregate models are obtained on the basis of a continuous average trip frequency variable and the average level-of-service and socio-economic variables, all pertaining to the 'average' individual in a zone. For the disaggregate model, the expected trip frequency of each individual is computed, and summation across all individuals gives the total aggregate travel demand. For aggregate models, each zone or zone pair represents one observation (individual): the 'average person'. The aggregate travel demand is then obtained by multiplying the trip frequency of the 'average person' by the size of the market in the zone. The additional effort involved in diaggregation is offset by the advantage obtained by the explicit selection of assumptions rather than the acceptance of unexplained or unidentified implicit assumptions inherent in the aggregate analysis approach, where the 'aggregation' problem is disguised.

While the disaggregate approach is clearly more realistic from a behavioural (demand) point of view, there are very real difficulties in actually summing across individuals, because of the heterogeneous nature of the population and the impossibility of computing the probabilities of choice for each individual, in order to obtain an estimate of the aggregate travel demand (the sum of the probabilities). The aspect of non-homogeneity can be shown by an example. Suppose we are concerned with predicting the effect of increasing the relative speed of buses. For *any* individual the resultant change in the value of the preference function $y[\,y = \alpha_o + \alpha_i x_i$

where α_i are parameters to be estimated and x_i are the values of the independent variables, and where the probability of taking a bus: $P_{\text{bus}} = e^y/(1 + e^y)$] is simply α_i times the change in the value of the variable x_i (assumed to be a relative value). But this identical change in y values will have different effects on mode choice for the particular journey purpose, depending on a person's current position along the curve representing the relationship between the probability of choosing the bus and y. If he is someone whose travel choice and personal characteristics make the bus a really inferior alternative, or if the person is captive to the bus, then the change in his choice probability will be very small. If he were at a point around the centre of the curve (a more competitive location) then the expected reaction to this same change in service characteristics is much larger. We must then know the current probability for choosing the bus (i.e. value of y) for each individual before we can predict the change in his probability. Some sort of averaging – aggregation – must be used, but it is argued that the method should not be like the present approach of aggregating the values of the variables affecting travel demand over the heterogeneous groups of individuals in a traffic zone whose demand is being modelled. An information loss occurs because no account is taken of the variability of the explanatory variables within the traffic zones in estimating the model coefficients. Assigning a zonal proportion (one point on the probabilistic curve) to *each* person in the zone, and then predicting on this basis, could lead to highly erroneous results if the people are distributed over a wide range of y values. We must concern ourselves with how the aggregation of individual travel demands may be accomplished more efficiently without losing information. There is no information loss in disaggregate models due to aggregation, because no aggregation is necessary to estimate the models. But the problem of aggregation and possible loss of information must be confronted *later* when using the model in aggregate travel demand forecasting and analysis. There is a need for the development of a practical relation between individual probabilities of choice and the corresponding aggregate shares.

The deterministic economic theory of consumer choice has been outlined in the context of an assumed single monetary budget constraint, and then criticised on the basis of its inconsistency with probabilistic consumer behaviour. There is another dimension of the neoclassical choice theory, however, which has received considerable attention within the framework of determinism, which relates to the allocation of time. Since a major economic benefit from transport investments is saving in travel time (ch. 5), and an important influence on travel choices (e.g. modal and route choice) is the relative travel times on the alternatives,[26] it is imperative that the modelling procedures used in the assessment of travel demand and choice should be used in the estimation of the value individuals place on savings in travel time. The improved behavioural disaggregate probabilistic methodologies, in particular the disaggregate recursive models of modal and route choice,[27] have been used with varying degrees of success to estimate the monetary value of travel time-savings, defined as the amount of money that an individual is willing to spend in order to save a unit of travel time. Before discussing the empirical and conceptual issues, it is important to outline the theoretical argument for incorporating considerations of time allocation, in addition to money allocation.

The neoclassical choice theory considered only the duration of the time-period for which the utility function is defined, without any allowance for the time that is available during this time-period to consume the particular commodity.[28] Given that an individual's actions are influenced by a complicated set of interactive constraints (including technological and institutional factors such as a determined work week), he is unable to allocate the desired amount of time to an activity; he may have to allocate too much or too little. In this chapter, consideration will be given to this problem. The consumer hence faces two constraints on his choice, namely the total time and money available. The combination of time and money is referred to as either the generalised cost or the implicit price of travel. The utilisation of this composite cost requires relative weights to be given to time and money. If it is desired to express the two inputs in like units (i.e. money or time[29]), it is necessary to estimate a value of time-savings in terms of money, or a value of money-savings in terms of time.

Bruzelius[30] has developed a 'general model'[31] framework in which to explain the theoretical relationships between goods and activities[32] in the context of the choice of consumption activities. The utility function is:

$$U(x_1, \ldots, x_n, t_1, \ldots, t_n), i = 1, \ldots, n$$

which is maximised subject to

$$\sum_{i=1}^{n} p_i x_i - wt_w - y_{ex} \leq 0 \qquad (1)$$

$$\sum_{i=1}^{n} t_i + t_w - T \leq 0 \qquad (2)$$

$$g_i(x_i, t_i) \leq 0 \qquad (3)$$

$$x_i \geq 0;\ t_i \geq 0;\ t_w \geq 0 \qquad (4)$$

where x_i = quantity of good i
t_i = time used along with the use of x_i
p_i = price of good i
w = wage rate
t_w = work time
y_{ex} = exogenous income
T = total time
g_i = an implicit function

Constraint (1) indicates the limits within which time and money can be allocated to goods and activities; (2) expresses the total time limit; (3) indicates the relationship between the consumption of time and goods variables; and (4) expresses the non-negativity requirement on the endogenous variables. In the case of inequality, it is assumed that the constraint is closed by a slack variable (t_{n+1}).

We will assume that (3) can be modified to conform with the constraint that for each x_i a minimum amount of time is needed but this minimum may be exceeded:[33]

$$g_i = a_i x_i - t_i \leq 0 \qquad (5)$$

where it is assumed that t_i cannot be chosen in positive quantities when x_i is non-positive (i.e. $x_i = 0 \Longleftrightarrow t_i = 0$). Restricted (flexible) substitution is a reasonable assumption for transport, where for example the capacity of the car and road congestion restrict the consumer to select a driving time for travelling between an origin and a destination, above a certain minimum level. From the first order conditions of maximum utility,[34] the marginal utility of x_i should equal the marginal utility of monetary outlays plus the marginal utility of *saving time in the particular activity* multiplied by a_i (the minimum time required per unit of x_i). The marginal utility of time in activity i should equal the marginal utility of time as a resource plus the marginal utility from saving time in activity i.

The special cases of this model are derived by varying the assumptions on the partial derivatives $\partial U/\partial x_i$, $\partial U/\partial t_i$, $\partial g_i/\partial x_i$, $\partial g_i/\partial t_i$. For example, if $\partial U/\partial x_i \neq 0$, $\partial U/\partial t_i = 0$, $\partial g_i/\partial x_i = 0$, and $\partial g_i/\partial t_i = 0$, then for all n activities, the general model would be nothing more than the traditional theory of demand involving perfectly timeless activities. The model above assumes restricted substitution, where $\partial U/\partial x_i \neq 0$, $\partial U/\partial t_i \neq 0$, $\partial g_i/\partial x_i \neq 0$, and $\partial g_i/\partial t_i \neq 0$. In DeSerpa's study,[35] also concerned with travel time-savings, he defined 'intermediate' goods from Tipping's[36] 'intermediate consumption' category to cover such activities as travelling to the shops etc. For these activities constraint (5) is binding.

The discussion above referred to time as a resource and the saving in time associated with a consumption activity. Since we are concerned with estimating the monetary equivalent of time, it is important to indicate the difference between the value of time and the value of *savings* time. The value of time as a resource results from the fact that time may be a scarce resource for the consumer, representing the monetary value that a consumer would be willing to pay to have an additional unit of time, *if this had been possible.* It is equal to μ/λ (where μ = marginal utility of time, and λ = marginal utility of money). The value of time-savings, however, reflects what the individual would be willing to pay to have time in an activity reduced and allocated to some other activity. The value of time savings is not necessarily equal between activities or the same as the resource value of time. DeSerpa has shown, in the framework outlined above, that the value of time-savings in an activity equals the difference between the resource value of time and value of time used in activity i. That is, $k_i/\lambda = \mu/\lambda = \partial U/(\partial t_i . \lambda)$ where k_i is the marginal loss in utility per unit of x_i from increasing the minimum time per unit of good i in an activity i. It is the value of time-savings that has empirical content:

> The value of time as a resource derives from its scarcity; it is an opportunity cost which is positive because the time resource is available in a limited amount. However, it makes little sense to consider the value associated with acquiring more of it, for such an increment is not possible ... in any meaningful sense. Time saving, on the other hand, is both possible and observable in many facets of human activity.[37]

The value of travel time savings has been obtained from binary choice models of mode choice[38] and route choice,[39] using the revealed preference or 'trade-off' approach. Situations were selected in which the traveller revealed (through questionnaires) a preference between alternatives involving a trade-off between higher (lower) time costs and lower (high) money costs. The assumptions necessary to justify the resultant conclusion, that a preference for a slower and less expensive alternative indicates that an individual values his time-savings at a rate no greater than the measured trade-off, are somewhat restrictive in terms of *demand* theory, since they imply that subjective preferences (non-time-cost influences) are not relevant. Any study which includes a constant term is not making the restrictive assumption, since such a term can be interpreted as a mode bias. The only choice criterion is the relative cost (money and time) of the various alternatives. Given that in the complete spectrum of situations facing all individuals, there is a definite proportion of individuals who face a situation where the preferred journey requires both time and money,[40] then 'other things' in the subjective preference function must be influencing the choice between alternatives, and hence travel demand. This leads to the suggestion that the present empirical approaches to the valuation of travel time-savings are not consistent with the foundations of choice and demand theory, but that in the absence of acceptable alternative procedures which allow for the trade-offs in terms of relative costs which include all the relevant subjective preference dimensions (such as comfort and convenience), it is assumed that the value of time-savings obtained from the traders only is representative of the values applicable to all travellers, including persons not presently facing a strict time-cost trade-off situation. This is a preferable assumption[41] to the widespread empirical approach which includes in the analysis of the calculation of the value of time-savings all individuals facing time-cost trader and non-trader situations.

The arguments here support the need for a determination of the relevant trade-offs for various individuals, and a possible composite trade-off function incorporating time as one of the ingredients of the estimation procedure. For example, perhaps we could trade-off (in accordance with subjective preferences) 'time plus effort' with money, because this might place more people in the sample in a trade-off with respect to the choice criterion. If the 'effort' dimension was time-independent,[42] then a linear additive function would give us the value of time-savings and the value of effort reduction, which with money cost (or time-cost) could be combined to produce a generalised cost (or time) of travel.

Empirical illustrations

The empirical studies that exemplify a range of issues related to the determination of the real demand for urban passenger transportation are relatively few. There are several reasons for this. Firstly the traditional transportation modelling system which still operates as the basic planning tool is essentially non-behavioural, with the models concerned with replicating the results of conditions existing at the time of data collection. These models provide little or no guidance to the effects on travel decisions of changes in traveller's circumstances or in the terms upon which they are offered competing alternatives in the transport environment. Secondly, the type of area-wide data typically collected by transportation studies (table 1) has been traditionally designed to conform with the replication criterion. Thirdly, the inability to handle large data sets at the level of the basic decision-making unit resulted in the grouping of users of the transport system on the basis of physical location (both origin and destination); in effect defining the heterogeneous geographical zone as the decision unit.

There are, however, a few recent studies which have taken existing transportation study data and modified them to allow for behavioural interactions. The better studies have been undertaken by Charles River Associates and Akiva, the former using the existing home-interview and network information collected in 1967 for Pittsburgh, and the latter extracting a sub-sample from a metropolitan Washington study home-interview conducted in 1968, together with network data. The Charles River Associates study is discussed below as a mechanism for illustrating the most promising approaches to understanding the demand for urban passenger transport. In addition, an aggregate simultaneous model will be presented to illustrate the type of economic demand model presently used in an operational role by a number of planning organisations.

A disaggregate recursive model

The Charles River Associates Model (CRAM)[43] of urban transportation choice behaviour is an application of the Luce model of the determination of choice probabilities. The approach already outlined above involves specifying the functional form of a probability condition:

$$P(x, S, i) = \text{Prob}[U(x_i, S) > U(x_j, S)] \text{ for all } j \neq 1, \ldots, J.\ j \neq i,$$

TABLE 1 *Typical transportation study data*

Basic Household Information

Number of separate families in a dwelling unit
Type of dwelling
Number of years the head of household has lived at the present address
Number of privately owned cars and utilities
Number of government and company cars
Number of all residents (excluding visitors) under 5 years old and 5 years and over
Number of resident visitors under 5 years old and 5 years old and over
Number of residents employed full time or part time
Total take home annual family income
Average take home income per resident 5 years old and over, and per employed person
Number of persons 5 years old and over making trips
Number of persons 5 years old and over not making trips
Number of car driver trips and car passenger trips by household member
Head of household job location change since living at present address
Relationship of each house occupant to head of household
Sex of each member of household
Age of each member of household
Driving licence status of each member of household
Employment status of each member of household
Occupation of each member of household
Industry of each member of household
Employment or School location of each member of household
Residential location zone
Main mode of travel to work or school of each member of household
Trip making propensity for travel to work or school of each member of household on survey day
Number of public transport passenger trips
Type of parking at work
Number of hours worked on day before survey
Previous address of head of household if moved in last 5 years

Trip Information

All trips made by each permanent resident and visitor 5 years of age or older at the address during past 24 hours:
- Trip origin zone
- Trip destination zone
- Time trip commenced
- Time trip finished
- Land use at origin zone
- Land use at destination zone
- Purpose of trip
- Mode of travel
- Car driver – Number of persons in car
- Car driver – Type of parking
- Car driver – Parking cost
- Trip time duration
- Shopping commodity group:
  - Connecting modes to and from railway station
  - Rail ticket type (season ticket etc.)

and specifying the variables in x and S, where x is a vector of attributes of an alternative i, and S is the socioeconomic characteristics vector of the individual. The operational version proposed for the CRAM is:

$$P(f) = g_6(S, A, L)$$
$$P(d/f = 1) = g_7(S, A_d, L_d), \forall\, d)$$
$$P(h/f = 1, d) = g_8(S, L_{dh}), \forall\, h)$$
$$P(m/f = 1, d, h) = g_9(S, L_{dhm}, \forall\, m)$$

(A, L are weighted averages across all alternative destinations.)

We shall illustrate this approach for the three choice acts of mode choice, destination choice and frequency choice. The sequence implied by the order of the conditional probabilities was used to formulate the composite variables L and A. The notation used has already been explained. The single journey purpose of shopping travel was selected because it displays greater short-run variability in the choice acts other than mode choice than does the work or school trip, the only other two journey purposes for which adequate data are available. Shopping destination and trip frequency are directly linked to mode choice, since they incorporate measures of disutility of travel as significant determinants of choice. The disutility measure is an inclusive price for a given trip, defined as the sum of the attributes of a given mode weighted by the parameters from the modal choice function for that purpose. The inclusive price concept differs from the generalised cost notion in that the latter is an expression in terms of a common unit of measurement, usually cents or minutes, whereas the former is simply a linear summation of weighted attributes, each not necessarily expressed along the same measurement dimension. Hence in the trip destination model, for example, the disutility of travel to each relevant shopping destination is measured by the attributes of that trip to that destination weighted by the parameter of each attribute as estimated in the modal choice model. This provides a natural measure of 'accessibility' of each destination to the tripmaker. The measure is a significant determinant of choice of destination and can be used to measure the effects on the distribution of shopping trips between zonal pairs resulting from selective changes in the transportation system.

The CRAM sample was a sub-sample of the total Pittsburgh sample, selected to include sections of Pittsburgh which are job and shopping centres, as well as a broad cross-section of inner-city and suburban residential neighbourhoods. Pittsburgh is essentially a two-mode city; car and bus. Data was initially obtained from a person and trip questionnaire relating to trips taken by a sample of households in the previous 24-hour period; from a household questionnaire which obtained a wide range of information on household socio-economic characteristics, and from highway and public transport network data such as assignment speeds. Information on alternative modes, destinations, travel times and costs were not available and had to be generated on an individual by individual basis. The final variables used in the models are door-to-door modal travel times and their components (in-vehicle, walk, wait and transfer times), travel costs (including the marginal cost of car usage for a given trip, parking and toll costs), travel times for alternative destinations, and various socio-economic variables.[44]

A statistical estimation procedure has to be selected for applying the disaggregate recursive model. In recent years, extensive testing of alternative estimation procedures[45] has shown that, on both theoretical and statistical grounds, the binary logit approach (and its multinomial extension) is the appropriate transformation to use in fitting the model to the base data and in predicting the effects of a change in the value of an explanatory variable on the probability of choice. The dependent variable is an expression of the log odds of choice of a particular mode. Binary logit maximum likelihood estimates for each explanatory variable (including the constant term) are obtained, together with measures of the statistical reliability of the parameter estimates, and various measures of the ability of the model to explain the data. The results for the conditional logit model of shopping mode choice are given in table 2 for four combinations of the explanatory variables which gave the most satisfactory results.

All coefficients in the four models have the expected sign; for example, if the in-vehicle time by car were to increase, then according to the model there would be a reduction in the probability of choosing the car for the journey to the shops (assuming a given f, d, and h). Models 1 and 2 are better than models 3 and 4 on the basis of the significance of the individual variables. Although the t-valves are low for bus walk time, the magnitudes of the parameters are quite stable even though the t-values decrease when additional variables are included. The coefficients of bus walk time, car in-vehicle less bus station-to-station time, and car operating costs less bus fares imply in model 1, a value of walk time of \$US5.46 per person hour and a value of invehicle time of \$US0.95 per person hour. The models provide good fits of the base-line data; for example in model 1 the probability of selecting the actual mode used is greater than 0.5 for 133 of the 140 observations, and greater than 0.9 for 116 of the 140 observations.

The results of the mode choice model are now used to calculate the inclusive price of the trip for each person, which is an explanatory variable in the next model, the destination choice model. CRAM investigated the choice of the trip to the actual destination for the chosen mode with the trips to the alternative destinations for the chosen mode. The possible alternative destinations for each observation are selected by dividing the city into zones and choosing all destination zones to which there is a trip in the sample from the

TABLE 2 *Empirical results for the conditional logit mode choice model. Choice of mode: 1 = car, 0 = bus. Estimates of Parameters. (t-statistics in brackets), N = 140.*

Explanatory variable	Model 1	Model 2	Model 3	Model 4
Walk time (minutes) for bus trip	0.374 (1.14)	0.398 (0.97)	0.300 (0.86)	0.274 (0.45)
Wait plus transfer time (minutes) for bus trip	–	–	0.0647 (1.61)	–
Station-to-station time (minutes) for bus trip	–	–	–	0.0532 (1.17)
In-vehicle time (minutes) for car trip	–	–	–	−0.0486 (0.51)
Car in-vehicle time less bus station-to-station time (minutes)	−0.0654 (2.04)	−0.0636 (1.60)	–	–
Car in-vehicle time less bus in-vehicle time (minutes)	–	–	−0.0287 (0.40)	–
Car operating cost less bus fares (dollars)	−4.11 (2.46)	−4.66 (2.27)	−4.10 (1.93)	−4.06 (2.32)
Ratio of number of cars to number of workers in the household	2.24 (2.02)	2.26 (1.98)	2.01 (1.93)	1.89 (2.48)
Race of respondent (0 if white, 1 if non-white).	–	−2.18 (1.73)	–	–
Occupation of head of household (0 if blue-collar, 1 if white collar)	–	−1.53 (1.39)	–	–
Constant (pure car mode preference effect)	−6.77 (4.07)	−6.20 (2.96)	−6.65 (4.31)	−6.37 (3.50)

Recent studies[46] have suggested that socioeconomic variables such as occupation should not be separately included in a model containing variables performing different roles, such as trip characteristics. Rather, they should either be used to stratify the data set (so as to assess variations in behaviour) or be directly related by a functional form to the trip characteristics, so as to allow for their direct effect on the perception of trip characteristics.

origin zone. Since the number of alternative destinations is likely to exceed two (the binary choice situation), then a multinomial logit procedure must be adopted to develop maximum likelihood estimates.[47] 63 observations on car travellers were used to test the destination choice model. Inclusive prices for each traveller were obtained by the formula (from the shopping mode choice model 1):

Inclusive Price = 0.0654 (car in-vehicle time) + 4.11 (car operating cost). Two additional variables are also included in the model. The ratio of retail employment in the destination zone as a percentage of total retail employment in the region is used as a measure of the attractiveness of a destination. An interaction variable designed to show the effect of a socio-economic variable on choice of destination is included in the form of the difference for alternative destinations between the product of the number of

TABLE 3 *Empirical results for the conditional logit destination choice model (Destinations i and j). N = 63*

Explanatory variable	Model 5	Model 6
Inclusive price ($\hat{p}$) of trip $= \hat{p}_{iz} - p_{jz}$, $z = 1 \ldots n$ persons	−1.06 (3.76)	−0.602 (3.78)
Index of destination attractiveness $= E_{iz} - E_{jz}$	0.844 (3.72)	0.832 (3.71)
Interaction effect $= (\text{PSC}_z)(\hat{p}_{iz}) - (\text{PSC}_z)(\hat{p}_{jz})$	–	−0.521 (1.52)

pre-school children in the household (PSC) and the inclusive price. The alternative destinations are unranked and vary between individuals. The results are given in table 3. The dependent variable is the log odds that one destination zone is chosen over a second destination zone. The inclusive price of travel is a highly significant determinant of the choice of shopping destination (t-value = 3.76). The sign of the estimate suggests that as the 'price' of travel to a given destination i increases relative to the individual's alternative destinations, the probability of travelling to that destination decreases. The same argument in terms of the relative size of the shopping areas suggests that the greater the relative trade opportunities at a given destination, the greater the probability of travelling to that destination to shop. With only three variables, model 6 predicts the actual destination about 46 per cent of the time. Despite an absolutely low percentage of correct prediction, this is an improvement over present aggregate models; and with more explanatory variables and observations on other (non-car) model trips an improvement in predictive capability can be expected.

The shopping trip frequency choice model is designed to investigate, among other considerations, the hypothesis that the frequency of travel to relevant shopping facilities is directly related to the accessibility of a household to these facilities. CRAM analysed a sample of 80 car-using households, of whom 59 recorded a shopping trip on the survey day. An inclusive price of a trip for non-trip takers is calculated by assuming that the distribution of destination preferences is that determined in model 6, and that utility has a separable form, implying that this distribution is independent of the distribution of tastes for choosing car trips. The overall price of shopping for household z is:

$$\hat{\hat{p}}_z = \sum_d H_z(d)\,\hat{p}_z(d)$$

where $H_z(d)$ is the estimated probability of household z selecting destination d, and $\hat{p}_z(d)$ is the inclusive price of travel for household z to destination d. The destination attractiveness index was also redefined as

$$\hat{E}_z = \sum_d H_z(d)\,E_z(d),$$

TABLE 4 *Empirical results of the conditional logit trip frequency choice model. N = 80*

Explanatory variable	Model 7
Inclusive price of trip (weighted time and cost using model 6 weights)	−1.72
$= \hat{\hat{p}}_z - 0$	(3.16)
Index of destination attractiveness	3.90
$= \hat{E}_z - 0$	(3.61)

where $E_z(d)$ is the percentage of the region's retail trade employment found in household z's destination zone d. $\hat{\hat{p}}_z$ and $\hat{E}_z$ are respectively measures of the cost of travel to shop for household z and the shopping opportunities which an individual from z receives if he takes a trip. The results of the best model are given in table 4. The dependent variable is the log odds of making a daily shopping trip. The variables, both significant and of a plausible sign, reflect the argument that the frequency of travel is inversely related to the time and cost of travel, so that if travel times or costs are reduced through improvements in the transport system the frequency of shopping travel should increase. The model predicts the actual decision with a probability of at least 0.5 for 75 per cent of the observations.

The disaggregate recursive model (CRAM) provides the planner with a relatively stronger tool for advising policy makers on the types of policies required to achieve a more efficient transport system; and at the same time it provides an improved mechanism for assessing the effects of selected policies. Also, these models suggest that the planner may 'have far stronger tools at hand for dealing with congestion than alternative modes of transportation'.[48] For example, changes in parking charges or fares which differentiate between areas of a region according to relative congestion will cause shoppers to rearrange their travel patterns and thereby spread out the traffic volumes over less congested areas of the city. Selective changes in transport variables will also cause appreciable changes in the amount of shopping travel. The extent of the change as a result of a policy can be compared with the expected modal switching (frequency assumed constant), by calculating the elasticity of trip demand, with respect to the attribute k. The elasticity measure for the logit model is:[49]

$$\epsilon_z = (1 - H_z)\theta_k x_{kz}$$

where k = attribute k
θ = estimate of parameter of attribute k
x = value of attribute k for each individual

Suppose we compare the elasticity of demand for modal choice with respect to a given transport variable, and the elasticity of demand for trip frequency with respect to the same given transport variable. For a particular individual displaying (for example) a 30 minute in-vehicle car time, and a 0.5 probability of currently choosing the car, and of currently maintaining a trip frequency, an across the board change in car time (to all destinations) would produce a mode choice elasticity of demand of 0.98, and a trip frequency elasticity of demand of −1.69. Hence, unless there are offsetting differences in the existing probabilities of choice, the trip frequency elasticity will be significantly greater than the modal choice elasticity. Often, the modal choice elasticities derived from disaggregate models are based on a sample of people facing a real mode choice only, and hence allowance must be made for the proportion of captive modal travellers (for the particular journey purpose) in an urban area. Thus if the captives are x per cent of the total mode m users, for example, then the short-run trip purpose elasticities for the mode m should be derived by multiplying the appropriate elasticity by $(1 - x/100)$.

An aggregate simultaneous model

Shepherd's direct demand model[50] is a good example of the aggregate simultaneous demand modelling approach. A non-linear work travel demand model is developed, replacing the traditional aggregate simultaneous model dependent variable – volume of trips – with a probabilistic interpretation – work travel choice probabilities for any zone – given by the observed trip frequencies for each zone. The general form of the model is:

$$\begin{aligned} T_{ijm} &= f_m(G_{ijm}, Y_i) \qquad & i &= 1 \ldots n \\ G_{ijm} &= f_m(c_{ijm}, vt_{ijm}) \qquad & j &= 1 \ldots n \\ & & m &= 1 \ldots k \end{aligned}$$

where T_{ijm} = number of work trips per worker from zone i to zone j by mode m

G_{ijm} = (average) generalised cost of travel from zone i to zone j by mode m

Y_i = (average) income level in zone i

c_{ijm} = money cost of travel from zone i to zone j by mode m

v = value of (in-vehicle) private travel time-savings

t = travel time from zone i to zone j by mode m

Weights of 1.0, 1.5, 1.5 and 2.0 were given to in-vehicle, walking, transfer and waiting times respectively, to indicate the relative disutility of each component of travel time. These weights were obtained from studies of the value of travel time components. The empirical analysis was simplified by considering only home-based work trips, aggregations of traffic zones (= districts), and districts with a specified minimum number of work trips (designed to reduce high sampling variance). The data was obtained from the 1970 Perth (Australia) Regional Transport Study and a 1966 home interview survey (2% sample). 34 of the 63 Perth area districts were accepted on the basis of the specified minimum number of work trips. The study was further restricted to two alternative destinations – the Central Business District (CBD) and non-CBD. 30 per cent of all work trips were attracted to the CBD, an area of 3.6km^2 out of a total 5390km^2. Two modes – car and total public transport – were considered separately for CBD travel, by linking trips involving several modes and grouping bus and train modes where both existed. The non-CBD work travel demand equations did not stratify by mode; the total number of non-CBD work trips from any district was derived from the difference between the estimated CBD work trips and total work trips from that district. Shepherd used a proxy variable for the non-CBD generalised travel cost. This variable, the ratio of labour force employed in district *i* to the labour force resident in district *i*, is assumed to be a proxy for both the price of travel by all modes to districts competing with the CBD and the attractiveness of these districts as places of employment.

The demand functions to be estimated are:

$$D_{iw} = f_w(G_{iw}, C_i) \qquad i = 1 \ldots 34$$
$$w = 1 \ldots 3$$
$$\sum D_{iw} = 1$$

where
D_{i1} = number of CBD work trips per worker from district *i* by car
D_{i2} = number of CBD work trips per worker from district *i* by public transport
D_{i3} = number of non-CBD work trips per worker from district *i*
G_{i1} = generalised cost of travel from district *i* to CBD by car
G_{i2} = generalised cost of travel from district *i* to CBD by public transport
G_{i3} = generalised cost of travel from district *i* to non-CBD districts
C_i = car ownership per head in district *i* (as a proxy for income level)

The dependent variables can be interpreted as the conditional probability that a worker from district *i* will make work travel choice *w*, given the values of the explanatory variables. The model cannot specify whether a *particular* worker will travel to the CBD by car when his generalised costs of travel are, say G_{sw} and his car ownership C_s. The model is only concerned with the set of all workers with values G_{sw} and C_s, and thus it is entirely probabilistic. Since the dependent variable is a probability, i.e. $0 < E(D_{iw}/G_{iw}, C_i) \leqq 1$, the appropriate estimation procedure is the logit transformation. Since estimators of the work travel choice probabilities for any district are given by the observed trip frequencies for that district, we can rewrite the above relation as $0 < P(w/\alpha_1 x_1 + \alpha_2 x_2 + \ldots + \alpha_n x_n) \leqq 1$. Since it can be assumed that more than two travel alternatives are available to the individual worker, the multinomial extension of the binary logit model must be used.

$$\text{i.e. } \log\left[\frac{D_{iw}}{D_{ir}}\right] = \log\left[\frac{P_w}{P_r}\right] = f(\alpha_1 x_1 + \alpha_2 x_2 + \ldots + \alpha_n x_n)$$

$$w, r, = 1 \ldots 3$$
$$w \neq r$$

The empirical results are given in table 5. Both equations are statistically significant at the 95 per cent level of confidence, with all coefficients displaying theoretically correct signs. While both the CBD generalised cost and car ownership coefficients are statistically significant at the 95 per cent level, the non-significance of the non-CBD generalised cost (x_{i2}) variable is probably related to the selection of the proxy variable. Since the probability rate values are determined by the summation-to-unity condition, it is possible to compare the observed and expected frequencies. The correlation coefficients between observed and expected choices over all districts were 0.96 and 0.92 for car and public transport CBD work choices respectively.

The model can be used directly to assess the likely short-term travel behaviour implications of alternative policies. Since Shepherd concentrated on work trips, the short term implications are essentially modal split effects, since a change in the total number of work trips caused solely by a change in some characteristic of the transport system does not arise. We will illustrate this for CBD work trips. The traditional elasticity measure (i.e. $p_w\, \partial x_{iz}/x_{iz}\, \partial p_w$) is inappropriate for the difference formulation of the generalised cost variable, because when the generalised cost difference between the two modes is zero, the elasticity of choice with respect to this difference is zero. The elasticity measure used by Shepherd is one of a number capable of overcoming this problem:

$$\epsilon(p_{1j} x_{iz}) = (p_1 + p_2)^{-2}\left\{p_1 e_{p_2}^{x_{iz}} - p_2 e_{p_1}^{x_{iz}}\right\} = -\epsilon(p_2, x_{iz}),$$
$$\text{where } \epsilon(p, x) = p\, \partial x/x\, \partial p.$$

TABLE 5 *Empirical results of the logit (weighted regression) demand model. N(Districts) = 34*

Dependent variable	Explanatory variables
$\frac{P_1}{P_3}$	$\exp(-0.109x_{i1} - 0.194x_{i2} + 2.695x_{i3})$ (3.63) (7.95) (4.37)
$\frac{P_2}{P_3}$	$\exp(-0.093x_{i1} - 0.134x_{i2} + 1.553x_{i3})$ (3.00) (0.556) (2.47)

$x_{i1} = G_{i1} - G_{i2}$, $x_{i2} = G_{i3}$, $x_{i3} = C_i$

Figures in brackets are t-values

The change in modal split (either overall or on a single district basis) resulting from a proposed policy can be estimated by varying the mean value of the appropriate explanatory variable or component of an explanatory variable. For example, suppose CBD car parking costs were doubled to 20 cents, increasing the average cost difference to 23 cents. Since the base probability that a worker faced with the average values of the independent variables will choose to work in the CBD and to travel there by car is 0.35 or by public transport is 0.30, the probability of this (representative) worker travelling to the CBD by car after the change in parking costs becomes $0.35 - 10(0.004) = 0.31$, or by public transport 0.34. 0.004 is obtained from the elasticity formula. This single result will clearly be an overestimate of the policy effect because of feedback effects. While longer-term feedback effects are not ascertainable, it might be possible exogenously to postulate likely second-order effects of the 4 per cent fewer worker car trips to the CBD (via speed–flow and speed–cost relationships), and then reconsider the effects of the real short-run effect of parking cost. For example, the consequent reduction in congestion might lead to a reduction in in-vehicle time of, say, 3 minutes for car and 1 minute for bus. The new in-vehicle time difference would be minus 7 minutes, which would increase the new proportion of CBD car and public transport users from 31 per cent to 32 per cent ($0.31 + 2(0.0042) = 0.32$), and 33 per cent respectively.

The discussion above has outlined the operational state of urban passenger transport demand modelling, which is still in its infancy with respect to the development and application of models in the many real world situations. Nearly all aggregate modelling has been confined to the relatively well-defined short-run work (fixed origin–destination) travel situation, with occasional application to shopping and social trips. However, the same common set of trip variables is generally used, which is contrary to evidence which suggests that each journey-purpose has a set of distinct explanatory influences not contained within another journey-purposes influencing set. For the results of a recent study by Hensher on the main determinants of the frequency and mode choice for shopping trips see table 6.

Conclusions

Almost any transport issue involves travel demand. In order to judge the wisdom of changing the amount or character of the transport system, we should have a good indication of the effects which the changes will have on travel demand. After all, travel demand in turn leads to the determination of such diverse indicators as system service for the user, economic feasibility, financial feasibility, and social and environmental impact. Without the ability to predict the response of travel demand to system changes, our ability to judge the wisdom of particular initiatives is questionable.

TABLE 6 *The major determinants of shopping travel, Sydney, Australia, 1973*

Mode choice	Number of trips	Number of trips by a mode	
Car passenger/bus Bus/car passenger	All modes	Car passenger	Bus
1. Overall time and speed	1. Able to do all or main shopping in one trip	1. Allowing for baby's stroller (pram)	1. Cost
2. Frequency and regularity	2. Being constrained by shoppers' full time employment	2. Multi-purpose journey requirement	2. Ease of travel
3. Convenience in general	3. General leisure activities	3. When food needs arise	3. Able to do all or main shopping in one trip
4. Shortage of goods	4. Fitting in with plans of other members of household	4. Dislike for shopping	4. Fitting in with other planned activities
	5. Buying fresh foodstuffs	5. Buying fresh foodstuffs	5. Limited finance
	6. Availability of local goods/services outlets		

Source: Hensher, D. A., *Consumer Preferences in Urban Trip-Making*, Commonwealth Bureau of Roads (Melbourne, 1974), 784.

The traffic forecasting models were successful for the work that was necessary in the 1960s. Will they be just as successful in analysing today's transportation issues? The problems of the 1960s are not the problems of the 1970s. In the near future, the transport planning process will have to become more short-term or problem-solving oriented to reflect current needs. Such planning will often revolve around the development sub-area plans, such as a plan for the central business district, which may be concerned with distribution systems, fringe parking concepts, traffic-free zones, the role of the bicycle, the taxi and the pedestrian, the movement of urban goods and the location of freight terminals. Plans for the remainder of the central area may focus on the development of fast public transport and methods to keep traffic off local streets so as to reduce the impact of arterial traffic on local residents.

There are certainly additional problems with today's models, which need to be addressed in the near future. It is difficult to use them in responding to the increasing number of environmentally oriented legislated requirements. For example, the Clear Air Acts in the USA which require plans for improvement in air quality to be drawn up and implemented, or the development of strategies for conserving energy resources, often result in a desire to control travel demand, yet that is the best way to achieve this end? Is the current state of the art in travel demand forecasting adequate for the evaluation of such options as: car free zones, a staggered working week, staggered working hours, priority lanes, traffic control schemes, bus pooling, jitney (a form of taxi service, permitting multiple hire), and changes in comfort and convenience?

While we are able to evaluate a few of these options, our ability to do so is embryonic at best. Even in the case of traditional alternatives, such as adding highway capacity, we often find our ability somewhat lacking. Perhaps the most frequently asked question involves the amount of additional travel which is generated when highway capacity is increased. While essentially all travel forecasting procedures produce a travel demand forecast which varies with system supply, we seem unable to respond directly to this issue. The question is complicated by the fact that the change in supply will also result in a change in land use. What is needed is the ability to predict the three-way equilibrium between level of service or system supply, urban development and travel demand (see chap. 10) and to express the result in such a way as to be meaningful to the decision-maker.

It is thus apparent that there is a clear need to move ahead in the area of the travel demand model development. But in what direction should we head? This chapter has worked through the development and application of the main alternative modelling procedures. As we approach a more general procedure, we are paving the way for models which will be able to handle more diverse options. The disaggregated models show desirable signs of being able to handle the more complex requirements that will need to be included in future travel demand models, either as direct influences or as constraints.

7

Urban freight

S. K. Hicks

Introduction

Any urban area depends for its existence on a massive flow of commodities into, out of, and within its boundaries. Yet the transport of goods remains a forgotten aspect of urban transportation study. An OECD panel study of future directions for research in urban transportation, in acknowledging the lopsidedness of its recommendations, which related entirely to passenger transport, said:

> the problem of urban distribution of goods remains largely unexplored, and the Panel's inability to treat this matter in detail can be taken as tacit evidence of the lack of an informed body of knowledge on the subject. Yet, the movement of goods in cities is so closely related to the movement of people, that a study of urban transportation requirements which neglects to take freight into account can be quite misleading. This is why a systematic inquiry into the problems of urban freight transportation is, in the Panel's opinion, a very urgent necessity.[1]

The joint carriage of both passenger and freight in one vehicle defies any simple distinction between passenger and freight transport tasks. The household shopping trip is one important case. The shopping trip is a journey for the purpose of selecting and purchasing particular commodities and carrying them back to the home. This suggests that the trip is a freight journey. Yet the housewife's presence at the store is an essential element of the journey and, indeed, if she is unable to find the goods required, she may return home without transporting any goods at all. This might suggest that the shopping trip is best treated as a passenger journey. The nature of the service vehicle journey presents a similar problem. It is unrewarding to attempt to separate the plumber from his tools, the fireman from his hose and ladder or the doctor from his medical bag. The problem extends to any truck journey. The truck driver is a passenger who performs functions apart from control of the vehicle. Certainly he is guardian of the commodities during transit, but he may also be responsible for their loading and unloading and for billing and the taking of orders.

In transport behavioural analysis, the important factor in determining whether a journey is a freight journey is the extent to which the vehicle type and its use are dictated by the decision to carry goods. The central purpose of the classification is not semantic – the affixing of a 'passenger' or 'freight' label to each jouney – but the distinguishing of a form of urban transport which, because of its own particular characteristics, is not amenable to application of economic planning analysis in the format that has been developed for the study of passenger transportation.

The unit of carriage in passenger transport is the individual person. In freight transport it is the *consignment*, the commodity or collection of commodities travelling together as a unit from a single dispatch point to a single receiving point. Unlike private passenger transport and more like public transit, the freight vehicle does not usually wait ready to take the load to its next destination; instead it moves on to pick up and deliver other consignments. Freight movement is undirectional: goods move from point to point and, unlike passenger transportation, are unlikely to return to the point of their original departure. Passenger transport must pay regard to the comfort and convenience of its passengers. Except for special problems of perishability, fragility and urgency, freight transport need pay no such regard: the ride can be rough, hot or cramped and the goods can remain loaded on the vehicle overnight. Where breakdowns occur in the passenger transport system, passengers provide quick and vocal notice of the difficulties. Goods consignments are voiceless. Finally, while passengers are able to step straight from other activities into the vehicle, freight consignments must be prepared for transport, packaged and perhaps stored, loaded and unloaded, documented and checked.

The different modes of freight transport have particular features which give each unique problems. For this reason, and due to the central importance of the motor vehicle as the feeder mode of other modes and as a competitor for the road space used by the major passenger modes, it seems sensible to concentrate the early stage of development of an urban freight planning model on the vehicular mode. As we will see, goods movement by motor vehicle is many-faceted and one must not risk losing sight of these facets in an attempt to cover too wide a field at once.

However, at no stage should the railway, waterway, pipeline and air modes be forgotten. They are of particular importance to the vehicular mode for two reasons. Firstly, insofar as they are practicable substitutes for vehicular-freight, they offer an opportunity to reduce freight traffic on roads and therefore to diminish the problems of road freight. Secondly, to the extent that road transport must deliver goods to, or receive them from, other modes, there will be difficulties and costs in transhipment, the establishment and operation of terminals and the congestion of streets leading to the transfer terminals.

Here, then, urban freight transport will be defined as all journeys into, out of, and within a designated urban area by road vehicles specifically engaged in pick-up or delivery of goods (whether the vehicle be empty or not), with the exception of shopping trips. The goods carried can be any form of non-human cargo, including livestock and self propelled items such as mobile cranes, mobile libraries, street sweepers and earth-moving equipment. With the plea that they should not be forgotten and in the hope that they will at a later date be integrated into an urban freight model if that is where they fit best, service vehicle jouneys and shopping trips are excluded on the subjective assessment that their nature is influenced more by the requirements of the passenger than of the goods they carry.Though non-vehicular freight modes are here excluded from direct attention, the need for the special and thorough study of their role in urban goods movement is not disputed.

This chapter reviews the state of present knowledge on urban freight. It begins with an examination of the nature of the urban freight problem and the costs of urban goods movement. An analytical taxonomy of these costs is proposed. The second section discusses the potential and difficulties of some of the most important measures that have been proposed to alleviate the urban freight problem. The central role of the government in the effective implementation of these proposals and the discovery of other urban freight strategies is argued in the third section. The nature of planning models needed for this role to be played is considered. The final section surveys the state of supply and demand modelling and the problem of heterogeneity of urban freight.

Cost and the urban freight problem

An old maxim says that once a problem is clearly defined it is more than half solved. In reality, the first problem in urban freight is the definition of the problem. Such factors as under-utilisation of vehicles, traffic congestion and inadequate loading and unloading facilities may be important elements of the problem and yet, without further research, it is intuition as much as knowledge which guides efforts to plot the dimensions of the urban freight problem. 'It is possible that the most important issues are yet to be discovered' observed a US National Transportation Report,[2] citing the possibility that the unexplored technological difficulties of improving urban goods movement may prove one of the gravest elements of the problem.

Demand for freight transport is a derived demand, the movement of goods being an imput in the production and consumption processes; it is a means, not an end. Thus the primary operative objective of the urban freight transport system becomes clear. The urban freight transport task should be performed at the lowest total social cost possible. The total amount of resources consumed and disbenefits created in performing the freight task should be minimised: efficiency is the goal, given any other social, commercial and equity objectives agreed upon.

This being the operative objective, then, the urban freight problem is that of achieving this objective. Specifically, the problem is this: the discovery and effective implementation of measures which will reduce the total social cost of urban goods movement to the lowest possible level commensurate with the freight requirements and objectives of society. The premise is that costs are not at present being minimised.

The economists' starting point is therefore the social cost of freight transport. For the purpose of looking at its elements in the urban area it is helpful to sub-classify this cost into four parts: *a.* Transport operation costs, *b.* Community costs, *c.* External costs, and *d.* Urban structure costs. Classification of costs is an old, and occasionally overwrought, economic analytical manipulation. It helps here to concentrate attention on the various aspects of a multiform problem. In examining them in turn, we must remain mindful of the interrelationship and overlapping nature of the cost elements.

Transport operation costs

Freight transportation incurs private costs for dispatcher, trucker and receiver. These *transport operation costs* include not only driver's wages and vehicle running costs, but also vehicle depreciation, registration and overheads, and the terminal costs of packaging, storing, loading, unloading, recording and insuring the goods. The qualitative characteristics of the transport used will not only influence the magnitude of these costs (e.g. higher packaging or insurance costs with more damage prone transport) but also can create additional transport operation costs of their own, which can be called *quality costs.* The damage, destruction or theft of uninsured goods, for example, involves a loss of revenue-earning potential for their owners, as can late delivery. Again, unreliable service may involve the dispatcher or receiver in the added wage costs of employees waiting for vehicle arrival or in time-consuming searches for 'lost' vehicles.

Depending on the nature of a commodity, the total transport component of its final demand price can vary widely. The outputs of service industries and of sectors producing goods with a high ratio of value to bulk have a low transport cost component, while goods with a low ratio of value to bulk, such as minerals or certain staple foodstuffs, can have very high transport cost components. Table 1 shows, for the US, the proportion of domestic transport operation cost in final demand price for a selection of sectors, varying from 1.1 per cent in the communications sector to 76.7 per cent for gravel, sand and stone quarrying.

For manufacturing industry as a whole, transport operation costs account for about 10 per cent of the total cost of producing and distributing goods.[3] Air transport makes up only a small part of this and, except for a few special commodities such as bulk fuels, so does transport by water and pipeline. The major part of the transport cost of commodities is generally made up by rail and road modes. No detailed figures are available as to the proportion of this cost incurred specifically within urban areas. Of course, certain transport overheads are common costs and are therefore beyond any simple

TABLE 1 *Direct and indirect freight costs as percentage of final demand price, selected sectors, United States, 1972**

Sector	Domestic freight component (percentage of final demand price)								
	Railway	Domestic water	Domestic air	Pipeline	Intercity for-hire trucking	Intercity ancillary trucking	Local for-hire trucking	Local ancillary trucking	Total
Communications	0.3	0	0	0	2	0.2	0.1	0.3	1.1
Electrical machinery	1.1	0.1	0.2	0.1	1.4	0.3	0.3	0.4	3.9
Textiles and apparel	0.9	0.1	0.1	0.1	2.8	0.4	0.4	0.6	5.4
Food and drugs	2.4	0.2	0.1	0.1	1.5	0.8	1.6	1.8	8.5
Petroleum and products	1.0	1.1	0	2.8	0.6	1.1	0.5	2.3	9.4
Paper and products	5.1	0.3	0.1	0.1	2.4	0.6	1.0	0.9	10.5
Timber and products	7.5	0.7	0	0.1	1.4	1.5	0.7	1.6	13.5
Scrap sales	14.5	0.4	0	0	1.2	0	0	0.6	16.7
Coal mining	10.8	1.0	0	0.1	4.6	1.0	0.1	2.6	30.2
Gravel, sand, stone	12.4	4.2	0.1	0.3	18.1	6.5	22.6	12.5	76.7

* Including freight costs of the inputs to the final product and freight services needed to transport the final product to the consumer.
Source: Department of Transportation, US, *National Transportation Report* (Washington DC, 1972).

division between urban and non-urban components. However, the great majority of freight transport trips will have at least one end, and often both ends, in an urban area. Therefore, in addition to local transport (which remains the almost exclusive domain of the truck), longer distance transport will probably include a quite large urban transport component. Except on very long journeys, line haul costs make up only a small proportion of the total operation costs of road transport. Even for a journey as long as 500 km, packaging, terminal handling, pick-up, delivery and other trip-end costs may make up two thirds of the total.[4] It is likely, therefore, that not far short of 5 to 10 per cent of the final price of manufactured goods is made up by urban transport alone.

If firms could be relied upon to minimise this amount in the pursuit of their commercial interest, policy attention could be focused on the community costs, external costs and urban structure costs of urban freight transport, in the knowledge that transport operation costs would be minimized at all times. However there are a number of indications that transport operation costs, though never consciously and unnecessarily increased, are not presently being minimised.

Firstly, some firms undertaking trucking tasks may lack transport and distribution management skills. As an atomistic industry with many small vehicle fleets and, in common with other forms of transport, a large element of joint production, so that any trip in one direction induces the problem of back-loads or empty vehicles in the reverse direction, its operation tends often to rely as much on 'seat of the pants' instinctive management as on any more scientific management approach. This may be particularly true of the smaller trucking firm where one or two men, whose skills lie more in truck driving than transport management or marketing, make up the entire employment, or in firms where transport is performed as a function ancillary to the main task of producing a particular good or service and is treated by the business management as something undeserving of detailed attention.[5]

Secondly, transport users and operators may lack the access to planning and coordination which would enable them to take advantage of economies arising from a greater utilisation of transport facilities. In Melbourne the average truck travels only 34.8 km daily, is on the road for 116 minutes, and carries an average of one quarter of its load capacity.[6] With greater knowledge of each others' activities and a willingness to cooperate, this low utilisation might be improved. Of course there is no economic reason why the available freight facilities should be used to capacity 24 hours a day and many reasons why they should not. There is not always a backload available. Trucks can be used for personal transport. Only through coincidence will a load exactly utilise the vehicle's full capacity and in cases such as the carriage of pre-mixed concrete a return load in unfeasible. In some situations there will be advantages in placing the vehicle on standby for unforeseen eventualities. Such reasons notwithstanding, however, there are certainly cases where with greater foresight and planning the quantity of empty and LTL (less than truckload) vehicles criss-crossing each other's paths could be reduced and the size of the total urban truck fleet diminished.

Thirdly, the demand for urban freight transport may be quite inelastic to changes in its cost. As an input making up perhaps 10 per cent of final commodity price, the proportionate decrease in final goods price resulting from a decrease in transport price will be only one tenth as great. Thus, for example, if transport operation costs of all commodities could be reduced by 20 per cent, the resultant decrease in the final price of the commodities would be only 2 per cent. In this way, exercises to decrease freight costs can appear to display little tangible reward for large expenditures of a firm's effort. Of course the point is that, in aggregate rather than from the viewpoint of the individual firm, savings in transport costs will be very significant. In the US, for example, a reduction in costs of local goods movement of 20 per cent has been estimated to produce a cost 'saving' of $US 8200 000 000 annually.[7]

Community costs

Community costs are those costs incurred by the general community, through its political representatives, in assuming responsibility for certain activities felt desirable to be performed by public authorities. In urban goods movement the most important community costs are the *track costs* of construction, maintenance and administration of the road network. Many attempts have been made to calculate the track cost 'responsibility' of heavy commercial vehicles.[8] The concern of these studies has been primarily to determine the charges that should be imposed on the road users in order to achieve certain equity or efficiency objectives. Regardless of the purposes and problems of these calculations, however, it is clear that heavy goods vehicles require certain road track expenditures which, in those vehicles' absence, would not be incurred. Pavement may need to be a number of times thicker and a metre or more wider for the heavy vehicle than it need be if only passenger cars were to use the road.[9] In addition, seal, shoulder, gradients, curvature, bridges, and parking provisions can require special expenditures to accomodate the truck. Once the roadway is constructed, periodic maintenance will be required to repair damage caused by the passage of the vehicles. One American study suggests that the passage of a heavy truck may cause as much damage to the road surface as that of 2500 cars, so that virtually all road wear is attributable to the heavy vehicle.[10] The relevant track costs extend outside the boundary of the urban area itself in cases where bypass roads are provided in order to divert traversing traffic from the area.

A second community cost is the government operation of freight services, such as garbage collection and post office services. A third community cost is the expense of governmental regulation and planning of urban goods movement. The enactment and enforcement of legislation and any planning strategies can involve the community in a large and continuing expenditure to ensure the proper functioning of the urban freight process.

External costs

The urban freight vehicle is also responsible for creating costs to other members of society. Although not always paying these costs directly through the price of the goods it consumes, society nevertheless must meet these external costs as well. They include the familiar costs of air and noise pollution, traffic congestion and road accidents.[11]

In Hindu mythology, Juggernaut, an idol of Krishna, was annually drawn through the streets on a giant vehicle under whose relentless wheels devotees threw themselves to be crushed. In modern times Juggernaut's name has been given to the heavy goods vehicle, implying that members of society similarly sacrifice themselves to its obdurate passage. The word is emotional, yet so also can be the reaction of those who feel adversely affected by the heavy vehicle. Their dislike can be based on a factual assessment of the external costs or on vaguer but no less real notions of the 'visual intrusion' of trucks or of dislike of truck operators appearing to profit out of being a nuisance. The trend toward enclosed loads (such as containers) and larger vehicles, and the way in which heavy freight vehicles loom over pedestrians and other vehicles with which they share the road, can evoke the primordial and quite human fear of things which are big. Such *psycho-social disturbances* can be a very significant external cost of the presence of trucks on the roads; they cannot be dismissed as mere foibles. They are likely to be diminished by a concerted campaign to make people more aware of the central importance of freight transport. For example, trucks might carry signs with such messages as 'Another load of bricks for the new Jonesville high school' in an effort to assist people to relate more personally to the cargo that goods vehicles carry.[12] Policy actions may be necessary to restrict the operation of certain freight vehicles or to ban them in particular places or at particular times, but these should be based on some analysis of the resultant costs and benefits (including the psycho-social) and should not be the direct *consequence* of psycho-social emotional concerns.

The costs of urban structure

In the purchase of one of its factor resources, land, the firm affects the cost of other inputs and its output. The reason is that, in purchasing the land, the firm simultaneously purchases a second 'commodity', location, which will influence the costs of labour and raw materials as well as the delivered cost of its output. When its location decision is based on the cost of moving its raw materials in and its finished products out the firm is described as *trans-*

port oriented. Of course, many other factors influence industrial location decisions: firms may be labour oriented, energy oriented or amenity oriented, there may be important external economies resulting from firms grouping together to share common facilities and gain personal contact with suppliers and customers, or less rational reasons may influence location decisions. Yet there can be no doubt that an often close connection between transport cost and location does exist. The modern tendency for firms to move out of a central city area to the side of major highways leading from the centre is sufficient to demonstrate this. Thus freight transport considerations may play an important role in determining the nature of the urban area, industrial (and consequently residential) location, the extent of urban sprawl and the vitality of the central business district. These factors in turn affect the quality of urban life and amenity. Only coincidentally will the amalgam of location decisions work towards the same social and environmental goals that the general urban community seeks.

As an urban area grows, it changes from a town serving a surrounding area to a city acting as regional centre. Traffic to surrounding areas becomes increasingly overshadowed by the transport generated for the area's own internal functioning. It produces a greater proportion of its own needs and these commodities must be distributed throughout its area. It may develop specialisation in the production of certain commodities and these it may export to other areas in great quantity. In turn, it may need to import the raw materials for the production of these goods. The city of Detroit provides an example of highly developed specialisation. As a city grows, and its population and traffic densities increase, the task of moving freight throughout its area becomes more difficult and more costly. Ports and railyards can become choked with consignments and the surrounding roads jammed with freight vehicles. Vehicles have difficulty moving through the traffic stream and finding parking spaces for pick-up and deliveries. Queues develop and speeds of delivery diminish. In some cases the viability of industries is threatened. Older urban areas are likely to suffer more from these problems because of the inadequacy of streets laid out long before the advent of the motor vehicle. In table 2 the indices of tariffs for vehicular pick-up and delivery of air freight illustrate the relationship between an urban area's transport cost and its population size, development density and age.

The search for solutions

In acting to reduce any one freight cost item other costs will almost certainly be increased. A successful 'trade-off' between these costs can hardly be performed without some knowledge of the effects of alternative proposals to reduce total social cost. Yet, in its present state, the body of knowledge on the workings of urban freight distribution is insufficient for anything but rudimentary guesses as to the viability of proposed solutions. Here we shall

TABLE 2 *The relative costs of urban goods movement in selected US cities**

City group	Relative cost index per 100 lb (45 kg) consignment
Nashville, Norfolk, Peoria Reading, Tallahassee	1.0
Binghamton, Providence, Sacramento, Tulsa, Wilmington (Del.)	2.0
Chicago, Cleveland, Pittsburgh, St Louis, Washington	3.0
New York City	5.7

* Based on air freight pick-up and delivery charges which are thought to reflect the relative costs of urban goods movement in various cities. Cities were selected at random from published rate tables and final selection based on similarity of rates.
Source: Urban Goods Movement Task Force, *Departmental Action Plan and Report to the Secretary*, Department of Transportation, US (Washington DC, 1973).

limit ourselves to a brief examination of some of the proposals that have been made for the reduction of urban freight costs.

Road investment

Perhaps the oldest and hardiest proposal for reduction of freight transport costs is for increased road investment. With the argument that traffic congestion is the prime enemy the suggestion is that roads be widened, freeways be provided, gradients and surface be improved and intersections be upgraded. Community costs are increased in order to achieve reduction of transport operation costs and hopefully, through improved traffic flow, the reduction of external costs. Through the development of road investment cost–benefit analysis this cost trade-off has received much greater attention than any of the trade-offs involved in the other proposals for cost reduction that have been made.

Technological and technical innovation

The extension of freight tasks undertaken by non-truck forms of transport has also been proposed. For example, solid waste disposal ordinarily undertaken by truck is replaced in a Swedish system by vacuum suction pipelines connecting residences to a central disposal silo.[13] The system is already operating in some cities. Consideration has been given to the use of pneumatic or conveyor based pipeline systems for more general goods distribution.[14] Buses and taxis might carry some smaller consignments without need for great changes in the present system and without greatly affecting their passenger carrying capacity. Mishan proposes use of urban rail facilities during off-peak periods or at night when they are usually closed down.[15]

Other possibilities include the provision of special trucklanes or the sharing of buslanes, the provision of underground roads for truck access to buildings, and the development of trucks which facilitate loading and unloading, such as the 'carousel truck' with its mobile storage bays within the body of the vehicle.[16]

Vehicle design rules

Almost any of the external costs of urban commercial vehicle movement could be reduced if the design of the vehicles themselves were changed. It is technologically possible to build trucks which are quieter, emit fewer pollutants, are more manoeuvrable, faster, more powerful and safer. There is no legal difficulty in setting up vehicle design standards to which manufacturers must conform, as many countries have shown in recent years. The deciding factor should be whether the costs of meeting higher design standards are offset by a reduction in other costs, especially external costs.

Temporal and spatial restrictions

Temporal separation of goods and passenger transport may assist the two forms of transport to exist more compatibly together. Passenger vehicles perform most of their travel during daylight hours and, in particular, in the morning and evening hours on journeys to and from the driver's place of work. Regulations might be formulated to direct commercial vehicle travel away from those hours when streets are most heavily used by private vehicles. These can take the form of commercial vehicle bans during certain times or the prohibition of deliveries at certain hours.

Freight deliveries at night have an obvious appeal. If undertaken throughout an urban area they would effectively separate much of the goods and passenger functions and decrease congestion faced by both. In 1968, the British Ministry of Transport, the Greater London Council, trade associations and unions cooperated in an experiment in out-of-hours goods delivery called 'Operation Moondrop'.[17] Four retailers and 21 distributors participated in the scheme, whereby shops remained open to receive deliveries one night a week from 6 p.m. to 10 p.m. After six months the project was abandoned. Many important lessons were learnt from Moondrop's demise, but the most important was the difficulty of running a scheme on only a limited and voluntary basis when it requires economies of large-scale operation to be successful. After only two months of operation the scheme had reached a stalemate: 'no expansion of the scheme could take place until it could be shown to be viable, and viability was not possible without expansion.'[18] As an exercise in decreasing the external and transport operation costs of congestion the project showed clearly how, if overall transportation operation costs of congestion the project showed clearly how, if overall transportation operation costs appeared adversely affected, firms soon lost interest in such experiments.

An alternative form of night delivery is the night-safe system in which night-time goods consignments are locked in safes to be removed by staff on their arrival next morning. The system is an extension of the already common practice of bulk tanker delivery of fuel to service stations at night. However, in addition to the cost of providing safes, this procedure has the disadvantage of eliminating the often important contact which the truck driver ordinarily makes with receivers for billing, taking of orders and so on. Night deliveries, no matter how they are undertaken, also risk causing noise levels which are unacceptable in residential areas during evening relaxation or sleeping hours.

There is room for greater coordination of work hours of those involved in urban freight. Pick-ups and deliveries are often frustrated by tea breaks and lunch hours which do not coincide between truck driver, consigner and consignee, by businesses which refuse to accept deliveries after 3 p.m. or during stocktaking, or by peak periods when vehicles must queue to use loading or unloading facilities. Many of these time consuming inconveniences could be eliminated through greater planning.

Spatial measures can direct goods traffic away from or towards certain routes or areas. Recent British legislation[19] requires local government authorities to prepare comprehensive plans to decide how and where trucks should be routed and parked in order to best suit the urban environment. The legislation places the authorities in the unenviable position of being compelled to develop freight policies with little knowledge of the nature of goods movement or the likely effects of alternative approaches, yet is an example of what may be the best available method of ensuring that those with political power in urban areas give thought to the problems of urban goods movement.

Road pricing

Economic theorists have suggested that more efficient use would be made of roads if vehicle operators were charged a price for their road use which made them aware of the external costs, especially congestion, that they cause when using a particular road at a particular time.[20] By charging the marginal social cost of road use the vehicle operation cost is enlarged to include external costs – an externality is internalised – and the vehicle operator is forced to take account of the costs he causes others by making his journey. Road pricing is thus an application of the theory of marginal cost pricing and no journey is undertaken if its marginal benefit is exceeded by its marginal cost.

The road pricing argument has customarily centred around the assumption of a homogeneous vehicle flow, specifically of passenger vehicles, and has had little to say on its application to goods vehicles. When the homogeneous vehicle assumption is dropped and more than one vehicle type is introduced into the analysis it no longer follows that the effect of road pricing on all vehicles *in toto* will be identical with the effect on individual vehicle classes. In fact, even if the road pricing charge on goods vehicles is higher than on other classes of vehicle (to account for higher marginal costs caused), it is possible that road pricing will result in an increased number of goods vehicles on the road or, at least, little change in their numbers.

Let us assume that demand for use of road space by an individual vehicle operator, i, is an inverse function of the generalised cost per kilometre (G_i) he faces, where, for any particular road,

$$G_i = M_i + v_i t_i.$$

M_i is the money cost per kilometre of running his vehicle, t_i is the time (minutes) taken to travel a kilometre of the road, and v_i is the value to him of one minute of travelling time. Upon the imposition of road pricing, the prospective road user must pay the new road pricing charge (p_i), while at the same time he finds the other money costs of running his vehicle diminished due to the improved traffic flow resulting from the pricing out of some road users ($\triangle M_i$). In addition the faster traffic flow results in a decrease in time costs ($\triangle t_i$). The vehicle operator's generalised cost per kilometre is now

$$G_i^{\star} = (M_i - \Delta M_i) + p_i + v_i(t_i - \Delta t_i).$$

Although the imposition of the road price will result in lower *total* effective demand for use of the road,[21] it is possible that the *individual* finds his generalised cost has decreased and that he therefore increases his use of the roadspace. The higher is his time value, v_i, the more likely this is. As commercial goods vehicles are likely to have a high time valuation,[22] it is therefore possible that their generalised costs of travel may diminish with road pricing and their road use consequently increase. Of course, the amount of change in demand is affected by elasticity of demand and, it would seem, goods vehicles are likely to be less elastic in their demand for roadspace than most passenger vehicles,[23] thus dampening the magnitude of any increase in demand. Moreover, with labour costs usually making up well over half of vehicle running costs, a congestion charge will be far outweighed by any driver overtime rates which need to be paid if a vehicle is scheduled outside normal hours of operation. Off-peak delivery is not likely to be encouraged if, to avoid the congestion charge, overtime wages are incurred.

If no trucks, or only a few, are removed from the road by a road price charge, a retort might be that trucks were simply not being charged enough and that the toll (p_i) should be increased, and continue to be increased, until a 'sufficient number' had been removed. However, this argument loses sight of the economic efficiency basis of road pricing. To take this approach is to make an arbitrary decision as to the amount of truck traffic to be allowed on the route. Taxation, not road pricing, is being used. Whether a road price can provide any impetus for the introduction of technological improvements in urban goods movement or for increased vehicle utilisation or changed hours of operation will depend on the extent to which the charge can be shifted from the shoulders of those who have the power to affect these variables. At one extreme, it is conceivable that no changes would occur in the urban freight processes at all and that any additional costs would simply be passed on to the consumers of final goods. This concept of 'shifting' comes from taxation theory: it is the economic and not the statutory incidence which determines the essential effect of the impost. It has been suggested that congestion charges be levied on the businesses which generate freight, rather than the operators of the freight vehicles serving them. Jacobi has proposed metered loading zones and the payment of the metered congestion fee by the firm being serviced.[24] The firm wishing to avoid the charge would schedule its freight loading and receipt to off-peak hours.

Road pricing opens various income distribution questions. These are difficult enough when the assumption of homogeneous vehicles is maintained: they are further complicated when the assumption is dropped. Road pricing will evolve a particular split between passenger and freight vehicles, yet this split may be unsatisfactory on equity grounds. It may be felt, for example, that the poorer man is being priced from the road whilst the richer man and his commodities are not.[25]

Also, it might be argued, as different industries have different proportions of total costs made up by transport expenses, the charge will be unfairly punitive for some, such as the quarrying and construction materials industries, where transport costs are a relatively large proportion of total costs. Alternatively, should road pricing be applied to passenger and not goods vehicles, the generalised cost of freight transport would certainly decrease, giving rise to the equity argument that cars were being priced from the road for the benefit of goods vehicles.

Parking, loading and unloading facilities

In the 24-hour day American trucks average three hours or less in actual movement over the road.[26] In New York, about one third of trucks do not move at all on the average weekday.[27] Decker has suggested that 'the truck "at rest" may be a larger problem for the urban planner than the moving truck'[28].

Business enterprises are loath to provide vehicle loading and unloading bays and rear access facilities unless they can foresee financial rewards in doing so. Equally, truck drivers show no willingness to make use of such facilities if they do not save time: 'The most carefully laid out servicing systems will not be used by lorry drivers if alternatives are open to them (including illegal ones) which save as little as two or three minutes during the delivery'.[29] In a study of Toronto's city centre, 19 per cent of all recorded freight vehicle stops were at office buildings with 'good off-street facilities with loading/unloading docks', yet 90 per cent of these stops made no use of the facilities.[30] To save time, unloading trucks block driveways and access roads, park on street corners, double park and occupy multiple-car parking spaces at kerbside. External costs are increased, particularly through delays caused to other vehicles, as may be community costs through the additional road capacity needs. To enforce regulations on illegal parking more stringently offers little help if adequate legal parking facilities are unavailable. A strong case appears to exist for compulsory provision and use of adequate off-street facilities.

Many transportation engineers favour the provision of only a limited number of parking spaces for passenger cars in urban areas because they believe that, as with urban expressways, supply of such traffic facilities creates its own demand. The principle operates in relation to passenger transport because of the alternatives to the car that exist. For much urban freight transport, however, there is no alternative to the truck and the principle cannot be applied. Lack of adequate parking facilities for trucks increases the costs of freight transport while having little effect on the number of trucks using urban roads. It would appear that the government should take a direct hand in ensuring either that sufficient kerbside parking is available, or that businesses provide facilities of their own, and that the facilities are used.

During non-working hours, the owner occasionally parks his goods vehicle in the street outside his home in a residential area not equipped to handle the presence of the truck. Often the parked truck will occupy a substantial part of the carriageway and, unlit at night, can constitute a major hazard to other vehicles using the road. The government authority may need to proscribe the habit by ensuring that vehicles are parked off-street, either on the owner's land or at a depot.

Terminal facilities

It is at the transport terminal that many have seen the greatest opportunities for the diminution of urban freight transport costs. Automation of terminals, standardisation of freight units and containerisation of consignments will speed delivery and cut wage bills. However terminal automation is likely to be expensive and the feasibility of standardisation or containerisation will depend largely on the nature of the freight. One might also expect that it will already have been adopted in those freight areas where major benefits to the trucker, consignor or consignee can be gained.

Consolidation of freight consignments has received perhaps more support than any other proposed solution to the cost problems of urban freight. Consolidation is quite simply the carriage of more than one consignment at the one time. As a means of increasing vehicle payloads and decreasing the number of vehicles on the road its advantage is clear. The bread delivery van, for example, does not carry each consignment – e.g. each household's loaf – separately but instead consolidates all those destined for a particular area and moves from house to house to deliver them.

One need not be an adept mathematician to realise that if trucks were to make greater use of their load capacity their numbers could be greatly reduced. It should not be too surprising to find, for example, that the goods delivered to a Chicago department store by 378 commercial vehicles daily could conceivably be consolidated into 20 trailers[31] or that the small consignments daily carried by 660 freight vehicles into the Columbus, Ohio, central business district could be consolidated into 70 or 80 vehicles.[32] The physical possibility of doing so is, of course, a somewhat different matter from its financial feasibility. It is possible that neither the trucker nor the transport user finds financial reward in making a single full truckload trip instead of a number of LTL trips. The trucker might well ask why he should meet the expense of setting up consolidation facilities to cut down on truck trips for which his customers have shown a willingness to pay. Speed of delivery is often of prime importance to the firm dispatching or receiving goods. The firm is willing to wait neither for a fuller truckload to be made up nor for a vehicle to visit other locations on its way to a pick-up or delivery.

To examine the financial feasibility of consolidation operations Vandenberge developed a simple analytical model for application to a hypothetical American town.[33] He found that in most cases the economies of higher vehicle utilisation would be far outweighed by the cost of operation of the consolidation terminals. At best he could find some profitability in consolidation of small consignments of around 50 kg and less. This conclusion is particularly interesting because, in that segment of the freight market where Vandenberge found financial feasibility for consolidation, its possibilities appear to have been well exploited already: witness the bread van mentioned earlier, milk, newspaper, grocery deliveries, parcel express companies such as the United Parcel Service[34] in the US, and (consolidation's patriarch) the Post Office. In a similar study for the city of New York, de Neufville and Wilson isolated two particular cases where freight consolidation appeared to offer financial reward: the collection of garbage and the servicing of aiports located some distance from their cities.[35] Again, consolidation of those sectors generally occurs already.

Like the simple physical mathematics of the exercise, the major conclusions of studies such as Vandenberge's and de Neufville and Wilson's should not be unexpected. They confirm the implications of a pioneering study by Horwood in 1958:[36] most financially feasible opportunities for freight consolidation are soon taken up by private enterprise and those segments remaining unconsolidated do so because consolidation is financially impracticable. The argument for increased consolidation of urban freight must revolve around the likelihood of decreases in costs other than transport operation cost or of greater cooperation between those providing or using freight transport.[37]

The government's planning role

There is no panacea for the urban freight problem. No single solution will minimise all elements of the cost of distributing goods in the urban area. To decrease the total social cost of urban freight, certain elements of this total must almost always be increased. Almost every proposal requires a commitment which, with the state of present day knowledge, produces the risk that the increases in some cost elements may not be adequately outweighed by the decreases in others. With many of the more adventurous or novel approaches this risk will be far too great to be undertaken by private business organisations. In any case, private business firms are unlikely to demonstrate great interest in activities which trade a decrease in external, community or urban structure costs for an increase in their own transport operation costs.

Moreover, many of the suggestions for decreasing the social cost of urban freight transport, such as road investment, road pricing and regulation of vehicle design can be undertaken only by those who have been entrusted with political power.

Where private firms are willing to persist with experiments aimed at diminishing the problems of urban freight, there may be need for a government body to 'mother' the firms, to encourage them should they commence to lose interest, to help them to work together where co-operation in large numbers is essential to the success of the activity, to referee their disagreements, to goad and cajole, and to publicise those experiments that prove successful.

To rely on initiative from private industry is to rely on a market mechanism which works imperfectly. Not only will an unimpeded price system inadequately reflect the externalities of many activities, but it will also result in occasional mistakes when the business is unable to accurately predict future influences. The firm's location decision, for example, must be partly based on an assessment of the future growth and activity in an area. The correctness of the decision is dependent on the location decisions of other firms. Of course, the working of the price mechanism is partly a matter of trial and error and responsive correction of past errors. But where mistakes are made in such long-term investment decisions they will not be corrected overnight. There is a possibility that location decision errors will consolidate one another, one firm's incorrect decision attracting other firms to locate similarly. Government policy will affect these investment decisions and their correctness: where future government plans are not made clear, firms may make investments which, on implementation of the plans, prove incorrect. Where government planning is vague or nonexistent, government policies and investments may, by becoming reactions to incorrect private decisions, consolidate private errors.

Regardless of any of these arguments for planned, active participation by government in the urban freight process, it must be recognised that, through a series of historical accidents and assumed responsibility, government bodies already actively influence the process in a great variety of ways. They build, maintain and administer the streets on which urban freight travels and operate certain freight transport services themselves. Governments generally assume responsibility for the ownership and control of non-vehicular transhipment terminals – ports, airports and (in many countries) rail stations. Zoning ordinances and the quality and location of government services affect private location decisions; these in turn affect the entire urban area's freight transport requirements. Laws and regulations greatly influence the types of freight vehicles using the roads, their dimensions, the size of loads they carry, the speeds they travel, the routes they take, their ownership and the tariffs charged. It should be remembered that, although stricter regulations have habitually been applied to long distance than to local freight transport, constraints on long distance transport are constraints on urban transport to the extent that the long distance journey starts in, terminates in, or passes through metropolitan areas. It is therefore improper to attempt to isolate the effects of intercity transport regulation from any examination of the influence of governments on urban freight transport. Financial incentives and disincentives, taxes, tolls, fees, and user charges will also greatly affect the nature of urban freight transport. Ultimately, of course, it is difficult to separate almost any governmental decision from the realm of urban goods movement, because of its influence on economic activity and therefore on quantities of goods to be transported.

There are two points being made here: firstly, if the urban freight transport problem is to be moved closer to solution, government should play an active part in the move; secondly, government already plays a significant role in influencing the nature of the urban freight process and it is difficult to see how it could withdraw this influence if this were thought desirable. It follows, then, that government activities which have influence on urban freight need greater researched planning than hitherto has been the case. In some cases existing activities may be found to give undesirable results; in other cases activities not previously undertaken by the government will be found desirable.

Rationality of government policy requires the setting of objectives and the enactment of measures which are likely to achieve those objectives to the greatest possible extent. Complete certainty is, of course, not possible. Some factors, such as future technology or changes in social order, defy certainty, and the further one attempts to peer into the future the less predictable they become. In seeking to direct urban freight towards desired goals, the government's influence is primarily upon the decision-making of the actors and institutions whose collective activities, in conjunction with the government's own activities, determine the operation of the urban freight process.

Any economic behavioural model, to remain within the bounds of practicability, must assume certain factors as parameters. Clearly, where the model is to be used for policy purposes, those factors which can be influenced by government policy should not be treated as constants. The government considering substantially increased vehicle registration fees for example, receives no help from the freight model which assumes vehicle imposts constant. While the point is not new, nor unique to urban freight modelling, it is yet to be wholly accepted. The reason is not so much lack of good intentions, nor often forgetfulness, but instead the theoretical and technical difficulty of describing relationships between urban freight behavioural variables and their determinants. When the US Department of Transportation finally recognised the need for some sophistication of treatment of urban freight, as late as 1968, it found that 'concepts such as feedbacks and interdependencies took on new meanings'.[38] No relationship was simple.

Without compromising their expense or usefulness, urban freight models should be as comprehensive as possible. The behavioural interaction of decision-making units is not fully described by models which relate to parts of the urban freight task in isolation from other parts, separate from the urban environment in which it is carried out, or over only the short period. Nevertheless, the urban freight model will begin as an incomplete and piecemeal construction.

Uncertainty acts as a constraint on the distance of the planning horizon. Long-term planning corresponds to a lower degree of certainty than short-term. At the present stages of relative ignorance, concentration may well be on short-term freight strategies of low capital intensity and consequently short-term models should receive early priority.

Table 3 describes a hierarchy of urban freight models. Basically, each level of the hierarchy acts as a building base for the next. The descriptive and behavioural foundation of each level constrains the content of the next. Thus segmentary models, which concentrate attention on the factors determining the freight which enters or leaves an area, a land-use type or an individual link in the system, act as inputs in the development of dyadic models which examine freight *flows* between areas, land uses or links. Attempts to develop dyadic models without the decision-making, freight generative information derived from segmentary models must weaken the behavioural content of the dyadic models and, in turn, diminish the conviction with which policy recommendations based on the models can be offered.

While a comprehensive freight model, composed of a series of dyadic or

TABLE 3 *The urban freight planning model hierarchy*

Model type	Description
1. *Segmentary models*	*Freight production – attraction, analysis of*:
Regional	Entire urban region
Zonal	Geographic subdivisions within region
Sectoral (land use)	Economic groupings (industrial, residential, governmental classifications and sub-classifications)
Link	Decision-making units (individual firms, shops, households, terminals etc.)
2. *Dyadic models*	*Origin – destination flow, analysis of*:
Inter-regional	Flow between urban region and other local, national or international regions
Inter-zonal	Flow between zones within region and/or between intraregional zones and extraregional zones
Inter-sectoral	Flow between sectors
Inter-link	Flow between links
Imparity flow models	Flow between dissimilar analytical units (between intraregional zones and external regions; between a link and regional zones; etc.)
3. *Urban freight model*	Integration of dyadic or segmentary models, including route assignment
4. *Urban transport model*	Urban freight model integrated with urban passenger model
5. *Urban planning model*	Urban transport model integrated with land use and urban structure models

segmentary models which interlock and act as inputs to one another is desirable, the temptation must be resisted to rush to levels of aggregation which conceal the heterogeneity of the urban freight task. Vehicles, the services they provide and the loads they carry are extremely heterogeneous – much more so than in passenger transportation – and consequently it is almost impossible to draw general conclusions from specific studies. A study of for-hire carriage may shed little light on ancillary carriage; a study of semitrailers (articulated vehicles) may not reveal very much about the operation of small vans; a study of traffic entering the urban area may provide little information about short distance pick-up and collection journeys within the area; a study of the distribution process from factory to warehouse may be largely irrelevant to the distribution process from shop to household.

Measurement units

In the study and planning of urban goods movement there is no generally applicable unit of measurement. Depending on the uses to which data is to be put, the ideal unit of measurement may be related to the flow of goods or the flow of vehicles. If studying consolidation possibilities, for example, the nature, mass, volume, frequency, origin and destination of goods consignments may need to be given priority. On the other hand, if studying measures to ease the street congestion caused by freight vehicles, data relating to the nature of vehicles, their size, times of travel and the journeys they undertake may be most important.

As a heritage of urban passenger transport planning, where it is relatively easy to relate vehicles to their loads, much of the information gathered in the past has been about vehicle trips. Using these data, a milk van's delivery of two bottles to each of 40 neighbourhood households in the early morning counts as forty trips (or forty-one, including return to base), while the journey of a pantechnicon through the entire length of an urban area at peak hour counts as a single trip. The nature of vehicles and the times of travel clearly need to be kept in mind if truck trips are used as the unit of measurement. Furthermore, trip unit take no account of the varying distances travelled. But, in turn, the measurement of freight traffic by distance travelled hides other information which may be relevant, such as the number of stops a vehicle must make for pick-up and deliveries.

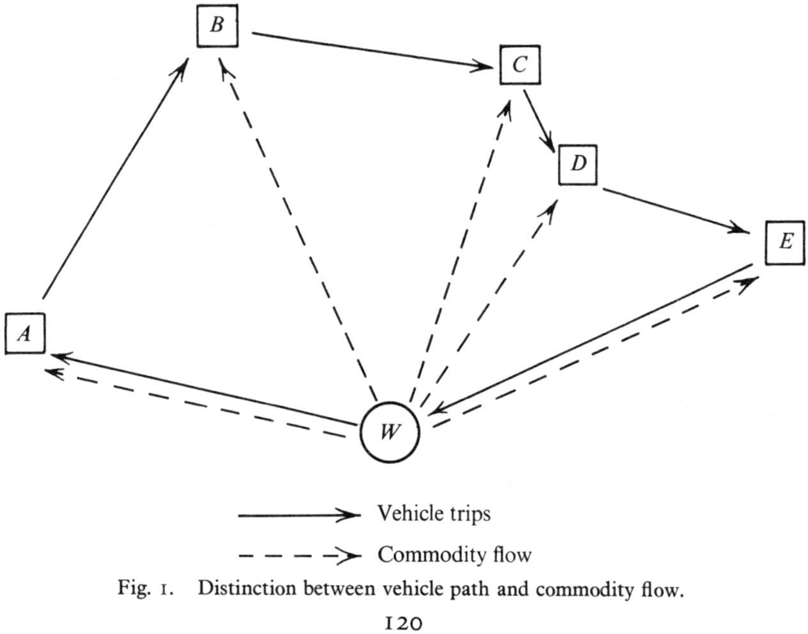

Fig. 1. Distinction between vehicle path and commodity flow.

Goods flows may not reflect the route the vehicle takes. In figure 1, freight is to be trucked from a transport warehouse, *W*, to the five retail stores, *A*, *B*, *C*, *D*, and *E*. In a 'round trip' (actually a collection of six trips, as indicated by the solid arrows), the flow of consignments (the broken arrows) gives no indication of the vehicle route taken. In one case, as with any empty return trip, the vehicle moves in the opposite direction to the freight flow: the vehicle trip is for origin *E* to destination *W*, while the commodity movement is from origin *W* to destination *E*.

Freight is often usefully measured in tonne-kilometres, a unit which takes account of both the mass of the goods carried and the distance they travel. But this measurement of volume, as a composite, hides the individual data on tonnes carried or kilometres travelled, which may be important in the consideration of particular freight strategies. On the other hand, if only mass or distance is measured, part of the identity of the urban freight task is also disguised. In yet other cases, the value of goods, their dimensions or their physical description may be important.

Only with a clear idea of the policy alternatives to which data are to be applied and the nature of the economic models to be developed is it possible to choose the measurement units which ensure that neither irrelevant data are sought nor relevant data are omitted during the data collection process.

Supply and demand

The modelling of urban goods movement is able to concentrate much less on a single blade of the Marshallian scissors than can urban passenger modelling. Supply of automobile travel, in particular, is largely 'dictated' by its demand – the supplier and demander being the same individual behavioural unit – so that urban passenger modelling has become basically *demand* modelling. Demand in passenger transport is for a particular *method* of supply. In urban freight, however, this does not usually apply. Demand for the cartage of a consignment from point A to point B may specify a range of times within which the goods must be picked up and delivered, but is seldom specific as to the precise method of carriage – the type of vehicle, the route it takes, the other consignments it carries, the stops it makes, and so on. Even where freight transport is provided on own account (ancillary carriage), the originating source is ordinarily an organisation, where those responsible for operating the vehicle fleet, purchasing vehicles, loading the vehicles, timing their departures, routing them, etc. are unlikely to be the same individuals as those who determine gross quantities to be carried and their destinations. This separation of demand and supply decision-making, though more like public than private passenger transportation, displays considerably greater complexity, decentralisation and flexibility of supply decisions than does public transit.

Demand for goods transport stems from the decision-making involved in economic production and consumption. The central factors are the community's output of goods, the nature, value and utility of these goods, the community's consumption patterns and the economic, geographic and demographic relationship between consumers and producers. Supply of goods transport represents the response to this demand by commercial enterprises, government and individuals. The nature of this transport supply is determined by decisions affecting the size and description of the vehicle fleet, the road network and terminal facilities, and the operation, scheduling and routing of vehicles. The supply and demand sides may share a concern for the level of transport operation cost; however, each side is determined by its own unique decision-making processes; demand relating primarily to goods consignments and supply relating primarily to vehicles.

It would be simplistic and economically improper to attempt to maintain a rigid distinction between the supply and demand sides of urban freight transport: their interrelatedness is total. Yet the distinction is useful. Symptomatic of hazy thinking on the matter has been the continuing difficulty in determining the relationship between urban goods movement and urban truck movement. Studies of trucks in the urban environment, in an origin–destination vehicle trip format similar to passenger transport studies, have often appeared under the misnomer of urban *goods* movement studies.[39] Examinations of urban freight transport have almost totally failed to approach the issue from its source. Instead they have started a few steps along in the analysis, looking at the transport supply response to demand for goods. If urban goods movement is to be fully understood it will be necessary to retrace the omitted steps and consider the need for goods and their movement through the utility they provide.

The intermediary between freight supply and demand is the vehicle loading factor, which brings the vehicle and consignment together. Meyburg and Stopher have proposed a *vehicle loading model* which, in an imperfect analogy with the vehicle occupancy rate (VOR) used in passenger transport analysis, would provide estimates of empty, loaded and part-loaded vehicle movements, given the goods transport task to be performed:

> The translation of consignment movements into vehicle movements will probably be related to the availability, by capacity, of vehicles; the characteristics of the consignment; the proportion of vehicle capacity required by each consignment and the total volume of consignments from each shipper in a specified time period; ability to hold back shipments until a full vehicle load is achieved; and characteristics of the desired pick-up and delivery pattern of the vehicle, e.g. one vehicle may pick up small packages from many desinations (particularly a for-hire carrier), while others may serve one origin and many destinations, etc.[40]

The vehicle loading model, however, assumes the size and nature of the vehicle fleet as exogenous and fails to examine the decision-making processes which have resulted, for example, in a recent decline in absolute numbers of medium sized trucks (those with a load capacity of two or three tonnes) in many urban areas. Of course, any such examination could not fail to consider the influences of government regulations on vehicle fleet composition.

Regression analysis. If demand for freight transport is dependent on the level and nature of economic activity in a community, a simple method of forecasting future aggregate demand for urban freight transport would appear to be the expression of the demand as a function of some measure of regional economic activity, such as real gross domestic product, population, developed land area or energy consumption. The resultant *demand coefficient* can then be applied to projections of the independent variable in order to produce a forecast of future aggregate demand.

For Australia, over the 15 year period 1957 to 1971, the relationship between real gross domestic product and estimated tonne-kilometres of freight carried by road transport[41] is expressed by the ordinary least squares linear regression equation:

$$Y_y = 0.99856\,X_y - 2.8718 \quad (R^2 = 0.99)$$

where
Y_y = tonne-kilometres carried by road transport (thousand millions), year y
X_y = GDP at 1967 prices (thousand millions), year y

The form of the equation suggests the quite accurate and eminently simple rule of thunb, for the short term:

$$Y_y = X_y - 3.0.$$

The simplicity of this equation, however, hides two pressing difficulties. The first is that the equation may be self-fulfilling, in that the crude estimates of the dependent variable are themselves based partly on the value of the independent variable where, in Australia, national surveys providing freight volume data have been conducted at only eight-year intervals. Though this criticism does not arise with equal validity in some other countries at the national data level, it is likely to be more relevant when the analysis is applied at the urban regional level where data sets are currently available only with a great deal of imprecision if at all.

The second hidden difficulty is the possibility that a causative relationship may be inferred from a temporal autocorrelation between variables. Of course, a regression equation with high predictive qualities does not prove a causal relationship or a derived demand. The argument on these pages that freight transport is a derived demand is intellectual, not statistical. Doubtless the divorce rate would also provide a healthy correlation with the volume of freight transport carried. To investigate the possibility of temporal autocorrelation Chisholm and O'Sullivan have calculated a regression between UK gross domestic product and total freight tonnage over the 16 year period 1953 to 1968 on the basis of first differences – i.e. annual *changes* in the variables.[42] They found a correlation coefficient (R^2) of only 0.29, which is unacceptable at the 99 per cent confidence level.

However this does not disprove a relationship between a community's output and its freight demand. As various sectors of the economy are likely to be differently affected by the periodic cyclical movements of the economy (displaying varying decision and production lags and sometimes counter-cyclical trends), one might reasonably expect predictive accuracy to be improved if freight volume is related more directly to the annual production of individual industries. Bayliss has been able to show good predictive accuracy using weighted indexes of the output of the major freight generating industries.[43]

While estimates, albeit often rough and ready, are available for both the dependent and independent variables at the national and occasionally sub-national level, they may need to be generated by the researcher himself at the level of disaggregation required. For estimates of such factors as regional domestic production, freight volume carried or trips undertaken at the level of the urban area, this can involve considerable work. Where time series analysis is used these variables must be projected backwards in time to provide a sufficiently large sample to determine a valid correlation. Where cross-sectional analysis is employed the variables must be calculated for other urban areas outside the researcher's immediate field of interest and, perhaps, expertise. In cross-sectional analysis the risk is also taken that data collected for other urban regions will reflect characteristics which do not apply to the region in question. Freight volume data collected for an industrialised seaport city, for example, may bear little useful comparison with those collected for a landlocked agricultural/residential city of a similar population size, if a cross-sectional correlation is sought between freight volume generated and regional population.

The relationship between freight demand and the indicators of a region's economic activity suggests that time-trend analysis can justifiably be used to predict future demand. Where a forecast of the determining factor, e.g. real gross domestic production in the region, is based on trend extrapolation and the estimates of future freight demand are then linearly based on this extrapolation, it is computationally simpler (and conceivably more accurate) to base the freight prediction on extrapolation of the demand trend itself. In fact, at the present early stage of freight demand study, Schneider reports that trend extrapolation may well provide more accurate long-term predictions than more 'sophisticated' methods.[44]

Using regression analysis or trend extrapolation to estimate freight demand, freight modelling can follow the path set by urban passenger transport modelling and employ an interactance model to distribute vehicles or goods between geographic zones within the urban region. Following the lines of past urban passenger modelling and its concentration on vehicle trips it has not been uncommon to apply the gravity model.[45] Though preferable to those approaches, which have provided no specific model for goods movement and simply apportioned a quantity of trips from the passenger gravity model according to passenger car unit (p.c.u.) equivalents, the use of the gravity model for freight transport is open to the same criticisms as its use in passenger transport. In addition, where present gravity models make use of the geographic zonal approach, they may be particularly inapplicable to urban freight transport. The gravity model in its basic form ignores the complexities of the business decisions that result in goods, though being required in zone j and being dispatched from zone i, not gravitating between the zones. Unlike passenger flows, freight flows between zones are not usually balanced by direction, there being no 'home zone' to which a freight consignment returns. And, to a much greater degree than passenger transport, freight travels to or from areas outside the urban region and can have only one or even no end within an urban zone.

The smaller the urban area under investigation the greater is the possibility that individual links will significantly influence total regional freight volume. A new factory, for example, may substantially affect freight flows into and out of a zone. For this reason, regression and time-series analyses of small urban areas should be treated with caution.

Land-use and input–output tables. A behavioural approach to urban passenger demand study has recently shown signs of growing support (see ch. 6), and it would seem that freight movement studies also have much to gain from the approach. The central features would be an emphasis on consignments rather than trips, and on land use rather than geographical zones. The initial efforts can be seen in attempts to look at freight produced at and attracted to individual production and consumption sectors in the urban economy and are prescient of future studies which will attempt to relate freight transport to its behavioural causes in the light of business, government and household consumption and production decisions, location decisions and the structure of the urban economy.

Table 4, though relating only to intra-city movement and to a city which is not necessarily representative of other urban areas, reveals some of the heterogeneity of the freight task given different land uses. From the table it is apparent that the greatest number of vehicle trips is generated by the residential land-use category. Most significant producers of freight volume, however, are the manufacturing and processing land uses, and largest attracters of freight volume are the service industries.

Recognising that the outputs of one industry are the inputs of another, Leontief developed the input–output table which shows, in matrix form, the transactions taking place between sectors. Although generally developed at the national level, input–output tables have occasionally been developed to describe inter-regional or, less commonly, metropolitan interactance between sectors.[46] More recently, the usefulness of input–output tables in

TABLE 4 *Truck trips and freight movement generated by land-use categories (intra-city movement), Melbourne, Australia*

Land-use category	(1) Trips generated (percentage)		Freight volume (tonnes) (2) From land use (percentage)		(3) To land use (percentage)	
Residential	28.0		4.3		7.0	
Retail and wholesale	24.6		10.6		13.7	
Foodstores		12.0		1.0		4.7
Other retail stores		8.0		3.4		3.4
Wholesale: durable goods		2.0		2.8		2.2
Wholesale: non-durable goods		2.6		5.0		3.4
Manufacturing and processing	15.9		43.9		24.5	
Brick, pottery, glass and cement manufacture		1.3		8.0		5.2
Chemical processing		1.1		2.5		1.7
Extractive industries		0.8		12.0		0.9
Food, drink and tobacco processing		2.2		5.6		4.4
Machinery and motor vehicle manufacture		2.6		2.0		3.9
Metal and metal fabricating industries		2.8		3.5		3.5
Paper and paper product processing		1.2		2.4		1.2
Petroleum and coal processing		0.2		2.1		0.2
Textiles, clothing and footwear manufacture		1.3		0.7		0.8
Timber and furniture manufacture		1.0		2.2		0.9
Other		1.4		2.9		1.8
Services	23.5		23.6		32.2	
Communications, public buildings and services n.o.s.*		10.9		4.1		5.6
Public utilities and rubbish dumps		3.4		4.1		10.4
Service stations and repair shops		2.9		0.5		3.2
Storage and junk facilities		2.6		9.9		4.3
Streets and highways		3.7		5.0		8.1

TABLE 4 *(continued)*

Land-use category	(1) Trips generated (percentage)		(2) From land use (percentage)		(3) To land use (percentage)	
			Freight volume (tonnes)			
Transportation	5.2		15.0		4.3	
Railway and transportation facilities n.o.s.*		2.2		5.1		5.4
Shipping facilities		0.9		4.6		4.5
Trucking facilities		2.1		5.3		4.4
Construction sites	1.6		0.8		6.4	
Open space and agriculture	1.2		1.7		1.9	
Total:	100.0		100.0		100.0	
	515,400 trips daily		209, 964 tonnes daily			

* n.o.s. = not otherwise specified.

Source: K. W. Ogden, 'Issues in Urban Goods Movement Planning', *Proceedings of the Seventh Australian Road Research Board Conference*, Adelaide, 1974.

transportation studies has been recognised. Stein and Mosbaek, for example, have proposed the use of a multi-regional input–output model in the estimation of effects of alternative transport investment proposals on economic activity.[47] Brown and Maultby have used input–output tables to forecast freight quantities in Great Britain with some success.[48] The input–output model has also been suggested as a method of predicting urban freight flows. For example, Demetsky proposes the preparation of input–output tables, specific in their elements as to commodity type, commodity volume, and land use and zone at origin and destination, in order to predict transactions subject to an impedance factor derived from time, cost, frequency of service, etc.[49]

The possibilities of input–output analysis in the study of urban freight demand remain almost uncharted. Not the least important cause is the apparently substantial data collection task. There may be opportunity to derive regional tables from national input–output tables and convert technical coefficients to physical freight flows.[50]

Freight generation and attraction. In a study of manufacturing plants in the Medway towns conurbation in Kent, Starkie found relationships between daily commercial vehicle trips generated by a plant and both employment and floor space at the plant.[51] The regression equations were linear in the logarithms, with correlation coefficients of 0.54 and 0.60 respectively.

Although these equations were 'perhaps acceptable to traffic planners for some purposes',[52] predictive accuracy was improved by classifying plants into industrial groupings. Thus, for the 37 engineering and allied trades plants in his sample, Starkie found the regression:

$$\log T_p = 0.4010 + 0.4996 \log E_p \quad (R^2 = 0.86)$$

where T_p = daily commercial vehicle trips, plant p
E_p = total employment, plant p

The curvilinear shape of these functions, whereby the rate of increase in trips declines as the industrial plant gets larger, was explained by Starkie as evidence of 'economies of scale' in trip generation caused by the use of higher capacity vehicles as plant size increases. This hypothesis, though yet to be fully tested, amply illustrates the problem of measuring freight demand in only one of its dimensions, in this case vehicle trips alone.

Atlhough Starkie's general findings have found recent support in the work of Maltby,[53] Redding,[54] Gaudio and Meko,[55] and (for rètail shops) Meyburg and Stopher,[56] agreement is yet to be reached on the nature of the independent variables which best explain trips generated at the various land uses.

Using regression analysis on Chicago Area Transportation Study data, Kolifrath and Shuldiner[57] attempted to relate truck trips to a measure combining both employment and floor space. This measure was employment intensity, defined as the number of employees per 10 000 sq. ft of floor area. They were unable to fit significant regression equations to the data, but were able to conclude that industry groupings with high employment intensities had a tendency to generate fewer truck trips.

Hutchinson and Kardosh used an inventory of daily truck trips to and from 240 manufacturing firms in metropolitan Toronto to obtain explicators of daily truck trips produced at and attracted to the firms.[58] For the aggregate of the firms, daily trips produced and attracted were best explained by the number of private trucks owned by the firms. The regression equations were:

$$P_f = 11.4 + 1.53\, Y_f \quad (R^2 = 0.81)$$
$$A_f = 12.5 + 0.86\, Y_f \quad (R^2 = 0.53)$$

where
P_f = daily trips produced, firm f
A_f = daily trips attracted, firm f
Y_f = total private trucks owned, firm f

On breaking the firms into industry groupings Hutchinson and Kardosh were unable to confirm Starkie's close correlation between trips and employment. In general, they found that the total number of private vehicles owned, together (in some cases) with certain elements of the firm's employment, best explained daily truck trips from and to the various industrial groupings.

As the regression analysis of trips production and attraction has met with some success, it is likely that more general conclusions will be attainable when further studies are undertaken. Furthermore, there should be an advantage in extending the analysis to examine the attraction and production of freight volumes (instead of traffic volumes) to and from land uses.

Segmentary analysis. Segmentary analysis examines the nature of freight generation in individual segments of the urban economy. Often limited to a small geographical area, it can take a less structured and more wide-ranging look at freight consignments and trips in the context of the actors, institutions and facilities in the segment.[59] It amounts, in effect, to a 'case-study' approach, where the contact of the investigators with the people involved, their decision-making attitudes and their region is essential to its success. Segment analysis can be used toward three main goals. Firstly, it can be used for project analysis in the area. For example, it might provide inputs to an examination of proposals to ease truck congestion in a regional shopping centre. Secondly, it should assist to isolate elements of freight demand behaviour for more widespread investigation. Decision-making processes are usually best studied in microcosm first. Thirdly, a more general urban freight model might be built from an interlocking set of segment analyses.

Conclusions

Central to the examination of urban freight transport are its costs. The search of operative methods of diminishing these costs, though not beyond the area of responsibility of private industry, should be taken up by government, as must their implementation. The various levels of government should recognise that their activities already substantially influence the nature of urban goods movement and should re-examine their present roles as well as seeking new solutions. The need is for planning and consequently, where possible, models of behaviour which will enable them to foresee the effects of their proposals.

Urban freight modelling is in its infancy. Often data are unavailable. Inattention to urban goods movement and the facile treatment of goods traffic in urban transport plans has left a great deal of ground still to be covered. The policy purposes of the models to be developed will require an emphasis on the decision-making processes of urban freight. Decision-making must be reduced to its basics. Goods consumers and producers are likely to have similar elements in their behaviour (for example, utility maximisation or private cost minimisation) though these decisions will manifest themselves in different ways due to the different nature of goods and individual requirements. The heterogeneity of the urban freight task defies any simple treatment of its problems. Generalisations are difficult and, with the present state of knowledge, it is difficult to determine the features which are common from one freight task to another.

Segmentary models will be a useful starting point, for their focus on the dimensions of urban freight and its problems and for their input into dyadic models. The entire urban freight modelling process must fit into the urban passenger process and modal choice in longer distance freight transport. Equally, it is important that these models fit into models of land use and urban structure.[60]

8

Integrated urban transport and location analysis

S. Hansen

Introduction

The nature of urban development calls for land-use planning models in which short-term as well as long-term aspects are simultaneously treated. The physical structure of an urban area consists of transportation systems and buildings with a very long life. On the other hand the socio-economic activities which are undertaken in this physical setting are continuously changing in response to changes in preferences and other demand parameters. Consequently planning oriented land-use models should aim at explaining and describing the interplay between the long lasting physical infrastructure and the continuously shifting use of it. Ideally then, the spatial allocation problem in an urban area should be studied in terms of dynamic interdependent investment planning, where interdependencies apply to time as well as space. Obviously this implies a high degree of complexity. In practice the full scale planning problem has been reduced substantially in order to derive operational models.

Desirable model characteristics

Indivisibility

Economic textbook theories are usually based on the assumption that all resource allocations are continuous and feasible, whereas in the urban reality adjustments in the physical infrastructure are extremely costly in the short run. Over a fairly long period of time, allocations of land resources, once decided, are virtually fixed. Furthermore, optimality considerations with respect to plant location indicate that one is really dealing with non-continuous, indivisible, immobile and specialised resources. A study of returns to scale in Swedish manufacturing industries[1] forecasts the number of plants in different manufacturing sectors assuming minimisation of long run costs to match the predicted market demands. The study indicated a significant increase in production scale and a drastic decrease in the number of plants, down to a duopoly in most sectors. This tendency becomes more pronounced the smaller the urban region in focus. There is little reason to believe this to hold for manufacturing sectors only. The service sectors seem to fit the same description and there should be no need to point out that indivisibilities are a main feature of the links of the transport system. Consequently there is a strongly pronounced need for allocation models designed to handle indivisibilities and economies of scale.

Interdependencies

Traditionally land-use planning has been clearly separated into two independent problems: transport analysis and activity location. Even these two major sectors are frequently structured so that independency can be assumed between activity sectors and/or between transport modes.

Typical of most transport studies undertaken is the assumption that a future land-use pattern can be treated exogenously. Consequently the problem becomes one of designing a transport system to cope with the predicted land-use pattern, ignoring the redistributive effects which are produced as byproducts when constructing the system.

Most activity location studies are, unfortunately, equally partial in nature, in that they accept a transport system as given and allocate activities, ignoring the congestive effects of this on the transport network. A further simplification often assumed in activity allocation studies is the separation of households from manufacturing sectors. One may therefore say that the three major types or interdependencies to be dealt with are between: The locational pattern of manufacturers; The transport system; The locational pattern of households. Further complications arise because of the interdependencies *within* each of these three major sectors. Such interdependencies must be carefully dealt with in order to derive an operational model where inter- and intra-sectoral interdependencies can be adequately studied. Obviously an optimal balance between transport facilities and land uses can only be achieved if the planner can capture the interdependencies mentioned above. It is therefore of the utmost importance to identify the principal features of the urban interdependency pattern.

The urban area can be said to be occupied by building stock, recreational land and transport systems. The latter are designed to handle the various intermediate demands for transport services between activities located in the building stock and/or recreational land. In a long-run context both the land uses and the transport network may vary considerably. The interplay between the two is fundamental.

In this long-term context we identify the interplay as inter dependency between physical infrastructure or as stock location interaction. Due to indivisibilities the capacity of these physical stocks is fixed and acts in the short run as a limitation on the potential use of urban space. The building stocks, recreational land and the transport facilities undergo only slow and gradual changes with manufacturing and household activities allocated accordingly. We therefore identify a second interdependency level dealing with the actual use of physical infrastructure by the various activities. We observe the need to simultaneously deal with transport behaviour and activity location.

Welfare criteria

In order to suggest particular allocations of land for the use of buildings, transport and recreation, some welfare and cost criteria are needed. Obviously, even an ideal practical urban land-use model will be highly aggregated. Consequently only coarse welfare measures are operational.

Experience in urban land-use planning indicate that three welfare dimensions are generally agreed upon: accessibility; local environment; costs. Accessibility measures the relative proximity of the activities in the region. Local environment is taken to include space standards, pollution levels, socio-economic integration, etc. Costs obviously measure resource scarcities. It is immediately clear that a high level of accessibility is promoted by compact building stock patterns and high capacity transportation systems, whereas the local environment indicator is high with a scattered spatial structure with transport investments allocated to peripheral zones. Since there appears to be a conflict between achieving good accessibility and a good local environment with limited resources available, one should aim at revealing the welfare trade-offs between such different urban structures.

Uncertainty

As stated above, substantial change in the physical infrastructure of an urban area is a time-consuming process. Preferences and relative resource scarcities may change substantially in such a long-term perspective. In addition uncertainties exist with regard to the traditional forecasts of traffic volumes and activity levels, and with regard to the relative future weights attached to the basic welfare measures (accessibility and local environment). The models should therefore be formulated so as to allow for the generation of a number of different *efficient* investment patterns, leading to urban structures covering the whole spectrum from compact to highly dispersed cities. This is felt to be an important model feature since the physical stock, once it is there, only changes very slowly and at a high cost. The welfare losses due to unsuccessful infrastructural investments will thus be substantial, and only in so far as emphasis is laid upon a substantial degree of freedom of investment action will such potential welfare losses be kept at a minimum.

Spatial and sectoral disaggregation

In order to apply the various transport and regional policy measures efficiently, the planning model must be specified in some detail with respect to geographical zones and activity sectors. The need for detailed information calls for a very disaggregated model structure, whereas operational limitations in practice are rather severe and allow only rather large geographical zones and sectoral clusters to be used in the models. It is therefore important to undertake very careful disaggregations of the regional economy in order to minimise information losses. Such losses are experienced because the within-zone variations may grow to such magnitudes as to dominate the between-zone variations (see ch. 6). One must therefore seek to group geographical zones so that the former variation is minimised relative to the latter. One possible source of information when clustering activity sectors is input–output tables. These reveal which sectors are highly interdependent and which are independent of each other. In searching for low transport cost regional patterns of location, it seems reasonable to use this knowledge in grouping together activities which have important direct or indirect association with each other, and to separate activity clusters by means of some measure of interactivity independence.

Foundations of behavioural theories

A land-use transport model attempts to explain and describe the location and transport choices made by individual decision units, such as households and manufacturers of goods and services. It therefore seems natural to approach the analysis in terms of well established theories of consumer and manufacturer behaviour, rather than mechanistic correlation models lacking behavioural underpinnings. The latter will obviously be inefficient in studying the effects of various specific policy measures that are explicitly aimed at influencing the choices of the decision units in question.

Economic models of land use/transportation

Having listed and discussed various characteristics to be included in realistic urban land-use/transport planning models, we are now ready to take a closer look at the theoretical foundations of such models. The theoretical development departed from traditional microeconomic static equilibrium analysis and considered the land-use structure of monocentric urban areas. Equilibrium models which treat space as a continuous variable form the best point of departure for an attempt to provide some insight into the spatial structure of urban areas and the ways in which it is affected by market forces and public policies. These models are fairly easy to understand, although seemingly marginal complications to the attempt to approach a better real world description may make it very difficult to achieve a mathematical solution of the model. These models are, however, mostly based on the use of the calculus of maxima and minima.

The monocentric urban area is, however, not at all representative of urban areas in general. Models dealing with multicentre urban areas are needed in order to give a complete theoretical underpinning of urban land-use allocation and equilibrium analysis. The mathematics of such multi-centre spatial models are, on the other hand, less familiar to the student of traditional textbook economics. Several such models require programming techniques, some of which are quite cumbersome.

This chapter will, however, concentrate on fundamental theoretical aspects of monocentric and multicentre urban equilibrium analyses, rather than mathematical solution problems. On the basis of the desired planning model characteristics and theoretical foundations reviewed in the first half of the chapter we shall finally review practically oriented planning models aimed at coping with the complex interaction between land-use and transport in an urban area.

Monocentric urban land-use models

The simplest behavioural spatial static equilibrium model deals with the way household demand for residential land is affected by travel costs in an urban area with one city centre. It is assumed that household demand for residential land depends only on the rental value of land and that the actual outlay on such land anywhere in the urban area equals the difference between travel cost to the city centre from the city limit and the point in question. Land rent is thus equal to travel cost savings relative to travelling from the city limit. Travel cost is assumed to depend on radial travel distance from the centre and on the total population of the urban area. The model assumes total residential land to be a function of distance from the centre and at each particular distance this amount is exogenous. Since the model is a locational equilibrium model, a market clearance relationship for residential land in the entire urban area is needed to complete the model. The equilibrium condition states that savings in monetary commuting outlays are equal to residential land costs.

This partial equilibrium model for residential land was developed by Wingo.[2] Wingo's partial household location model has been elegantly extended by Muth.[3] In this model household utility depends on the consumption of housing services and other goods (including leisure). Utility is maximised subject to a generalised income constraint where income is defined to include not only money income but also income forgone in the consumption of leisure. The time cost of commuting to the centre where all employment is located is partly paid in terms of forgone leisure and in part in forgone money income. In addition, monetary travel costs are distance related. The households behave as if market prices are not influenced by their behaviour, but the price of housing services is distance dependent. The other element of Muth's model is the supply of housing services. These services are produced with land and non-land inputs, using the same production function for all such services. Input and output prices are distance dependent but exogenous in the eyes of the producers. Producers maximise their profits but the competitive market assumption implies zero profit regardless of production site.

The equilibrium of the model is assured by letting the urban area extend as far as is necessary to equate the supply and demand of housing services. By means of this model Muth showed the behavioural conditions under which population density will be a negative exponential function of distance from the city centre, as frequently assumed in the land-use literature.

The role of transport is passive in these two models. Land used for transport purposes is exogenously determined, as is the number of commuters. These land-use models are therefore partial in several respects. Emphasis is on location decisions in the household market, whereas other manufacturing sectors are preassigned to the city centre. All commuting will therefore take place to and from the centre. Land used for transport is predetermined. Consequently, residential activities are located on the basis of a given transport system and a given location of manufacturers.

In attempting to generalise the land-use model to simultaneously treat residential and manufacturing land uses, Alonso[4] developed a static spatial equilibrium model including manufactured goods as well as time costs. The model consists of a spatial theory of utility maximising households and a spatial theory of manufacturers of other goods and services, who maximise profits. The household utility is a function of goods, housing, and travel distance from the centre. The goods prices are assumed fixed and spatially independent, whereas housing and commuting costs are distance dependent. Household income is exogenously determined. Maximising utility yields a so-called bid price function. Bid price is a function of distance from city centre and is constructed as a constant utility curve indicating the highest land rent the household can pay at each site. Thus there is one bid price curve for each level of utility. In order to find the equilibrium location of households, a function showing the market price of land at each distance from the centre is required. The tangency between the bid price curve and the price structure curve then determines equilibrium location. Alonso's spatial theory of the firm assumes revenue and non-land costs to depend on quantity sold and location. Land costs to the firm depend on location and the quantity of land demanded, but the firms behave as if land rents are exogenous to them. Maximising behaviour yields the firms' bid price function, and locational equilibrium is established in the same way as for households.

Based on these submarket models a theory of urban land market equilibrium is sought. The model unfortunately, does not allow for such a general equilibrium analysis unless some stronger assumptions are introduced. The failure of the model is a result of trying to combine two partial equilibrium models whose basic underlying assumptions are inconsistent when viewed simultaneously. In solving each partial location model the location of the other activities is located with respect to the city centre. Consequently one does not gain much in the direction of a more general equilibrium location model by this approach. With respect to the land use – transport interaction properties the criticism presented in connection with the works of Wingo and Muth also holds true for the Alonso model.

Further development along these lines of thought has been carried out by Mills.[5] His final extension[6] represents the most elegant and advanced model based on the behaviourally oriented calculus models of single centred spatial systems, with land being a continuous variable around a city centre.

In his 1967 study Mills takes the view that the basic characteristics of cities are to be understood as market responses to opportunities for production and income. He claims that factor substitution and technology are the most dramatic factors of urban structure. Consequently, the attention is essentially production oriented in contrast to the demand oriented models by Wingo, Muth and Alonso discussed above. Actually the household demand side is almost excluded in order to focus on and solve the problems Mills thinks of as essential in this context.

The model assumes three different activities to take place in the urban area: production of goods; intra-city transport; housing. Production of goods justifies the existence of the city for one or both of the following two reasons: favourable location; increasing returns to scale. In either case production will take place in a single area and the model implies that this area plays the role of the Central Business District (CBD). The goods production function is assumed to be Cobb–Douglas with three input factors: land, labour and capital.

The model further implies that the households are located in the suburbs around the CBD in a pattern determined by their bids for land. It is worth noting that goods are defined as outputs of those production processes which, for reasons of locational efficiency or returns to scale, locate in the CBD. Other production activities will locate adjacent to households to minimise transport costs and will for convenience be included in the housing activity. The housing production function is also assumed to be Cobb–Douglas, defined over the same three input factors. In this case, however, constant returns to scale is assumed. Transport is the activity that links the CBD with the suburban areas. Mills is aware of the importance of factor substitution in this particular activity and the need to develop optimal transport programmes for the urban area. Different modes of transport require highly different input–output coefficients relating the three inputs to transport services. The model does not, however, deal with this challenging substitution topic. It limits itself to using an exogenously determined coefficient relating land input to transport volume. This again implies an exogenously determined mode split. The model is based on competitive factor markets with an exogenously given wage rate and capital rent. The land rent is an endogenous function of the distance from the CBD. The output market for goods is assumed to be monopolistic, as a consequence of increasing returns to scale. The goods demand has a constant elasticity.

The city centre of this urban area will be circular and its size will be endogenous. CBD land uses will compete with suburban land uses. Land rent at the CBD boundary determines the amount of CBD land, and the city population is determined by the number of workers demanded at the exogenously determined wage rate. The CBD rent is assumed to be high enough to absorb any monopoly profit and it must be at least as high as the land rent at the CBD border. This requires increasing returns to scale, which were assumed above. A competitive housing market operates in the suburbs. Housing comsunption per household is assumed constant regardless of distance from the CBD. Not all workers living in the suburbs commute to the CBD. The model assumes that a fixed fraction of the workers are employed in housing activity in the suburbs.

The travel cost per passenger mile is proportional to land rent and increases as one approaches the CBD, since land is used in the production of travel services. The increase in travel cost may also be interpreted to express increasing traffic congestion as one approaches the CBD. The urban land market is such that urban land users are able to bid land away from rural uses at the outer limit of the urban area. The opportunity cost of using land for urban purposes is exogenously determined in the model, thus providing an initial land value.

The equilibrium of this urban land use model requires that all land in CBD and suburbs be used for something: either goods production or transport facilities in the CBD, and housing or transport in the suburbs. Finally the model is completed by stating that all workers must live somewhere.

This simultaneous model is cumbersome to solve, although each particular segment of it has been enormously simplified as compared with the real world. On the basis of exogenously given production function parameters, goods demand parameters, factor prices on labour and capital, proportions of workers producing housing, housing demand per worker and opportunity cost of urban land, the following are determined within the model: land rents at each site; amount of land allocated to goods production, transport and housing; population density; CBD size; urban area size; population of urban area; output prices in the three submarkets.

Although the model describes an abstract city of a very particular nature, it sheds light on several issues raised at the beginning of this chapter. In contrast to the previously described demand oriented models of Wingo, Muth, and Alonso, Mills' model is explicitly concerned with the interplay between transport and land use. In addition to allocating land between transport and other uses, the model also describes roughly how travel costs change as one approaches the CBD with a predetermined transport technology and mode split.

As mentioned earlier, a typical observation in urban processes is the slow and gradual change in the physical infrastructure (building stock and transport network) and the much quicker change in the use of this stock. Mills' model suggests that urban traffic congestion is a result of the existence of these two urban development characteristics and not a consequence of city size as such.

Five years after the presentation of this interaction oriented model Mills published his important book *Studies in the structure of the urban economy*,[7] where he presents his most recent developments, attempting to explain and describe car oriented urban structures. This study contains empirical as well as theoretical analysis and much effort is developed to further improvements of the modelling approach of 1967. His 1972 model differs from the 1967 version described above in several respects. Mills has solved both models by means of numerical analysis and evaluated them empirically by the use of what he considered representative parameter values. He has also carried out some valuable sensitivity analysis to help in evaluating the realism of the theories.

We shall concentrate here on pointing out the main differences between the 1967 model described above and the 1972 model, and shall indicate the relative merits of each. The 1972 model is in some respects simplified compared with the 1967 version. Simplifications were sought where the loss of realism was minimised and the gain in mathematical simplicity was significant. Complications were introduced where a need was felt for a more realistic treatment of basic structural features. Some endogenous variables of the 1967 model were exogenised in the 1972 version. These were inputs and outputs in goods production in the CBD, and consequently the labour force of the urban area.

Land allocated to transport was endogenous in the 1967 model and the use of the variable constitutes a major step in the direction of coping with interdependencies in urban land-use analysis. On the other hand it may well be that the role of transport in this interplay is more realistically handled by explicitly introducing a travel market with an exogenously determined capacity. Exogenising transport capacity (or land allocated to transport) is then justified in the 1972 model, since changes in this type of physical infrastructure come about slowly and as a result of public and not private decisions. On the other hand, the 1972 model is complicated relative to the 1967 model by the explicit introduction of the demand for urban CBD oriented travel. Each worker is assumed to make one daily round trip and total travel demand is therefore determined by the residential location pattern.

A typical feature of urban rush-hour traffic is that use of the transport system exceeds its design capacity, causing congestion and delays. Commuters' travel costs are therefore expressed as a sum of the uncongested travel cost plus an element which represents the effect of congestion on travel costs. Thus the effects of congestion on the urban structure may be studied. Another complication introduced in order to improve realism is the demand for housing. As mentioned earlier, housing consumption per worker was assumed constant in the 1967 version, whereas the 1972 model contains a Cobb–Douglas housing demand function in income and own price. This makes it possible to study income and housing price effects on the urban structure. The 1967 model contained income only as a factor price in the production functions.

The other relationships and variables are quite similar, but all in all the changes mentioned here are substantial and the models cannot be expected to yield similar empirical results in sensitivity analyses. The sensitivity analysis carried out on the 1967 model yielded some empirical consequences counter to intuitive economic reasoning. First of all, exogenous increases in factor prices, such as the wage rate and capital costs, are expected to reduce factor use, output and urban area. The 1972 model is compatible with this reasoning, but the 1967 model is not. Secondly, technological improvements in the production of housing services reduced the size of the urban area in the 1967 model as a consequence of the exogenisation of housing demand. The 1972 model assumes price elastic housing demand and the opposite (and in real life expected) effect is achieved. Thirdly, technological improvements in the production of transport services led to reduced urban area in the 1967 version, whereas the 1972 version produced an increase, as would have been expected on the grounds of pure intuition.

One feature of the model that deserves more attention in studying the land use – transport interaction is the role of commuting costs. Travel demand in the model is related to the commuting costs experienced typically by a car-using commuter of today. He is faced with an average commuting cost which, as a consequence of congestion, is increasing. Consequently social marginal commuting costs are higher, but not fully reflected in the cost faced by the commuter, and the discrepancy increases rapidly as congestion becomes severe. His travel demand will therefore exceed what would be optimal in welfare economic terms. Since the correct evaluation of transport system improvements is dependent on the use of efficient prices and evaluation coefficients, it would be tempting to test the effects through the model of introducing a social marginal cost oriented pricing system on CBD oriented travel. Mills could not resist this challenge and his 1972 study culminates with a presentation of a slightly modified model version specifically developed to reveal the implications for urban size and structure of an efficiently priced transport system.

The modification relative to the above mentioned 1972 model consists in assuming that the price of travel services at each distance from CBD is the marginal cost of land used for transport and that equilibrium on the travel market is attained. Since other production factors are fixed in such a way that only land enters the transport production function, the marginal cost of land use in this sector equals the marginal social cost. As it is assumed that this sector is competitive, marginal cost also equals average cost. This modification implies that land allocated to transport is endogenously determined in a way similar to the 1967 model. The final task is to compare the urban size resulting from the model with exogenously determined transport land areas and inefficient transport pricing with that resulting from an efficient allocation and pricing scheme.

On the basis of Mills' numerical parameter values and the use of numerical analyses and sensitivity tests, the conclusion is clearly that a much larger and lower density urban area results if the efficient policy is chosen. Land rents and travel costs decline compared with the situation based on an inefficiently priced and exogenously determined transport system.

The total amount of land used for transport is more or less independent of whether transport supply is endogenous or exogenous, so long as the exogenously determined transport land use is chosen to be representative of large US urban areas. However, its percentage of total urban land is much smaller in the model where it is endogenously determined, the reason being that an efficient pricing system results in land being devoted to transport only where it is needed. These models certainly support the intuitive feeling that improper pricing of urban transport services leads to large distortions in the allocation of resources. Improper pricing leads to congestion which makes travel expensive. Consequently residents are induced to avoid long trips to and from the CBD searching for residential location near the CBD.

Multicentre urban land-use models

The monocentric models reviewed above have substantially extended our knowledge of how market forces and public policies affect the land-use structure and land rents in single centred circular urban areas with only radial transport systems. These models have not, however, been found suitable for the study of the suburbanisation of production activities and the resulting need for, and use of, tangential transport systems.

With the increasing decentralisation of economic activity in urban areas, a realistic model cannot ignore the possibility that many journey-to-work decisions are made from a fixed residence, in contrast to the fixed job location implicit in the monocentric models. Assuming urban employment sites in subcentres outside the CBD obviously complicates the equilibrium analysis substantially. It is therefore felt that the study of multicentre urban areas is best approached by first reviewing a simple partial equilibrium model dealing with the way people locate their worksite with respect to fixed residential sites and a fixed transport network. Since residence sites are fixed, home location rent does not vary with the siting of the job location. The spatial equilibrium is then determined by the disutility of commuting and the utility of income from working at that site. Such a model has been developed by Beesley and Dalvi,[8] who further assume that the number of job opportunities increases with willingness to commute. The model thus focuses on the relation between income and distance, and each individual seeks to maximise the income that remains at his disposal after paying his transport cost (including time costs) and the fixed location rent. The equilibrium condition states that the worker will commute up to the point where marginal income with respect to commuting distance is equal to marginal commuting cost with respect to distance. One immediately sees that the higher the value of time, *ceteris paribus*, the less the willingness to travel. It is also realised that this model is limited so as not to deal with the question of changing residential location once the optimal commuting distance is found to be very long.

We are therefore automatically forced to look into more general equilibrium models in our search for more realistic descriptions of the urban market forces. We will concentrate this review on two such modelling approaches and some extensions of these, which have eventually led to practical land-use–transport planning models containing explicit treatment of the interaction between transport and urban structure. The two approaches reviewed below represent two complementary approaches to a static and deterministic study of urban land and transport use. Dynamics and uncertainty will not be discussed until the last part of this section.

Our starting point is the spatial general equilibrium model developed by Lefeber.[9] The point of departure is the classic Walrasian general equilibrium model. This is extended to a well behaved spatial problem where a few interdependencies of production, consumption, location and transport are taken into account. A finite number of spatial locations (coordinates) are pre-fixed as possible sites for consumption and/or production activities. The model further contains a finite number of consumption activities, production activities, transport activities and production factors (resources). These resources are classified, according to their degree of mobility, into four subgroups.

Initial quantities of products and input factors are exogenously located at the various sites. The input factors can be used at their initial site or transported to another production site, thus incurring transport costs. Each site is connected with all the others by means of a transport network, and transport services used to move input factors and output products are produced by a transport sector which itself does not use transport resources. Due to overall resource scarcity the allocation between transport and other activities must be undertaken simultaneously. The optimal spatial structure and resource use are sought by maximising social welfare (which is a function of individual utilities) subject to four sets of restrictions:

i. Total household consumption of a commodity at a given site must not exceed total deliveries of that commodity to that site.
ii. Transport demand must not exceed transport capacity.
iii. Total use of a commodity must not exceed total production capacity for it.
iv. The use of each input factor supplied at a particular site must not exceed supply.

By further assuming that no external effects are present and that all submarkets are perfectly competitive (constant returns to scale), a spatial general equilibrium solution is achieved through the optimisation procedure in which the resulting factor rent structure reflects the dual of the quantitative location and transport decisions. The model has been developed both in the general Walrasian case and as a linear programming model. It is worth noting that the problem of interdependencies is dealt with in only a rather limited way. Firms deliver outputs to a household via a common product pool. Households deliver their factors directly to firms in exogenously determined locations. Firms never use each other's outputs as inputs. The model thus does not recognise direct interdependencies between firms.

The basic problem encountered by those attempting to use the Lefeber approach as a point of departure for urban spatial allocation studies is that two essential urban characteristics are typically assumed away in the Lefeber model: externalities; indivisibilities (economies of scale). If externalities are introduced, the equilibrating pricing and rent system must be completed by the addition of a number of taxes and subsidies, in order to achieve a stable spatial equilibrium. If economies of scale are to exist in one or more urban sectors, this simultaneous equation system has no unique solution which can be reached by a traditional decentralised market mechanism. Our conclusion is therefore that the Lefeber approach is challenging in its attempt to cope with simultaneity, but too unrealistic to form the basis for urban land-use planning and policy evaluation.

The discouraging discovery that no linear price system on plants, on locations and on commodities in all locations will sustain any assignment was made by Beckmann and Koopmans in their famous 1957 paper[10] on assignment problems and spatial location. The assignment approach proceeds as follows: The whole of any activity is allocated to a whole location, the location eventually becoming fully utilised. It is a procedure specifically developed to deal with the allocation of indivisible resources where interdependencies between firms are recognised, in the search for an optimal land-use pattern. Assuming first that no transport resources are forgone in moving factors between locations, it can be shown that a linear price system yielding an efficient equilibrium solution is attainable. Making the model more realistic and introducing transport costs complicates the assignment problem and appears to defeat the linear price system as a means of sustaining an optimal assignment, since there will always be an incentive for someone to seek a location other than the one he holds.

On the basis of these two approaches one is tempted to conclude that planners should either delete transport costs and assume the existence of indivisibilities or assume the existence of transport costs, but at the same time assume away indivisibilities. In both cases a stable spatial equilibrium solution is attained, unfortunately at a very uncomfortably high price: the total loss of urban real world contact. If this conclusion is not acceptable one has to look for other ways of securing an equilibrium market solution. This idea was suggested by Moses in 1958.[11] A consistent mathematical solution to these problems within a spatial general equilibrium model with indivisibilities was given by Andersson and Marksjø in 1972;[12] they showed that a nonlinear pricing system is able to allocate efficiently, thus providing at least a theoretical solution for a basic difficulty in urban land-use–transport analysis. The practical problems of how to implement such a pricing policy efficiently in practice are severe. Andersson and Marksjø conclude their analysis:[13]

> An introduction of a price discrimination in the form of a progressive tax on the scale of operations in a spatially separated firm would then be a welfare increasing device securing an optimal spatial dispersion of production, employment and population. To this end the proposed techniques for derivation for a nonlinear shadow price system would presumably be an efficient aid. It seems, however, to be more difficult to insure workable competition in the market as a whole with the aid of a progressive tax on the scale of operations within firms, because of the possibilities of trust or cartel control of the pricing policy in the spatially separated, but organizationally coordinated firms.

Modelling urban land-use – transport interaction in practice

What then, should the urban land-use–transport planner do in practice? He obviously would like to incorporate the model characteristics described at the beginning and at the same time develop an operational and policy oriented model. The most commonly used applied model is the urban transportation modelling system (UTMS), which has been frequently used and refined in applied urban transport planning in the past 20 years. This approach is discussed in detail in chapter 12 (see also ch. 6). The section above on desirable model characteristics referred to the importance of simultaneous treatment of transport and activity location in land-use models. We will therefore now turn to attempts to recognise such interdependencies by outlining the approaches of two studies.[14]

In order to integrate a land-use model and a complete transport model (UTMS), Putman[15] has recently presented a promising way of handling the interdependencies that occasioned our strongest criticism of the UTMS. Putman's modelling process begins with a set of initial spatially defined activity levels along with initial transport system characteristics for the case of freely flowing traffic. These two data sets are used to generate a preliminary inter-zonal trip matrix. For this initial traffic estimate one can load the projection year network in order to reveal the travel times and costs that would be observed if there were no change in the spatial activity distribution relative to the base year. These network characteristics, base year spatial data and projection year totals can then form the basis for generating a forecast on the spatial activity distribution of the projection year. This projected distribution forms the basis for a new trip matrix which is then loaded on the network to derive modified network characteristics. On the basis of these the projection year control totals are relocated spatially and this distribution is compared to the first estimate thereof. In case of significant differences, new trips will be generated and loaded on the network and further iterations made until no significant differences occur. An equilibrium is then reached and the principle failing of most applied land-use–transport models has been eliminated, by explicitly introducing feedback loops.

Empirical testing on the basis of this model has clearly indicated that disregard of the interdependency between transport and land-use is virtually certain to introduce significant errors in model results. The model tests further suggest policy possibilities much in line with those derived from comparison of Mills's continuous models reviewed in the previous section. Both Mills' and Putman's empirical testing led to the conclusion that congestion of networks produces tendencies towards centralisation of economic activities and land use in metropolitan areas. Relieving the networks of congestion by means of transport pricing and/or investments produces tendencies towards decentralisation of economic activities and land use and an increase in the urban area.

A more ambitious approach has recently been developed by a research team engaged in developing the so-called TRANSLOK model for the Stockholm region in Sweden. They spent a considerable time on the questions regarding desirable model characteristics reviewed earlier, and we shall end this chapter with a brief review of how this group integrates the above mentioned theoretical findings and operationality in order to improve active integrated land-use–transport planning in a metropolitan area.[16] The work of the TRANSLOK group has been consciously developed to give optimal *strategies* for investments in the communication system and in the real capital of different sectors of the economy, distributed over space. To cope with the almost insurmountable computational problems, the whole theory has been developed as a decomposed group of interrelated models going from the most aggregated to a successively more detailed level of analysis. The basic planning philosophy is in many respects quite similar to the Australian systems approach.

Although it is an *intra-regional* planning theory, the realism of the whole analysis is dependent on reasonably correct forecasts of the development of production, employment and total capital in the different economic sectors of the region as a whole. An inter-regional theory of growth is thus needed as a foundation for the intra-regional planning analysis. The various regional and sectoral resource and activity levels used in the intra-regional study are made available for a number of inter-regional transport policies for base and future planning years by means of a mathematical model of optimal growth[17] applied to Swedish national statistical data.

We now turn to the specification of the TRANSLOK decomposition scheme.[18] This follows the interdependency levels identified in the earlier section on desirable model characteristics and has resulted in the pattern schematically outlined in figure 1. The arrows show the structure of interactions. We observe the mutual interrelations between transport networks and zonal contents both on the stock capacity side and on the user side. Moreover, we note the principally hierarchical dependence between capacity planning on one hand and activity location on the other and between aggregate/disaggregate activity analyses. This observation is crucial for obtaining a computationally feasible decomposition of the total problem. However, as indicated in figure 1, the decomposition is not strictly hierarchical, since more detailed user analyses may show inconsistencies with assumptions made on the capacity planning level. In the event of severe inconsistencies, the introduction of feedback loops may be needed. The fundamental assumption underlying the decomposition scheme is, however, that the intensity of such feedback interactions is low, compared with the main flow of impact. This is of primary importance for the computational efficiency of the model framework.

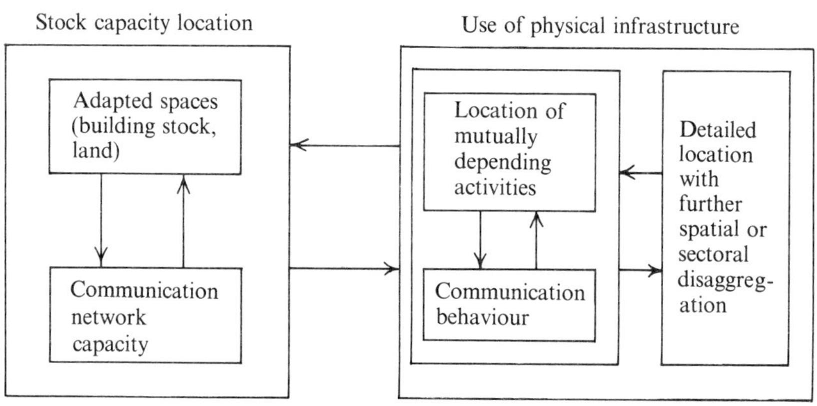

Fig. 1. Spatial interdependency pattern.

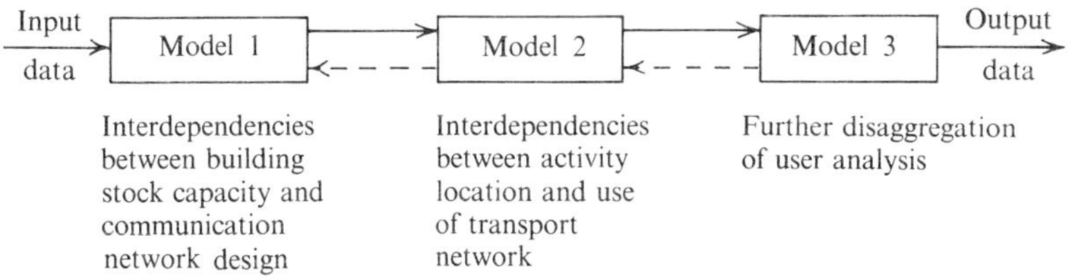

Fig. 2. Model framework.

The identification of three levels of interaction suggests that the model framework should operate with three separate submodels. In figure 2 the basic characteristics of the model chain are outlined. The socio-economic objective to be optimised is composed of regional accessibility indicators and local environmental indicators. It should be stressed, however, that the model framework is flexible and the submodels may easily be adapted to other measures of urban welfare.

The purpose of model 1 is an explicit treatment of the inter-dependencies between investments in building stock capacity and communication network capacity. Given the limited manpower and capital resources in the construction sector, the growth of building stock demand should be allocated and the communication networks should be expanded in order to meet the socio-economic objective. Good accessibility properties of an urban structure are generally obtained at the expense of local environmental quality. The aim of the stock capacity location model is to generate a set of development patterns with basically different accessibility and local environmental properties. The whole range of solutions is characterised by the fact that they are efficient with regard to the supply of investment resources. The model attempts to combine optimal network design and optimal allocation. The potential building stock location area is divided into a set of N disjoint zones, each represented by a single node. The nodes are connected by the existing communication network links. A finite number of possible extensions of the communication network is specified in advance. This is a common limitation in most transport planning models. However, at a very high level of aggregation (few zones) (for computational reasons and with the aim of limiting the study to high capacity links having marked structural effects on the location pattern), the assumption of a predetermined set of possible transport projects should not be very restrictive.

In order to evaluate the accessibility properties of a location pattern, some model of transport behaviour has to be employed. Without specific knowledge of the use of the building stock (this is studied at the model 2 level), this model has to be crude. It should give an approximate picture of congestion effects and route choices. Velocity fields are used in combination with shortest route traffic assignment. For the existing urban structure this means that a matrix of generalised travel costs (or distance frictions) can be calculated. By investments in new transport projects the velocity field is changed and by the shortest route algorithm this influences the matrix of generalised travel costs. The actual degree of freedom of action is studied in terms of the two welfare indicators, by introducing a marginal rate of substitution which is then varied over a wide range.

In order to solve the problem formulated, the model is transformed into a purely combinational one. This is done by dividing the total amount of building stock into a finite number of equally sized 'projects'. The solution procedure is based on heuristic tree-searching.[19]

The key questions for any decision-maker would now be: What degree of freedom is inherent in the problem? To what extent can regional accessibility be increased and what does this cost in terms of local environmental quality? What do the efficient, compact and dispersed investment plans look like and what are the consequences on the zonal level? These questions may be answered without further information about the preference structure of the decision-maker. By varying the marginal rate of substitution between zero and infinity the set of efficient solutions is gradually scanned. This gives political bodies an opportunity actually to choose between basically different investment plans. The process can be seen as a two stage resolution of preferences: Agreement on the socio-economic indicators which are components in the social welfare function; A posterior determination of the marginal rate of substitution by choice among efficient alternatives.

With input data from the Stockholm region, model 1 was run for the time period 1970 to 1985. The total area was divided into 12 zones. Twenty-five structurally important extensions of the transport system were collected from a number of proposed plans during the 1960s. The anticipated velocity field for the year 1985 was used to calculate travel times in the initial transport system. The impact on these of each potential new link was then estimated, as well as the impact on zonal areas. The technological coefficients measuring the use of investment resources (labour, capital) per unit of building stock and per transport link were projected by means of estimated production functions of the Cobb–Douglas type applied to local data. Consistent forecasts of population growth and development of production potentials were developed, from which the demand for building stock and total supply of investment resources were obtained. In order to fit the approximate solution procedure, the total demand for building stock investments was partitioned into six projects.

With a decreasing marginal rate of substitution between average accessibility and average environmental quality, the structure of the investment pattern becomes gradually more concentrated. In terms of building stock location, the expansion strategy changes from a markedly scattered character, with the emphasis on peripheral zones, to a relative concentration on highly accessible zones in the central or semicentral part of the region.

The communication investments show a somewhat more stable pattern. Some of the projects are common to all solutions, while others are due to variation according to the building stock location pattern. Changes in building stock allocation influence the availability of resources for network design and thus transport services, as measured by average interaction costs, and finally environmental consumption, as measured by the environmental congestion costs. Taken together these effects concern both the choice set and priority order of transportation investments. Thus a particular resource-consuming railway project appears in solutions where the building stock is allocated to semicentral zones with low consumption of resources.

The size of the labour force has only an upper limit (set by maximum immigration) in the model. The actual level is endogenously determined by the allocation process. To achieve a balanced growth of residential activity and production activities in the region as a whole, a set of equations is introduced relating the labour market to the housing market. The depreciation of the building stock and changes in it due to investments or demolition are taken care of by the updating formula. The relation between building stock and building activity is given by the capital/output ratio. Finally the rate of change in the activity pattern may be subject to restrictions for social or economic reasons.

At the transition from the stock capacity level to the study of the use of physical infrastructure, several consistency issues are raised. Consumption and supply of resources, the growth rates and the accessibility and local environmental indicators have to be transmitted between model levels in a consistent way. The disaggregation in itself may, however, lead to suboptimisation. As model 1 does not take the interaction intensities of different activities into account, the proposed network structure may be suboptimal with respect to the location pattern determined by model 2. There are at least two ways of reducing the suboptimality. One way is to take the detailed demand structure of model 2 as a starting point for an optimum network calculation. This process will locally improve the solution. In order to receive a stable global fit, several iterations between the spatial allocation of activities and network optimisation might be required. To avoid convergency problems of such iterations, an alternative way of reducing suboptimality is to choose a number of the best solutions found in model 1 as inputs for the model 2 calculations. In this way a number of alternative allocation strategies are produced, providing a rough sensitivity analysis.

The accessibility indicator of model 2 seeks to segregate the activities according to their relative interaction intensities. Spatial clustering is neutralised by the claim of high environmental standards and the limited capacity of communication network links. The aim of model 2 is to generate a set of development patterns with different characteristics as regards accessibility, environmental consumption and transport. The dynamic allocation model at this level of interdependence has a quadratic programming structure, with a quadratic objective and linear restrictions. The model has been used for prediction in the Stockholm region using 3-year periods between 1970 and 1979.

The development over time of the activity location pattern for two quite different trade-offs between accessibility and local environment shows that in the compact solution providing good accessibility properties, the growth of the residential activity is concentrated in the central zone, while the production activities are allocated to the southern semi-central areas and to some extent to the north western peripheral zone. Increasing the weight on the environmental indicator gives rise to a scattered allocation of activities. The most space consuming production activities are moved to the peripheral western zones, while the remaining production activity and most of the residential land-use are directed to the eastern areas. Behind the regional measures of average accessibility and average environmental quality is hidden a spatial distribution of accessibility and environmental conditions. The properties of such distributions can be expected to be crucial in an actual evaluation of plan alternatives.[20]

In a long-term perspective the preference structure may be subject to qualitative changes. One possible way of handling these questions is to analyse the adaptivity of development strategies. The purpose is to take into account the multistage character of an investment strategy. The gradual resolution of uncertainty through time makes it favourable to postpone structurally binding decisions until more thorough information is at hand. By analysing the possibilities of altering the later stages in an investment scheme according to future conditions, the adaptivity of initial decisions can be established. An adaptive strategy in these terms aims at optimising future freedom of action. The adaptive or robust initial decisions leave a maximum of 'good' end-states open to future decisions. By good end-states are meant optimum or near optimum end-solutions, relative to the expected variation of external future conditions.

On the basis of the empirical results mentioned above, six transport projects and one single location for building stock were common to both the compact and the dispersed urban structure. A strategy with maximal adaptivity to changes in trade-off between accessibility and environmental quality is likely to give initial priority to these projects.[21] The price of increased adaptivity is generally paid in terms of a lower dynamic efficiency in relation to a specific preference function.

Let us now examine the second level of interdependence in the TRANSLOK model package. The purpose of the model 2 stage is to perform a more detailed analysis of the use of building stock capacity and transport network capacity. The interdependencies between activity location and communication behaviour are considered explicitly much in line with the models developed by Sharpe and Brotchie[22] in Australia and Putman in the

USA. An exogenously projected growth of production activities and a balancing number of households should be allocated in order to maximise the socio-economic objective. The allocation is performed subject to limited resources in the construction sector. At this stage a dynamic spatial allocation model for land, residential activity and production activities is formulated. The accessibility and environmental indicators are formulated by strictly disaggregating the objective function elements in model 1.[23]

The restrictions express the exogenously determined growth rate of production levels, the limited availability of labour and construction capital, and the balance of supply and demand in the land and housing markets. There are also updating relations transforming inputs between time periods by depreciation and activity relocation. The labour restriction permits substitution between construction sectors and other production activities.

The land available for allocation of activities in each zone and each time-period has to be produced by investments in local transport links and other service facilities (water, sewerage, electricity, etc.) or to be freed by the demolition of old building stock. A balance of supply and of demand for available land for allocation is thus enforced.

The aggregation level in model steps 1 and 2 is high. Geographically the region is divided into 12 zones and the total production activity is split up into 6 to 8 functionally identified clusters in model 2. To be of relevance in many practical planning situations, a more disaggregated treatment of spatial and sectoral elements is necessary. For example, the analysis of detailed spatial patterns of location has to take into account local intra-zonal conditions. In the same way, the better production sectors should be allocated (within respective cluster locations) with regard to intra-cluster heterogeneities. These analyses are performed with an approximate knowledge of the overall regional location pattern, and therefore the average distance from one zone to the various activity clusters may be considered as given. Thus the treatment of inter-sectoral interdependencies is simplified. Instead it is possible to give a wider attention to indivisibilities and economies of scale in production.

Conclusion

In order to develop planning tools to cope with the complicated interaction between transportation and land use, it is necessary to identify the typical characteristics of the development of urban structures. In the search for appropriate models of this kind one is naturally led to review the theoretical foundations of behavioral spatial equilibrium models. By relating these models to the initially listed urban development characteristics, one immediately reveals both theoretical shortcomings and a lack of relevance to real urban planning situations. One should, however, recognise the spatial equilibrium models not as planning models, but rather as behavioural-theoretic interaction hypotheses which form an important basis for the development of practical planning models, where explicit policy parameters enter as exogenous variables measurable by means of accessible statistics.

Not many practical planning models have so far been developed to satisfy the criteria listed early in this chapter. This is in part due to the cumbersome mathematics implied by the characteristics identified once one attempts to transform such characteristics into a behaviourally consistent theoretical framework. One is also seriously hampered in this process by the constraint that the mathematical planning model must also be computationally operational, and that the endogenous and exogenous variables should be uniquely identified to be measured by means of characteristics observed in the urban area. It is felt that further development of actual integrated planning models depends more on the development of operations research and computer programs, than on a new behavioural hypothesis of the spatial activities of firms and households. Computer and operations research is undergoing a very rapid development; the models reviewed in this chapter indicate only the very beginning of a new and exciting era of integrated spatial planning, and hopefully the end of the era of partial spatial planning.

9

Transport and land-use determinants of urban structure

J. Paterson

Introduction

In this chapter a discussion is presented of the way in which activity patterns influence urban structure. The emphasis is placed on means of conceptualising transport and land use within a general equilibrium context. The centralised general equilibrium models are taken as a point of departure, and the key relationship between accessibility and rents or location premiums are illustrated in the context of this class of conceptual models. A critique of the implicit structural assumptions of the centralised models is offered. This is based on their failure to embody the readily observable phenomenon of the dual or reciprocal effect of externalities, whereby land uses frequently create 'two-way' externalities, which are important in the transfer of goods and services to establishments within a city, and in the dynamic adaptation of urban activities to new conditions. A further criticism is made of the overemphasis which is generally given to the work trip, both in conceptual and empirical models of land-use determination. It is suggested that establishments recognise the value of proximity to so many poles of attraction within a city that they tend to visualise their environment in terms of multi-dimensional accessibility surfaces, rather than one or a few specific points of attraction. Spatial competition is capable of transforming the structure of a city so as to move the choice of residential location, or choice of factory site, toward virtually any desired pattern, and is likely to be efficient in doing so. Visualisation of the city in terms of a multitude of overlapping fields of accessibility permits a more flexible approach to the modelling of land-use–transport interactions than is possible within the context of the centralised general equilibrium models. Empirical evidence is offered of the adaptability of land-use characteristics to transport conditions.

Simple transport-based relationships

The economic models of urban spatial and locational equilibrium, in the line of development through Wingo,[1] Alonso,[2] Muth,[3] and Mills,[4] have been erected on the basis of a geometrical frame with an exogenously determined 'centre', which may be a point (Alonso) or may have area (Mills) but which, in either case, is the focus of all location choices by the establishments whose optimising behaviour underlies the equilibrium space, location, and rent structure. In these models all establishments look only toward the centre, and are oblivious to the locations of other establishments, either between themselves and the centre, or between themselves and the periphery.

In the simplest paradigm (fig. 1), travel cost increases as a linear function of distance and, for a resident at i, rent amounts to the difference between his travel costs and those of a resident at the margin; each site commands a premium or rent equal to the travel cost saving which it confers relative to a site on the urban fringe. With given transport plant, R_1 is the rent at the centre of population P_1, and F_1 the distance to the fringe with the same population.

This simple model, which is close to the form published by Wingo, has limited practical application, and can be criticised on many grounds, some of which are developed in this paper and others of which have been raised by Mills.[5] Nevertheless the essential interrelationship between urban land rents and accessibility, or transport costs, forms the basis for all systematic discussions of transport and land-use interaction, and the simplicity of the relationship offers an invaluable heuristic device for the urban theorist in his thinking about how urban space is organised. The rent–distance relationship in figure 1 can be expressed as in figure 2. With constant population, transport capacity and a build up of traffic, leading to a proportionate increase in congestion and travel time at all distances, the rent gradient curve can be expected to rise from R_1F_1 to R_2F_1, once a bigger transport cost saving is available at any location than was available before, relative to the fringe. This is only the first step in the adjustment process, as the new rent levels will increase equilibrium densities at all intra-

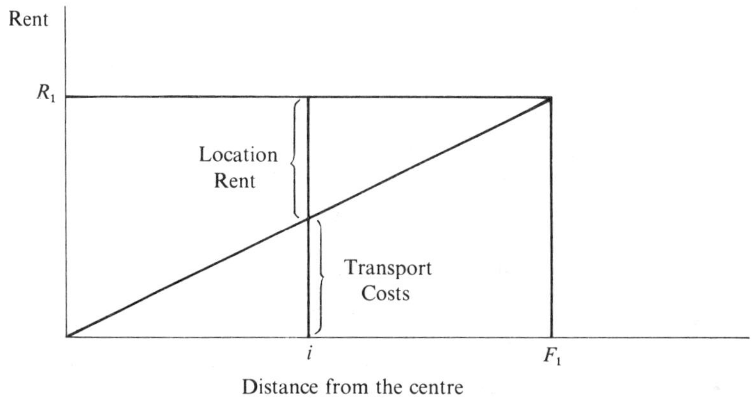

Fig. 1. The basic relationships.

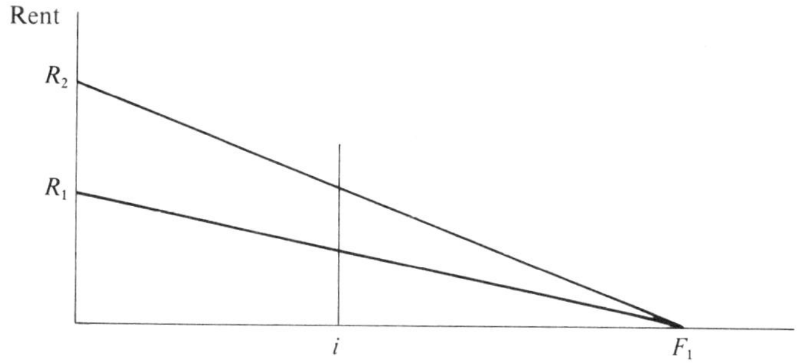

Fig. 2. The rent–distance relationship.

marginal points. This second round effect goes beyond the capabilities of the simple Wingo model, but was picked up and developed by Alonso and more recent workers. Broadly, and without becoming too specific about the space and location preferences of households, it would follow from classical price theory that increased rent (i.e. increased land and housing costs) would tend to reduce unit consumption of space, or in other words to increase equilibrium residential density. The extent to which increased travel costs are translated into increased densities, or carried as higher travel costs at densities similar to those originally prevailing, will depend broadly on the value which the typical household puts on the marginal square metre of land in his homesite. Consequently the final equilibrium rent gradient will be somewhere between R_2F_1 and R_1F_2 in figure 3: R_2F_1 if the price elasticity of demand for space is near zero so that no density increase occurs, and R_1F_2 if the density adjustment is sufficient to restore total rent and transport costs to near their original level.

Many other effects can be followed through in an approximate way dia-

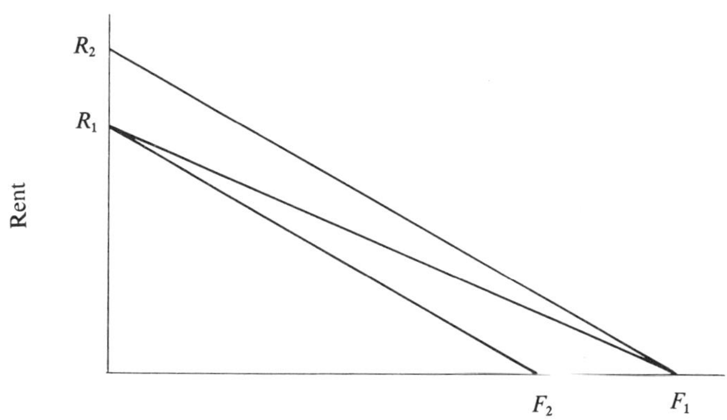

Fig. 3. Determination of final equilibrium rent gradient.

grammatically. An increase in the interest rate will raise the cost of space relative to transport and tend to increase densities; an increase in incomes which leads to a higher valuation of travel time-savings will tend to have an effect similar to an increase in congestion, raising the location premium on centrally located sites, increasing the intensity with which these are used, and thus densities.

If generalised travel costs are defined to include a time and vehicle cost distinction (see ch. 6), and households are segregated into time savers and money savers, a crude theory of residential segregation emerges. If consumer preferences are introduced, and also residential space, as goods whose value varies between households with a given income, the spatial behaviour of the suburban and the inner urban man emerges. Alonso produced the extensions which embody the most highly developed theoretical description of equilibrium seeking behaviour of households and firms. Finally, the basic framework has been used by Mills to elaborate a simple model of production in a radial context. Mills probably represents the most developed, and probably last, significant contribution in an intellectual tradition which put urban structure fully within the framework of classic general equilibrium theory. This tradition has been criticised by people outside the economics profession, such as Angel and Hyman,[6] and it has certainly produced little in the way of practical tools. On the other hand, it established a new level of analytical rigour in the analysis of urban structure.

There are several directions which might be taken in the search for 'realism' and practical computability. One is toward increased eclecticism, and reduced theoretical clarity, through the introduction of further location and space variables in the analysis of the market in urban space and location. This path is advanced by Richardson *et al.*,[7] whose interesting results (discussed below) are taken as a reason for retreating from the quest for analytical rigour in favour of a more eclectic theoretical basis. Another is to generalise the concept of accessibility and to free it from the geometry of the centralised models, by avoiding prior definition of 'the centre'.

Asymmetric centralisation

From a practical point of view the major weakness in this analytical tradition stems from the *asymmetry* implied in an over-literal treatment of place and space; in these models households and firms fix their gaze steadfastly on 'the centre' and arrange themselves at various distances from it in the process of maximising their utility or profit functions. In the real world a two-way process operates, with effects which are important.

In most cities there is a recognisable centre, which does offer a major proportion of total metropolitan jobs, which does attract a significant proportion of the workers living in each suburb, and which does constitute the major focus for urban density gradients and for the location rent surface of the metropolis. The centralised models seek to capture the essence of the actual situation in that they focus on the pre-eminence of 'the centre' which is taken to be exogenously determined, and to act as a focus for all other space or activity organising processes. In doing so they implicitly assume a qualitative difference between 'the centre' and all other sites. This is not only at variance with observable reality but, more seriously, complicates rather than simplifies the resulting theoretical paradigm. The paradigm is based in *geometric*, rather than *economic* space and based, what is more, in geometric space with rather peculiar properties.

This introduces a major difference between the model and the reality which it seeks to capture. Conversion from the inappropriately specified asymmetrically centralised model into real world economic space populated by reciprocally attracting entities, scattered in a virtually random fashion throughout the real urban area, is virtually impossible.

Before elaborating this assertion, the use made here of the term 'asymmetric' needs to be explained. Externalities have been widely recognised as a major factor in shaping urban development, and structuring human settlements. A park, a place of employment, or a place of trade attracts households to it, because each generates external benefits which can be enjoyed by those who settle nearby. The benefits are usually external in that the employer or the trader does not *directly* receive payment for the benefit which proximity to him confers on adjacent sites. While externalities have been given their due in general discussions of urban processes, in agglomeration theory (i.e. in the theory of why activities tend to cluster in various groups within cities) the importance of the reciprocal, or two-way, nature of many positive externalities has not been generally recognised. Indeed it has been *defined out* of the class of economic models discussed above, in which external benefits are asymmetric; access to the centre confers a benefit (expressed through the rent or location premium payable for an intra-marginal homesite) but by definition access to homesites bestows no benefit on 'the centre', since it is unique by assumption, and therefore not in a situation in which comparative advantage can apply.

Generalising even to the extent that a second centre is permitted, it can be seen that the value of a site in one centre will depend in some way on the size of the part of the catchment in which it has an absolute cost advantage, in terms of access to households who supply it with labour. Consequently the presence of each centre confers external benefits, in the form of job opportunities on adjacent residential populations, but the residential population confers an external benefit on the centre, in the form of a labour source available to be tapped. It is this second element of the equilibrium-seeking process (the element which, in reality, helps determine the relative size of centres within a hierarchy or any other nucleated system) which is excluded from the equilibrium urban models, and which therefore makes them a very special version of the usual model of markets, in which demand and supply are both variables. The number of buyers to whom a seller can offer a price advantage over any other seller determines the volume of sales achieved by the seller or, in other words, the size and density of his catchment determines the transaction rate in the market. The equilibrium models treat 'the centre' as a monopolistic seller facing a market of predetermined size and density. In reality, establishments, whether they are at the centre or not, compete for labour and for sales, and their size is controlled by what they are forced to pay for labour, and by the number of consumers whom they can reach at a competitive price.

Proximity to desired destinations is valued by the location decision-maker; this is true whether the optimising entity is a household seeking proximity to work, family, friends, schools and recreational facilities, or a firm seeking to control its transport costs by locating close to its markets or sources of supply. So much is common ground. What seems to be missing from received theory is the reciprocal effect of *A* choosing to locate close to *B*, on the value of *B*'s own location to *B*. Taking a simple example, if a residential location close to the factory gate is valued by worker *A*, it will also be true that the proximity of worker *A* will increase the site value of the factory, because it commands a 'captive' labour unit. Similarly, with other things equal, *A* will offer a higher rent for a residence closer to the residence of his friend *C*, while the newly established proximity of *A* will raise the value which *C* attaches to the site he occupies.

Consequently the value of land in the total system is a function of the arrangement of activities within it. The insights which follow from this approach cannot all be obtained from the 'pole of attraction' framework, within which most general equilibrium models of urban structure have been erected. One heuristic model based on the pairwise or reciprocal nature of the land-value determination and spatial equilibrium conditions is that of Lowry.[8] Lowry postulated a city as a finite set of sites, each of which can be occupied by either no user or one user. Each site has location (i.e. a specified place in an (x, y) plane), and terrain (i.e. it is high or low, flat or broken, etc.). A finite number of establishments exists, and each calculates the rent it will offer for each site. Site owners let their respective sites to the highest bidder in each case and a pattern is established. Given a base pattern, each establishment (household or firm) can review its location in the light of the pattern and bid for the site occupied by any other establishment if this gives it a benefit relative to the base allocation.

The Lowry paradigm proved to be a blind alley from a theoretical and practical point of view,[9] but it contained the germ of an important idea in that its mechanism was one of reciprocal site value determination. If the pairwise structure is dropped in favour of a generalised accessibility structure, little of the heuristic value of the Lowry framework is lost while, on the other hand, the model becomes quite tractable from a logical and computational point of view. The use of accessibility measures eliminates the geometrical problems which arise in simultaneously determining the demand for a location and for space at that location, and which plague the Alonso model. While something is undoubtedly lost in using the aspatial accessibility measure, much is gained.

Some regression models of land prices estimated on Melbourne data can serve as an illustration. Prices, based on mean sales prices (in 1972) per metre,[2] were expressed in natural logs (ln) to linearise the distribution of prices for use in linear regression equations. The independent variables are accessibility measures. To illustrate how these were constructed, take the case of a variable, APW_i, which represents the accessibility to work places of residents in zone i.

$$APW_i = \sum_j \frac{NPW_j}{D^2{}_{ij}}$$

where

NPW_j = the number of people at work in zone j.
D_{ij} = straight line distance from the centroid of zone i to zone j.

A zone i has a high accessibility to jobs if APW_i has a high value; generally the higher accessibility scores are found in the inner suburbs or around major suburban employment nodes. The exponent on D_{ij} offers a means of controlling the influence of distance on the score; a higher exponent will make local employment patterns relatively more important, while a lower exponent causes the index to resemble a measure of urban centrality. The unit in which APW_i is denominated can be described as 'jobs per km squared'.

Using similar logic to that above, it is possible to construct, in addition to indices of accessibility of jobs to population, indices of the accessibility of particular subsets of population to subsets of jobs, or jobs to population.

APW = access of residential zone to all jobs.
AWCW = access of residential zone to White Collar jobs.
AWCR = access of employment zone to White Collar residents.
ABCR = access of employment zone to Blue Collar residents.

The denominator is travel distance squared in all four cases. The variable *AWCR* can be taken as a crude surrogate for the social standing of a sub-region, since it stands for accessibility to white collar households which generally reflect higher social rank. Commercial land prices appeared to depend mainly on the size of the commercial agglomeration:

$$\ln(LPC) = 2.31 + 0.0036(AWCW)$$
$$t = 6.8$$
$$R^2 = 0.49.$$

This accounts for only half of total variation in unit prices and it is thought that the low explanatory power of the equation arises from the importance of micro effects on the price of commercial sites – mean price by Local Government Authority (LGA) is not a particularly suitable measure. The unexplained 51 per cent of variation probably arises from planning variables (relative location of shopping centres, site planning, etc.). On a broad zonal basis, it is unlikely that this can be improved without specifying the detailed nature of the commercial land use – office sites will fetch different prices from retail sites.

The accessibility to White Collar jobs (*AWCW*) variable is an important determinant of Industrial Land Price (*LPI*), as is accessibility to White collar residential areas (*AWCR*). This *AWCR* variable probably represents an opportunity cost effect; premium residential terrain requires a higher industrial land price if the land is to be allocated to industrial use. An alternative explanation would be that management bids higher for sites closer to home. The negative effect of accessibility of potential Blue Collar workforce to industrial land (*ABCR*) appears consistent with either of the above hypotheses regarding the influence of upper-class work and residential areas.

$$\begin{aligned} \ln(LPI) &= 0.65 + 0.0043(AWCW) + 0.0031(AWCR) - 0.0014(ABCR) \\ t &= \qquad\quad (6.6) \qquad\qquad\quad (3.1) \qquad\qquad (-1.1) \\ & \qquad\qquad R^2 = 0.69. \end{aligned}$$

The coefficient of *ABCR* is not statistically significant, but was left in to improve the specification of the effect of the other two independent variables.

The Residential Land Price equation gives a higher level of explanation than the Industrial and Commercial equations:

$$\begin{aligned} \ln(LPR) &= 0.617 + 0.0018\,(APW) + 0.0010\,(AWCW) \\ t &= \qquad\quad (12.0) \qquad\qquad (3.0) \\ & \qquad R^2 = 0.83. \end{aligned}$$

The accessibility to jobs (*APW*) term accounts for 83 per cent of variance, and the *AWCR* term, basically accessibility to White Collar residential area, can be taken as a crude measure of social status: it is likely to intercorrelate with terrain quality and accessibility to beaches, views, etc.

The price explanation derived from the accessibility measures varied between the three broad forms of land use. Accessibility accounted for most of the variation in residential land prices and for only about half of total variation in commercial land prices. The equations mask the effect of certain variables which are known to influence land prices. For example, the results obtained in predicting residential land prices arise in part from the fact that the character of residential buildings, and more particularly the average intensity of land use, is in itself correlated with accessibility, because the city was built outward from the centre. Areas of high accessibility were built at times when site intensities were greater than in the modern era, so that price per hectare of land area also tends to be high.

The equations suffer from all the usual limitations which arise from use of aggregate data, and of course a major component of variance in prices, the variance *within* zones, is eliminated in the process of aggregation. The variance *between* zonal aggregates is, however, quite well 'explained' by accessibility considerations, and it is at this level that accessibility would be expected to make itself felt.

These highly aggregative reduced form equations are only suggestive but, to the extent that they capture a real structure, they indicate that residential land prices differ between broad areas of the city in terms of the availability of jobs from the respective residential areas. Industrial land prices are influenced by access to a population from which a workforce can be drawn. Commercial prices are primarily influenced by agglomerative factors, that is by the size of the tertiary workforce employed in the locality.

Residential preferences and dimensions of accessibility

Work travel accounts for a little over one-third of weekday trips in most cities. Work trips are the longest class of trips and on average they account for approximately half of the total time spent travelling on weekdays. They account for a somewhat smaller proportion of *distance* travelled, since work trips are performed in general at lower speeds than others. Average distances travelled for non-work purposes are less than those travelled for work purposes. The work trip is of major concern to the transport planner, since it generates most of the coincident peak demands within an urban transport system. Its significance may, however, be less from a *locational* point of view, since the shorter average length of non-work trips can plausibly be interpreted to indicate that people choose their residential locations more with a view to minimising the length of non-work than of work trips. Many people choose a residential location which puts them close to relatives or friends, close to schools, or close to outdoor recreational areas, and so on. The widely observed short average length of shopping and school trips does not necessarily indicate that distance as such is a greater deterrent to school and shopping travel than it is to work travel, since the relative homogeneity of school facilities and shopping centres and their relative ubiquity throughout an urban area means that intervening opportunity effects would lead to rapid attenuation of such trips, even if the will to travel were there. An intervening opportunity effect is simply the effect of a local opportunity on the probability that someone will travel to a more distant opportunity of the same kind. For example, if there is an acceptable shopping centre within half a mile, then there will be no reason for the shopper to travel two miles to any equally suitable shopping centre, even though in the absence of the first he may be perfectly willing to do so.

Social and recreational trips in most cities account for approximately one eighth of weekday trips and, again, these are usually shorter on average than work trips. Transportation studies have been overwhelmingly concerned with weekday travel and very little data exists on weekend travel behaviour. Lansing[10] found that in a number of North American suburban situations, social and recreational trips accounted for 50 per cent of all weekend trips. Consequently, on a full week basis, the total number of social and recreational trips is only slightly less than the total number of work trips and, again, on a full week basis, non-work trips account for about three quarters of all trips. In view of these considerations, it is at least possible that the almost exclusive emphasis which has been given to the work trip in transport and land-use models as a major organising force within urban areas could be misplaced. The work trip quite properly dominates the consideration of the urban transport planner, but the step from this observation to the easy assumption that it also dominates choice of residential location by households, while rarely questioned, has never to my knowledge been rigorously demonstrated. The possibility that access to non-work opportunities is influential offers at least a plausible alternative to the approach customarily used for modelling urban structure.

Circumstantial evidence may be derived from various sources to indicate that considerations other than work travel have a major influence. The homogeneity of social areas within a city is a widely observed phenomenon.[11] Social area analysis regularly reveals that over quite extensive areas of residential development, households tend to cluster within fairly homogeneous neighbourhoods. People tend to settle near to others in similar circumstances to themselves. The main conditions for development of social networks appear to be propinquity and homogeneity. The clustering of homogeneous groups within urban areas is not incompatible with the predictions which arise from the general equilibrium models, but it can also be accounted for by a causal hypothesis based more on social processes than on maximisation of work travel convenience.

Within small residential areas, social homogeneity may be pronounced and yet a wide range of directions and trip lengths of work travel can be observed or, in other words, at the small area level, social homogeneity tends to be more pronounced than homogeneity of orientation to work places. Places of employment, of all but the least specialised kind, tend to draw their labour force from widespread and socially diverse residential areas. Work trips, as well as having greater mean length than non-work trips, also have a greater variance than most classes on non-work trips.

The influence of non-work variables on the locational behaviour of certain social groups is sufficiently powerful to be directly observable in many cities. Commonly, the influence on the observed city shape of outdoor recreational facilities, such as beaches and water bodies, or of a high point with a commanding view of the surrounding terrain, can be readily observed. High income people, in particular, select locations to capture these forms of amenity, even at the expense of long work trips. Melbourne's south-eastern bayside suburbs, Sydney's more distant northern suburbs, and Adelaide's hill face zone, are all cases in which people who largely have upper income, central area, white collar jobs, choose remote locations, and long journeys to work, in numbers sufficiently large to give a pattern of metropolitan expansion which is far from efficient in terms of the narrow objective of minimising work travel.

Finally, from a dynamic point of view, the observed pattern of intra-urban decentralisation in the post-war period in most cities of the western world must also give pause to any theory which depends heavily on residential orientation to work opportunities. Decentralisation of work places has come about through the establishment of places of employment in the suburbs. While there are instances in which very large establishments open their doors well beyond the existing urban fringe, the more characteristic pattern of movement by firms is to areas which are already well established from the residential point of view. Broadly speaking industry has followed people to the suburbs, rather than people following industry.

Richardson, Vipond and Furby[12] approached the problem of testing theories of urban structure by means of an econometric analysis of determinants of housing prices. They used a sample of data derived from 1176 house sales in Edinburgh in 1966 and amassed a large amount of background information about each property, in such a way that they were able to test the separate effects of characteristics of the dwelling itself, of its local neighbourhood, and of its location within the larger urban area. It is this third variable which is overwhelmingly stressed in the economic models of urban structure. The data assembled by Richardson et al. permitted them to test the relative weight of centrality factors compared with other influences on house price. Their work suggested that there was no statistical basis for emphasising accessibility or centrality influences on influences on house price, and that housing characteristics, location in the macro-region, and local environmental characteristics were all at least as effective in explaining house prices as were accessibility variables of the kind incorporated in general equilibrium models. The authors concluded that their study does not lend strong support to any single residential location theory, but rather suggests that the determinants of relative urban house prices include housing characteristics, general spatial variables, accessibility and environmental quality considerations. The residential site choice, and the price–quality trade-off, is a much more complex decision than conventional theory suggests.

In conclusion, it has been argued that an overemphasis on the work trip in transport and land-use models may have imparted a false direction to the leading work in this field, and that an alternative approach, in which accessibility to a much wider range of opportunities is considered, could be more fruitful.

A sketch of an electric theory of urban structural equilibrium

If it is asserted that excessive emphasis has been given to the role of work travel in the transport-based models of urban equilibrium, then it should be possible to indicate an alternative approach which is free of this structural mis-specification, and which can offer at least a heuristic basis for consideration of transport and land-use issues, if not, at this stage, a formal mathematical model. The two points of departure for a new formulation are:

i. Avoidance of the asymmetrical centralisation which requires an exogenously defined starting point for the determination of equilibrium.
ii. Avoidance of excessive concentration on the journey to work.

It will be argued that these simplifications, which have been presumed to facilitate formulation and solution of a model, have in fact actually had the effect of making urban models more complicated than necessary.

The first step is to decide just what needs to be explained by a useful model of urban spatial equilibrium. The received models have concentrated on explaining how activities are arranged around a point in such a way as to crudely reproduce the centrally-focused pattern found in most large existing cities. I would argue that a general equilibrium model need not, and indeed probably should not, have asymmetric centrality built into it. Asymmetric centrality has already been discussed and has been broadly defined as an activity pattern in which the centre influences its hinterland, but the hinterland does not simultaneously determine the role of the centre. If the economic forces which create a centralised system are present in sufficient strength to create a highly centralised city, then such a solution should emerge from solution of the model rather than by initial definition. If these forces are not strong enough, a decentralised solution should be able to emerge, an outcome which is excluded by definition in the leading economic models.

From an empirical point of view, a properly specified general model, which embodies realistic contemporary parameters, will almost certainly not have an equilibrium solution of a highly centralised kind. All the evidence points to a steady move away from the historically-given centralised pattern in most cities. The forces producing decentralisation of activity patterns are evidently quite strong, since historically-given urban plant, particularly road and rail networks, port and railhead locations and existing office cores, all tend to build in the historically-determined centralised pattern, and yet even these influences are insufficient to nullify contempory forces, which are downgrading the role of the centre and decentralising activity in almost every city of the western world.

Consequently, it is to be expected that a model which accurately captures the equilibrium-seeking processes is unlikely to produce a solution which looks realistic, since a realistic pattern or, in other words, a reproduction of an existing city, will not emerge as a product of contemporary equilibrium-seeking forces. Contemporary urban structure is a very durable historical survival, which persists in spite of forces operating to change it. A properly specified model will produce something which looks like a contemporary centralised city only if it is constrained to do so by explicit embodiment of the durable infrastructure and the existing building stock. A truly general model would undoubtedly be capable of reproducing such a pattern if constrained to do so, but such a constraint must be explicitly introduced rather than implicitly built into the model formulation. The equilibrium models with asymmetric centrality built into them are anything but general. To the extent that they produce realistic results, they do so by their implicit embodiment of a constraint which stands for an obsolescent pattern of infrastructure and building stock and which resists the achievement of an efficient intra-urban activity pattern, where efficiency is defined to include only the contemporary processes of a kind with which the equilibrium models explicitly deal.

The residential density gradients observed in contemporary cities are predicted by the theoretical models, but even on the evidence of Muth, one of the leading contributors to the development of these models, this occurs largely because successive rings of suburbs have been laid down at successively lower densities, under the influence of successively higher incomes and successively more economical vintages of transport technology.[13] The correlation of lower densities with higher incomes, from which Alonso[14] drew comfort, was evidently spurious, since Muth has shown it to be related almost entirely to the preference of the rich for areas with better quality building stock. With the exception of a few notable fashionable inner suburbs, which exist in most inner cities, better quality buildings are, in general, newer buildings, and newer buildings are predominantly outer area buildings.

Having decided that a truly general model cannot have the property of asymmetric centrality, the second step is to choose a method of reflecting the key force that holds the city together – the force which arises from economising behaviour in choice of location by any establishment, whether a household or a business. This key force arises from the fact that, other things being equal, a short trip will be preferred to a long one, and that this is true whether the trip is to work, to shop, to school, to visit friends, or to travel to ex-urban outdoor recreational sites. The destinations or opportunities which offer some attraction to a household are likely to be scattered over a wide area, to vary in their force, and to include many which are rarely, if ever, chosen but which are valued as options. Accessibility to each type of destination is likely to appear as an attribute of consumption with a positive value in the utility function of the household. Access respectively to labour, to customers, to specialist services, and to the managing director's club, is likely to be valued by the profit maximising enterprise. The bid which any establishment will make for any site will be determined by the weight which it attaches to each constituent of accessibility and by the degree of accessibility to each of these constituents which the site enjoys. The location choice of the household may be visualised in a spatial setting as a series of trade-offs between various poles of accessibility in fixing a price which the household is prepared to bid for any site – a price identical to Alonso's bid rent concept.

Taking the simplest case of a household which values only access to work and to outdoor recreation, that household can be imagined as making calculations of the number of job opportunities per mile of travel at each potential residence and the number of outdoor recreational opportunities per mile of travel at each potential residence, along lines similar to those in the accessibility formulae set out on page 159 above. The household will make its own subjective weighting of the disutility involved in a mile of travel or, in other words, will choose the exponent on the distance term used in the summation, in a way which reflects its own valuation of the vehicle and time costs involved in travelling. For each of the respective purposes, namely work travel and recreational travel, the household, by these means, computes accessibility surfaces, so that for each point in the urban area it can then trade off between two dimensions of accessibility: to work and to outdoor recreational opportunities. The shape of the perceived accessibility surfaces will be unique to each household, given that the valuation placed on each of the destination opportunities, and on the cost of travel for each purpose, is likely to be distinctively related to the household's characteristics.

It can be seen that the economic attributes of space can be fully defined from the point of view of the household without it being necessary to specify any geometrical characteristics of the Cartesian space within which the household's economic space exists. The great simplification arising from this approach emerges not from the way in which the household formulates its bid rent surface which is, to all intents and purposes, identical with the method of formulation presented by Alonso. Simplification is possible because, on the supply side, urban sites can be produced in a way which is freed from the restrictions of a centrally dominated space.

Within the centralised model, it is not possible to produce more usable space at any distance from the centre, even though there may be very substantial bunching of demand, say, at the periphery or at the centre of the urban area, or even in the middle-distant suburbs. Within the centralised model, the supply of space is totally inelastic and the model simply allocates it between competitive bidders. Once space is freed from the dominance of an arbitrarily defined centre, it is immediately possible to create additional urban space with almost any combination of accessibility characteristics. If, for example, households predominantly express a demand for access to ex-urban outdoor recreational sites, together with ready access to jobs, but do this within a city in which jobs are predominantly centralised, the occurrence of residential development at the fringe will create an unsatisfied demand for locally accessible jobs in those fringe locations. No feasible response exists to satisfy this demand in the centralised model but, in reality and in a generalised accessibility model, spatial competition will produce the required result, as employers seek to capture access to the workforce by moving job locations towards areas of new development. If these moves occur in industries with strong agglomerative properties then new fringe nuclei will emerge; if they occur in industries which do not seek contact between establishments then a scatter of new establishments will occur around the fringe.

The generalised accessibility framework is far more appropriate as a basis for practical transport planning models than the centralised economic models can ever be, since a generalised accessibility model can handle a region of any shape, inhabited by economic entities with any spatial distribution, and can still produce continuous accessibility or potential surfaces which act as the decision criterion for the entity seeking a location within the urban space.

The pattern of accessibility within a city can change for any number of reasons, but those of most significance from a transport planning point of view are the following:

i. Changes due to construction of new facilities which reduce travel costs between some areas of the city.
ii. An increase in the level of activity of some kind at a particular point in the urban area, which changes the pattern of accessibility relative to that type of activity.
iii. Changing travel patterns, including increased vehicle usage, which increase loads on the existing network and have a differential impact on the relative time and cost of using different routes within the city.

All these influences on accessibility patterns are likely to be in operation at any given time, and only the larger scale, or grosser, measures are easily identifiable by empirical techniques. To complete the present chapter, a brief consideration of these aspects of system dynamics is in order.

Joint adaptation of transport and land-use to scale change

At the most aggregative level of analysis, one would expect to find that trip lengths are influenced by city size and by travel costs, given a constant distribution of activities. Voorhees *et al.*[15] used cross-sectional data from 23 United States cities to examine the effects of scale and network speeds on trip lengths. The cities ranged in size from Los Angeles, at 6.5 million, to Beloit, at 33 000, in work trip duration from Philadelphia, with an average work trip of 20.1 minutes, to Hutchinson with 6.1 minutes, in mean trip length from Los Angeles, with 8.7 miles, to Hutchinson, with 2.0 miles, and in terms of average trip speed from Lexington, at 37.6 miles per hour, down to Hutchinson, at 19.2 m.p.h. The following equation was estimated from these data:

$$\ln \bar{L} = -5.86 + \underset{(0.02)}{0.20} \ln P + \underset{(0.20)}{1.49} \ln S$$

$$R^2 = 0.85$$

where $\bar{L}$ = average trip length (miles)
P = urban area population
S = average network speed (m.p.h.)

The standard errors of the coefficients are shown in parenthesis. The equation can be written as:

$$\bar{L} = 0.003\ P^{0.20}\ S^{1.49}$$

This suggests that work trip lengths increase with population size, but at less than the fourth root of population, so that a 1 per cent increase in population leads to an increase of only 0.2 per cent in the work trip length. More importantly, the cross-sectional equation suggests that trip lengths increase *significantly faster* than average travel speed, so that a 1 per cent increase in mean network speed produces a $1\frac{1}{2}$ per cent increase in average trip length.

Making the (rather heroic) assumption that these results, obtained by cross-sectional analysis from 23 different cities, can be applied to changes *within one city* over time, several implications would follow. Firstly, the population exponent is less than one might expect in a circular city with all employment at the centre, growing by addition of concentric bands of residential areas (after the manner of Alonso, Wingo and so on). Mean travel distance, given a radius of r miles from the centre to the periphery, would be $r/\sqrt{2}$, and in a model of this kind, the relationship between population and work trip length would be

$$\bar{L} = KP^{0.5}, \text{ where } K = (2\pi d)^{-1}.$$

The exponent on population is 0.5, compared with that in the estimated equation by Voorhees *et al.* of 0.2. The substantial, and statistically significant, difference between the exponent in the totally centralised city model and that estimated from a cross-section of 23 cities indicates the influence of mean size of city on city structure, since it can only come about through a process of progressive dispersion of work places, which moves the pattern of employment steadily away from the centralised paradigm as scale increases. Without this adjustment, work travel costs would rise much more rapidly with urban scale than is evidently the case. This is evidence of adaptive response or economising behaviour within a city, which produces structural change to a more economical pattern as city size increases.

Longitudinal studies, of which the classic example is that of Hoover and

Vernon[16] on New York and, in the Australian context, Paterson[17] on Melbourne, have shown this pattern of adjustment to occur in a highly systematic way in response to changing circumstances within a growing city. With a road network of constant capacity, an increase in urban population will lead to a significant slowing down of traffic, once the urban network is operating near to its design capacity. Again, while recognising the statistical problems which can arise in extrapolating from cross-sectional to longitudinal processes, the trip length equation can indicate the conditions under which population growth would lead to increasing, constant or declining trip lengths. Leaving aside the question of whether the system responds to work travel conditions or to average daily travel conditions, it appears that total daily travel costs on a road network start to increase markedly as the network as a whole approaches a mean volume capacity rate ratio of about 0.5, at which level a significant proportion of links are operating at to volume capacity ratios >1. User costs for the journey to work increase well before this point is reached. Once the network approaches a critical capacity limitation, a functional relationship becomes established between population size and network speed for a constant capacity network, provided work travel patterns do not change. A change in pattern can permit less heavily loaded routes to be more fully utilised, and thereby handle a greater volume of travel without pushing the system to the critical level at which the flow ceases. It is of interest to follow such a process through, taking Melbourne as an example.

The equation predicts that for a city of 1 909 000 people (Melbourne in 1961), and an average network speed of 25 m.p.h., average trip length would be 6.55 miles. Melbourne in 1961 had a mean work trip length of about 6.3 miles. Between 1961 and 1966 Melbourne's population grew by 10.4 per cent to 2 109 000. Mean work trip length increased by about 2 per cent. In terms of the equation, this is consistent with a constant network speed for the given population change: a constant trip length would have called for a reduction of 1.2 per cent in mean network speed.

There are any number of reasons why the apparent agreement between the relationship estimated from American cities and the observed situation in Melbourne, Australia, can be attributed more to chance than to the inherent validity of the equation. The Voorhees equation is presented here only as a device for data summarisation, but superficially it does appear to summarise Melbourne's situation quite well. At a more detailed level, the pattern of adjustment underlying the change in the state of the urban system can help illustrate the response of the city to changing relative accessibilities between work places and residences, brought about in part by a deterioration in service quality on the radial network and involving, whether as cause or affect, a rapid decentralisation of work places.

The motor car arrived in strength in Melbourne only after the Second World War. Travel data for metropolitan Melbourne are only available in any substantial form for the years 1951 and 1964. Between 1951 and 1964, there was a substantial decline in the number of people walking to work: in 1951, 23.5 per cent of the workforce used no motorised transport for work travel, a proportion which fell to 13.7 per cent by 1964. Over the same 13 years there was a slight decline in employment within the Central Business District, but the number of CBD workers travelling in private cars increased from 19 700 to 46 300. Employment other than in the CBD increased from 420 000 to 680 000, but the number of non-central workers using public transport as their main travel mode declined marginally from 198 000 to 193 000, while the number of non-central workers travelling by car increased from 94 000 to 370 000 over the same 13 years.

This transition called for major readjustments in tramways and rail operations. Between 1953/4 and 1965/6, passengers carried annually on the suburban system by the Victorian Railways declined by just over 10 per cent, but train miles run actually increased from 8.19 to 8.46 million miles; load factors on the rail network declined. Trams suffered far more heavily, with a decline of approximately 31 per cent in the number of passengers carried between 1953/4 and 1956/6, but they succeeded in reducing the number of miles run by about 24 per cent, so that the decline in average loads was less precipitous for trams than for trains.

In terms of the conventional orders of spending which have followed in the wake of major transport plans, the amounts actually spent on the road network during this period of major transition were negligible. Total spending on the main road network in Melbourne was less than $10 million in 1965/6, and less than $2 million in every year up to 1959/60. This very low level of spending occurred at a time of severe capital rationing in the Australian economy as a whole, and in the public sector in particular. Nevertheless, the transport systems of Melbourne kept operating, in spite of a more than four-fold increase of total vehicle stock between 1947 and 1966. A road network and rail system that differed very little from the basic system laid down in road rights of way before the 1850s, and in rail capacity before the 1880s, served the city at least adequately until the 1960s, with virtually no expenditure on capacity expansion. While the Metropolitan Transportation Study of 1964 found many roads to be operating at above practical capacity, traffic conditions in the mid-1960s were, by contemporary standards, perfectly reasonable.

The outcome of the combined impact of a rapid increase in the use of private motor vehicles and a negligible increase in radial road capacity was an absolutely dramatic change in the pattern of employment growth in the metropolitan area. From the centrally-dominated pattern which had characterised Melbourne since the earliest years of the city, there was a sudden explosion of non-central employment locations, and a complete change in the process of population growth in as little as five to ten years. Some of the effects of this can be seen in table 1. The analysis on which this summary table was

TABLE 1 *Summary of work-travel in Melbourene: 1961 and 1966*

	1961			1966		
	Persons ('000)	Total miles travelled ('000)	Average travel (miles)	Persons ('000)	Total miles travelled ('000)	Average travel (miles)
Place of residence						
1. Central	102	222	2.2	90	206	2.4
2. Inner ring	272	1068	3.9	283	1111	3.9
3. Established	235	1342	5.7	264	1416	5.4
4. Growing: West	68	339	5.0	948	462	4.9
5. Growing: East	86	769	8.9	139	1138	8.2
6.. Other (fringe)	29	235	8.2	57	431	7.5
	792	3975	5.0	932	4763	5.1
Place of work						
1. Central	405	2518	6.2	399	2629	6.6
2. Inner ring	174	652	3.7	197	791	4.0
3. Established	144	387	3.4	166	629	3.8
4. Growing: West	45	196	4.4	66	286	5.8
5. Growing: East	38	142	3.7	75	306	4.1
6. Other (fringe)	16	79	4.9	27	123	4.5
	792	3975	5.0	932	4763	5.1

based was conducted at the municipality level, with municipalities aggregated into six groups as shown in figure 4. Distances are in crow-flight miles, which must be multiplied by 1.3 to represent road miles.

Average work travel distances increased only marginally, from 5.0 to 5.1 miles, or approximately 2 per cent, over a period in which the workforce growth was almost 18 per cent. Average distances travelled by residents of all groups of *LGA*s, except the Central and Inner groups, declined by varying degrees in the face of declining radial accessibility by private transport.

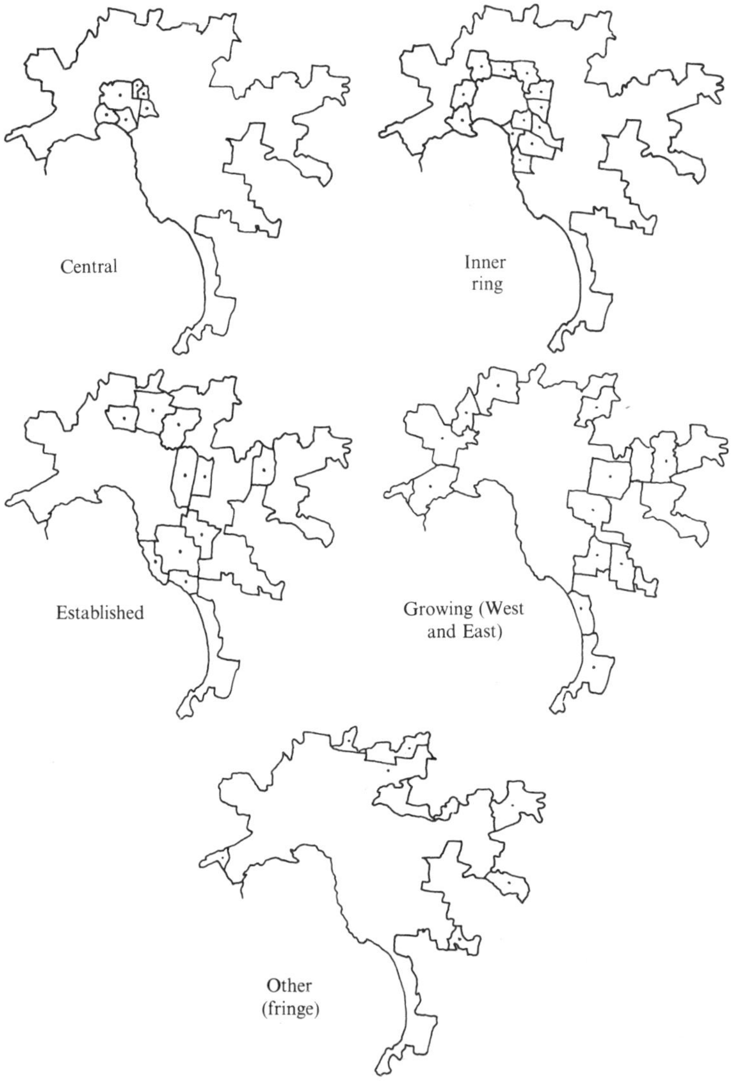

Fig. 4. Municipal groupings in Melbourne.

Average travel distances to work in all municipal groups except 'Other' *increased* to varying degrees; in other words, non-central employment catchments spread and, from most residential origin areas, the *proportion* travelling to the centre declined, as local employment opportunities were seized in the face of increasing costs of access through the radial network. Even with their extended catchments, the suburban work-places drew their workers from distances less than the city-wide average travel distance in 1961. Employment at the metropolitan Centre declined marginally, having grown steadily in absolute terms throughout the previous history of Melbourne.

Although Central employment *declined*, the number of travel miles generated by the Central group *increased* by 4.4 per cent, which constituted 14 per cent of the total increase in work-travel miles generated in the metropolitan system as a whole. The average travel distance to work in the Central group increased from 6.2 to 6.6 miles. This came about as a result of the combined effects of a reduction in the number of people travelling to the Centre from settled inner- and middle-distance residential areas where new employment opportunities were emerging, and their partial replacement by people travelling to the centre from the fast growing fringe areas, where small local job availability causes a high proportion of new fringe settlers to travel right to the Centre. Analysis of the pattern of rail usage over the period indicated that the rail usage towards the centre declined substantially from inner and intermediate suburban areas, and that it was only growth of population at the extreme ends of the railway lines, oriented to Central employment opportunities, which restricted the decline in commuter rail travel to as little as 10 per cent. The tram network did not cover the growing fringe and tram patronage declined absolutely.

In terms of the argument presented earlier in this paper, the interpretation to be put on these events is fairly clear. The relative pattern of access-

TABLE 2 *Change in work-travel between individual municipalities in Melbourne Grouped 1961/6* Persons '000)

	Place of residence						
	(1)	(2)	(3)	(4) Growing	(5)	(6)	
Place of work	Central	Inner ring	Established	West	East	(Fringe)	Total
1. Central	−12.8	−8.5	−7.8	6.1	9.8	6.7	−6.2
2. Inner Ring	−0.3	7.3	3.6	4.6	4.4	3.0	22.9
3. Established	0.5	7.1	24.5	2.3	13.3	4.3	52.2
4. Growing: West	0.2	3.5	2.1	13.23	0.6	1.8	21.5
5. Growing: East	0.2	1.8	5.2	0.2	23.2	5.8	37.3
6. Other (fringe)	0.0	0.4	1.3	0.5	1.9	6.8	11.0
	−12.1	11.7	29.0	27.0	53.2	28.4	140.9

ibility changed dramatically, as a network of virtually constant capacity was increasingly loaded by the growth of private vehicular traffic. Rather than a breakdown occurring in the road-based travel systems, there was a rapid response in the pattern of destinations, so that the system was kept operating continuously close to the margin of capacity, by reorientation in the pattern of demand. It is likely that the suburbanisation of employment would have occurred even in the face of a significant increase in road network capacity, but it is equally likely that this would have been accompanied, not by a decline in average work travel distances of the kind seen in Melbourne, but rather by an increase in average work travel distances, of a kind which has been measured in studies in some of the more accessible American cities.

Conclusion

The adaptive properties of the city are strongly indicated by the pattern of response which can be observed in Melbourne. Travel and transport undoubtedly play a major part in shaping cities, but they do so in a way which is complexly interdependent with the contemporary pattern of technological change and the change in average incomes, tastes and institutions.

10

Transport decision-making and its spatial repercussions[1]

P. J. Rimmer

Introduction

If the weak links between academic discussion, research and development, and policy-making on transport are to be strengthened there is a need for a larger picture of the transport decision-making process and its spatial repercussions, particularly as social science knowledge is widely fragmented among various disciplines and by different ways of thinking.[2] As a means of exploring the interrelationships between the transport decision-making process and the spatial structure of socio-economic activities, this chapter provides a conceptual framework to help shape our understanding of the 'real world'. The framework also, in part, regulates any future modelling approach because it suggests 'what may be accepted as significant "facts", what are already assumed to be data and what remains problematic with reference to that conceptual scheme'.[3]

Such a general framework has to embrace the decision by the transport agency in locating facilities and offering them for use and the subsequent decision by transport users as to whether and how intensively the facilities will be used.[4] The highlighting of these decisions is apposite because net socio-economic benefits stemming from changes in the transport system, transferring people and goods between separate physical locations, may not meet community values, goals and objectives. The need thus arises to mitigate such failures by providing a deeper understanding of the policy control and communication process both within the transport system and in its interrelationship with the social system in which it is embedded. Hopefully, the general framework will assist our comprehension of this process by providing a focus for subsequent empirical studies.

What we need in designing the general framework is 'a description of the choice process that recognizes that alternatives are not given but must be sought; and a description that takes into account the arduous task of determining what consequences will follow on each alternative'.[5] If purpose-ridden man is not to be a substitute for rational economic man it has to be borne in mind that the bulk of a decision agent's behaviour is directed to threat aversion or maintaining relations and flexibility.[6] Goal-seeking, involving changes in relationships or opportunities for relating, is only part of life, but it is the particular focus of interest here.

Of pivotal importance in progressively building up the general framework to encompass goal-seeking behaviour is the recognition of the role performed by the actor as the conceptual unit in the transport decision-making process. While the initial task involves recognising and defining the expected behaviour or plans of action associated with a particular role, the centre of attention is not role definition as such. The prime focus is on the role playing (and role taking) that occurs when one actor interacts with at least one other and engages in the plans of action described in the definition. Interactions of particular interest in the transport decision-making process are those generating either passenger and goods flows, vehicle movements, track and terminal capacity or resource availability. A common basis is established for examining these interactions by assuming that they revolve around two role players functioning either as producer or consumer.

The next stage is to use each producer–consumer interaction unit as a building block to integrate the separate sets of role players into a conceptual framework, in such a way that the resulting system of 'interactive relationships', based on a constellation of roles, provides a schema for allocating facilities and rewards.[7] When the interrelationships between the decision process and the spatial structure of socio-economic activities are understood, ways of controlling the allocation of transport facilities and regulating conflicts and competitive processes to meet society's perceived values, goals and objectives with regard to the distribution of income can be investigated; the role of the planner is considered in this regard.

Roles in the transport decision-making process

The system of interest in the transport process consists of 'a number of interlocking, mutually interdependent subsystems', each revolving around the *role* performed by an actor on a particular area of land.[8] We begin by recognising and defining the general character of each role. 'All role definitions include a unique configuration of many types and aspects of behavior, systematically arranged so that the parts are somewhat consistent with each other and with the counter-roles that form a part of the larger system to which they all belong'.[9] Although only a few of the courses of action available will be considered when the actor is faced with a problem at a particular point in time, an extensive range of options is given in defining seven key roles in the transport decision-making process. 'traveller' or 'shipper', 'prime contractor', 'vehicle owner', 'track and terminal operator', 'administrator', 'activist', and 'impactee'.[10]

The identification of the set of interacting role players emphasises a range of differing viewpoints in the transport decision-making process. However, the seven specified role categories can only be sustained by assuming that the set of interlocking, partly inconsistent, functions performed by transport suppliers and users are divisible and can be allocated to the appropriate unit.

Private car owners, for instance, have to be apportioned between the traveller, prime contractor and vehicle owner categories. The functions of firms with ancillary equipment are distributed among the shipper, prime contractor and vehicle owner categories. Similarly, the functions performed by railway authorities have to be assigned between the prime contractor, vehicle owner and track and terminal operator – a powerful source of intra-organisational conflict as the components in a role set grate against each other.

No attention in role definition has been given to the fact that an individual role can have its own internal organisation and problems of horizontal and vertical integration. The track and terminal operator's role, for example, embodies both executives and employees; if employees withdraw their labour the role's mission cannot be satisfactorily accomplished. Similarly, the administrator's role could be viewed as a coalition of politicians, public servants, political parties and voters at federal, state and local levels. A fuller specification of all roles must necessarily take account of their substructures and capacity for conflict. However, our immediate concern is not with the internal structure of a role but with the concept's use as an aid to understanding the interrelationships between the transport decision-making system and the spatial structure of society. Attention is focused here on identifying the role players and describing their distinctive attributes.

Role definition

As, above all, transport systems are for people, we begin by defining the role of the traveller or shipper. Parenthetically it is assumed that the shipper (the owner of the goods) has a similar range of alternatives to the traveller in overcoming the problem of distance as, to some extent, they are substitutes; people can either be moved towards raw material, production or marketing centres, or goods can be shifted to places where people locate themselves.[11] The traveller's response, once motivated, is restricted in the short term by the fixed network as to where and when to go, how frequently, what mode to employ and which route to take.[12] These individual decisions depend on the perceived prices of transport which when aggregated constitute the demand for transport.

In the long term the transport network is a permissive factor because the political, economic and social actors can exercise a wide range of options about the location and scale of their activities, which strongly affect the demand for transport over time by altering the distribution of population and economic activity. These demand shifts are difficult to control because changes in the spatial pattern of activity systems respond not only to transport changes but also to external forces (e.g. housing subsidies or mortgage policy). As the external forces are controlled by a myriad of public and private decision-makers, many of the activity system options are treated as exogenous inputs in most transport studies. However, some control may be possible in coordination with such non-transport options as land-use control via zoning. Whether controllable or not, the full set of transport and activity system options have to be encompassed.[13]

The second role in the transport decision-making process is performed by the prime contractor who determines operational policies such as time scheduling and routing of vehicles, pricing, types of service offered (including auxiliary services such as meals), handling methods and reliability. Collectively, these policies help set the level of service available to the traveller or shipper in terms of time, cost (to the user and non-user), comfort, convenience, safety and other variables.

A third role is played by the vehicle owner, whose function involves varying options about the number and types of vehicles that can be used over a range of differing distances and terrain. This facility includes purchasing new vehicles, modifying existing equipment, re-positioning vehicles and leasing equipment.

The fourth role is enacted by the track and terminal operator, who controls changes in network structure and characteristics. Such a function can embrace the addition or abandonment of links or nodes. Alterations in link characteristics are also involved, such as dredging channels, widening roads and providing control signals. In addition, variations in network configuration can occur when, for instance, a new motorway is implemented and new carrier operating rights are assigned in a particular market.

The administrator engages in the fifth role. A dual function is involved, which encompasses the allocation of resources to the transport sector and the establishment of operational norms (what, who, how, when and where) governing the reciprocal relations between actors in the transport decision-making process, in such a way that they are sensitive to changing resources and standards for judging services. Such a role involves the provision of a level of satisfaction, either in terms valuable to the administrator or by those to whom he is accountable, while simultaneously maintaining a dynamic balance (in a budgetary sense) between other claims on scarce resources.[14]

Where the state of affairs is out of line with current governing relations the administrator can intervene to regulate the transport decision-making process. Hence, the failure of the free market system to achieve allocative efficiency through competition in terms of social values as perceived by governments, due directly or indirectly to monopolistic or oligopolistic control, has prompted government intervention in transport activities through regulation, taxes, subsidies or public ownership.[15] Such a strategy makes it difficult to ascertain whether the market or government intervention is the root cause of observed difficulties.

A concomitant failure of the market system to get agents to pay for the costs or benefits arising from transport, such as pollution, traffic congestion and the destruction and modification of the physical and social environment, has prompted the demand for the administrator to devise a system of taxes and subsidies in such a way that prices and public investment in transport and the economy as a whole reflect social costs.[16] There is also a felt need to employ taxes and subsidies in a discriminatory way to achieve a preferred distribution of real income between different groups. A neglect of considerations of 'territorial distributive justice' leads to a spatial form which embodies in its structure a pattern of income and opportunity out of line with what is desired by those affected.[17]

The sixth role is fulfilled by the activist who can lobby to subvert the anticipated impacts of decision-making.[18] In some instances the lobbying has been extended to include citizen or public participation.[19]

Finally there is the impactee, whose role embraces beneficiaries and victims of the economic and environmental effects of transport.[20] For example, transport developments can raise property values through increased accessibility, or reduce them via noise and air pollution. Some of the human consequences of physical decisions can be compensated in monetary terms but intangibles can only (if at all) be identified, classified and ranked according to weightings supplied by those affected.[21] Indeed, the recognition of the impactee emphasises that transport can act as an impure public good in its discriminatory impact on the access of various socio-economic actors to jobs, education and recreation, particularly for the poor, young, aged and the ethnically disadvantaged on the periphery of society, as it decreases the welfare of one group to the benefit of some others.[22] The impactee's perception of the possible range of alternatives, the technical feasibility of particular adjustments, the efficiency of reactions and the function of social constraints, bear a striking similarity to those of people affected by floods.[23] However, the parallel does not end there because, like transport, interest in flood problems has 'centred more upon planning engineering work and judging its economic feasibility than upon the effects of that work'.[24] Thus, in ascertaining transport's differential impacts it is necessary to estimate the current level of inefficiency and inequity. 'Who gets better service with a prospective change? Who gets worse? Who pays? And how do they all change the way they work, live, and relax as a result?'[25]

Role playing

Role definition specifies the expected behaviour or plans of action associated with a particular position. As such it does not encompass all of the propositions encountered by an individual actor in making a decision. 'In addition to role premises there will be premises about the state of the environment based directly on perception, premises representing beliefs and knowledge, and idiosyncratic premises that characterise the personality'.[26] The full range of these propositions can be incorporated in analyses of choice behaviour by reference to the 'action space' which comprises the social beings and non-social objects that the actor perceives or remembers in examining available courses of action and possible outcomes in a choice environment.[27] Our concern here, however, is not with delineating the 'action space' of an individual actor but with the role playing that ensues from engaging in the expected behaviour or plans of actions associated with the position. Even then the emphasis is not focused on the individual actor but on the *interaction* between two (or more) role players in situations that involve their mutual perception, consciousness and memory; an 'interaction space' potentially more complex than the 'action space' of an individual actor.

Interaction occurs when one role player desires to change his own action, thereby affecting the other role player; this result is achieved by sending a message to generate a response in the counter role player's available courses of action, possible outcomes, or the choice environment. Such messages can initiate, increase, or reduce either cooperative or conflicting behaviour because they contain information capable of modifying the probability of choice, the efficiency of alternatives and the value of outcomes to participants. Information flows, therefore, are critical in examining situations involving the interactions between two (or more) role players.

Interaction space

Four sets of interactions between pairs of role players are deemed pertinent to the understanding of the transport process. Travellers, shippers and prime contractors generate passengers or freight flows, prime contractors and vehicle owners initiate vehicle movements, vehicle owners and track and terminal operators set track and terminal capacity, and track and terminal operators and administrators establish the availability of resources. In these categories the perceived interaction space will be influenced by expressed values and goals, conceptions of the perceived space and the ability to recognise opportunities. Hopefully, an exploration of the interaction space created by joint needs, interests, attitudes and training will provide an understanding of how the role players think and feel in a particular behavioural setting.[28]

The investigation of a real life behavioural setting necessarily entails an overview of the social setting within which the agents operate.[29] A survey of this operational milieu 'allows us to take into account such factors as who owns and controls the means of production in a given society, what set of socio-economic relations are generated around those means, who creates and develops the transport technologies, and what ends they serve'[30] Indeed, transport, unlike mobility, is not necessarily an end in itself, but is conditioned by the pervasive values, objectives and goals of society governing supply, demand and priorities in resource use and the criteria for evaluating its performance. If society's goals are specified in profit maximising or social surplus maximising terms, the interactions must be considered within the system of such values. As behavioural settings are necessarily dependent on the personality of the interacting agents, attention is confined here to indicating the general nature of their perceived interaction space before discussing how each set of interacting role players can be included in a common frame.

Four sets of interactions

A series of paths or arcs is used to represent the perceived interaction space of the traveller or shipper and the prime contractor, given the short-run assumption of fixed production and attraction locations (fig. 1A). Each arc is tagged by price, total travel time and frequency. Other indicators, such as comfort, may have to be added to be fully representative of the user's multi-arc movement space. As it is presumed that the traveller or shipper chooses between arcs on the basis of their subjective characteristics, separate paths would, for instance, be required for freight services by air express, road express, air cargo, fast road, express rail, general road, rail freight and sea cargo. Perceived distinctions of the traveller or shipper mean that the arcs do not necessarily relate to any fixed facility on the ground or organisational entity.

As it is assumed that the individual traveller or shipper will choose the arc offering least disutility or perceived cost, surveys of attitudes, preferences and reactions will be necessary to expose the user's subjective perception of the spatial movement alternatives for satisfying his need set.[31] If the emphasis on an individual's behaviour is to be retained in deriving the number of passengers or goods using an arc, the probabilistic modelling of disaggregated travel behaviour will have to be employed.[32] Ideally, a single equation will incorporate the trip probability variables of trip frequency, destination zone, mode of travel, time of day and route. While such disaggregate models may overcome the problems of using zonal data and the ecological fallacies inherent in modelling aggregate behaviour, they are still static and preoccupied entirely with demand analysis. Indeed, there is a pressing need to delve into the nature of the interrelationships between demand and supply posed by the concept of interaction space.

A three-dimensional diagram encompassing the spatio-temporal aspects of vehicle motion is used to demonstrate the perceived interaction space involving the vehicle owner's capability of offering a varying range of units in response to the prime contractor's demand for transport space at differing speeds and frequency on particular routes (fig. 1B). Two dimensions (x and y) represent nodes and links of the fixed network and the other (t) allows the vehicle to be depicted in time and space by a point. If size (seats or freight capacity), range of vehicle and status measures (meals, etc.) are added to a fuller version of the time – space domain, it would be possible to establish load factors (e.g. seat kilometres) and some level of service features, including frequency, convenience, comfort and travel time. However, fares and

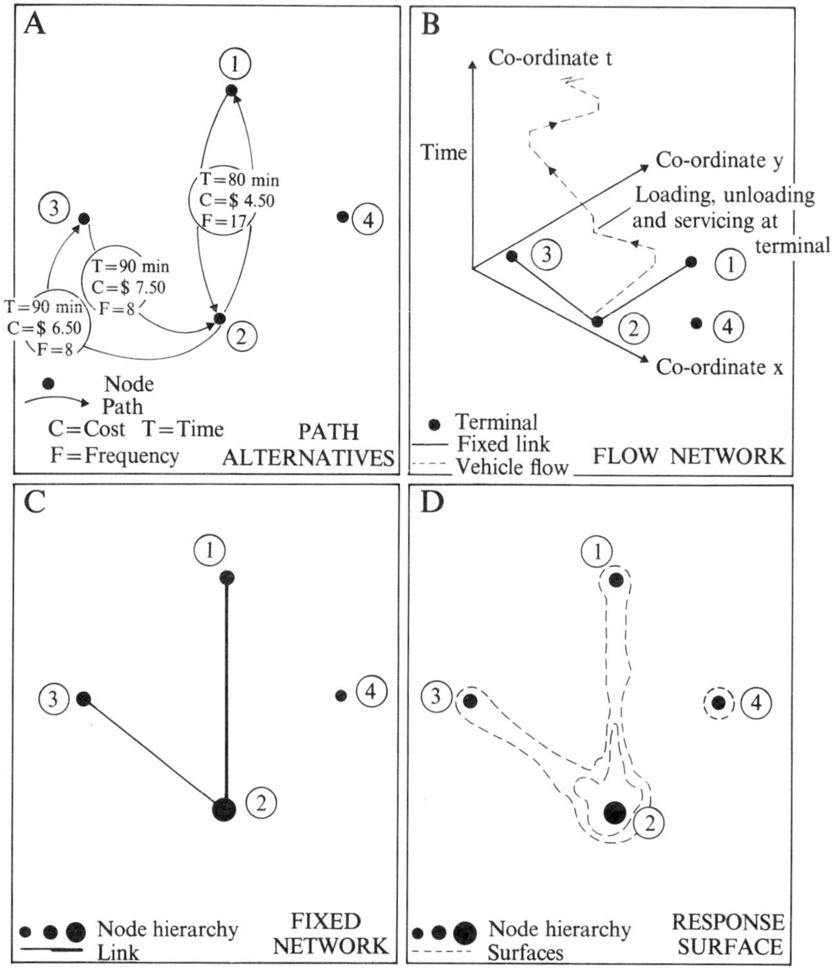

Fig. 1. A symbolic representation of the perceived interaction space of the four pairs of role players. (A): traveller or shipper – prime contractor; (B): prime contractor – vehicle owner; (C): vehicle owner – track and terminal operator; (D): track and terminal operator – administrator (diagrams *A*, *B* and *C* adapted from E. K. Morlok, 'A Goal-directed Transportation Planning Model', *Transporation Research* (1970), 199–213.

freight rates are not decided in this interaction, because they do not necessarily follow from vehicle capability, although the time properties do. Thus the main emphasis in this interaction is on the minimum time required to travel between each pair of access points. The essential time properties are encapsulated in four parameters. These are terminal stops involving deceleration, dwell and acceleration; cruising speeds on way links; turn-around speed between discharge and loading; and additional time incurred in passing through intersections.[33]

The interaction between the track and terminal operator and the vehicle owner hinges on the effectiveness of the physical plant provided to satisfy the demand for vehicle space between specific points. A description of the perceived interaction space is facilitated by employing graph theory to convert basic structural features to abstract equivalents. Points or nodes represent terminals and intersections, while lanes or links symbolise railroad tracks, highways, sea lanes, air lanes and conveyor belts (fig. 1C). In assessing the ability of fixed track and terminal facilities to accommodate varying numbers of vehicles, the most common measure is their maximum capacity, though more sensitive indicators of physical performance have been developed.[34]

Once the administrator has determined the overall balance of investment priorities in all sectors, attention in the interaction with the track and terminal operator can be turned to directing the flow of resources to determine the broad configuration of the network.[35] Decisions to add, subtract, improve or neglect links, nodes and modes are reflected not only within the operations of the network but also in the interstitial areas around and between the skeleton formed by the web of routes and nodes (fig. 1D). The administrator is able to exploit the varying degrees of permeability offered by alternative transport modes to structure and differentiate the spatial response surface. In this way fixed capital investment can be allocated to vary accessibility. If the prospects for the most disadvantaged territory are to be as great as possible, the resulting distribution of income should be such that the needs of a territory's population are fulfilled, resources are allocated to maximise spread effects within the territory and any extra resources are assigned to problem areas.[36]

While the perceived interaction space of each unit can be explored in isolation, there is a need to determine the common structure underpinning changes in their behavioural relationships and interdependencies over space and time. By assuming one role player is cast as a producer and the other as a consumer, a supply–demand model can be invoked to provide the necessary structural base to account for interactive events. Decision-theory provides a general analytical model for examining interactions in terms of alternatives, pay-offs and future events or states of nature, under conditions of certainty, risk and uncertainty.[37] However, it is preferable to examine spatio-temporal changes in the supply and demand for transport on the premise that the interactions of producer and consumer occur within an information feedback system.

A framework for producer–consumer interaction

A feedback loop is embodied in the producer–consumer interaction, which brings the result of the past action of the system via information channels to regulate future action. An examination of this information feedback system is initiated by indicating the output and functioning mechanism: the alternating levels and rates.[38] Levels (or stocks) are integrations or accumulations of rates of flow through time. They are the state variables which describe the system's spatial structure at any point in time. The levels are symbolised by rectangles. Rates (or decision points) determine how rapidly the levels or states of the system change through time by altering action streams or flows to overcome discrepancies between goals and observed conditions. They describe the change in a system at a point in time. The rates are symbolised by valves. Together, rates and levels are sufficient to describe the interaction

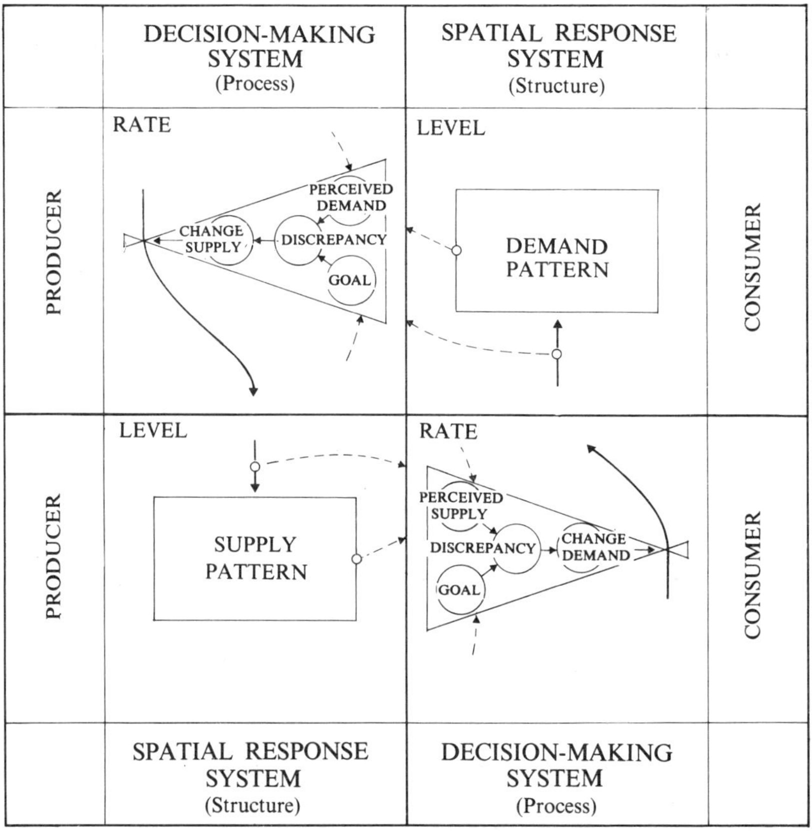

Fig. 2. The information feedback system embodies the interaction between producer and consumer. Changes in the supply pattern can be interpreted in terms of either the choice mechanism or material flows. The locational patterns of supply and flows provide the setting in which the consumer matches his changing preferences against what is offered. Modifications of the demand pattern can be explained as either the product of decisions or flows of orders. The locational pattern of demand and flows furnishes the framework within which the producer examines his need set. Both the goals of the producer and consumer are subject to revision in the light of fresh information inputs.

between producer and consumer and its consequences for the supply of and demand for transport over space and time (fig. 2).

In the output and operation of a transport decision-making system, the producer (seller) cannot arbitrarily decide on a supply rate and create it immediately with any degree of certainty.[39] A new demand pattern at a particular point in time has to be matched against the producer's available labour and capital equipment resources. While in the long term the producer may be able, subject to indivisibilities, to alter supply capacity by hiring extra labour, ordering new equipment and obtaining extra space, and may endeavour to influence demand through advertising, the present supply rate involves an implicit decision dependent not only on what is wanted but on the true value of current resources. If there is a discrepancy between anticipated and perceived situations, the producer responds as far as he can by varying the supply of a commodity or the quantity and quality of the transport service offered (process).

The new pattern of supply (structure) is perceived by the consumer (buyer or user) and matched against his goal or need set and buying power. power. Any apparent discrepancy occasions a change in demand (process) which alters the flow of orders for different quantities and qualities of transport services. Unlike covert paradigm-selection procedures the conscious, purposeful, 'overt' decisions of the consumer wanting or attempting to change demand stem from available, but not necessarily true, information on the supply pattern. The result of changes in demand occasioned by overt decision-making is recorded in the new pattern of demand (structure). This new pattern is perceived by the producer and matched against his goal conceived as maintaining a desired inventory level. If there are discrepancies between goals and the observed situation the supply–demand cycle is continued and further adjustments are made. Thus, decisions taken by the producer are not continuously adapted to consumer choices, as both actors make independent decisions even though their actions are ultimately linked via information, prices, and inventories.[40]

Time delays, amplification and information distortion

The reactions of the producer and consumer are not instantaneous in the operation of the system, but subject to temporal and spatial leads and lags occasioned by the properties of the information feedback system. Some of the properties stem from the way parts of the feedback loop structure are interrelated, but others are occasioned by time delays, amplification and information distortion.[41]

Delays occur in the initiation of production and the availability of the resulting item and are occasioned by delayed responses and hold-ups in inventories and the flow of orders and shipments. In a British motorway project, for example, the decision-making phase, including obtaining planning consent and finance is, on average, eight years, and the construction time, embracing site development and building, accounts for two to four years, while the expected life of the project is over twenty years.[42] Further, long lead times in providing capital equipment prevent a vehicle owner switching rapidly from one form of equipment to another. It takes an oil company in Australia six to twelve months to add an extra rail car and twelve to fifteen weeks to add a prime mover and tank to its fleet 'in normal times', but delays in providing road equipment have taken nine to twelve months. Such delays are critical in the operation of the information feedback system, because they lengthen the reaction time, causing problems to be separated in time and space from prime causes.

Amplification is 'manifested when an action is more forceful than might at first seem to be implied by the information inputs to the governing decisions'.[43] The amplification of orders and supply capacity above demand levels occurs at several places within the supply–demand system because the producers and consumers, operating under conditions of uncertainty, overreact when their images and conceptions of what they perceive differ from the desired goal towards which they are striving by searching and planning. In these circumstances the consumer has no guarantee that the supply requirements will be available; likewise the producer, in spite of attempts to influence demand, has to make decisions without knowing the actual structure of demand over time and space.[44] Extrapolating on the basis of past growth trends only accentuates the propensity towards amplification.

Information distortion can be induced by means other than time delays and amplification before it reaches the decision point even though information of the true state of the system cannot be depleted like the flow of orders or material. Sources of distortion range from the aggregation and distillation of raw data, differing perceptions of the producer or consumer, purposeful distortion in advertising by the supplier, error and unidentified disturbances. The inclusion of these biases emphasises that apparent information rather than true information is the basis of decision-making.

Structure and process

With or without the recognition of time delays, amplification and information distortion, examinations of the output and operation of the supply–demand system have generally been considered in terms of either the spatial or temporal expression of the respective structural and process attributes of producer and consumer. The pattern of consumer demand is reflected in space by trip distribution and, over time, by variations in expenditure allocation (fig. 3). In response to the changed pattern of demand, competition occurs among producers, which is manifest in space by variations in modal flows and changes in infrastructure and reflected through time by managerial quality, expressed, for instance, in responsiveness to innovations. The resulting supply pattern is manifested in space by the distribution of access points and over time, through variations in the quantity and quality of transport options. Learning is important in the consumer's reaction to changes in the spatial structure of supply. Over time this feature is expressed in mode loyalty, whereas in space it is demonstrated by repeated place patronage.

As Andrews[45] has shown, it is possible to study each of the spatial and temporal aspects of the structural and process attributes of both producer and consumer in isolation, because a set of appropriate techniques is available (see fig. 3). However, the pressing need is to study the output and operation of the system as a whole. A single functioning unit is required which incorporates the relationship between the output and processes over space and time for both the producer and consumer, together with the interrelationships between structure and process. In this way the states of behaving (functioning), becoming (evolving) and being (morphology) can be considered as an identical process.[46]

	DECISION MAKING SYSTEM (Process)		SPATIAL RESPONSE SYSTEM (Structure)		
	Spatial	Temporal	Spatial	Temporal	
	Competition				
PRODUCER	Spatial births and deaths	Management	Trip distribution	Expenditure allocation	CONSUMER
			Learning Behaviour		
PRODUCER	Network configuration	Specialisation	Place loyalty	Mode loyalty	CONSUMER
	Spatial	Temporal	Spatial	Temporal	
	SPATIAL RESPONSE SYSTEM (Structure)		DECISION MAKING SYSTEM (Process)		

Fig. 3. This diagram parallels the phases of fig. 2. It indicates the respective spatial and temporal patterns and processes of the producer and consumer. Each can be studied in isolation.

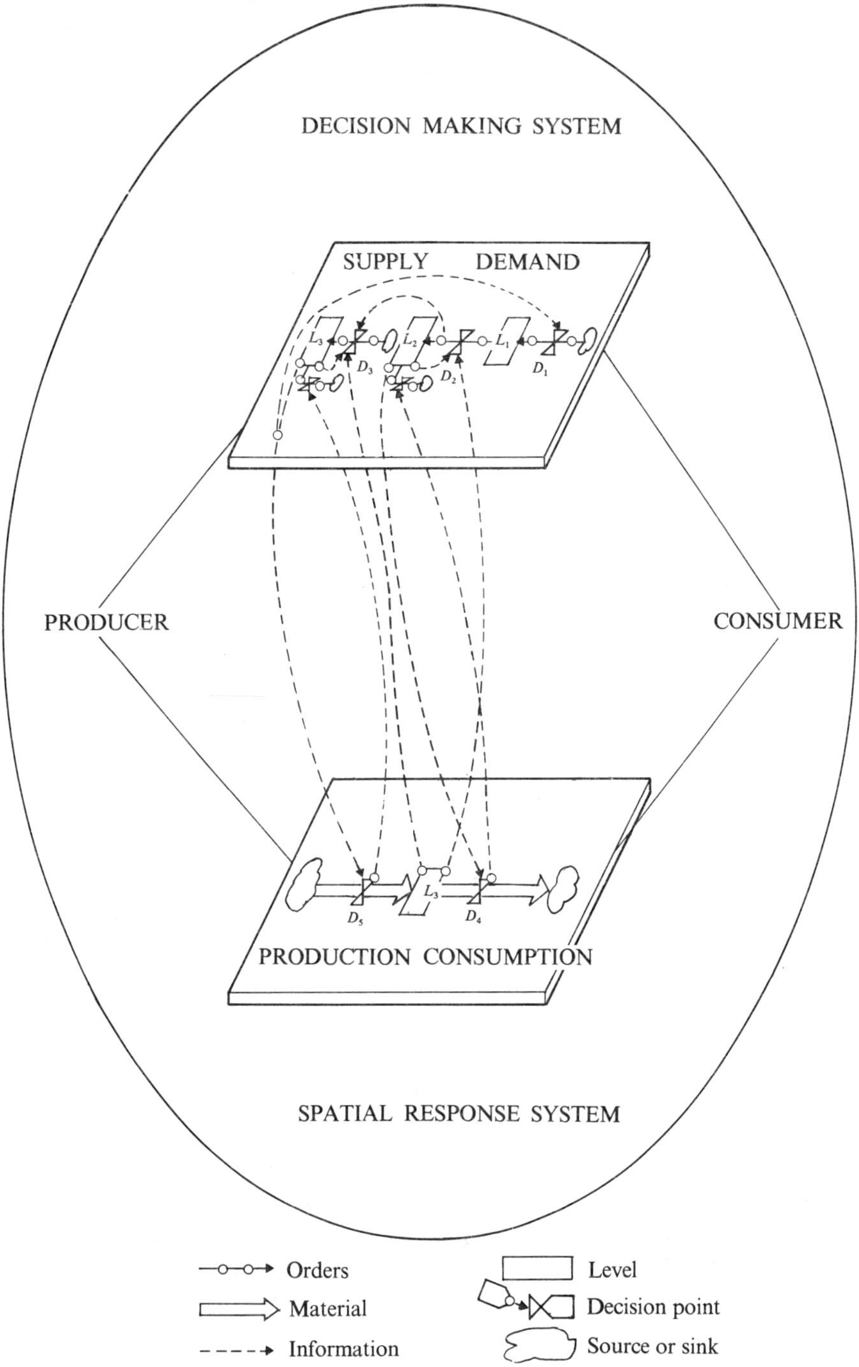
DECISION MAKING SYSTEM
SUPPLY DEMAND
L_3
L_2
L_1
D_3
D_2
D_1
PRODUCER
CONSUMER
L_3
D_5
D_4
PRODUCTION CONSUMPTION
SPATIAL RESPONSE SYSTEM
Orders
Material
Information
Level
Decision point
Source or sink

A single functioning unit

The equilibration of supply and demand within the producer–consumer interaction can be demonstrated by conceiving decision-making and the spatial organisation of socio-economic activities as occurring on separate surfaces within an information feedback system (fig. 4). In this system a continuous flow of orders (contracts and requisitions) consolidated from individual decision-making 'events' passes across the decision-making surface. The initial decision point controls the generation of the potential consumers and the second decision point controls the flow of orders after the decision has been made to purchase; these orders accumulate as demand. Such orders are transmitted to the spatial response surface to occasion changes in the size and magnitude of flows. A conversion coefficient exists in the information links to transform orders into the relevant flow units. The rate of consumption of available stocks is communicated to the third decision point. At this point the producer determines the rate at which the stocks will be replenished.

As the flows on the decision-making and spatial response surfaces accumulate at the various levels, it is possible to describe the condition of the producer and consumer by status variables – functional, structural and existence attributes that have both spatial magnitude and geographical location.[47] In the interaction the levels and channels represent adapted spaces, while the waxing and waning of flows depict changes and adaptation of activities within them. Indeed, a reciprocal 'dialogue between activities and adapted spaces is characteristic of man's development as his activities become differentiated in time and space'.[48]

Fig. 4. Interactions between producer and consumer are conceived as occurring on separate decision-making and spatial response surfaces. On the decision-making surface potential orders are generated by the consumer from a convenient source and accumulate at the first level or inventory. When a decision is made to purchase on the basis of information about the existing spatial response system, there is a flow of orders through the second decision point to the second level, where they accumulate as demand. These orders are communicated by the producer to the spatial response system to draw off production from the single inventory, which disappears into a consumption sink. As the inventory has to be replenished by the producer its state has to be communicated back to the supply decision point on the decision-making surface, where it is matched against existing demand. Once the supply decision is made orders accumulate at the third level on the decision-making surface before they are transmitted to the production decision point on the spatial response surface, which releases supply to replenish the inventory. The producer is not a passive participant in the interaction but endeavours to influence potential demand by communicating with the first decision point. Indeed, the classic case in which consumer needs and preferences are transmitted into the market and the producers respond quickly is not generally applicable to the transport industry. While consumers (users) are not captive to any mode and can exercise a wide range of choice, consumer sovereignty does not necessarily prevail. Transport is a producer-dominated industry where operations and investments are undertaken in a regulated market. Lumpy investments and long lead times can result in the type of service being inappropriate when it is offered.

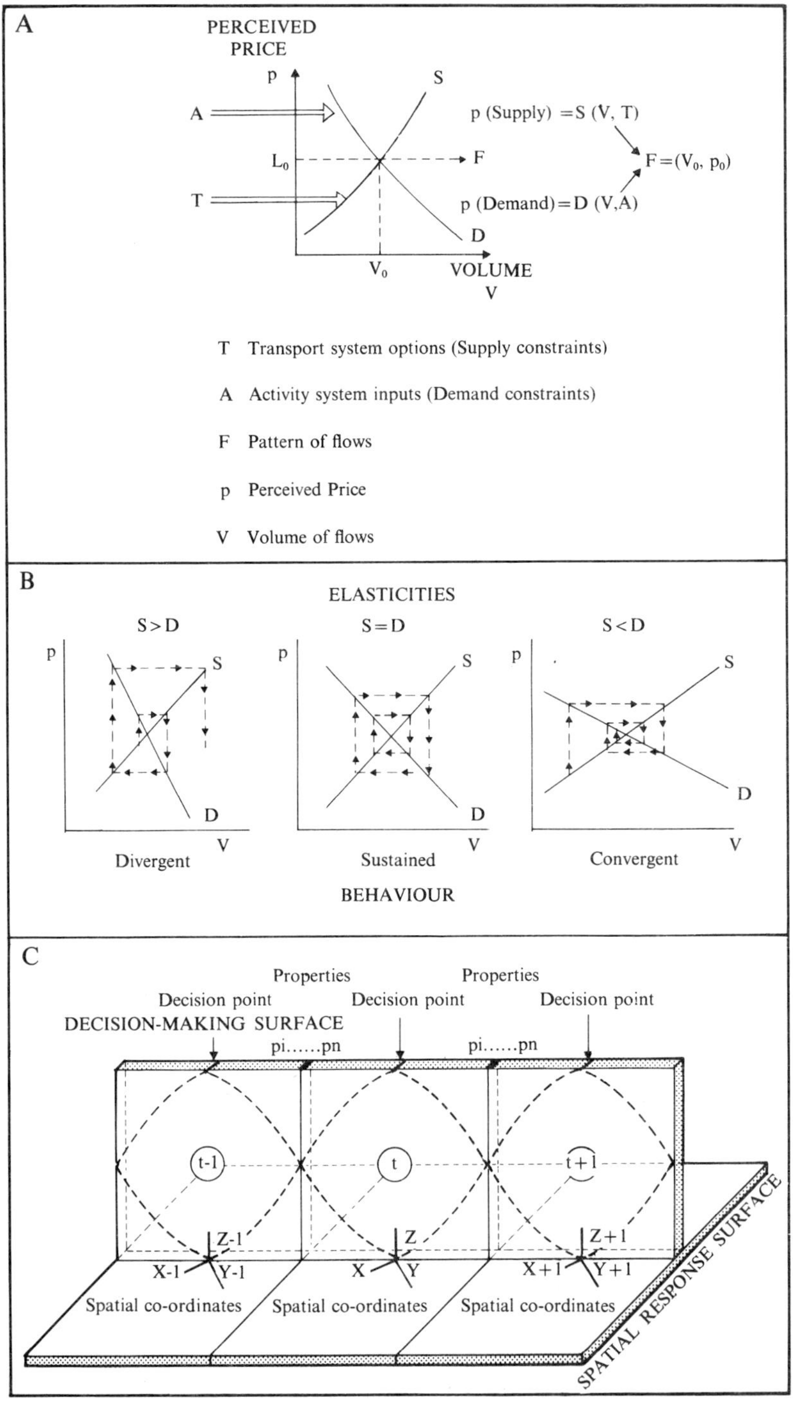
A
PERCEIVED
PRICE
p
S
A
p (Supply) = S (V, T)
L0
F
F = (V0, p0)
T
p (Demand) = D (V,A)
D
V0
VOLUME
V
T Transport system options (Supply constraints)
A Activity system inputs (Demand constraints)
F Pattern of flows
p Perceived Price
V Volume of flows
B
ELASTICITIES
S > D
S = D
S < D
Divergent
Sustained
Convergent
BEHAVIOUR
C
Properties
Properties
Decision point
Decision point
Decision point
DECISION-MAKING SURFACE
pi……pn
pi……pn
t-1
t
t+1
Z-1
X-1
Y-1
Z
X
Y
Z+1
X+1
Y+1
Spatial co-ordinates
Spatial co-ordinates
Spatial co-ordinates
SPATIAL RESPONSE SURFACE

Incorporating the lag

Attention in operationalising this rudimentary system is focused on the flow rates (fig. 5A) because they provide a sensitive indicator of stress. However, the communication of system instability and fluctuations in parameters associated with stress are not instantaneous, because of the indicated lag between the initiation of orders and the availability of the resulting flows.[49] Hence, the simple equilibrium model has to be recast as a cobweb model, to accommodate causally-related variables that are linked in a non-instantaneous manner.[50]

The cobweb model assumes 'production initiated in one period is only and wholly available in the next'.[51] Thus, flows initiated at period $t - 1$ affect decisions at time t. Orders initiated at period t determine the flows at period $t + 1$ (fig. 5B). Any disturbance in the system, such as a sudden increase in consumption, can trigger convergent, sustained or divergent oscillations, which focus attention on the period between peaks and the damping factor (fig. 5C).

No allowance in the operation of the one-lagged response system is made for the fact that the producer may not respond solely to orders in the preceding period, but may base his expectations on two (or more) previous (or future) periods. Other factors intervening between the initiation of orders and flows occurring include the availability of goods and services and time spent by the producer in determining an appropriate response and making an investment decision. There is also the problem of incorporating the perceptual lags of the consumer. As the reverberations of decisions take time to work themselves through the system via the price mechanism before a new order is established, the time lag itself may cause variations in the quantity, quality and direction of flows because of leakages.[52] Any accommodation of multiple lags necessitates replacing the sudden adjustment from the equilibrium point in one period to another in the next by a process of continuous adjustment.[53] The change from the period to the rate form of

Fig. 5. A: The pattern of flows, *F*, is the equilibrium solution to the supply and demand relations defined as the perceived prices and volumes that will actually occur for a given set of activity system inputs (demand constraints, including social and political factors) A, and transport system options, T, (based on M. L. Manheim 'Search and Choice in Transport Systems Analysis', *Highway Research Record Number 293*, 1969:57). B: Geometrical analyses of the cobweb model, which assumes straight line demand and supply curves and more or less fixed capacity (at least in the medium term). A lag has been introduced into the supply equation but demand has been left as a function of this year's perceived price (level of service). Thus, this simple text-book example is far from the complexities of the transport market (based on D. L. Meadows, *Dynamics of Commodity Production Cycles*, Cambridge (Mass.), 1970:10–18). C: A framework designed to show that the spatial coordinates (height, length and volume) at t + 1 are based on a decision at time t. In turn the decision at time t is based on information on the spatial coordinates at t − 1. The effect of the decision is reflected in the properties of the decision-maker, which indicate changes between t − 1 and t and t + 1 (see D. Harvey, *Social Justice and the City*, Edward Arnold, 1973:38–40).

analysis requires the revamping of the twin surface model, to incorporate not only multiple lags but also the constraints imposed by a fixed productive capacity. The recognition of such a non-linearity is important, because non-linearities and discontinuities in function effectively contain the divergent oscillatory tendencies, so that the system is bounded by the availability of resources at the upper limit and zero activity at the lower.[54]

In any revamped model the assumption of a fixed network needs to be relaxed. A mechanism is required to vary the number, location and capacity of levels as activity flows change. Even if on-going changes in network structures can be incorporated, a mechanism for recording the consequences of flows is still required to help determine the desirability of regulation.

Regulation and impacts

Habit, tradition and conformity already act as control processes in producer–consumer interaction and there are policies providing rules for repetitive behaviour. Where problems are 'new, unstructured and consequential' fresh policies are required.[55] However, the producer and consumer do not interact in a vacuum. Their choice processes are impinged upon by the activist and administrator, in addition to the other influences emanating from the changing, complex environment in which they operate. In turn, their decisions have consequences for transport users, transport operators, the government and the impactee.

> Transportation differs from most other market goods and services. A market is the forum for transactions between willing buyers and willing sellers, where prices serve as a cybernetic control to determine quantities and distributions. But in . . . market economies, the transportation activity is thoroughly regulated by public and semi-public institutions that usually set prices and often the supply quantity, frequency, and terms of service. Buyers, and most especially sellers, have little range in which to engage in the processes of bargaining, comparison, and adjustment that are implicit in the paradigm of a market.[56]

When such a regulated 'quasi-market' is viewed as an information-feedback system, control in the transport decision-making process is exerted through the decision point in the supply sector, while attention is focused on conditional forecasts from the demand sector. The effects of changes in the supply of transport on the user, operator and government can be made in terms of variables such as cost, frequency, speed or returns. As transport has the acknowledged propensity to dislocate social relations and destroy the physical milieu of the impactee, territorial indicators of social well-being have also to be recorded.[57] With this information attention can be given to evaluating short-run trade-offs between efficiency and equity. However, problems of 'distribution and retribution' for the individual cannot always be satisfactorily resolved by regulation. Alonso, for example, says 'transport markets are controlled and regulated *but unplanned*!'[58] The task of information collection, forecasting and the design and evaluation of alternatives devolves on the previously unidentified role player – the transport planner.

The transport planner

An integrated view of the transport decision-making process is created by invoking a potential user category and absorbing the pairs of interacting role players into a single system (fig. 6). Within the system's social setting there is a power and communications structure in which all decision-makers can make choices and in the process expose their attitudes, ideals and motivations.[59] The structure is created by interconnecting the levels and decision points to establish a chain of subsystems or a cascade. A potential user category (traveller or shipper) is added to the set of roles because this assists in examining the generation of transport need and the impacts of advertising on travel deferrability. Once the potential user pool is established attention can be paid to the other roles and in particular to the trunk connections between the traveller or shipper and the transport infrastructure on the one hand and the society system, via the administrator, on the other.

In the cascading structure of the transport decision-making process, orders from one subsystem become the input for the adjacent subsystem; such a strategy leaves a measurement problem because of the need to generalise events into continuous flows. The cascade's input and output process is represented as a series of canonical structures – the simplest components performing standard functions.[60] Within this framework the decision points not only govern the flow of unfilled orders into the levels, but create the through-put for the adjacent subsystem. It is also at these key control points that interacting role players resolve their problems, subject to the intervention of the administrator and activist (see inset fig. 6). The critical import of the decision points is carried through to the next stage, which links the cascading system of orders with the spatial response system. If the component role players are described in terms of their relationships and status variables the system may be susceptible to the microanalytic modelling techniques developed by Orcutt *et al.* for simulating regional economies.[61] However, our attention is restricted to delineating the system's structure.

No systemic role is specified for the transport planner functioning as an anticipatory decision-maker. In a sense all transport role players engage in planning when they consciously evaluate alternative options before they take action. Where disfunctional occurrences indicate conditions are out of phase with expectations, it is possible for interacting decision-makers to resolve the sensed problems by alterations to existing programmed or adaptive decision-making mechanisms. Such localised action is feasible because the dispersion of decision points throughout the system helps resolve instances where actual results differ from those desired; unlike engineering systems, therefore, control is from within.[62] If the difficulties identified cannot be dealt with by existing programmed or adaptive decision-making machanisms the problem is unique and requires a unique solution.[63]

While interacting decision-makers are capable of providing the strategies

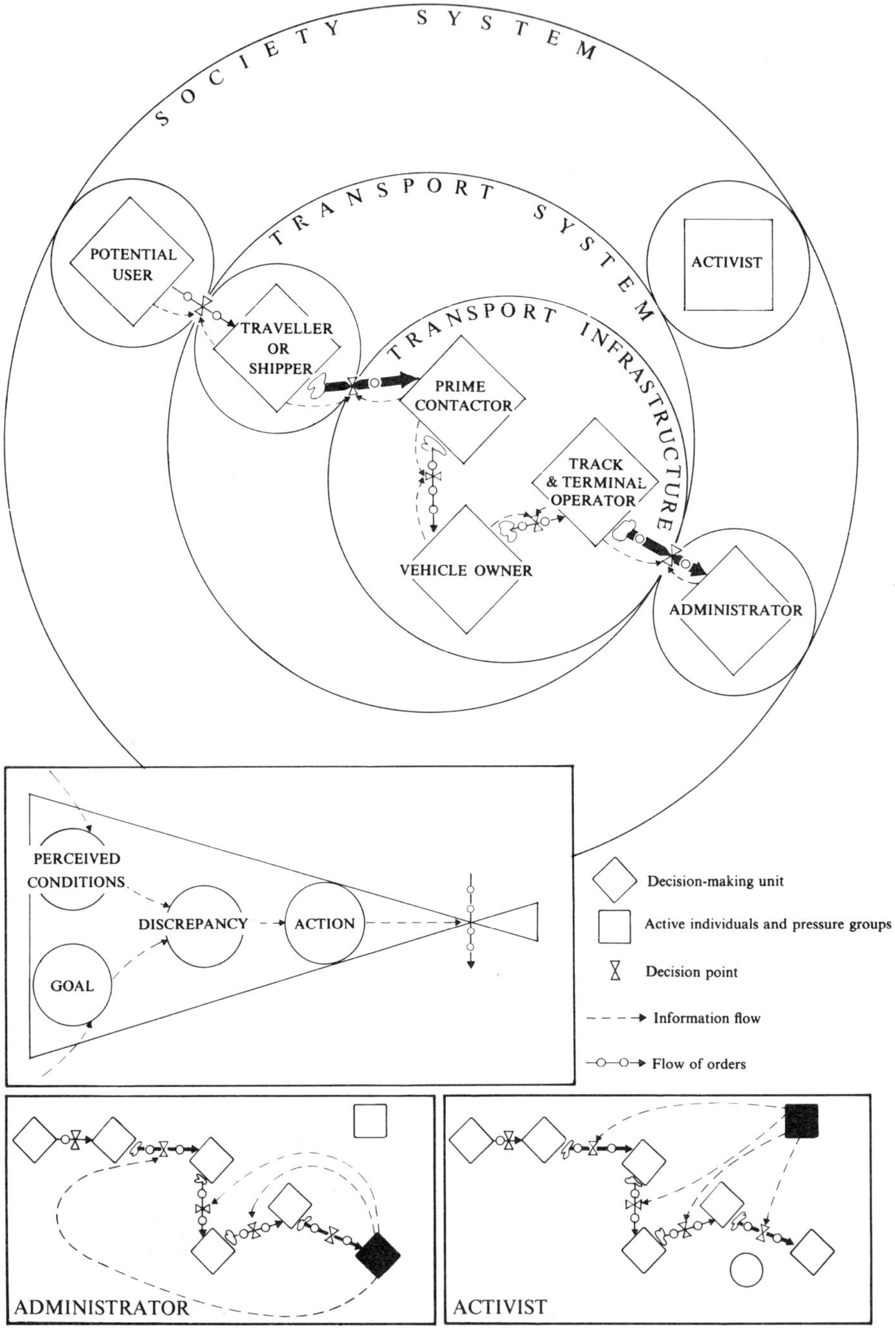

Fig. 6. The transport decision-making system.

required in problem solving there is no guarantee that their choices will be conscious of and sensitive to social, collective and individual goals within the system and its environment. Such compatibility stems from a responsiveness to society's changing values and needs in the short and long term.[64] The task of motivating role players to adapt their actions to these changing requirements belongs to the transport planner. Indeed, there are some similarities with the role of a social systems engineer, who is thought capable of interfering with and modifying the feedback processes within the multi-level and multi-goal framework.[65]

As all transport role players are participants in the planning process, a separate surface has to be invoked in considering the transport planner's innovative, preventative and remedial role – a controlling 'overlayer' which reaches into the role playing units to influence and respond to them (fig. 7).[66] The incorporation of the planning surface enables the role player, through learning and creative action, to respond to the needs of the entire system.

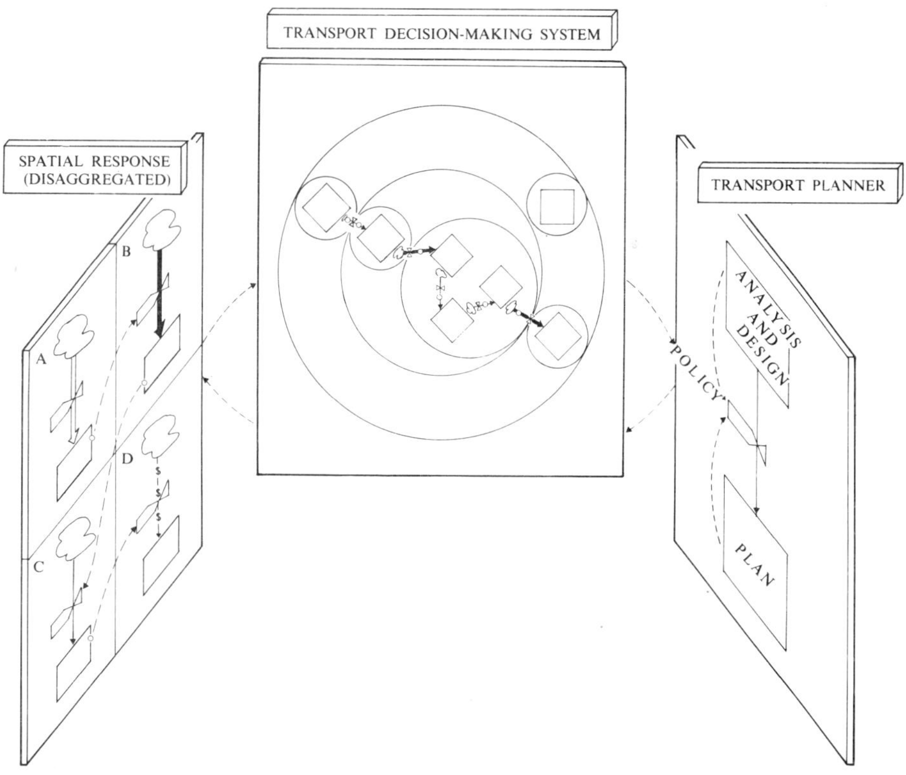

Fig. 7. The decision-making, spatial response and planning surfaces. The spatial response mechanisms refer to: A: passengers or freight, B: vehicle movements, C: track and terminal capacity, and D: resource availability.

In this way knowledge can be disseminated and a commitment made to transport policies and programmes and their attainment.[67]

The planning process in theory

As planning evolves over time it embodies a set of research, development and implementation procedures for a series of on-going reviews. Only the programme's outline is indicated here, because the discussion's purpose is to suggest how the general framework for the appropriate urban, regional, national and international context could dovetail into the transport planning process (fig. 8).

The planning process is set in motion when the continuous scanning of information derived from the levels in the decision-making system indicates that past actions have produced (or will produce) either partial or total misfit states, when matched against expressed values, goals and objectives. Then follows a statement diagnosing the nature and magnitude of the problem. This reveals the need either to improve system behaviour, to create a new system with satisfactory behaviour or, in the more usual case, to anticipate public or market action by adding or replacing existing structures to satisfy behavioural criteria. A description of the system identifies its parameters. Its modelling helps create the problem symptoms of interest and to predict their outcome – a means of building up the planner's image and understanding of the problem.

In the succeeding design-stage system, components–rights of way and terminal locations, operating, financial and planning resources–are used to synthesise and formulate alternative plans (programmes or policies) to overcome unacceptable social conditions.[68] An explicit recognition of the uncertainties inherent in long-term planning is detected in the representation of the step by step strategies over time as decision trees (network programming). The consequences of adopting a particular set of options can, in theory, be examined at a more tactical level by simulation or other appropriate techniques, but their cost may be prohibitive. Feedback from undertaking such an exercise can be employed in modifying values, goals and objectives, stimulating a fresh search for alternatives and as the basis of evaluating, ranking and choosing plans (programmes or policies) in terms of risks and gains set against priorities and resource limitations.[69]

In selecting the plan of action based on the predicted consequences of alternatives, the policy objective is to avoid all misfit states. Beyond that the aim of the process is to foster states of the system with 'wide-fit' choice characteristics. Each plan of action emerging from the weighting of conflicting value judgements is an option in a series of actions constituting the pre-implementation programme. As it is easier to get agreement over actions rather than objectives (which are rarely stated), the programme is directed at providing technological fixes for keenly felt problems.[70] However, if a systematic pattern is to be incorporated in short-term solutions dispatched to the decision points, the socio-political choices involving trade-offs between options and impacts have to be seen as part of a long-term future-oriented policy for shaping the environment to meet society's

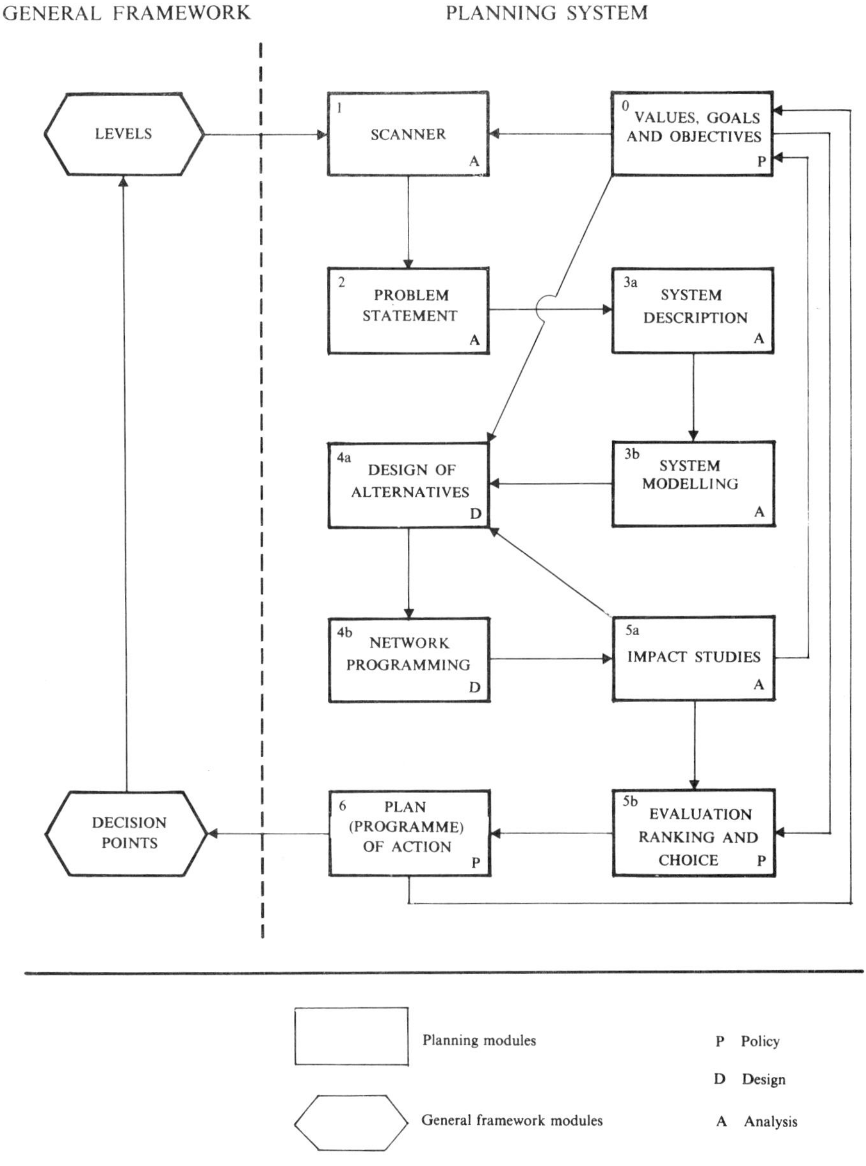

Fig. 8. Planning modules and their relationship with the general framework. The planning system and allocation of modules between policy, design and analysis is a composite framework based on Chadwick, Manheim and Wilson.

evolving aspirations.[71] Thus, planning is an evolutionary trial and error process which, through the continuous evaluation of information, permits a revision of values, goals and objectives and conceptions of actions in searching for and choosing between alternatives.

The planning process in reality

The plans and programmes for the future-oriented policy will be constrained by the transport planner's appreciation of the problem, the plan's objective and the time and resources available for its preparation and implementation. Indeed, the planner is not conceived as a super-being but, like the *planned*, subject to control. Any planning decision implemented has to be evaluated–a function involving the planner forecasting the outcome of a decision, matching it with the actual outcome and taking corrective action.[72]

In reality the transport planner does not always function as conceived. The role performed is often more akin to that of the transport analyst who works fitfully on data remnants almost unconscious that the resulting 'objective' observations, assuming the status quo, can have a differential effect on socio-economic groups.[73] However, the information generated by the transport analyst is usually localised in its impact, as administrative control is dissipated among individual spatial units without an overview of the decision-making system or any strong guidelines. Invariably, the situation is aggravated by the mismatch between the wide span of transport problems and the narrow institutional span for making transport policies;[74] it is also exacerbated by the fact that computer-based transport modelling, seen as a panacea by decision-makers, has had a questionable record of usefulness.[75] In these circumstances it is not surprising that with conflicting and competitive substructures, the attention of role players is squandered on producing *ad hoc* plans for altering segments of the physical fabric. Thus, if the planner is to have a creative role he cannot continue to be cast solely as the transport analyst but must facilitate the task of increasing the efficiency of the range of responses decision-makers are able to make, or extending the awareness of the goals they might successfully pursue.[76]

There is much still to be done in delineating the transport planner's role, including the determination of the variety of organisations for the exercise of his functional responsibility and the establishment of the exact nature of interdependencies between units and their spatial responses.[77] Yet a rich field inquiry has been revealed. The specification of the general framework does identify role players and even at this level of investigation provides the basis for classifying a host of disparate transport studies. Hopefully, the strategy outlined here will provide a deeper understanding of the transport decision-making process and the complex world it is designed to structure and control in the progress towards a super-system capable of subsuming transport and other divisions of interest into an integrated framework.[78]

11

The sociology of urban transportation planning a socio-political perspective[1]

P. Healey

Introduction

Donald Schon discussed the capacity of organisations to fight very hard in order to stay the way they are and termed this 'dynamic conservatism'.[2] Pahl has indicated recently that there is a lack of a detailed ethnography of planning, or even a good sociology of planning professions.[3] Even in the absence of this, however, there can be little doubt that the definition of problems and the provision of solutions in transport planning has traditionally been dictated by organisational and professsional constraints, and that transport planning organisations have fought hard in the recent past to retain their capacity to constrain problem definitions and solutions by the incorporation of a range of 'soft' social sciences, such as sociology, into their activities.

This chapter will argue that transport planning has increasingly experienced a changing social environment, characterised by uncertainty and turbulence. The incorporation of sociology into transport planning in certain specific periods can usefully be seen as a mechanism of adaptation to this environment. Without stretching an ecological analogy too far, it can be said that this has created a tension for sociology in transport planning between on the one hand engaging in activities appropriate to maximising the survival potential, in traditional terms, of planning organisations, and on the other attempting to develop methodologies for planning which the perspectives of sociology might indicate to be more appropriate to contemporary needs. The sociologist in such a situation has to choose between on the one hand accepting the professional demands of the planners, or on the other engaging in the formulation of a revised planning activity, which may well intensify certain popular demands for basic changes in the institutions of planning and decision making.

The organising framework for the present discussion is derived from several interrelated sociological propositions: the 'perception' of society is a theoretical activity, and even the most innocently common sense or deliberately objective observations of social events will be based upon implicit conceptual explanatory theories; these conceptual explanatory theories have socio-political implications and consequences related to the social position of both those holding them and those exposed to their empirical consequences; and the theories, along with other intellectual concerns, will alter with changes in social structure and general social context. This approach therefore relates an analysis in terms of elements of social structure and social change to perspectives in the sociology of knowledge.[4]

Models of social explanation

The subject matter of the social sciences, especially sociology, consists of systems[5] of social relationship.[6] Social relationships, however, are theoretical constructs, in the sense that they have no objective existence outside the meaning which is attributed to them by the actors involved in them and comprehended by observers of them. Meaningfulness, and the theoretical systems which support meaningfulness, are the essence of social relationships as opposed to simple coincidental occurrences.[7] As Weber explains: 'a mere collision of two cyclists may be compared to a natural event. On the other hand, their attempt to avoid hitting each other or whatever insults, blows or friendly discussion might follow the collision, would constitute "social action".' Social action, therefore, 'is confined to cases where the actor's behaviour is meaningfully oriented to that of others'.[8] The implications of this for the social scientist in the study of social systems are indicated by Wirth: 'If, then, the social sciences are concerned with objects that have meaning and value the observer who attempts to understand them must necessarily do so by means of categories which in turn depend upon his own values and meaning'.[9]

Explanations of events in social science must, therefore, be located within an understanding of the assumptions, values and theories of the proposer of the explanations. A sociological analysis of social systems operates at two levels, firstly positing explanations, and secondly reviewing those explanations reflexively as social phenomena, themselves requiring analysis and explanation. For the most part disciplines and professions in social science, other than sociology, have emphasised the validity of explanations at the first level without considering their status at the second.

Assumptions and values may be explicit or implicit in theories of social explanation. Perhaps those of greatest significance are those that are implicit, which operate as basic social paradigms[10] for the observer and define for him that which is 'obvious' and 'common sense'. Wirth observes that: 'The most important thing . . . that we can know about a man is what he takes for granted, and the most elemental and important facts about a society are those that are seldom debated and generally regarded as settled.'[11] In other words, what may seem to be obviously the case in social relationships and be promoted as such, may in fact upon closer examination, or examination from within an alternative theoretical or conceptual model, appear to be quite different. Social reality is thus a very slippery animal.

The socio-political implications of social theories derive from the relationship between those theories and the position in the social structure of a society of the person or group holding them. Individuals do not construct or hold theories in isolation. They do so firstly as members of particular societies and cultures, and secondly as members of groups within those societies. It is because, in the international social system, nation states and other social entities are ranked in terms of differential control of power and other resources, and within individual social systems social groups are ranked in a like fashion, that social theories assume a socio-political significance. Social theories in the sense in which the word is used here are therefore ideologies. Because ideologies are a function of social structure (although it is a functional relationship involving a high level of reciprocity), changes in social structure will be closely allied to changes in theories and ideas.

Applying this discussion concretely to transport planning, it is possible to say that transport planners (in common with other physical planners) for some time operated implicitly with a crude and extremely positivistic consensus model of society, and that this had the socio-political consequences of ignoring distributional issues and system interactions. Changes in the distribution of power through the articulation of disadvantage or concerned interests, however, required a modification both to this implicit model and the methodologies which served it. The articulation of active interests effectively altered the structural context of the planning activity, with a resulting introduction of strains and inconsistencies into the application of the planning paradigm. The incorporation of social sciences, such as sociology, was an attempt to adjust the existing paradigm to changed conditions as painlessly as possible, by introducing elements of an alternative 'conflict' model of society. The longer-term effect of this introduction of social science, however, is to aggravate the inconsistencies and hasten a more basic paradigm change.

Social paradigms

Consensus models

Consensus models of society emphasise the structural and normative integration of social systems, and reduce social conflict to the status of an aberrant or transitory phenomenon. Societies are conceived within this framework as having an optimum condition (equilibrium), in terms of which functional integration is assessed, or as characterised by a consensus on values and norms, including those governing distributional and stratification factors. Sociological consensus theories, such as structural functionalism, developed through biological analogies from nineteenth-century organicism, stressing the functional unity of the social organism comparable to the functional unity of living organisms.[12] In organismic models, the analysis of social phenomena or institutions proceeds in terms of the relationship of the part to the effective survival of the whole, and integrated functioning or consensual social activity is defined as a necessity for survival of the social system.[13]

The significance of this type of analysis for the present discussion is that it relegates social conflict to a minor role in social systems, deriving from failures of socialisation rather than structural inconsistencies. It also requires analysis of social activities in terms of the well-being of the whole social system on the basis of both necessity and agreement. Sociologists such as Coser[14] have endeavoured to introduce conflict into functionalist analysis, by asserting that it too can be functional to system survival, and Parsons, the grand master of functionalism, has indicated that normative consensus may be broadly shared, rather than unanimous.[15] Despite these, and other modifications to censensus models, however, the problem of explaining conflict, and the assertion of communality of interests to whole societies, remain fundamental to them.

Conflict models

Contrasted to consensus models of society are models which emphasise the endemic and structural nature of social conflict. In this view social conflict is seen as ubiquitous and rooted in the basic structure of social relationships of a society. Conflict occurs around the relationships of distribution of such socially valued items as economic resources, power and status, and is characterised by the constraint of some members of society by others. As Rex indicates, conflicts may range from peaceful bargaining in the market place to open violence, and will produce a situation in which opposing groups emerge, defined according to their interests.[16] One such group will usually become dominant, although, in the long term, changes in the balance of power between and among groups may result in either the extreme of revolution or, more likely, compromise and subsequent reform.

Within such a model, the search for a 'true' model of the social system is the pursuit of a chimera. Society is a plurality of values and beliefs, and separate values and beliefs which correspond to the range of conflicting material interests within the society.

The transport planning activity

The role of sociology in transport planning can be usefully discussed with reference to four broad phases of post-war development in road planning: the descriptive and prescriptive phases, the phase of rejection, and the phase of restudy.[17]

Not all countries will demonstrate the same stage of the process through these stages at the same time, and similarly it would seem to be the case that not all the responsible authorities within a country, especially nations which are federations of states, may be at the same stage simultaneously. It may be for example that there is a lag between federal and state road authorities in this development, as well as discontinuities between states.[18] A valuable aspect of this presentation of stages is that it permits an identification of the period of paradigm tension, which leads in the longer term to a change in the social model with which transport planners operate.

The descriptive and prescriptive phases

In the post war period the problems of urban transport, the increasing dominance of the car as a private transport mode, and general employment considerations, created for transport planning the problem of anticipating traffic demand and providing the road infrastructure investment to meet the demand. The social objectives of transportation in the descriptive phase are therefore subsumed within an acceptance of the market as the arbiter of desirable development, and neither the imperfection of the market as an allocation device, nor the imperfection in wider social terms of the consequences of market-derived planning objectives, are seriously considered. Transport planning is effectively reduced to road construction for the benefit of road users, and the outcome of this dedication to market decisions is accepted as socially optimal.

In this descriptive phase, the market-oriented consensus model of the road planner is the lynchpin of his professional activity. Not only does it permit him to assume that the market mechanism is effective, and indeed just, in the identification of social needs, and to justify his planning decisions on the grounds of aggregate community welfare, but it also allows him to define his role as that of an objective functionary concerned to fit revealed community aspirations to resource limitations through the application of objective technical expertise. In this process most socio-economic and political consequences of planning decisions are ignored, because professional decisions derive from a model of society which adequately incorporates all diverse elements in its general assumptions of organic and consensual social functioning. Possessing a social paradigm which 'solves' the key problems of planning, the planner is able to define his activity solely in technical terms.

In this phase the transport planner is typically the engineer, latterly aided by the economist. For the engineer, roads are seen primarily as physical facilities which are constructed to respond to the demand for transportation expressed in terms of actual and projected traffic flows. The questions to be answered by the engineer in road planning deal with traffic demand, engineering feasibility, and construction, maintenance and operating costs.

In the prescriptive phase, a range of techniques is developed within these basic orientations, for use in more sophisticated engineering and economic transport planning. The need for urban transport models, modal split, and trip generation and origin and destination data is appreciated, as is the requirement for an efficient accounting procedure, such as cost–benefit analysis, which can bring resource allocation in the public sector into line with practices in private enterprise. Using all these tools, planners then attempt to prepare a rational plan for an optimum transportation system for an urban area. The approach is essentially the same at project and strategic level, but the major edifice of transport planning which is erected in these phases is the metropolitan-wide transportation study. As the visibility of faults increases with scale, the grand studies (discussed in the next chapter) can be used illustratively in the present argument.

The failings of the metropolitan transportation study in sociological terms, lie precisely in the emphasis on long term-goals (the '1995 syndrome'), and orientation to the network level. It creates a situation where project-level (i.e. local) decisions are justified on the basis of a planning framework which is removed in both time and space from the actual site of the consequences of the decision. The process is consensus seeking, in that it assumes that a transportation system can be designed which will produce an aggregated net social benefit, usually at the regional level, conceptualised in terms such as the public interest or community welfare.

Cost–benefit analysis employed in this phase as a public sector accounting device pursues the same goals, for 'the aim of cost benefit is to guide the decision-maker into channelling resources into projects which will yield the greatest gain in net benefit to society'.[19] The requirement to construct roads for cars on the basis of market demand, elevated through cost–benefit analysis to the concept of consumer preferences, is therefore absolute in this period, and even if the metropolitan scale studies do not always produce results, at the project level roads are constructed using closely related methods.

The planning profession in the descriptive and prescriptive phases

Just as implicit models and assumptions will be reflected closely in the methodologies, results and consequences of empirical research, there will be a high degree of isomorphism between both these areas and the professional organisation of the activities.[20]

In the descriptive and prescriptive phases, the planning establishment is dominated by a hierarchist ideology rooted in a one-way causal paradigm. The philosophical basis of this, as has already been indicated, is an organismic model of society emphasising essential unity and the undesirability of diversity and conflict. Scientifically, this philosophy reveals itself in methodologies seeking one-way causal relationships and relying on positivist procedures for inferring the future directly from the past, either deterministically or probabilistically. Epistemologically, the existence of one ascendant truth is stressed, which will commend itself to all people if information is supplied in the correct amount and form.

In the planning process these elements have several concrete manifestations. Planning organisations are hierarchical and inegalitarian, with a decision-process which is elite oriented, and planning procedures based upon the concept of the expert. The community is viewed as ignorant, incapable, lacking expertise and limited in scope, and therefore to be kept uninformed, or only sufficiently informed to ensure agreement. The paradigm also requires certain methodologies in the assessment and analysis of projects, and these will be returned to below.

The phase of rejection

The transition from the period of descriptive and prescriptive planning to that of rejection does not occur entirely abruptly, although it may happen in a relatively short space of time. It occurs through the demonstration of cumulative inconsistencies and tensions between the activity of the transport planners and the reception of the consequences of that activity by elements of the society in which they operate. In the last analysis it may occur because the transport planner can no longer carry out his basic commitment to construct facilities. As a concrete historical example in the USA, the assumptions of the prescriptive phase of transport planning mirrored the general climate of conservative optimism concerning the development of western society into a post capitalist form based upon consensus and an end to ideology.[21]

By the middle 1960s in the field of transport planning, the fantastical nature of the 'end of ideology' thesis, and its damaging consequences for the planning activity were becoming apparent. As Bellomo *et al.* indicated, 'Where it has not suffered internal collapse from its own methodological shortcomings, the transportation planning process and the plans it spawned have been brought to a halt by its very constituents'.[22]

The reason for this was the development of popular opposition to the nature of transport planning, which was not simply concerned with disputes over technical issues, but was a profound rejection of the political and social assumptions of the planning process. In other words, it was a dispute over ideologies and basic values.

Historically the tide of general political rejection and protest grew to a flood in the latter half of the 1960s. It consisted of an opposition displaying disillusion with unrestricted economic growth, a fierce concern by certain groups with questions of what came to be referred to as the quality of life, and also involved mobilisation over specific issues, such as the Vietnam War and certain national liberation movements throughout the world.

In the planning arena generally, the phase of rejection manifests itself in an increasing concern with what is often rather poorly conceptualised as the environment. The environment becomes a generalised category, standing for all quality of life issues excluded by a market-dominated and growth-oriented planning process, and it is used to subsume both physical environmental and social factors.

It is hardly surprising that in periods of general value conflict, transport planning should suffer from rejection of its dominant models and assumptions, or that the failings of the prescriptive phase of transport planning should be seen in the phase of rejection as being essentially socio-political rather than technical in nature. In essence the failings consist of the exclusion of the social consequences of physical planning decisions, particularly the exclusion of their distributional implications. These failings are inherent in the implicit social model of the planning process, and they manifest themselves procedurally in evaluation objectives and methods, sequential decision making, modal bias, closed shop planning, and the lack of account of the interaction between transportation and certain physical systems (e.g. land use) and social system factors in general.[23]

Sociology and the phase of rejection

The introduction of sociology into transport planning is a function of the paradigm uncertainties produced by the phase of rejection. The issues raised by the phase of rejection indicate that a form of analysis is starting to be required that goes beyond the capabilities of engineering and economics in transport planning, to a consideration of sociological and political questions.

Initially, however, the social sciences, including a reorientation of the role of welfare economics, are not introduced into transport planning in order to ensure the transition from the existing consensus paradigm to the sort of conflict social model which is being forcibly asserted by the rejectionist movements (including previous clients and recipients of transport planning services and facilities). Rather the role of the social sciences is to modify existing transport planning sufficiently to allow it to continue without fundamental alterations to planning practices. The social sciences are adopted at first, therefore, as a mechanism of minimum adaptation for survival of the professions and institutions of transport planning in an altered social environment.

This role of the social sciences can be demonstrated by an examination of the problems that this period addresses, and the methodologies which are employed to solve them.

Issues in transport planning

The social conflict model which transport planning is forced to confront in the phase of rejection depicts society as a plurality of diverse and conflicting interests and goals, in which group interests will be effective (not normative) if the group possesses the power to make them so. It indicates, therefore, the primacy of distributional issues, including the question of the distribution of power and other resources, and the necessity of examining interrelationships of activities and institutions in social systems, and between social activities and the physical environment. The concept of the system is important in this phase, emphasising as it does the interconnectedness of apparently unrelated activities. In brief, the phase of rejection challenges the two main assumptions of the prescriptive phase: the consensual nature of social systems and the role this allocates the planner, and the acceptability of the market as a mechanism for the identification of social priorities and the distribution of resources and opportunities.[24]

This alternative perspective identifies in prescriptive transport planning a range of previously ignored issues. The position of transport minorities and the implications for modal split, the distribution of the costs and the benefits of planning decisions, the question of compensation for negative effects of decision, and the difficult problems of the interrelationships of transportation and other physical and social systems. It also calls into question the imposition of local and sectional costs in the pursuit of abstract objectives embodied in long-range and strategic-level planning, and in this process requires that some opening of the closed planning shop occur, to allow access to interested or affected parties.[25]

The initial reaction of transport planning to demands articulated in the phase of rejection is an attempt to modify the dominant transport planning paradigm without fundamentally changing it, through the incorporation of a range of impacts of planning decisions, coupled loosely with the institutionalisation of participation as both a methodology and a public relations exercise. What does not change in this response to rejection is the basic commitment to consensus seeking models, and the dominance of the market in setting goals and evaluating alternative courses of action.

The response: Cost–benefit analysis (CBA)

Cost–benefit analysis is discussed in detail in chapters 4 and 5. The issues it raises will not be dwelt on here, except in so far as they relate to the role of sociology in transport planning, in that cost–benefit analysis represents one avenue by which sociology enters the planning field in the phase of rejection.

As cost–benefit analysis is incorporated into transport planning in the descriptive and prescriptive phases as a public sector accounting procedure, its development as a methodology for assessing certain socio-economic dimensions of planning decisions is a logical one. In the rejection phase it is an attempt to introduce social welfare considerations into physical planning decisions. It therefore represents, at least conceptually, proof of the felt need of transport planning to adapt its paradigm and procedures in order to take into account a broader range of factors and achieve some kind of trade off amongst them.

It does not, however, mark a qualitative discontinuity with established methodologies, with which it shares both assumption and models. It had, firstly, a consensus-seeking methodology; secondly, it is market oriented; thirdly, it operates on the basis of aggregate welfare assumptions which can include a distributional perspective only with great difficulty if at all; and fourthly, it is only an evaluation tool for the consideration of projects generated on conventional traffic flow criteria.

A basic assumption of CBA is that: 'The objective function of maximising net benefits can . . . be constructed as a function which channels resources into their 'most preferred' uses, as viewed by society itself.'[26] It is interesting in a discussion oriented to social theories and their bases in what are essentially philosophical positions, to locate this assumption in the context of its obvious historical antecedent, with which it shares its faults and shortcomings. This antecedent is to be found in nineteenth-century social philosophy, in the Utilitarian propositions of Jeremy Bentham, concerning the desirability of pursuing the greatest happiness of the greatest number in any decision. The modern cost–benefit ratio is a quantitative version of Bentham's felicific calculus: 'his elaborate schema for estimating amounts of pleasure, which assumes that the intensity of a pleasure can be set against its duration, its duration against the likehood of its being enjoyed, and so on, as if these and other properties were all amenable to a single standard of measurement, and could be multiplied together to get a quantity of happiness, as length, breadth and height are multiplied to get a volume'.[27] The point is precisely that Bentham did assume that different persons' felicities could be aggregated, and despite the debate over interpersonal comparisons of utility, latter day Utilitarians, in the form of welfare economists in the phase of rejection, assume the same.

Bentham's model, like cost–benefit analysis, was consensus seeking, in that it posited that felicities could be elevated at some level to a common form, i.e. that differences in pleasures were quantitative, not qualitative, and that a common measure which represented diverse interests could be derived, which adequately traded off all states of pleasure and pain (or benefits and costs), and arrived at the best possible solution for everyone concerned. In this process Bentham ignored distributional issues by concentrating on net aggregate felicities, rather than the social characteristics of those enjoying them. Plamenatz observes that: 'the felicific calculus is useless, not only because we cannot in practice get the required information but . . . because a 'sum of pleasures' (as Bentham defines it) is a logically absurd notion.' 'Benthamism is optimistic and liberal and also inadequate.'[28]

For optimistic and liberal cost–benefit analysis the sum of pleasures is derived through the market. The concept of consumer sovereignty appears in CBA in the form of revealed consumer preferences said to be normative for public resource allocation decisions. In other words, costs and benefits are calculated on the basis of individual ability to pay, which is usually stated as their willingness to pay. In common with all methods based on a model of rational economic man, CBA must assume equality of resources (income, information, power) and ignore contrary distributional realities.

In terms of the principle underlying the evaluation of alternative courses of action in resource allocation decisions, the net aggregate benefit assumptions of CBA are expressed clearly in terms of Pareto optimality, which states that if one person gains and nobody correspondingly loses there is a net gain in welfare. If some gain while others lose, however, the method can give no guidance about a correct course of action. The ultimate admission of these limitations of CBA is the Kaldor–Hicks criterion that an allocation of resources is warranted if those that gain could in theory compensate those that may lose. As is explained in other chapters, this does not require that compensation actually take place, nor that gainers and losers be identified.

Social impact analysis

In the initial stages of the phase of rejection, transport planning continues to be hierarchical in nature and as a consequence continues to be beset by problems of opposition. These problems can become acute if opponents at a popular level exercise influence as constituents in the political system. The elected political representative, if he is the formal decision-maker in transport planning matters, may respond to the pressures of his constituents by overriding the recommendations of the planning organisations. For the organisations this creates a perplexing situation, in which their recommendations based on technical rationality are rejected for reasons derived from the political rationality of the formal decision-maker. This conflict of decision models reflects the articulation of diversity and conflict of interests in the social system at large. It also indicates that the technical rationality of the planner is rooted in socio-political assumptions which may become unacceptable in a changed social environment.

The discontent in the phase of rejection is with consensus seeking (and assuming) models, and market-oriented non-participatory decision-processes, and therefore CBA as a methodology deriving from these same bases does not supply an answer to socio-political problems of planning. After a period of development and exploration the planner turns to the soft social sciences (the 'human' sciences) to introduce into the CBA a broader range of perspectives and variables. Sociology enters CBA and transport planning, in the form of social impact analysis.

The characteristic evaluation procedure of an hierarchist planning process is impact analysis. Deriving from the one way causal paradigm (i.e. excluding interaction), a planning project is depicted as the cause, and the community at large is considered to receive cultural, social, psychological and economic effects. In the analysis of these effects, a range of predetermined categories is employed. The categories are presented as exhaustive, mutually exclusive, and applicable to all situations, in that they are universally valid and comprehensive. Analysis is then carried out according to one theoretical model, with attention to cultural and social context considered to be irrelevant because of the universal validity of the model.[29]

Sociology is introduced into CBA in order to enlarge the formal catalogue of effects and enter them quantitatively in the calculation of a community felicific calculus. The task has several interrelated aspects: the sociologist is to identify hitherto unrecognised market costs, note any physical costs and cooperate in formulating quantitative indices for them; lastly, and perhaps most importantly, he is to identify and quantify the intangibles.

The following schema of effects indicates that the role of sociology in social impact analysis is to fulfil a service function in economic evaluation.

Benefits	Costs
1 User (of the new Highway)	1 Construction
A Saving to existing traffic	2 Maintenance
i. Market	3 Operating
ii. Non-market	4 Environmental
B Value to generated traffic	
i. Market	
ii. Non-market	
2 Non-User	
A User of alternative facilities	
i. Market	
ii. Non-Market	
B Effects on the environment	
i. Market	
ii. Non-Market	

Weiner says of this schema:

'When all the items that are included under the categories above have been taken into account, the result will be a dollar estimate of costs and benefits of the project for its estimated service life.'[30]

The schema includes both engineering and CBA criteria of evaluation, and expands these to include a range of economic intangibles.

There are three stages in the incorporation of social impacts:

i. the identification of an effect,
ii. the development of a method of analysis of the effect (in order to determine if the effect is present in a particular situation),
iii. the consideration of some way that the effect may be quantified in order to fit in into the economic framework.

Identification of effects. The identification of effects is initially academocentric but becomes at a later stage 'endogenous'.[31] Academic definitions of effects are derived from discipline based analyses of the likely consequences of transport planning. These can be anticipated on the basis of available theoretical frameworks and articulated into a preparatory typology of effects for the transport planner.

Endogenous identification of effects is of considerable and enduring significance in the development of transport planning. Firstly, it represents the attempt in the phase of rejection to institutionalise the swelling demand for participatory planning. Secondly, it marks the initial step away from a planning process which is closed not only politically, but methodologically as just a formal exercise, and a step towards an open and dialectical socio-political process. Thirdly, as a corollary of this, it has profound implications for the kind of methodology which can in the long term be employed in planning, for it opens up the question of not simply what methodology may be dictated professionally by planners, but what methodologies may be acceptable socially and politically. These latter two points are considered in detail later in this chapter.

Research to identify effects may, therefore, consist of any one of a range of procedures, from sample surveys, which presuppose an analysis and simply require quantified data, to genuine endogenous open and in-depth investigations, with a minimum of preconceptions. It is probable at this stage, however, that techniques of the former kind will be those most extensively employed. The essence of these procedures is a conception of the public under examination as a source of raw information which can be legitimately procured for the professional purposes of the planners. The techniques are thus in varying degrees exploitative, in that those supplying information have no control over the use to which it is put, or the decisions which may be based on it. For the sociologist this must raise ethical questions inseparable from the technical issues. Such questions as the extent to which it is proper to view important aspects of the lives and opportunities of individuals and groups as data in a technical trade off and decision process; the degree of control those respondents ought to have over the use that is made of their responses; and the problem of being sure, as a social scientist, that the products of the technical process will not be hostile to the interests of the respondents, or at odds with the scientist's own value system. In policy research, which may result in decisions about the allocation of social resources for the pursuit of certain objectives, and which will have real consequences for various groups and individuals, these are fundamental issues on which the social scientist must adopt a position in his professional activity.[32]

Methods of analysis. The analysis of effects in this period concentrates on the translation of commonsense notions into a formal presentation. In keeping with the organicist, anti-urban, preoccupations of physical planning, the concept of community is a major organising framework for social analysis in this phase, not necessarily because of its heuristic value but because it is easily comprehended as relevant. The sociologist in planning has both to establish his legitimacy and, being in a service function, to supply an input to the planning process which is understandable by those who control the process. If he does not produce any analysis, or produces material which cannot be understood within the requirements of the dominant paradigm, the sociologist sacrifices credibility and loses legitimacy. For this reason, the contribution of sociology to planning at this stage of the phase of rejection is inevitably trivialised. The disservice that this can do, for both the sociologist and the planners, is that the latter may consider that the trivialised version of sociology is the only version, and may consequently develop a longer term disregard for it as an activity.

In these terms, that part of sociology which is most relevant to transport planning is the area of community studies. Despite notable exceptions, community studies are, however, one of the most theoretically barren areas of sociology, lacking methodological or conceptual rigour, and being poorly integrated into general sociological theory. The concept of community itself is open to such diversity of operational definitions[33] that it has been influentially suggested that one should not be 'concerned to study community because this is a non-concept.'[34]

Despite the emphasis on community, or perhaps because of it, social impact analysis in the phase of rejection does not employ distinctively sociological frameworks. System and stratification effects are ignored, and an ad hoc approach is adopted in the identification and listing of individual effects. Most significantly, attempts to employ sociological analysis rigorously are resisted, because of the implications for the dominant planning paradigm. The kind of effects identified in this period are mainly concerned with disruption and relocation, expressed in terms of compensation costs or dollar costs which are imposed but uncompensated. Housing resumption (compulsory purchase) costs can be employed as a proxy monetary cost of impact to allow for unidentified additional costs. These effects, plus monetary consequences of projects for those adjacent to the right of way, considered in terms of the stages of construction, are the main areas of examination. There may also be some continued emphasis on the economic effects of town bypasses estimated through trading and tax data, in the context of concern with inter-urban or interstate highway construction.[35] The broad goal of the social impact analysis is to produce a comprehensive cost based environmental impact statement, which will array for CBA all the impacts upon the social environment, considered either as direct monetary costs or in terms of proxy or surrogate prices.

Quantification of impacts (evaluation). The concept of the social system and a preoccupation with social stratification are basic sociological concerns. As Encel suggests: 'The task of the social sciences, and especially of sociology begins with the exploration of the social division, cleavage and conflict arising from the tension between natural equality and established social inequality.'[36] Bottomore also indicates the salience of stratification in sociological analysis. 'The division of society into classes of strata, which form a hierarchy of prestige and power, is an almost universal feature of social structure which has, throughout history, attracted the attention of philosophers and social theroists. But it is only with the growth of the modern social sciences that it has been subjected to critical study and analysis.'[37]

Sociological analysis is, therefore, in a very fundamental sense incompatible with the requirements of CBA evaluation, stressing as the latter does the identification of effects rather than interactions, the general validity of effects rather than their contextual specificity, and the irrelevance of distributional issues within the dominant consensus-seeking model. Sociology is, in its inception, a relativising science. It is concerned to examine the specific social and cultural contexts within which phenomena occur, and although attempting to generalize from these specific observations, maintains as a basic perspective the contingent nature of social reality. The assumption of formal CBA, that interpersonal comparisons of utility are possible by reducing personal utilities to a market denominator, is at odds also with this sociological position. CBA is not only consensus seeking, however, it is consensus enforcing. As Mishan indicates, the methodological constraints of CBA override any other consciously espoused principles, such as that those adversely affected in planning should be allowed to assess the value of their loss or disadvantage. Discussing the Roskill Commission in the UK, he writes: 'The compensatory sum for (a householder who would not move at any price) was placed, arbitrarily at £5000. If these people mean what they said, the compensatory sum would be infinite and this would obviously wreck any cost–benefit criterion.'[38]

The role of arbiter of social preferences is allotted to the economist, therefore, and he is forced to dismiss the issue that various individuals and groups may not value things in different amounts, but in different ways: a distinction of quality, not of quantity. When faced with a qualitative assessment by respondents, the economist is required to reduce this to a quantitative value consistent with both the methodology and his own evaluations.

As has been shown in other chapters, it is not easy for CBA to produce planning recommendations which will not have adverse distributional consequences within the social system. As well as the reasons raised above, there is the issue of the disproportionate 'benefits' generated by sectional interests in CBA: freight time savings in urban areas, or the 'business tycoons and Majorca holiday makers'. If these are in any sense real, rather than fictions created for the analysis, they represent substantial advantages to already privileged groups, with no guarantee that benefits will be passed on through the market, or that compensation be paid to those upon whom impacts fall.[39]

The present concern is with the social system, rather than with the consequences of the phase of rejection for the consideration of the ecological system. It is of significance to note, however, that the incompatibility between important elements of the analysis of social system and cost–benefit analysis is parallelled by the demonstration by Pearce of the incompatibility between 'maximum economic welfare' defined as 'the maximum difference between the benefits of economic activity and its associated social costs', and the ecological system goal of dynamic equilibrium or a steady state.[40]

The idea of a steady state or dynamic equilibrium has been accorded a normative significance by ecologists. As it maximises the probability of species survival, it has been assumed that: 'A steady state system in which man is a dominant species will, by analogy maximise survival probabilites for man.'[41]

A steady state is defined by three characteristics:

1. population birth rate equals population death rate,
2. energy intake equals energy dissipation,
3. materials intake equals materials outflow.

Pearce bases his analysis on condition 3, which defines the capacity of a system to assimilate material without disequilibrium. Relating it to the economic concept of externalities, he argues that the issue of pollution is precisely that the level at which it is economically justifiable to pollute an ecological system will always be in excess of that which is consistent with the maintenance of a steady state condition. His conclusion is that employing a CBA frame of reference: 'a steady state situation must always occur at activity levels less than those that define economic optima. If steady state conditions are preconditions for survival, it follows that an economy which is planned to allow for externalities will not maximize survival probabilities.'[42]

An alternative social impact framework

A positive outcome to a cost–benefit analysis does not guarantee a planning activity which can meet the articulated demands of the phase of rejection. An alternative form of social impact analysis is available in this phase, however, which attempts to examine comprehensively the impacts of transport plans. This alternative form of social impact emerges parallel to physical environmental impact statements, with which it shares common procedures.[43]

This type of social impact analysis typically identifies 'affected groups and describe(s) how these groups are affected. Where possible, these effects are reduced to numbers. Impact studies, however, typically pay more attention to the way benefits or effects are distributed among affected groups than to the reduction of these effects to a final number, benefit–cost ratio, or rate of return. Impact studies do ordinarily identify and array all relevant effects even though these can seldom be added together or to user effects to provide a net amount of impact.'[44]

This kind of evaluation procedure, therefore, permits the analysis of highway impacts in a series of overlapping contexts. Impacts can be seen as taking effect within a temporal, spatial, political, economic and social context. They can be estimated also for the phases of project planning and construction, for different geographical areas, and for groups with differential economic and social characteristics and resources.[45]

This form of social impact analysis attempts to come to terms pragmatically with opposition based on conflicts of interest in society. Its significance is, perhaps, that it considers that consensus has to be sought rather than assumed, and acknowledges implicitly that this process of seeking consensus must be a political trade-off among various interests. For this reason the model marks a small qualitative change from previous planning procedures, in that it is a tentative step in the direction of explicitly relocating the planning activity in the political system. Despite this, it continues to be consensus seeking and market oriented in the identification of the need for transportation, including roads. There is an explicit intention to employ techniques which will allow the political issues to continue to be internalised in the technical process, thereby assuming that technical solutions can be found to political problems.

Popular participation in this stage is an important aspect of a methodology for 'minimizing conflict and proceeding to an orderly location and design process'.[46] It is approached as a methodology through which information can be fed to concerned groups in order to bring their perceptions of desirability of the planning process and goals into line with that of the transport planners. Considerable emphasis is placed on the problem of the perceived irrationality of popular responses to transport planning decisions. This represents a continuation of the hierarchist rejection, on aggregate welfare grounds, of popular opposition as in some degree anti-social and misguided.

The intention with this model is to acknowledge conflicts of interests in society, which will have important consequences for transport planning, but to impose rules of the game within which conflict will be transformed into competition. The distinction is of great importance, for, as Coser observes (generally of conflicts within social relationships), 'conflicts which concern goals, values or interests that do not contradict the basic assumptions upon which the relationship is founded tend to be positively functional (i.e. beneficial) . . . conflicts in which the contending parties no longer share the basic values . . . threaten to disrupt the structure (of social relationships).'[47]

The role of sociological analysis in this alternative social impact analysis is broader and more challenging, yet it is vitiated by an obvious contradiction. As this form of analysis has abandoned the market as a mechanism for maximising welfare, the more sophisticated the analysis of effects and impacts becomes, in sociological terms, the greater is the evaluation problem of trading-off and in some way aggregating effects for and against a particular planning alternative in order to reach a decision. Stacey indicates, for example, the possibilities of a detailed analysis of the structure of social relations in defined localities. Having rejected the notion of community, she suggests that the focus of study should be 'institutions in a locality, particularly to examine whether there are any connections between them'.[48]

Stacey reiterates the view of Frankenburg[49] that community studies have been little used in the development of sociological theory, and suggests that in order to improve the theoretical status of this area studies should in future concentrate upon the elaboration of 'a series of interrelated propositions about social relations in localities . . . in the light of general sociological theory.'[50] Stacey indicates what such an analysis might consider. 'Some specific aspects about which it seems possible to speak at the moment are–(i) the establishment and maintenance of a local social system; (ii) some circumstances under which an existing system might be modified or destroyed; (iv) certain interrelations between systems and their parts; (v) the interaction of the local and national system.'[51]

In this perspective, the typical planning question, concerning the impact of projects upon communities, becomes an analysis of patterns of interaction, and other characteristics (theoretically conceived), on which the project will impinge, particularly the processes by which effects are transformed into impacts through the mediation of local issues and problems.

Social impact analysis through the phase of rejection is, however, local, specific, and essentially short term in its approach. Arising from particular problems created by prescriptive planning, it addresses them piecemeal. The activity of addressing them raises a series of contradictions, however, which cannot be resolved within the existing models or methodologies. Significant amongst these are the manifest inadequacy of the consensus paradigm, the problem of the role of participation and, as a corollary to this, the question of decision-making.

Thomson comments on the tensions of the phase of rejection for the social sciences. He indicates that social impact continues to mean that 'everything within reason' should be done to minimize the adverse effects of a project – say a motorway – on the environment, but 'within reason' never includes the possible rejection of the project itself on environmental grounds.[52]

The phase of rejection is a major learning period in transport planning, in which dominant paradigms are subjected to scrutiny and reevaluation. By the end of this phase it is apparent that the incorporation of methodological modifications into the planning process has failed to answer satisfactorily the questions of rejection and, in so doing, bring about an adaptation of planning to the changed social environment. Rather, what has occurred is that the institutionalisation of participation, and the introduction of social sciences such as sociology, has both illuminated and created contradictions and tensions in the planning activity, which can only be resolved by very basic changes.

At the end of the phase of rejection it is admitted that 'current transport planning techniques have not yet adequately integrated community values, environmental quality, ecology and intangible costs and benefits into the equation for determining the allocation of resources, the program priorities, or the location of transport corridors.'[53]

Solutions to these anomalies in the normal procedures of transport planning are sought in new directions in the phase of restudy. In this phase there is a crystallising of many radical departures hinted at in the phase of rejection. Paradigm change does not reveal itself abruptly, but becomes apparent through the efforts of planners to articulate the requirements of their situation as they come to perceive it.

The phase of restudy

Many of the chapters of the present volume are typical products of the phase of restudy.

The phase of restudy attempts to produce a transport planning process which consciously overcomes the problems of the previous phases. For this reason it is characterised by an acceptance of a range of perspectives and methodologies quite different from those employed previously, and an initial lack of effective theoretical frameworks for handling them. As a consequence emphasis shifts from the requirement to produce concrete results to a preoccupation with the process by which results are produced. Also, because the major issues perceived in this phase are political, salvation for transport planning is increasingly sought in political science, in the examination of social decision processes.

The phase of rejection confronts the issues of consensus-seeking models, market-oriented planning and the significance of distributional questions, and accepts the inability of existing techniques to cope with them. In attempting to understand the questions of the phase of rejection and develop methodologies to incorporate them, the transport planning profession and its institutions undergo a degree of change away from a rigid hierarchist model and towards a mutualist form.[54]

The ideal-type mutualist-planning form stands in marked contrast to the hierarchist model. The mutualist-planning paradigm emphasises the participatory nature of planning, in which the community is viewed as possessing resources of ideas and information, and planning organisational structure becomes more fluidly non-mechanical and interactionist. The concept of interaction is of central significance, for a mutualist orientation stresses mutual causal loops and networks of interrelation in society. In the assessment and analysis of planning projects, examination is directed to such mutual causal loops between the project and the cultural, social and psychological aspects of the community. These are conceived in terms of changeable, situation-specific categories, which can be generated by members of the community in accordance with their culture and their structure of relevance. All analysis is carried out and interpreted in its cultural and social context.

Contexts of analysis in the phase of restudy

In the phase of restudy, the transport planning activity can be conceptualised in terms of a series of organising contexts: the spatio-temporal context, the distributional context and the institutional–normative context. Emphasising the interactionist orientation of this phase, the contexts are depicted as mutually reinforcing and overlapping, and an adequate approach to transport planning is seen to require consideration of each of them, together with their interactions. In this phase, the sociological activity emerges as an integrating conceptual framework for the planning process, dealing as it does with many of the perspectives that the restudy exercise addresses.

Spatio-temporal context

Responsive rather than prescriptive planning is the aim of the phase of restudy. Planning can only be responsive, however, when it is not locked into large-scale capital-intensive transport plans, oriented to target years far in the future. The desire for responsiveness is essentially pragmatic, in that large-scale planning requires a degree of certainty about future events which is in general unsupportable in practice. The emergence of an interaction perspective in planning indicates the likelihood of changes occurring which will seriously diminish the possibilities of large-scale plans being realised. The concept of social and physical systems as networks of interrelations suggests that changes which could influence plans may be unpredictable, in that they could originate in any part of the system and be transmitted through the network to the sensitive planning area. The possibility of a complete dynamic understanding of networks of relationships which would allow the prediction of such events is remote and therefore the emphasis changes, to support a planning process which is short term and incremental. In such a process, changes to any system can be implemented and tested against experience, before further modifications are introduced.

Similarly, there is a move away from strategic and network transport planning, based on aggregate welfare assumptions and aggregate transportation data, and an increasing unwillingness to impose local costs and problems on this basis. Because of the traditional orientation of physical planners, the spatial framework which receives most attention is that of the relationship of land use to transporatation. Rather than the one way causality of previous models, the interaction of land use and transportation is of prime interest, especially as this interaction affects the urban form and relates to social system factors.

One conclusion arising from a shorter-term incremental approach is that upgrading existing road ways may be, whenever possible, a preferred solution to embarking on the construction of major new networks with highly uncertain long-term or system consequences.

A development in the phase of restudy, which is really a matter of the level of analysis, but also reflects the concern with responsive planning that is not locked into deterministic large-scale plans, is the analysis of transport demand in terms of behavioural models, discussed in chapter 6. Militating against highly aggregated zonal data employed for long-range forecasting, behavioural analysis employs a range of economic and psychological models, in order to assess the composition of demand for transport and employ this information to render transport provision more relevant to the requirements of users. While this approach employs formal modelling, is user oriented and also is still derived from market assumptions, it does mark a development towards transportation provision based on the requirements of users assessed in other than traffic flow terms. This development is working towards transport planning deriving from the user needs of individuals rather than zonal trip patterns.

Distributional context

In the phase of restudy, the transport planner comes increasingly to accept the plurality of diverse interests and values which characterises society, and to comprehend the inevitable discrepancies between the values of many groups and those of the planners. As Gans remarks: 'when I studied people and communities, it turned out that their notion of the good life . . . had little to do with land uses, public facilities, and expressways: they were concerned about work, income, health, family, neighbours, friends, church, and if they were home owners, space, comfort and property values'.[55] The transport planner further acknowledges that the articulation of these diverse interests occurs in physical and social systems which differentially distribute both the opportunities for their expression, and the costs and benefits of changes of those systems.[56]

In approaching the social distributional issues, popular participation becomes an essential element. Three problems are of particular salience with reference to this, however: the difficulty of reconciling participation with varying spatial and temporal contexts of planning; the problem of appropriate methodologies of research and evaluation; and the conflict between participation and decision-making.

The demand of the phase of rejection is for direct democracy rather than representative institutions, and it is this direct democratic model which underlies discussions of participation in the phase of restudy. Because of this emphasis, the problem of participation in planning activities which involve other than local consequences is acute. At the project level, both information gathering and the evaluation of alternatives can be devolved to popular participation forms, but in strategic-level or longer-term planning the solution is not so obvious. There is, however, an obvious compatibility between the concern for participation and the emphasis in the phase of restudy on short-term, incremental planning.

Attempts are made to work out the participation problems of larger-scale planning, accepting that there will be instances where this is appropriate. These take the form of professionally managed representative participatory structures, consisting of the integration of various levels of spatial and temporal analysis in a process which is iterative between and among levels, and interactive in all its components.[57]

Methodologically, participation raises the problem of not simply how it is to be structured in the planning process, but what implications it might have for other areas of the process. Just as the metropolitan transportation study excluded participation by the very nature of the problem it set itself, certain methodologies may be antithetical to participatory processes. Following Illich, it is useful to conceptualise such methodologies as 'high energy', where energy refers to the whole range of inputs to an activity, and is a much broader concept than cost.[58] An example of a high energy methodology would be formal computer modelling in transport planning.

If the sum of energies required to produce and utilise a model is calculated, it will be obvious that it is far in excess of the resources of most public groups demanding participation in planning. Energy requirements of modelling include expert training, including extended education, expert model construction, calibration of models, data collection, computer operation, data analysis, and the attendant time and money costs of these items.

If planning processes are to rely heavily on high energy methodologies, popular participation in the processes becomes highly problematic. As Drake observes, 'The clients for transport modelling must have money ... the question of whether it is desirable to spend so much on modelling per se is something else again.'[59] This realisation led Illich to the conclusion that 'Participatory democracy demands low energy technology ... '[60]

Formal modelling is very much a technical activity which arises in the specific context of a hierarchist planning establishment employing a one-way causal paradigm. In this sense it services the professional needs of the planning establishment, rather than originating in the necessities of transport problems. Interestingly, modelling was never a successful form of transport planning, even in the prescriptive phase. Drake facetiously, but pointedly, observes after an extensive and up-to-date examination of a large number of models: 'It might be said (with due apologies) of computer based, transportation modelling that "Never before in the history of human conflict has more money been spent, by more people with less to show for it." It certainly involves conflict since all too often the clients and modellers end up in total disagreement concerning what was done, what was to have been done, and who was to have done it.'[61]

In the phase of restudy only two avenues of development appear to be open with regard to this kind of formal modelling: either it is abandoned entirely or it is institutionalised under popular control. If the computer is to assume the role of decision-maker, both it and those who serve it need to be brought under the same system of democratic sanctions which operates for the political decision-maker. The issues this approach raises are complex, however, especially when professional government bureaucrats control the modelling activity.

What is certain is that methodologies which are based on the unequal distribution of resources are of concern in the phase of restudy. Doubt is also cast on high energy methodologies in terms of their relevance for policy research. Given the pragmatic and often crude approach of policy making, the logical sophistication of modelling may come to be seen as less appropriate than lower energy methodologies, which will meet a range of political goals (e.g. for popular participation), and also satisfy the requirements for research and analysis in policy making.

The tension between participation and formal decision-making is also acute in the phase of restudy. If participation is defined as any activity which introduces additional actors, variables or perspectives into the planning process, there is little or no problem. If, however, participation is seen to involve the right not merely to supply information and express a preference among alternative strategies, but also to decide which alternatives shall be adopted, the problem of the legitimacy of the decision body arises, especially where allocation of public funds is concerned.

The translation of information through decisions into action, including resource allocation, is inherently a political process involving trade-off decisions within a social system of conflicting interests. In the descriptive and prescriptive phases, it is presented as a purely technical process, and the transport planner is encouraged by formal political decision makers to view it in these terms. Even in the phase of rejection, the planners attempt to adjust their activities to social changes by internalising the political process in technical methodologies, and are lauded for accomplishing this. As Mishan, with reference to Roskill, observes of the problem of quantifying intangibles in cost–benefit analysis: 'the research team has not yielded to the temptation to hand back part of its brief to the political process which had offered it to the economists in the first place.'[62] With the broadening of social analysis, however, and the development of participatory processes, the visibility of conflicts in the social system renders indefensible the confusion of technical and political processes. As indicated in chapter 5, the result in the phase of restudy is that the political decision making function is handed back to the formal decision-maker, in the person of the democratically elected represenitive.

The explicit relocation of the decision-process in the formal political arena makes the technical planning analysis into a procedure for deriving and supplying information, and rendering recommendations on courses of action. Ideally such recommendations would be accompanied by a statement of the assumptions and goals towards which they are directed, and would prevent the technical mystification of devices such as cost–benefit ratios.

Handing political decisions back to formally elected representatives may solve a number of problems for the transport planner, but it raises a range of issues for the social scientist, concerning the nature of decisions in public affairs. Political science in the analysis of formal political processes, and the sociology of politics in the analysis of informal processes, identify such key issues as the nature of information supplied to decision makers, the role of professions and organisations supplying it, and the internal dynamics of the decision process, including its socio-political context. Underlying these is the question whether, if the political agent has to make a trade-off among the interests of different groups, he will be inclined systematically to favour one type of group rather than another.

One significant role for the sociologist in the phase of restudy is therefore to relate the activity of the planner to its socio-political context, through the consideration of the nature of decision-making institutions, i.e. representative democracy and the coalition of interests in politics, business, and military circles; the question of influence and control (Is the formal office holder really the decision maker?); the formation and operation of pressure groups (Are the most visible groups the most effective?); the structural forces making for oligarchy – the distribution of power-related resources such as wealth, income and other property; and even the institutional arrangements for the dissemination of dominant ideologies, e.g. education.

While this may seem a demanding framework for transport planning in the phase of restudy, it is only through an examination of these questions that planning in any area can become politically mature. It is, of course, precisely these questions which have been raised in the quest of the natural sciences for a socially responsible role. The implication of this perspective for participatory planning is that, even if decision-making is handed back to the political agent, the process of decision-making must be subject to perceptive and informed scrutiny at a popular level, and in the last analysis to popular control.

The constitutional and normative context

Closely related to the concern in the phase of restudy with distributional questions, there develops at the level of government an orientation towards normative social planning directed to achieve equity goals. Equity objectives, concerned with the evenness or fairness of the distribution of income or goods and services (e.g. transportation), as contrasted with efficiency criteria for maximising social welfare for a given pattern of distribution, can be seen to emerge in some part from the interest in fitting facilities to needs (or preferences and demand), in behavioural transport analysis.

Normative social planning is designed to pursue explicitly articulated social goals, through the implementation of integrated and comprehensive policy programmes. It is, as Rein has indicated, an approach to social reform and city planning with an ideological commitment to introduce social innovation, new programmes and new ideas, that will reduce or eliminate social problems.[63] Normative social planning adopts a network and stratification perspective on social organisation, and searches for complexes of interaction in the planning activity. The innovation of this planning approach is not the introduction of a normative orientation, however, but the desire to make the values underlying the planning process visible and explicit. It accepts the socio-political reality that all planning is normative, both because of value positions which reside in assumptions and methodologies, and because of the implication of planning decisions within the social system.

Gans describes the broad process of normative social planning. He distinguishes three levels: societal goal articulation, which is any kind of goal adopted by the government for the society; societal planning, concerned with evaluating social goals and developing in broad outline the kinds of programmes to achieve the goals chosen; and social programming, which, may be defined as the programmes for goals adopted by societal planners.[64]

Normative social planning is idealistic in the sense that it assumes that the social world can be influenced by men's imagination, ideals and hopes,[65] but it is not utopian, because it acknowledges the necessity of a political understanding of the role of power in social relations. This form of planning rests on a conflict model of society in that, while goals are articulated by elected representatives, no pretence is made of the general acceptability of these goals and a minimum consensus on competitive relationships is viewed as goal rather than a given of the political situation. It is understood that goals and their attendant programmes will inevitably militate against some interests in society, and this is introduced into the analysis as a constraint factor. In this context the distinction between scientific and utopian social planning is important. This distinction was first discussed in detail, although with an orientation towards dialectical materialism, as the only scientific social science, in Engels' 'Socialism, Utopian and Scientific', which should be required reading for all social planners.[66]

Engels' position, slightly abstracted and highly summarised, is that all intervention in social processes should be based on an analytical understanding of social structure and social change. Any intervention which does not comprehend these questions will be utopian, in the sense of proposing goal states for social relations which will be rendered unachievable by constraints existing in the social context of the proposals. Only by identifying the forces which make for invariance, therefore, can social science become an invariance-breaking activity. 'If we are to intervene in the social, economic and political processes of the city we must better appreciate both the nature of such processes and the nature of the intervention process itself.'[67]

That social systems in their institutional framework are not amenable to deliberate change can be illustrated with reference to the recent Australian Federal Government experience in the area of urban improvement programmes. 'One of the things that experience with the Area Improvement Programmes has shown is that they begin to throw up the many constraints which exist in our society, constraints which exist not only in the systems of government and public administration, but the constraints which exist also in the system of law, the systems of public accounting and finance, and the availability of appropriately skilled people generally, all of which combine to make it extremely difficult to do anything that is new and without precedent.'[68]

Social assessment and Transportation Planning

In the phase of restudy, multi-disciplinary social analysis is inseparable from the transport planning activity. At the level of values the task is to assist in the articulation of social goals, and consider how these may be effectively rendered into programmes, even in the context of unsympathetic political agents. In practical terms the task is the analysis of problems and issues in keeping with the goal orientation, and to assist in the formulation of programmes for public resource allocation to address the problems. Social assessment in this process has two main areas: at the macro-level, it is the analysis of social structure and social change, in order to understand how intervention in social processes may be effective, and the nature of the constraints which may render it ineffective. It is this theoretically informed analysis of structure and change which distinguishes the sociological from the welfare approach to planning. While both may emphasise short-term and incremental solutions to problems, the latter acts with no understanding of the aetiology or structural basis of problems, which are identified in an *ad hoc* manner, and approached piecemeal and in isolation. The former sees relationships in systems of interaction which produce problems and aspires, through an understanding of these relationships, to derive comprehensive and effective solutions. At the micro-level, social assessment consists of the formulation of a socially and politically responsive analysis of issues through popular participation, including programmes for raising the political awareness of participants, such as will allow them to undertake an informed scrutiny of the government processes of goal articulation and the fashioning of social policy.

Macro-social assessment is the distinctive contribution of sociology to transport planning in the phase of restudy. Contrasting markedly with the fragmented local orientation of social impact analysis, social assessment is a central element in normative transport planning. This is clearly seen in the consideration by transport planners of alternative transport technologies designed to eliminate many of the problems of the car. Social assessment would direct attention not simply to the user benefits or the social impacts of alternative technologies, but to such issues as the consequences within the economic system of directing demand away from car usage. This is a structural question of available transport modes, and an understanding of it will be of more importance in times of unemployment and inflation than even the most sophisticated analysis of the composition of demand, the needs of transport minorities, or marketing strategies for non-car technologies.

The changed orientation of transport planning in the phase of restudy can be illustrated further, in the light of the preceding discussion, by reference to the nature of solutions which are devised to solve apparently transport problems. Solutions may be of a transport, non-transport, or integrated form, characterised by low capital intensity or high capital intensity. One could also add that solutions may be short or long term, or incremental, i.e., linking short-term provisions with a longer-term normative orientation. The typical transportation study of the prescriptive phase considers little more than long-term, high capital intensity, transport solutions. In many situations, these will be least efficient: for example, the position of the transport disadvantaged may best be dealt with by low capital use solutions, such as bus priority measures, or integrated solutions in which these measures would be interim in a longer-term activity to relieve the bases of disadvantage (e.g. low income). The combination of solutions which these eight dimensions produce could be elaborated at length. In the present context the examples serve to illustrate the comprehensive and coordinated approach of transport planning in the phase of restudy, designed to ensure that in the enduring condition of limited resources, the allocation of public money should be as effective as possible in solving problems. For this economic principle to be followed, problems must be defined as precisely as possible in comprehensive planning frameworks, rather than approached piecemeal within the constraints of traditional, institutional assumptions.

Conclusion

The sociology of transport planning has been presented as an activity which involves two conceptually distinct levels of analysis. At the micro- or operational level, it considers the role of sociology as a methodological device for exploring concrete problem areas. At a macro-level it proposes a framework which locates transport planning in its socio-political and historical context, as an institutional system intimately related to elements of social structure and processes of social change. This distinction between the micro-level, consisting of sociology *in* transport planning, and the macro-level, the sociology *of* transport planning, demonstrates the functional interrelationship of the two levels. Sociology as a methodological device entered transport planning as a result of pressures in the wider social system and subsequently acted as one vehicle for change in the planning process.

The nature of social paradigms, and their role in legitimising professional planning activity, has been examined in the context of social changes, which create cumulative tensions and inconsistencies in the application of the paradigms, through appropriate methodologies, to planning problems. Organisations in planning attempt to adapt their procedures marginally in order to accommodate to social change, but this adaptation in a continuingly turbulent social environment simply aggravates the tensions and inconsistencies. The result is a longer-term modification of the prevailing consensus paradigm, not merely to acknowledge the pluralistic and conflict management nature of social systems, but actually towards a framework of analysis which is founded on this perspective.

The consequence for transport planning in its contemporary manifestation is a much more messy and complex field of enquiry than the formal modelling or linear processes of earlier planning activities. The framework within which this enquiry operates can be assessed in terms of a series of overlapping socio-political and economic contexts, which serve to illustrate both its inherent possibilities and the problems it undeniably raises. This approach also indicates that these problems are common to both transport planning and other areas of planning, and that integrated and comprehensive solutions have therefore to be pursued. At present, the vanguard of transport planning is located at some point in the phase of restudy. What remains to be seen is if the impetus to normative planning can be sustained and developed, or if further pressures of social structure and social change will require yet another orientation. It may be, for example, that, in the immediate future, the luxury of normative planning, born in part of the relative economic prosperity of the post-war period in the western world, will find itself under attack, as economic recession causes a renewed concern with basic material issues of efficiency and the market.

12

The urban transportation study[1]

L. A. Duhs and J. J. Beggs

Introduction: transportation study methodology and some general problems

The preparation of metropolitan transportation plans became something of a boom industry during the 1960s, with many large cities commissioning comprehensive transportation plans charged with the responsibility for devising appropriate transport arrangements for some twenty or thirty years into the future. These reports have formed the basis of recommended investment in road and public transport facilities costing hundreds of millions of dollars. Not surprisingly, they have been anything but free of criticism, and our task here is to provide an overview of the methodology typically employed in metropolitan transport planning, together with illustrative reference to a number of capital city transportation studies.

In essence, one might distinguish several distinct stages in this methodology:

i. *Data inventory.* Collection of basic data relating to the size and distribution of urban population and employment, to present transport system characteristics, to the modal preferences of commuters, etc.

ii. *Analysis and projection.* Construction of appropriate analytical models to facilitate study of trip production and trip attraction by zone within the urban area, of trip distribution between the respective pairs of zones, and of the determinants of commuters' modal preferences between two or more modes of travel for a given journey. The obvious interconnection between the pattern of urban land use and the number and size distribution of trips makes some form of land-use modelling also important.

iii. *Evaluation.* Evaluation of the advantages and disadvantages – monetary benefits and costs – of a set of alternative possible land-use transportation plans.

A conspicuous feature of this methodology, as it has been applied in most of the comprehensive plans prepared to date, however, is that the studies have tended to be essentially engineering documents. The relationship of economics to the plans has all too often been rather like that of Cinderella to the ball – lucky to get in, and packed off home before the real event was scheduled to start. Apart from this quite common general neglect of meaningful economic analysis – despite the sums of public money involved – several specific difficulties can be alluded to immediately. Among the more apparent problems is the obvious fact that it is impossible to predict with complete accuracy the relevant traffic density, population and other data twenty or thirty years into the future. Planners now recognise this and the treatment of uncertainty has therefore become of critical importance; nonetheless such treatment has been grossly underplayed in virtually all the studies done to date. If policy-makers really are to be given a comprehensive picture of the likely consequences of endorsing this plan rather than that, it is apparent that single-valued, or point, estimates of a project's net benefits could be seriously misleading. What is ideally required is a probability distribution indicating the likelihood that (say) traffic density will be x vehicles per hour and thus that there is a given probability of achieving a net present value of $\$y$.

A second problem relates to the scope of demand analysis and form of the models (ch. 6), and is made increasingly important as technology develops and provides new alternatives to conventional urban land-use patterns and so to conventional trips. The fundamental problem is that present models do not 'explain' urban travel behaviour, but merely identify interesting correlations between variables at the zonal level. One result of such analysis has consequently been a tendency to preempt many possible planning solutions. This tendency has naturally been most pronounced with regard to long-range economic analysis, in which urban travel may be seen as only one component of the overall urban communications system. In the long run, both the amount of urban travel and the associated urban form will reflect the cost, and the rate of development and diffusion, of new technology (including the influence on office location of remote terminal computers and closed circuit television). Demand analysis with this enlarged scope is yet to receive much detailed attention in urban transportation studies, but it seems intuitively apparent that the growth of new forms of communication has played a role in weakening city-core influence in some American cities.

A third general problem relates to the first stage of the standard methodological framework outlined above, i.e. to the collection of the necessary underlying data on present, and likely future, travel habits and trip characteristics.[2] In modelling future trip patterns, the studies typically employ some form of cross-sectional analysis, relying heavily on the known trip production and modal choice behaviour of specific groups[3] in the present urban community. Since a great deal of transportation planning is done in the form of big one-off 'studies', chiefly as exercises in political one-upmanship, by individual local and state legislators, there has not been a great deal of past enthusiasm for moving transportation planning on to a continuing basis. However the current trend is towards continuous transportation planning and this will undoubtedly encourage the collection and use of time-series data. In the case of cross-section analysis, the difficulty for transportation planning, of course, is that the behaviour of a specified group or category cannot simply be regarded as constant over time, i.e. on moving one rung up the income ladder today's $4000 income family is *not* likely to duplicate the trip making of *today's* $5000 income family, since many other factors will, or at least may, change over the same time. Technology, urban form, relative transport costs and qualities, etc., will all change, and not the least of these is the opportunity for discretionary policy[4] quite deliberately to manipulate the determinants of modal choice in any desired direction. In particular, the limits to which the transportation authorities may choose to take discretionary policies in the future are in no way bound by the limits within which these policies have operated in the past,[5] and hence – irrespective of the analysis used, or the accuracy of fit of analytical equations to past data – there may be no valid, empirical precedent to serve as a basis for predicting future travel behaviour when modal split and other parameters are taken beyond their previous range. Extrapolations based on regression analysis cannot simply presume linearity, and cross-section data would be non-existent outside the past range of values for the policy parameters.

A fourth general problem relates not so much to the methodology of economic evaluation as to the practical difficulty of giving explicit and precise treatment to an almost endless list of pragmatic problems. A variety of non-monetary effects may well be important, including both the *fear* of accidents and the aesthetic appeal of urban form and system design, which may of course be of considerable importance to local residents. Similarly, particular groups of persons (e.g. pedestrians, cyclists, conservationists) may see themselves as affected differentially by the alternative system designs under consideration, and they may see positive or negative benefits in terms of (say) health through clean air and opportunities for exercise. Such factors have typically been ignored for the obvious reason that, while they are difficult to quantify, they are believed to be of relatively minor importance. In any event this is a reason for being more exacting rather than less exacting in the treatment of the more readily quantified factors of construction and maintenance costs, time savings, accident savings and vehicle operating cost savings. After these more usual factors have been evaluated, it at least becomes clear that any intangible benefits favouring plan option two over plan option one have to be judged to be worth at least the differential net present value otherwise favouring option one before any reversal of rankings is economically justified. More serious perhaps is the differential impact of alternative system designs on the number and type of home resumptions required to provide for freeway routes etc. Little evidence of a sociological nature has been employed in urban transport studies to date, but the increasingly vociferous complaints of those whose houses are resumed suggest that problems remain in this area both for theory[6] and for practice. In the Brisbane context, one study suggests that '10% of the population of Brisbane (70,000 people) will be relocated.'[7] (see chs. 5, 11).

Predictive models

After collecting relevant data for a base year, metropolitan transportation studies largely centre on the construction of models for the analysis of traffic flows. The acceptability of any set of models is tested by calibrating against base-year data and examining how well they reproduce existing travel conditions. Final formulae will be approved on the ground that, when combined or aggregated, they accurately duplicate the base-year data. Some reasons remain for caution in interpreting the predictive power of such models, however, as already indicated.

Obviously enough, the accuracy of prediction will reflect the quality of the underlying information system and the validity of the model. Over-simplified models may result in specification error, e.g. the representation of a non-linear relation by a linear one, or the omission of explanatory variables from the model. Specification errors may result in biases and inconsistencies in the predictions so obtained. Similarly, relevant variables may be inaccurately quantified if the information system is poor, and this measurement problem is one that compounds, since the relative magnitude of the errors tends to increase when mathematical operations are performed on the data containing them. The information system and model actually chosen will of course reflect the relative cost of removing specification and measurement errors, as well as the value placed on different degrees of accuracy in the forecasts. Decision-makers should naturally be made aware of the limitations of any modelling tools employed in a transportation study.

Specifically, the sub-models for analysing traffic flows may be categorised as follows: land-use models; trip-generation models; trip-distribution models; modal-split models; traffic-assignment models.

The virtue of this approach is to be found in the practical difficulties of model building for large systems, e.g. if a city is zoned into 200 possible origin and destination zones, and each trip can be made by one to two modes on any of three routes, we are already dealing effectively with 240 000 different commodities.

Land-use models

Land-use modelling attempts to describe and predict the geographical location of economic agents in an area. The location of work places, household residences, retail shopping centres, places of recreation, etc., has a crucial effect on the pattern of traffic flows within a region.

While land-use patterns clearly determine traffic flows, the cost of trip making conversely affects land-use patterns. Though this proposition is intuitively obvious and has a long history in the theory of economics,[8] it appears to have been overlooked and is disregarded in a number of transportation studies (see chs. 8, 9).

The interdependence of the transport network and the spatial form immediately suggests that there a wide range of alternative combinations of the two which could be used in any city. With the exception of the Perth Study (PERTS),[9] the Australian studies tend to imply that transportation facilities are supplied merely as a response or reaction mechanism to some given immutable traffic volume. As far as land-use planning is concerned, the Hobart, Brisbane, Adelaide and Melbourne land-use estimates merely reflect trend planning, rather than an assessment of what is desirable. As such they may simply be self-fulfilling.

Trip generation models

Trip generation models are concerned with the number of trips leaving each origin and the number of trips arriving at each destination. They do not attempt directly to link pairs of origins and destinations, but treat each as a separate entity.

Trip generation models are normally based on the premise that 'land use generates journeys'. The amount of traffic originating at any point, or destined for any point, will depend on a large number of factors. These can, for convenience, be divided into two groups:

i. socio-economic variables, which measure the desire or potential of a household to make trips. The variables normally considered are household income, household size, car ownership, workers per household, occupational status, etc. *Business economic* variables, such as workforce, the size and type of business enterprise, etc., will have similarly important effects on the number and pattern of non-home based trips;

ii. *locational* variables, which reflect the spatial separation of households from each of the amenities which they desire, for example workplaces, shops, schools, recreational places, etc. Locational variables should reflect the attractiveness of alternative destinations. In practice, many transportation studies do not include locational variables in trip generation models.

At present there are *two* techniques available for estimating trip generations, namely:

i. Least Squares Regression.

ii. Category Analysis.

The more commonly used method has been *least squares regression*, in which a response surface is fitted to observed data utilising the principle of least squares.

In many transportation studies the expertise required for correct application and interpretation of regression results has not always been applied, and there is little doubt that, in many cases, insufficient care has been taken in the design and testing of regression models.[10] When dealing with economic data it is not always possible to comply rigorously with all the assumptions of ordinary least squares regression, but the various statistical tests associated with the least squares model may become invalid when the basic assumptions are violated. Further, as mentioned above, these models are not explanatory. They have simply sought to link variation in one variable with that in another.

In fitting data to the 'consumers' response surface', the ordinary least squares model assumes a linear function of the independent variables. The variables need not be in their original form, and transformations such as logarithms, reciprocals, etc., are often used. The choice of the response surface to use is clearly a very difficult task. To date, however, Australian transportation studies have made no attempt to use more appropriate transformations to overcome the inherent restrictiveness of linear regressions.[11]

It is important to note that none of the trip generation equations developed for these studies has included the price of travel as a relevant variable in explaining the total amount of trip making.[12] This has important ramifications. If trip makers are, in fact, insensitive to changes in the cost of travel, then clearly there is no need to build any more roads – in the attempt to reduce travel costs – and the *raison d'être* of the transport plan and the road construction authority is lost. Clearly this is an absurd proposition. Equally ridiculous is an equation which attempts to explain quantity demanded without considering price.

A recent development in trip generation modelling techniques has been that of *category analysis*, which is used in the 1970 Brisbane Study (SEQBRPTS).[13] Unlike least squares regression analysis, category analysis does not require the formulation of any direct mathematical relationship between trip making behaviour and the independent variables. The problems of category analysis can be divided into two groups: those associated with allocating households to categories in the base year and forecast year; and those associated with deriving trip rates which accurately describe the behaviour of the households in each category, in both the base year and the forecast year. To determine the total amount of trip making, the number of households in each category must be multiplied by the appropriate *trip rate* for that category, and then summed over all categories to give the total number of trips.

The assumption of category analysis is that the trip rate for each category will remain constant, while over time more households will move into the higher trip making categories. This means, for example, that a four person household, on $6000 real income per year, with one person employed and owning one car, would exhibit the same trip making characteristics in 1992 as in 1973. This appears an untenable assumption. Not only does it imply a constant pattern of consumer preferences, but it also assumes away a wide range of important policy variables designed to influence trip production rates. Further, there are many problems in allocating households to meaningfully defined categories. Categories are normally cross-classified (arbitrarily) by such variables as household income, car ownership, household size, persons employed, etc. Due to the complexities of the joint density function, which describes the probability of a household falling in each category, it is often difficult to add additional, and perhaps desirable, cross-classifications.

Despite much of the recent enthusiasm for category analysis techniques, the approach is rather restrictive. The 'appropriate' application of regression methods would seem to offer a more fruitful field for research. The fitting of the 'consumer response surface' for transport demand has greater appeal than the segmented approach adopted in category analysis.

Trip distribution models

Trip distribution models, as discussed here, will take the land-use pattern and the amount of trip making emanating from any particular area as given. Intuitively, the availability of alternative destinations should affect the amount of trip making and also various location decisions. Consequently such models are a somewhat artificial device which separate the choice of location, the decision to travel and the choice of destination, but this is again part of the urban transportation methodology which is the subject of the present discussion.

There are four main models which are currently used for handling trip distribution, namely: the growth factor model; the crude gravity model; the Wilson gravity model; the intervening opportunities model. The earliest trip distribution models used the growth factor method[14] of predicting traffic growth. This model is a single extrapolation, which assumes that travel demand is independent both of the cost of travel and of the shape of the city, as it affects the availability of alternative destinations. The model assumes that the status quo of urban travel should be extrapolated unaltered into the future and that roads should be built to meet this apparent demand for trip making. Such a model, when used in a long-term plan, embodies a major statement of policy and allows no room for the consideration of alternative economic action, which might produce more desirable results.

Early forms of the crude gravity model are to be found in such formulations as Reilly's Law of Retail Gravitation and Black's measure of the attractiveness of retail shopping centres.[15] The full analogy of trip making to Newtonian physics is attributed to Stewart, who advanced the proposition 'that the demographic (gravitational) force F of the attractiveness between two groups of N_1 and N_2 average Americans separated by a distance r is given by

$$F = \frac{N_1 N_2}{r^2}$$

where F acts along the line joining the two groups ... and the potential which group N_1 individuals produce at a point where the second group is located is given by

$$V_2 = \frac{GN_1}{r}$$

where G is a gravitational constant.'[16] This is a familiar trip-distribution model and is the one used in *all* the Australian state capital city transportation studies. It has some acceptable features from the point of view of economic theory. The attractiveness of any destination (the determinant of trip making) is related to the characteristic bundle offered by that destination. The measure of the attractiveness of a destination's characteristic bundle is taken to be the number of trips terminating at that point, given by D_j. In this case D_j will have been derived from the trip generation equations and may not be the best possible measure of destination attractiveness. The second feature of the model is that it incorporates a deterrence funtion. The greater the separation between i and j, the less the attractiveness (potential) of j which is exerted on i. The greater the travel distance (and travel cost) of reaching a destination, the less attractive that destination becomes.

The derivation of the functional form of the gravity model is, however, at best heuristic and is based on a simple analogy with Newton's gravitational laws in the physical sciences. Like other such relationships, such as the K distribution or rank-size rule,[17] the crude gravity model is essentially an empirical rule. A more theoretically elaborate justification for the gravity-type distribution model has been formulated by Wilson.[18] This form of the gravity model was used in the South-East Lancashire and North-East Cheshire (SELNEC) study. The model is a statistical theory based on an analogy from a branch of physics known as statistical mechanics. The actual model is an entropy maximising model and is a variation on the micro-canonical ensemble method for analysing the movements of particles in a closed system, for example, molecules of gas.

From an economic point of view, however, we can dismiss the analogy with the physical sciences as inappropriate. As Fisher and Paterson[19] point out, any closed system is known to run down to a state of maximum disorder and minimum free energy, and in no real world city does this increasing disorder assumption actually apply. In fact the better established the city is, the greater the tendency for specialisation in economic activities and the more the segregation of social groups in residential areas. Further, at a more philosophical level, there is considerable doubt as to whether statistical entropy, as a measure of disorder, can also be interpreted as the physcial probability of the occurrence of a corresponding macrostate (tripmatrix).[20] Although the Wilson gravity model is more mathematically complicated than the crude gravity model, it appears to have little or no normative significance and could only be validated as an empirical rule. This, however, would require the publication of appropriate empirical evidence which showed that the rule did work within tolerable levels of accuracy.

Another sophisticated approach to trip distribution modelling is the intervening opportunities model.[21] This is essentially a probabilistic model, which considers a trip maker setting out from his origin in search of a desirable destination. As he comes to each potential destination he will examine it to see if it suits his likings – if it does, he will terminate his trip there, if not, he will proceed to examine more.

It is argued that the intervening opportunities model is superior to the crude gravity model because it is based on a more rigorous theoretical derivation. This, however, may be regarded as a doubtful proposition. The intervening opportunities model fails to incorporate an effective travel cost variable.

Let the traveller be first placed in a situation where he wishes to make a shopping trip and can travel to any one of four shops, which are one, two, three and five miles respectively from his point of origin, and second where he wants to make the same shopping trip but the shops are now five, ten, thirty and one hundred miles from his point of origin. In each case the intervening opportunities model will give exactly the same trip making decision. The intervening opportunities model can rank opportunities by distance, but takes no account of the cost of trip making relative to other items in the traveller's budget; nor does it take account of other desirable features of the destination.

Modal choice models

A central parameter in an examination of the demand for urban travel is the traveller's choice of transport mode. As has been the case throughout the rest of this discussion, the modal choice problem is treated separately from the decision to travel (trip generation) and the choice of destination (trip distribution) (see ch. 6). Given this artificial segmentation of the components of the trip making decision, the following discussion will examine the alternative techniques available for handling modal choice, and the appropriateness of their underlying behavioural assumptions.

There are many techniques available for handling modal choice and the following more important ones will be considered:

i. Trend Extrapolation
ii. Category Analysis
iii. Multi-variate techniques
  linear regression
  probit and logit analysis
  discriminant analysis
iv. Route Choice or Diversion Curves
v. Direct Survey Techniques

Both the Hobart (HATS) and the Brisbane (BTS) Transportation Studies[22] of 1965 simply extrapolate recent declines in public transport usage. The BTS forecasts, for example, foresee a vehicle ownership factor of 0.26 vehicles per capita in 1960, 0.30 in 1964 and 0.41 in 1981, and a parallel fall in public transport trips per capita from 0.76 in 1960 to 0.50 in 1964 to 0.30 in 1981.[23]

HATS explicitly espouses the well-known 'downward spiral' argument regarding public transport services – i.e. fares rise, patronage falls, and services are cut, followed by further fare rises – in revealing its (naive) conception of the division of institutional responsibility. One is accordingly forced to question the rationale of the HATS recommendation that the suburban rail network warrants closure. This HATS approach might be compared with PERTS, which gives an economic reason why it is beneficial for a community to subsidise its public transport system, and with the Brisbane Study (SEQBRPTS), which sees cost-based fare increases as inevitable, without being explicitly concerned about maintaining (or achieving) similar price/cost ratios for alternative modes. SEQBRPTS finally assumes a 50 per cent public transport subsidy, after rejecting as impractical two (wrongfully) supposed policy extremes of 0 per cent and 100 per cent subsidy. This 50 per cent subsidy is then even rationalised as being desirable, without further consideration of whether or not a 60 per cent subsidy might have been even more desirable. Recent public transport policies in Brisbane have also been characterised by an acceptance of this 'downward spiral',[24] although it has here been suggested that this represents a deliberate policy on the part of the Brisbane City Council to compel the Queensland State Government to take over the running of passenger transport in Brisbane.

Diversion curves were used by traffic engineers long before the finer theoretical details were developed. They were initially used to establish how much traffic would travel on the old road and how much traffic would travel on the new road when an existing road link was duplicated by a bypass.

The user of this method would establish a scale on which to measure total personal costs. In the simple case, when one is establishing how much traffic might travel by alternative road links, the total person cost measure might simply be travel time. In a more complicated situation, such as the choice of travel mode in an urban area, more sophisticated measures of total cost (or disutility) must include the value of walking and waiting times, and the values of comfort and privacy associated with different transport modes, etc. Diversion curves have been used in PERTS and SEQBRPTS. While this approach has some appeal to the economist, it does not show how relative disutilities might be measured cardinally (see fig. 1).

In their predictive models, most of the Australian studies use multiple regression analysis in analysing modal split, but PERTS rejects this technique in favour of a cross-section approach, because of non-linearities in the relationship. This latter approach, however, is *also* seriously deficient, as indicated above.

It is with respect to this issue that the absence of local, empirical (sample survey) data on the determinants of modal split is felt. The Hobart (HATS) and Brisbane (BTS) studies of 1965 both provide regression-based deterministic forecasts of what the future modal split will be, and thereby obscure the fact that the transportation authorities can manipulate this modal split within wide limits, at their discretion. Particularly once outside the relatively narrow band of price–quality policies influencing the public transport–private car split in the past, non-linear responses are likely, and the determinism of the HATS and BTS forecasts can only be regarded as naive.[25] One possibility is to survey directly a sample of commuters and confront them with hypothetical relative price–quality combinations that *might* be effected for public and private transport, and tabulate the hypothetical responses.

A major study of this type has been carried out by Duhs and Gibbings.[26] The advantage of the approach is that it allows a clear distinction to be made between behavioural cost and resource costs.[27] A behavioural cost is that cost function which best explains people's travel behaviour, and therefore allows it to be predicted. A resource cost is the actual quantified measure of costs (see ch. 6). The distinction is necessary because people may

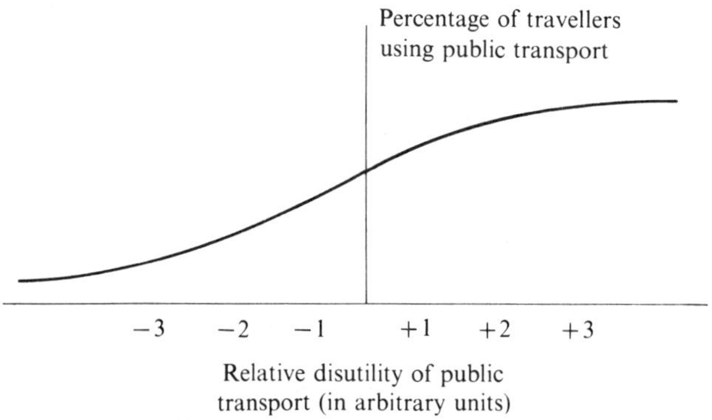

Fig. 1. A typical diversion curve.

base their behaviour on imperfect perceptions of costs. For example, there is considerable evidence to suggest that people significantly underestimate the cost of running cars. The mileage cost that best explains and models their travel behaviour may be different from the strict engineering assessment of marginal mileage cost.[28] Planning engineers in particular dislike this approach – since commuters do not always do what they say they would do – but in the absence of other valid data relating to the given community for the foreseeable range of movement of the modal split parameters in the future, the neglect or dismissal of such evidence raises some difficult questions for orthodox economic methodology.[29] Neglect or dismissal has been the standard procedure, however, and the sample surveys conducted in order to collect data for the Australian state capital city transportation studies do not run to questions about hypothetical responses to significant new relative price–quality combinations which might be effected in the urban transport system of the near or distant future.

Evaluation of alternative plans

After making the necessary predictions of employment and population distribution, of traffic flows, and of the relative cost–quality bundles of public and private transport which are to be provided, the next necessary step is to express the foreseeable benefits and costs of each alternative project in the form of some summary criterion, so that a comparative evaluation of the respective alternatives may be made. Needless to say, practical affairs permit the detailed comparison of only a relatively few discrete alternatives, and the selection of these alternatives for study is obviously important. Commonly enough, quite significant alternative plans have simply been omitted, and policy-makers are not necessarily well placed for rational decision-making, having no comparative data on (say) a system of busways as against railways, or on modal split given free or nominal public transport fares, or on transportation requirements given a different town plan. Future studies might well do more to seek out a reasonable compromise between comprehensiveness and the costs of computer modelling, by first applying 'rule-of-thumb' guides to (say) ten or fifteen alternative transport – land-use plans in skeletal outline as a guide to the selection of the smaller number of plans which warrant thorough investigation. For whatever reason, plans have generally simply disregarded specific terms of reference in this regard (to investigate alternative land-use plans and their implications for transportation requirements, etc.), and rarely provide a very explicit rationale for those discrete alternatives which they do choose to consider.

Some form of cost–benefit analysis is typically employed, although the differences in worth between the economic evaluations offered in the different studies are large, with some studies indeed providing no economic evaluation worthy of the name. Major difficulty occurs in the evaluation of benefits. Capital cost and maintenance costs can generally be estimated with reasonable accuracy (in current prices) even 20 years into the future, though problems remain, of course, in the estimation of the less tangible environmental costs of noise, air and visual pollution. Benefits, on the other hand, are more difficult to value, since, apart from the presence of non-monetised gains, such as reduced driving frustration, even the regularly quantified benefits of time-savings, accident-savings and reduced vehicle operating costs defy precise evaluation. Reduced wear and tear on vehicles resulting from the more consistent speeds made possible by expressways, etc., may be estimated accurately enough, but no definite value can be placed on human lives saved or human suffering spared, nor even on the value of work time and leisure time saved as a result of higher network speeds. A wide range of essentially arbitrary values has been placed on leisure time, with some studies valuing it at one quarter the worth of work time and others at two thirds the latter value (see ch. 6).[30] Moreover, time-savings typically bulk large in the empirical calculations of annual plan benefits, often accounting for more than 50 per cent of estimated annual benefits, and inaccuracy in its unit valuation may therefore significantly distort the overall cost–benefit calculations for the respective plan alternatives. Further problems arise from the fact that time-savings per trip will frequently be no more than a few minutes, so that there are few options open for what may be done with the time saved. Thus, a frequency distribution of time-savings is necessary to avoid the error of valuing sixty one-minute savings as equivalent to one sixty-minute saving. This is rarely, if ever, provided in the empirical evaluations completed to date, even though, on Tipping's[31] estimate, the oversight probably results in an overstatement of the true value of total time savings by 60–80 per cent. In the context of Brisbane's 1965 report, it might be noted that time savings account for 46 per cent of estimated annual benefits, and that a 50 per cent reduction in the value of aggregate time-savings[32] would mean a 23 per cent reduction in the *overall* annual benefits claimed by the consultants. In the context of non-Australian studies, it may be noted that when leisure time is included (excluded), time-saving benefits account for 89 per cent (69 per cent) of overall benefits in the United Kingdom M1 study. Similarly, the Victoria Line study attributed 80 per cent of its benefits in its first year of operation to savings in travelling time, and the Third London Airport Study saw 34–38 per cent of 1975 net benefits as arising in the same way.

A further point, on which there is anything but universal agreement, is the rate of interest to be used for discounting future benefit and cost streams back to their equivalent present worth. Controversy has raged in the cost–benefit analysis literature as to the appropriate place of, and magnitude of, the concepts of social time preference (STP) – reflecting the relative value of consumption at different points in time – and social opportunity cost (SOC) – reflecting the alternative investment options open for the deployment of society's scarce resources (see chs. 4, 5). It will also be noted that some annual benefits accruing in the future will be reflected in financial flows, e.g. reduced expenditure on vehicle repairs, while others will be non-financial in nature (e.g. reduced driver frustration). As such, some benefits are of a 'savings' nature and are capable of reinvestment on accrual and, in the absence of institutional constraints (e.g. compelling the investment of parking revenues in parking facilities) are thus capable of generating a further benefit stream reflecting the social opportunity cost rate of return. Non-monetarised benefits have to be consumed at the time they accrue, however, so that beautified city squares are either appreciated or not at the time in question, and SOC reinvestment rates are therefore not available for these benefit streams. Rather the STP rate is relevant here. It is apparent that the application of any single discount rate to heterogenous benefit streams is itself misleading, and that capitalisation of the benefit (and cost) streams to a terminal date is required in order to reflect the specific reinvestment possibilities open to the respective streams. Given the different time profiles of the benefit streams accruing to alternative projects, and the possibility of appreciable differences between projects in the proportion of reinvestible to non-reinvestible benefits (e.g. since accident-sufferings and aesthetic effects will vary between projects), there is a substantial reason for preferring what Mishan calls his 'normalisation procedure'[33] to the more conventional procedure of discounting all annual benefits and costs to a present value at a given discount rate, and then presenting the findings in the form of one or other of the conventional criteria, i.e. net present value, cost–benefit ratio, internal rate of return, etc. Empirically, this normalisation procedure has been shunned, however, and interest rates ranging from 5 per cent to 12 per cent have typically been employed. Another side effect of this is that the separate criteria of cost–benefit ratios, net present value, and internal rate of return – each of which has been used in one study or another – do not necessarily give consistent rankings of the various alternative plans under study, and will be consistent only after 'normalisation'. In short, plans which have ranked project *A* as superior to project *B*, as measured by the conventionally-defined cost–benefit ratio, may be misleading to policy-makers simply because of the method of presentation of the summary results. Use of the internal rate of return criterion may have reversed the rankings.

The uncertainty attaching to the accuracy of the underlying population/employment/car-ownership data, to the predictions of future traffic flows, and to the question of just what the discount rate should be, suggests the need for significant effort in providing sensitivity studies, i.e. for studies showing the impact on the ranking of the project alternatives of deviations from the 'most expected value' of the discount rate or of future traffic densities, etc. Many studies now include sensitivity tests, to the extent of ranking the relevant alternative plans at each of (say) three different discount rates, but rarely has a more comprehensive attempt been made to allow for uncertainty. In principle, a probability distribution could easily be attached to such key parameters as future traffic flow so as to provide policy-makers with a probability distribution of cost–benefit results. Single-valued estimates of net present values or cost–benefit ratios have been the order of the day. Comparison of two or more alternative projects is obviously much more meaningful if one is able to see that project *A* entails a 90 per cent chance of yielding a net present value of $100 000 or more, while the probability of project *B* achieving this result is only 60 per cent, etc. This is easily facilitated by running 100 or 200 simulated trials, and finding the resultant net present value distribution following from the 100 or 200 possible traffic flows selected.[34]

Attention to sub-plan detail can also have a significant impact on a plan's overall economic worth, but this kind of partial-system planning has all too often been grossly neglected. Despite the overall economic acceptability of a particular plan, important specific elements of it (e.g. major freeway interchanges or city rail facilities) may be capable of redesign at a different standard[35] or different location, etc., so that an acceptable overall economic result is not necessarily the most acceptable or optimal result.[36] For instance, the Melbourne Study could benefit from more detailed analysis of its Underground proposal, showing the impact on the system of failure to reach the predicted Central Business District (CBD) employment figure of 216 000 in 1985. Similarly, and perhaps more importantly, the *timing* with which the different plan elements (freeway links, etc.) are constructed may also significantly affect the overall result, but again this is commonly neglected. For the most part the Australian studies plan for a twenty-year time horizon, and only the Melbourne study offers an explicit attempt to phase system construction over time in an economically optimal way. More usually, phasing over time is governed by engineering expediency, rather than an attempt to maximise the net present value of committed resources.

One might also add that existing institutional arrangements are not inviolate, and could possibly be amended to good effect. This includes the possibility of manipulating peak-period traffic flows by staggering office hours,[37] or of banning private vehicles from inner-city streets, etc., and again reflects the possibility that plans will simply accept existing institutional arrangements as given and quite unnecessarily foreclose certain options. None of the studies gauges the impact on the economics of the recommended plan of a significantly less-peaked traffic flow induced by a discretionary staggering of office hours. More generally, one common problem in urban transportation planning is the fact that there is often a tendency for excessive compartmentalisation in existing institutional arrangements, with perhaps as many as eight or ten different government departments all making decisions that directly affect metropolitan traffic arrangements. One of the more prosaic, but nonetheless important, aims of metropolitan transportation studies has therefore come to be the recommendation of a suitable, integrated, transportion authority with responsibility over the rail, bus, private car, highway construction and other facilities so frequently handled at present by many different local government and central government authorities.

The Australian state capital city transportation studies: an illustration

Each of the Australian state capital cities now has one or more transportation studies (table 1). There are very real differences between these studies in the quality of their economic analyses, and only the Perth (PERTS) Study approaches adequacy in this respect. For the most part the Australian studies neglect at least some of the relevant alternative systems (Brisbane – BTS, SEQBRPTS, Adelaide – MATS, Hobart – HATS, Sydney – SATS); give very limited attention to alternative land-use plans (Brisbane, Adelaide, Hobart, Melbourne – MMTS, Sydney); give little attention to rigorous, comprehensive economic evaluation of alternative systems (Brisbane, Hobart; and Adelaide, Sydney and Melbourne in some degree); none has any local empirical data on the public's likely response to the discretionary manipulation of modal choice incentives; and the studies mostly provide only point estimates of future traffic levels without sensitivity tests. What cost–benefit analysis is provided, then, gives only point estimates of cost–benefit ratios (or net present values or internal rates of return) rather than a range of possible ratios with associated probabilities. This is a serious deficiency, and indeed each of the Australian studies is deficient in at least one important way.

The Perth study alone presents a comprehensive analysis of that range of alternative highway/public transport/land-use plans selected for consideration and, moreover, a more detailed rationale is offered for the selection of the (five) particular alternative systems which were considered than is the case in the other studies. We have already commented generally on the predictive models of these studies, but it should further be noted that only PERTS has anything like an aggressive discretionary policy to achieve desired modal split levels (via higher CBD parking charges and improved public transport services), although the Adelaide and Melbourne studies and both Brisbane studies also see reduced road and parking expenditure attributable to improved public transport as a gain. Even Brisbane's public transportation study of 1970, based on the announced urgency of encouraging people to use public transport, combines policies of quality improvements and fare *increases*. Given an average car occupancy for work trips typically in the range of 1.3–1.4, one can see the importance for the

TABLE 1 *Australian transportation studies*

Study and year	Capital cost ($m) recommended	Recommended capital cost ($m) specific to public transport	Overall saving in user costs $m/p.a.	Average length work trips (mins.)	Accident savings	Discount rate	Average car occupancy for work trips
BTS 1965 (Brisbane)	357[1]	8.3	73[3]	14.5 (car)	0.54¢/ vehicle[5] mile	nil	1.33
SEQBRPTS 1970 (Brisbane)	239	239.0	n.g.[4]	13.8 (car, 1960) 36.0 (public transport 1966)	n.g.	nil	1.35
MMTS 1969/70 (Melbourne)	2616	355	n.g.	20 white collar car 16 blue collar car 46 train 30 bus + train	n.g.	3, 4, 5, 7, 10[7]	n.g.
MATS 1968 (Adelaide)	544 + 30 for extra parking facilities	107.5	44[3]	n.g.	[6]	6%	1.27
HATS 1965 (Hobart)	51	nil	9.4[3]	9.1 car 14.7 public transport	0.54¢/ vehicle[5] mile on freeways	nil	1.46
PERTS 1970 (Perth)	398 + 15 for extra CBD parking facilities	51.5	43.6[2]	17	$6250/ casualty	Internal rate of return	1.23 (region) 1.32 (CBD)

TABLE 1 *Australian transportation studies*

Study and year	% Total trips oriented to CBD	Work trips as % of total CBD trips	% Home-based work trips by public transport	Public transport usage (%)	Public transport usage for CBD trips	Expected person trip increases over plan period (%): Car driver	Car passenger	Public transport
BTS 1965 (Brisbane)	35 (1960) 19 (1981)	n.g.	48 (1960)	45 (1960) 30 (1964) 15 (1981)	45[10]	138	99	Fall of 9% bus + train Fall of 4% train
SEQBRPTS 1970 (Brisbane)	25 (1965) 16 (2000)	n.g.	50 (1960)	28 (1968)[8] 25 (1981)	40 (1968)[11]	200 (approx.) Car person trips for Region		145 (approx.) (Region)
MMTS 1969/70 (Melbourne)	18 (1964) 9 (1985)	49 (1964) 51 (1985)	42 (1964)	38 (1964) 22 (1985)	72 (1964) 68 (1968) 60 (1985)	private transport 203		36
MATS 1968 Adelaide)	n.g.	n.g.	44.9 (1965) 44.5 (1986)	20 (1965)	n.g.	107	93	42
HATS 1965 (Hobart)	29 (1964) 23 (1985)	n.g.	31.0 (1968)	26 (1964) 21 (1985)	35 (1964)	139	88	47
PERTS 1970 (Perth)	28 (1966) 14 (1989)	33 (1966)	19 (Region)	n.g.[9]	n.g.	?	n.g.[12]	

Notes to Table 1

1 Thought to be greatly underestimated. This figure is now believed to be closer to $1500m.
2 PERTS also gives the annual operation maintenance and repair costs for the completed plan as $18.31 m/yr. The other studies typically do not provide this figure, though MATS gives an annual maintenance cost of $5000/expressway mile and $3000/arterial mile.
3 No allowance is made for the progressive build up of congestion over time.
4 n.g. = not given.
5 This figure was empirically derived in the USA.
6 Assume freeways will halve the death rate and reduce the injury rate to one-third.
7 As given in Technical Report No. 10 (1970), but not in MMTS itself. It appears that the basic discount rate is felt to be 5–7%.
8 Note that the 1970 public transport report also reveals declining patronage in absolute terms till 1981 – giving consistency with the 1965 forecasts – but then shows a marked increase in absolute numbers.
9 Chapter Five (of PERTS 1970) indicates that public patronage apparently rose by about 14% during 1961–9, however.
10 Note that car person trips to the CBD are expected to rise by 171%, while public transport patronage is expected to fall to 59% of its initial level over the plan period.
11 Table 2.13 (all tables in note refer to SEQBRPTS 1970) gives this as 39.5% on a typical week day in 1968, while table 5.3 gives it as 47.1%! Further, the figure for the year 2000 is given as 44%–48% (for the four alternative plans considered) in table 5.3, but table 5.5 would give a different figure. Also, table 5.5 indicates a 113% increase in public transport trips to and from the CBD, while table 5.3 indicates only an 83% (approx.) increase. Table 5.5 shows 234 190 public transport trips to and from the CBD in 1968, while table 5.3 shows 1 643 000. Paragraph 5.30 is ambiguous as to whether table 5.3 is meant to apply to trips *to and from* the CBD or merely to trips *to* the CBD.
12 Table 10.1 (in PERTS 1970), however, implies an increase of 196% in car vehicle (driver) trips.

Australian state capital cities of fairly exhaustive testing with respect to this modal split issue. SEQBRPTS confines its consideration of parking fee policy to a possible doubling of CBD parking fees by the year 2000, but there is no integrated modal choice study showing the impact on system economics of alternative parking policies, etc. PERTS, on the other hand, studies the impact of alternative CBD parking charges of 68¢/day and $1.20 per day in 1989 (in 1966 prices).

The value of time savings figures as the major benefit in each of the Australian studies accounting, for instance, for annual benefits of $33.6 million out of a total $73 million in the BTS study. The valuation of this benefit has been somewhat arbitrary and highly inconsistent, however, with leisure time valued at 60¢ per hour in the Brisbane and Melbourne studies, 58¢ per hour in Perth, $1.25 per hour in the Adelaide study of 1968, and apparently at about 40¢ per person hour in HATS, where the value is explicitly put at 60¢ per vehicle hour.

It might also be pointed out that even in the PERTS study, the recommended plan was preferred to another plan which actually had higher net economic benefits, on the ground that these 'higher benefits' were achieved via 'undesirably high' parking charges. That is, 'benefits' and 'costs' had been ill-defined and this was not really a higher benefit at all – merely a higher efficiency benefit bought at a still higher intangible (equity) cost. Further, despite the obvious superiority of the economic evaluations in the Perth study over the other Australian studies, PERTS was nonetheless found wanting, and a supplementary Perth Regional Transport Study was produced in 1972, in order to analyse two further plan alternatives which had not been considered in the original 1970 study.

In short, doubts remained about the suitability or optimality of the busway system[38] recommended on the basis of the 1970 comparative evaluation of five possible systems, and further evaluations were called for, which would (*a*) retain the existing suburban rail network while placing the central city station below ground level (thus removing the barrier to the northward expansion of the city); and (*b*) divert the through-city section of the suburban rail line to follow part of the inner-ring freeway, and provide transport links from a new city railway station(s) to the commercial centre. Rail electrification was assumed in both instances, in the interests of stimulating public patronage. This subsequent economic appraisal quickly eliminated the rail diversion alternative, and then confirmed the original busway plan in its pride of place over the 'rail sink' possibility. Certain sensitivity tests were included in this analysis – including the supplementation of the basic 10 per cent discount rate by calculations at rates of 7 per cent and 15 per cent. Capital costs of both rail and bus improvements were allowed to be varied by ±20 per cent, railcar and bus capital operating costs were allowed to vary by ±10 per cent, person time savings by ±50 per cent (reflecting the greater probability of large error in this estimate), and accident cost savings by ±50 per cent. While the busway plan invariably retains its cost–benefit ratio superiority on a case-by-case comparative basis, table 5.13[39] of PERTS–1972 makes it clear that reversals of ranking are not impossible, and a more comprehensive, probabilistic, simulation analysis would have been quite possible and more helpful. We could then compare the probability-profiles of the possible cost–benefit ratio results of the two plans, and attach a probability to the outcome of ranking the Rail Sink plan superior to the re-endorsed busway scheme.[40]

While even the quite comprehensive evaluations in PERTS–1970 could have ranked the original five alternatives differently under a net present value (or other) criterion, and could have given an ogive of probable NPV results, it stands in marked contrast to BTS and HATS, which include no real economic analysis, no appraisal of alternative plans, no discretionary manipulation of the modal split through price–quality policies, no discounting, no sensitivity analysis, no consideration of alternative land-use plans, no attempt to value pollution costs, and only a contentious valuation of time-savings. It is merely claimed by BTS–1965 that a capital investment of $357 million will obviously be justified many times over by direct user benefits of \$73.4 million per year, arising from accident, time and operating cost savings.[41] Similarly, MATS calculated cost–benefit ratios (alone) for four alternative *road* networks (i.e. excluding public transport facilities), without imputing any value to savings of *leisure* time, and then gives its reasons for preferring the recommended plan as that it has (i) the highest cost–benefit ratio (2.67) for the highway improvement element; (ii) the highest annual road-user benefit; and (iii) other cost-oriented advantages, e.g. the MATS–III system has the lowest average annual cost both for public transport improvements and for overall improvements. Plainly enough, these items relate only to particular components of the overall system and do not constitute very meaningful evidence on the economics of the *overall* system (though (ii) and (iii) may have relevance for the investing authority in terms of the ease of financing the alternative schemes under existing institutional arrangements). MATS provides single-value estimates of the annual rail and bus revenues and the number of future passengers with assumed fares 'based on present fare structures'. There is no manipulation of the modal split for a given physical network, no allowance is made for any progressive build up of congestion, and some elements were refined *after* the recommended plan had been selected. The subsequent 'Adelaide Transportation 1970 Report',[42] produced after the rejection of MATS, more fully endorses public transport but does so in a way quite devoid of any analysis.

Brisbane's second study – SEQBRPTS 1970 – considers four alternative public transport systems, but the differences between them are not great, price policy is not regarded as a discretionary determinant of modal split, and there is no cost–benefit analysis of the alternatives. There is no real integration with the earlier 1965 study,[43] and there is certainly no overall cost–benefit evaluation of the combined freeway and public transport recommendations of the two Brisbane studies. It may be noted that despite the professed SEQBRPTS aim of stimulating public transport, patronage does not begin to increase in absolute terms until 1981 (the target year of the 1965 study, and to which date this earlier study saw a continuing public transport decline).

In recommending an amended version of its plan 5 – CBD employment of 90 000 versus 120 000 bus rapid transit versus rail transit, and CBD parking at 68¢ per day versus \$1.20 – PERTS alone explicitly discusses the difference between the perceived cost of private car use (9.1¢/mile) and the real economic cost, including congestion effects (12.8¢/mile), and recognises this as an argument for subsidising public transport.[44]

Something of an inconsistency remains, however, between the PERTS concern to close the gap between the perceived and social costs of car use and its reluctance to recommend plan 5 unamended because of a fear that the higher (\$1.20/day) parking charges of plan 5 will infringe 'personal freedom of choice'.[45] The amendments to plan 5 reduced the internal rate of return from 14.9 per cent to 12.9 per cent.

MMTS states that seven alternative systems were evaluated but no details of economic analysis are provided in MMTS itself. Technical Report No. 10 provides some incomplete cost–benefit analyses of particular system components over a forty year (vs. twenty year) horizon, at discount rates ranging from 3 per cent to 10 per cent. This Technical Report states that the cost–benefit calculations completed to that date have been confined to peak CBD trips. It is not clear what modal choice policies underlie MMTS thinking. MMTS recommended a $2616 million investment in transport facilities, apparently in advance of the completion of the comparative economic analysis.

No real economic evaluation at all is involved in HATS, BTS and SEQBRPTS. The 'less than' ogive in figure 2 shows simulated cost–benefit ratio results for the 1965 Brisbane freeway system.[46] What is needed for decision-making, of course, is a similar ogive for some alternative plan, so as to facilitiate comprehensive comparison. It is apparent from the ogive that there is a 72 per cent chance of the cost–benefit ratio for the freeway system being less than unity, and that the median ratio is approximately 0.84. Note that the ogive is not perfectly symmetrical, its shape reflecting the type of variability in the underlying parameters. This ogive was computed by applying triangular probability distributions to six central parameters relevant to the BTS freeway system (The total number of trips made per day was varied from 1.4 million to 2.6 million, around a most likely value of 1.85 million, while average trip length was allowed to vary from 6.0 miles to 7.2 miles around a most likely value of 6.5 miles. Trip speed, value of travel time, construction costs and discount rate were similarly varied). Should problems of time, expense, or data availability make a detailed analysis of uncertainty impractical, there remains at least a need for greater circumspection in the interpretation of the limited single-value results than has been common in the past.

The Adelaide, Perth and Brisbane 1970 studies all call for the establishment of Regional Transport Authorities – to secure better integration of services – yet their own analyses often reflect a false *institutional separation* between public transport deficits and overall system economics. Hence the SEQBRPTS–1970 concern 'to protect the ratepayer' from increasing operating losses on buses, and thus the rising bus fares in a plan specifically seeking to attract bus patronage. Despite the recommendation of a Single Regional Transport Authority, SEQBRPTS does not free itself from all the policy consequences of present institutional division and parochialism and there is no clear intention that the new Authority be guided by relative price–cost ratios for different modes. Even the aggressive PERTS policies for the manipulation of modal split never include fare *reductions* on public vehicles, although this appears to be basically because it is believed that increased parking costs for private cars will achieve the desired effect, as against a fear of increasing operating deficits.

Regional Transport Authorities, and the adoption of programme budget-

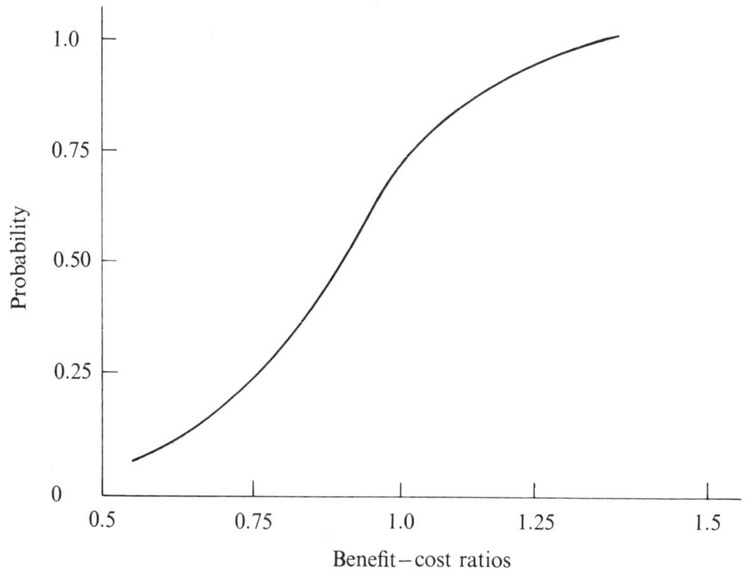

Fig. 2. Less than ogive of possible cost–benefit ratios for the 1965 Brisbane Transportation Plan. (Source: J. Beggs 'Urban Travel Demand' (unpublished B.Com. thesis, University of Queensland, 1973).)

ing systems, would obviously help rationalise what is at present often a foolish system of institutional division. The fragmented institutional structure of the past has (understandably) led the various transport authorities to become preoccupied with their own internal finances, at the cost of neglecting important 'externalities' or interdependencies with other modes of travel. A *single* Regional Transport Authority is obviously much better placed to consider simultaneously *all* the cost (and benefit) elements involved. Given adequate 'external' gains (e.g. reduced 'road needs'), increased bus operating deficits might even be welcomed.

Conclusion

There exists a clear gulf between what has so far been done and what could or should be done, in major metropolitan transportation studies. Two avenues are open in the future. One is the introduction of more rigour to a more comprehensive evaluation of plan alternatives, so as to eliminate the tendency to incorporate predetermined solutions and to allow better for uncertainty. The other is to turn away from the notion of the one big, comprehensive transportation study, committing resources twenty years into the future. A rolling plan which regularly updates data and reviews decision options is clearly necessary, and – in an effort to keep options open and political interference minimal – it may be more reasonable to forgo the consultant-produced studies and use instead the internal resources of highway authorities to plan more flexibly on a corridor by corridor approach. Cynics, of course, have already dismissed the transportation study syndrome as an exercise in confusion, i.e. they see the purpose of such studies as being to produce an impressive report indicative of a weighty study, so as to conceal rather than reveal the processes that really resulted in the final decision-choices, processes that often reflect institutional factors, technological determinism and the 'prevailing ethic'.[47]

In criticising the weaknesses of the economic evaluation in the Australian (and other) transportation studies, one should of course also bear in mind that this economic evidence is not the only evidence, and that it too rests on premises which may not be universally valid. Cost–benefit analysis reflects certain implicit value judgements, which policy-makers may sometimes (reasonably) wish to reject. Nonetheless it is difficult to conceive how trade-offs can easily be made, if their price in terms of the orthodox notion of efficiency is not first known.

Notes

Notes to chapter 2

1 E. J. Mishan, *Cost–Benefit Analysis* (Allen and Unwin, London, 1971).
2 E. J. Mishan (1971).
3 See for example: I. M. D. Little, *A Critique of Welfare Economics*, 2nd edn (Oxford University Press, Oxford, 1957), ch. 11; H. M. Kolsen, *The Economics of Road–Rail Competition* (Sydney University, Press. Sydney, 1968), ch. 2.
4 See for example: E. J. Mishan (1971); Ajit K. Dasgupta and D. W. Pearce, *Cost Benefit Analysis: Theory and Practice* (Macmillan, London, 1972).
5 G. J. Ponsonby, *Transport Policy: Co-ordination Through Competition*, Hobart Paper No. 49 (Institute of Economic Affairs, London, 1969).
6 See further: M. E. Beesley, *Urban Transport: Studies in Economic Policy* (Butterworths, London, 1973), ch. 10, esp. 322–5.
7 One of the best examples is still the frequently quoted article by C. Foster and M. Beesley, 'Estimating the Social Benefit of Constructing an Underground Railway in London', *Journal of the Royal Statistical Society* (1963).
8 See further: H. M. Kolsen (1968), 62–9.
9 See M. E. Beesley, 'Regulation of Taxis', *Economic Journal* (1973).
10 One of the earliest and most comprehensive arguments for this was given by A. A. Walters in the 'Theory and Measurement of Private and Social Cost of Highway Congestion', *Econometrica* (1961), reprinted in D. Mundy (ed.), *Transport* (Penguin, London, 1968); A recent summary appears in M. E. Beesley, *Urban Transport: Studies in Economic Policy* (Butterworths, London, 1973), ch. 9.
11 See further: M. E. Beesley *Economic Journal* (1973) and H. M. Kolsen, 'The Taxi-Cab Industry in Sydney', *Economic Monograph No. 280*, Economic Society of Australia and New Zealand, NSW. Branch (1966).
12 See further: Kolsen (1968), 40–4, 77–80.
13 R. Sherman, 'Congestion Interdependence and Urban Traffic Congestion', *Journal of Transport Economics and Policy* (1972).

Notes to chapter 3

1 F. P. Ramsey, 'A Contribution to the Theory of Taxation', *Economic Journal* (1927).
2 P. Diamond and J. A. Mirrlees, 'Optimal Taxation and Public Production', *American Economic Review* (March and June 1971).
3 M. Boiteux, 'Sur La Gestion des Monopoles Publics astreints a l'equilibre Budgetaire', *Econometrica* (1956), Translated as 'On the Management of Public Monopolies subject to Budget Constraints', *Journal of Economic Theory* (1971).
4 A. A. Walters, *The Economics of Road User Charges* (World Bank Occasional Paper, No. 5, Baltimore, 1968), ch. 4, appendix.

5 A. M. Henderson, 'The Pricing of Public Utilities', *Manchester School* (September 1947).
6 M. S. Feldstein, 'Equity and Efficiency in Public Sector Pricing: The Optimal Two Part Tariff', *Quarterly Journal of Economics* (1972).
7 W. Oi, 'A Disneyland Dilemma: Two Part Tariffs for a Mickey Mouse Monopoly', *Quarterly Journal of Economics* (1971).
8 M. S. Feldstein, 'Distributional Equity and the Optimal Structure of Public Prices', *American Economic Review* (March 1972).
9 See W. Baumol and W. Bradford, 'Optimal Departures from Marginal Cost Pricing', *American Economic Review* (1970).
10 As does British Rail to an extent, see S. Joy, 'Pricing and Investment in Railway Freight Services', *Journal of Transport Economics and Policy (1971).*
11 Except, for example A. A. Walters (1968).
12 For example, see C. D. Foster, *The Transport Problem*, revised edn. (Croom Helm, London, 1975).
13 For example see H. M. Kolsen, *The Economics and Control of Road-Rail Competition* (Sydney University Press, Sydney, 1968), ch. 2.
14 Information on the UK situation can be found in the Transport Act, 1968, and the Local Government Act, 1972.
15 For example, Pigou accepted the general desirability of using such taxes to affect distribution, but considered them to be too blunt an instrument for practical application. A. C. Pigou, *A Study in Public Finance* (Macmillan, London, 1947), ch. IX.
16 See A. B. Atkinson and J. Stiglitz, 'The Structure of Indirect Taxation and Economic Efficiency', *Journal of Public Economics* (1972).
17 For example, W. Baumol and W. Bradford (1970). For a concise analysis of some of the issues see A. K. Dixit, 'On the Optimum Structure of Commodity Taxes', *American Economic Review*, (1970), and also A. P. Lerner, 'On Optimal Taxes with an Untaxable Sector', *American Economic Review* (1970).
18 See A. A. Walters (1968).
19 See W. Baumol and W. Bradford (1970). R. Rees has developed a model which analyses the implications of a budget constraint along with other second-best difficulties, though the results become quite complex. See R. Rees, 'Second Best Rules for Public Enterprise Pricing', *Economica* (August 1968).
20 See A. B. Atkinson and J. Stiglitz (1972).
21 See P. Diamond and J. A. Mirrlees (1971). See also F. Hahn, 'On Optimum Taxation', *Journal of Economic Theory* (1973).
22 Which state that a second-best solution may require all conditions for first-best optimisation to be violated. See R. G. Lipsey and K. J. Lancaster, 'The General Theory of Second Best', *Review of Economic Studies* (1956–7).
23 M. S. Feldstein, 'The Pricing of Public Intermediate Goods', *Journal of Public Economics* (1972).
24 J. Stiglitz and P. Das Gupta, 'Differential Taxation, Public Goods and Economic Efficiency', *Review of Economic Studies* (1971).
25 See M. S. Feldstein, 'The Pricing of Public Intermediate Goods' (1972), 57.
26 *Ibid.*, 58.
27 W. J. Corlett and D. C. Hague, 'Complementarity and the Excess Burden of Taxation', *Review of Economic Studies* (1953).
28 For example, by P. Diamond and J. A. Mirrlees (1971) and A. B. Atkinson and J. Stiglitz (1972).
29 M. S. Feldstein, 'Distributional Equity and the Optimal Structure of Public Prices' (March 1972).
30 M. S. Feldstein, 'The Pricing of Public Intermediate Goods' (1972).
31 For example, Baumol and Bradford, quote the results approvingly, and justify railway pricing policies in terms of them.

Notes to chapter 4

1 K. J. Arrow and T. Scitovsky (eds.), *Readings in Welfare Economics* (Allen and Unwin, London, 1969), 1. A useful outline of the major issues in welfare economics is given in D. M. Winch, *Analytical Welfare Economics* (Penguin, London, 1971).

2 For example, E. J. Mishan. *Cost-Benefit Analysis* (Allen and Unwin, London, 1971); R. Layard (ed.), *Cost–Benefit Analysis* (Penguin, London, 1972); and Ajit K. Dasgupta and D. W. Pearce, *Cost–Benefit Analysis: Theory and Practice* (Macmillan, London, 1971).

3 M. S. Feldstein, 'The Inadequacy of Weighted Discount Rates' in Layard (ed.). (1972).

4 The whole question is discussed in A. K. Sen, 'On Optimising the Rate of Saving', *Economic Journal* (1961).

5 W. J. Baumol, 'On the Social Rate of Discount', *American Economic Review* (1968), 788–802.

6 K. J. Arrow and R. C. Lind, 'Uncertainty and the Evaluation of Public Investment Decisions', *American Economic Review* (1970), 364–78.

7 E. J. Mishan, 'Uncertainty and the Evaluation of Public Investment Decisions: Comment', *American Economic Review* (1972), 161–4.

8 S. A. Marglin, 'The Social Rate of Discount and the Optimal Rate of Investment', *Quarterly Journal of Economics* (1963), and *Public Investment Criteria* (Allen and Unwin, London, 1967).

9 E. J. Mishan, 'Uncertainty and the Evaluation of Public Investment Decisions: Comment'.

10 R. F. F. Dawson, 'The Economic Assessment of Road Improvement Schemes', *Road Research Technical Paper No. 75* (HMSO 1968), 9.

11 For a good discussion of this see R. Millward, 'Road Investment Criteria', *Journal of Transport Economics and Policy* (1968), 183–200.

12
$$V = C_0 + \frac{B_1 - C_1}{(1 + r)} + \ldots + \frac{B_n - C_n}{(1 + r)n}$$

where B_1 = gross benefit in period 1
C_1 = cost in period 1
V = net present value
r = discount rate
When $V = 0$, r = internal rate of return.

13 There is a considerable literature on the relative merits of IRR and NPV. See, for example, R. Turvey, 'Present value versus internal rate of return – an essay in the theory of the third best', *Economic Journal* (1963); and M. S. Feldstein and J. S. Flemming, 'The problem of time-stream evaluation: present value versus internal rate of return rules', *Bulletin of Oxford University Institute of Economics and Statistics* (1964). See also n. 5.

14 R. F. F. Dawson (1968).

15 E. J. Mishan, 'A Proposed Normalisation Procedure for Public Investment Criteria', *Economic Journal* (1967), 777–96; E. J. Mishan, 'Normalisation of Public Investment Criteria: Erratum', *Economic Journal* (1969), 980; and E. J. Mishan, 'A Normalisation Procedure for Public Investment Criteria: A Reply', *Economic Journal* (1971), 125–9. See also E. J. Mishan, *Cost–Benefit Analysis* (1971). Chapters 3–6 of this book deal with the topic adequately and are somewhat easier reading than the articles.

16 N. Lichfield, 'Cost-Benefit Analysis in Town Planning: A Case Study, Swanley', *Urban Studies* (November 1966); N. Lichfield, 'Cost-Benefit Analysis in Urban Expansion: A Case Study, Ipswich', *Urban Studies* (June 1970).

17 Economists have traditionally been wary of making interpersonal comparisons but Lichfield says of his method 'there is not much hesitation' in making the comparisons. N. Lichfield (1966), 223.

18 For a pertinent comment see W. H. Rahmann, 'The Theory of Benefit and Cost Measurement – A Note', *Australian Road Research* (December, 1973).
19 J. E. Meade, 'External Economies and Diseconomies in a Competitive Stituation', *Economic Journal* (1952), reprinted in K. J. Arrow and T. Scitovsky (eds.) (1969).
20 A. K. Dasgupta and D. W. Pearce (1972).
21 R. H. Coase, 'The Problem of Social Cost', *Journal of Law and Economics* (1960), 1–44.
22 E. J. Mishan, *Cost–Benefit Analysis* (1971), 111.
23 For example, by E. V. Morgan and A. D. Morgan, *The Economics of Public Policy* (Edinburgh University Press, Edinburgh, 1972), 37.
24 J. W. Knowles, 'Cost-Benefit Analysis of Railway Closures: The Criterion and Other Points', *Chartered Institute of Transport Journal* (November 1972), 34.
25 N. Kaldor, 'Welfare Propositions of Economics and Interpersonal Comparisons of Utility', *Economic Journal* (1939) 549–52.
26 See Little's criticism of this. I. M. D. Little, *A Critique of Welfare Economics* 2nd edn (Clarendon Press, Oxford, 1957).
27 See, for example, the recent controversies over expressways displacing housing in inner-city areas and the case of the second Sydney Airport – which it is proposed to build in an area favoured by middle-class executives for residence. These people form a large proportion of the air travellers. It is argued that till now the pollution effects of Sydney's air traffic have been borne by low-income groups who can rarely afford air travel themselves.
28 This aspect is discussed in J. K. Stanley, T. M. Hogg and D. J. Delaney, 'The Theory of Benefit and Cost Measurement, With Reference to Residential Disruption Costs of Urban Road Improvements', *Australian Road Research* (June 1973), 23–35.

Notes to chapter 5

1 A. Williams, 'Cost–Benefit Analysis: Bastard Science? And/or Insidious Poison in the Body Politick', *Journal of Public Economics* (1972), 199–226.
2 The arguments contained in this section are developed in greater detail in C. A. Nash, D. W. Pearce and J. K. Stanley, 'An Evaluation of Cost–Benefit Analysis Criteria', *Scottish Journal of Political Economy* (June 1975).
3 H. Neuburger, 'User Benefit in the Evaluation of Transport and Land-Use Plans', *Journal of Transport Economics and Policy*, vol. 5 (1971), 52–75.
4 The concept of averaging is not difficult if one favours the approach we suggested earlier of evaluating projects as if all affected persons had mean income. Practical problems of measurement still exist, however.
5 C. A. Nash, *Public versus Private Transport* (Macmillan, London. 1976).
6 C. A. Nash, 'The Treatment of Capital Costs of Vehicles in Evaluating Road Schemes', *Transportation* (1974), 255–262.
7 D. A. Hensher, *The Consumer's Choice Function: A Study of Travellers' Behaviour and Values*, unpublished PhD Thesis, School of Economics, University of New South Wales, (October 1972) and D. A. Hensher, 'Valuation of Commuter Travel Time Savings: An Alternative Procedure'. *Travel Time and Travel Choice* (ed. I. G. Heggie), (Oxford University Press, Oxford, 1976).
8 H. Neuburger, 'Perceived Costs', *Environment and Planning* (1971), 369–76.
9 R. Albert Berry, 'A Note on Welfare Comparisons Between Monopoly and Pure Competition', *Manchester School* (1971), 39–57.
10 H. Hotelling, 'The General Welfare in Relation to Problems of Taxation and of Railway Utility Rates', *Econometrica* (1938), 242–69.
11 H. Neuburger, 'User Benefit in the Evaluation of Transport and Land-Use Plans'.
12 P. J. McIntosh and D. A. Quarmby, 'Generalised Costs and the Estimation of Movement Costs and Benefits in Transport Planning', *Highway Research Record No. 383*, Washington DC, Highway Research Board (1972).

13 H. Neuburger, 'User Benefit in the Evaluation of Transport and Land-Use Plans'. A case study in which just such a misuse of traffic forecasts occurred is discussed in D. W. Pearce and C. A. Nash, 'The Evaluation of Urban Motorway Schemes: A Case Study – Southampton', *Urban Studies* (1973), 129–43.

14 See D. W. Pearce and C. A. Nash.

15 Even vacant urban land is frequently used for recreational purposes. Although methods have been derived for valuing recreational facilities it is doubtful whether they could be applied to purely local facilities of this nature and they have not been to date. See M. Clawson and J. Knetsch, *Economics of Outdoor Recreation* (Johns Hopkins Press, Baltimore, 1966) on methods of valuing recreational land.

16 A. Downs, 'Uncompensated Non-Construction Costs which Urban Highways and Urban Renewal Impose Upon Residential Households', in J. Margolis (ed.), *The Analysis of Public Output*, New York, National Bureau of Economic Research (1970).

17 Urban transport improvement frequently demolishes older property, forcing those displaced to move to newer, more expensive housing. Similarly, long-standing tenants may enjoy rents below current market levels.

18 It may be of interest to note that the UK government can pay a house-loss payment to occupiers of compulsorily acquired property who have been resident there for more than seven years as compensation for the 'psychic' costs of leaving.

19 See, for example, A. D. Flowerdew, 'Choosing a Site for the Third London Airport: The Roskill Commission's Approach', in R. Layard (ed.), *Cost–Benefit Analysis* (Penguin, London, 1972).

20 E. J. Mishan, 'What is Wrong with Roskill?', *Journal of Transport Economics and Policy* (1970), 221–34; M. Whitbread and H. Bird, 'Rent, Surplus and the Evaluation of Residential Environments'. *Regional Studies* (1973), 193–223.

21 E. J. Mishan, 'Evaluation of Life and Limb: A Theoretical Approach', *Journal of Political Economy* (1971), 687–705.

22 D. J. Reynolds, 'The Costs of Road Accidents', *Journal of the Royal Statistical Society, Series A (General)*, vol. 119 (1956), 393–408.

23 R. F. F. Dawson, *Cost of Road Accidents in Great Britain*, Report LR79, Crowthorne, Road Research Laboratory (1967).

24 E. J. Mishan (1971).

25 R. F. F. Dawson, *Current Cost of Road Accidents in Great Britain*, Report LR309, Crowthorne, Road Research Laboratory (1971). A naive defence of this approach might take the following lines: zero consumption (i.e. death) implies zero utility, so that if the objective function is to maximise the sum of utilities, the loss of utility due to the lost consumption of the victim is the cost of his death.

26 T. C. Schelling, 'The Life You Save May be Your Own', in S. B. Chase (ed.), *Problems in Public Expenditure Analysis*. (Washington DC, Brookings Institute 1968).

27 M. Jones-Lee, 'Valuation of Reduction in Probability of Death by Road Accident', *Journal of Transport Economics and Policy* (1969), 37–47.

28 See A. Williams (1972).

29 P. M. S. Jones, 'The Use of Cost–Benefit Analysis as an Aid to Allocating Government Resources for Research and Development', in J. N. Wolfe (ed.), *Cost–Benefit and Cost–Effectiveness* (Allen and Unwin, London, 1973).

30 Cost-effectiveness analysis of past government expenditures on accident prevention measures usually suggests that the more spectacular and public the death is likely to be, the more expense the government is likely to incur to prevent the death.

31 A. Lassiere and P. Bowers, 'Studies on the Social Costs of Urban Road Transport (Noise and Pollution)', *Report of the Eighteenth Round Table on Transport Economics* (ECMT, 1972).

32 R. Ridker, *The Economic Cost of Air Pollution* (Praeger, New York, 1966).

33 D. N. M. Starkie and D. M. Johnson. 'Loss of Residential Amenity: An Extended Cost Model', *Regional Studies* (1973), 173–81.

34 E. J. Mishan (1970).
35 D. W. Pearce, 'The Economic Evaluation of Noise-Generating and Noise-Abatement Policies', in *Problems of Environmental Economics* (OECD, Paris, 1972).
36 J. Diffey, 'An Investigation Into the Effect of High Traffic Noise on House Prices in a Homogenous Sub-Market', London, Centre for Environmental Studies (1971).
37 C. A. Nash, D. W. Pearce and J. K. Stanley.
38 Harsanyi (1955) distinguishes between 'subjective' preferences, what a person actually prefers, and 'ethical' preferences, preferences based on impersonal social considerations alone. J. Harsanyi, 'Cardinal Welfare, Individualistic Ethics and Interpersonal Comparisons of Utility', *Journal of Political Economy* (1955), 309–21.
39 C. A. Nash, D. W. Pearce and J. K. Stanley.
40 C. A. Nash, 'Future Generations and the Social Rate of Discount', *Environment and Planning* (1973), 611–17.
41 S. J. Bellomo and S. C. Lockwood, 'Metropolitan Transportation and Land Use Planning, An Evaluation', Paper presented at *University of Southampton Conference on Transportation and Environment – Policies, Plans and Practice*, Session 5 (April 1973).
42 We ignore social considerations which are rightly part of the evaluation process, but which are discussed in ch. 12.
43 B. Weisbrod, 'Collective Consumption Services of Individual Consumption Goods', *Quarterly Journal of Economics* (1964), 471–7.
44 K. M. Gwilliam, 'Economic Evaluation of Urban Transport Projects: The State of the Art', *Transportation Planning and Technology* (1972), 123–42.
45 J. R. Meyer, J. F. Kain and M. Wohl, *The Urban Transportation Problem* (Harvard University Press, Cambridge, Mass., 1965).
46 A. K. Dasgupta and D. W. Pearce, *Cost–Benefit Analysis: Theory and Practice* (Macmillan, London, 1972).
47 A. R. Prest and R. Turvey, 'Cost–Benefit Analysis: A Survey', *Economic Journal*, vol. 75 (1965), 685–705.
48 This holds with even greater force to evaluation in some other sectors of the economy. It is only because the concept of evaluation has well and truly arrived in transport that it is possible to be critical.
49 A. J. Harrison, 'Transport: A Case Study', Paper given at the Royal Economic Society Conference on *Resource Allocation in the Public Sector* (Cambridge, 1974).
50 S. P. C. Plowden, 'Transportation Studies Examined', *Journal of Transport Economics and Policy* (1967), 5–27.

Notes to chapter 6

1 See ch. 12, and R. Lane, T. Powell and P. Smith, *Analytical Transport Planning* (Duckworth, London, 1971). Analytical Transport Planning is a science developed to attempt to predict travel patterns in different areas with different transport systems.
2 The urban transport modelling system as a Newtonian analogue is discussed below and in ch. 12. A discussion of research into the fundamental basis for applying the Gravity-law-type-of-forecasting models is given by A. G. Wilson, *Entropy in Urban and Regional Modelling* (Pion, London, 1970).
3 This interaction is described in M. Wohl, *Transportation Investment Planning* (Lexington Books, Massachusetts, 1972), ch. 3, 37–61.
4 The phrase 'urban passenger transport' should be interpreted broadly to include considerations of all 'phases' of the demand process, and hence includes overall travel (number of trips over a given period of time, for example) as well as direct modal issues.
5 While such sensitivity parameter estimates might be the 'best' available operational tools, they are frequently of restrictive use because of an inability to extend reliably beyond the standard deviation of the mean value of a variable associated with the present level of usage. The empirical derivation of elasticities is illustrated in A. Talvitie, 'A

Direct Demand Model for Downtown Work Trips', *Transportation* (1973). The derivation and use of direct probability estimates is illustrated in F. X. DeDonnea, *The Determinants of Transport Mode Choice in Dutch Cities* (Rotterdam University Press, Louvain, 1971).

6 Behavioural theory refers to notions of user and non-user decision-processes leading to acts of choice.

7 This phrase was coined by Van Praag. B. Van Praag, *Individual Welfare Functions and Consumer Behaviour* (North-Holland, Amsterdam, 1968), 24. See also S. B. Linder, *The Harried Leisure Class* (Columbia University Press, New York, 1971).

8 See S. Hansen, 'Behavioural Structure of Disaggregate Choice Models', *Issues in Behavioural Travel Demand Modelling and the Valuation of Travel Time*, Transportation Research Board Special Report (Washington DC, August 1974).

9 D. W. Katzner, *Static Demand Theory* (Collier-Macmillan, New York, 1970), 163–4.

10 A recursive structure is a dependency relationship that is uni-directional.

11 H. Neuburger, 'Transport Demand Models', Department of the Environment (London, 1972), appendix (mimeo).

12 See R. E. Quandt (ed.), *The Demand for Travel: Theory and Measurement* (D. C. Heath and Company, Lexington, 1970), chs. 4–9.

13 The research of Charles River Associates is the major contribution along these lines. Charles River Associates, *A Disaggregated Behavioural Model of Urban Travel Demand*, US Department of Transportation (Washington DC, March 1972).

14 The major work in the area is Moshe E. Ben-Akiva, 'Multi-Dimensional Choice Models: Alternative Structures of Travel Demand Models', *Issues in Behavioural Travel Demand Modeling and the Valuation of Travel Time*, Special Report of the Transportation Research Board (Washington DC, August 1974).

15 H. John Green, *Consumer Theory* (Penguin, London, 1971), 150–6.

16 D. A. Hensher, 'Perception and Commuter Mode Choice – An Hypothesis', *Urban Studies* (February 1975).

17 Moshe E. Ben-Akiva, The Structure of Passenger Travel Demand, unpublished PhD Thesis, Department of Civil Engineering, MIT (July 1973), 25.

18 D. Brand, 'Separable vs. Simultaneous Travel Choice Behaviour', *Issues in Behavioural Travel Demand Modeling and the Valuation of Travel Time*. Special Report of the Transportation Research Board (Washington DC, August 1974).

19 Brand (1974), 17.

20 Ben-Akiva (1973) 140.

21 Charles River Associates, *A Model of Urban Passenger Travel Demand in the San Francisco Metropolitan Area*, Report prepared for the California Division of Bay Toll Crossings (Cambridge, Mass., December 1967); R. P. Plourde, *Consumer Preference and the Abstract Mode Model*, Boston Metropolitan Area, Research Report R68-51, Department of Civil Engineering, MIT (Cambridge, Mass., 1968); A Talvite (1973). L. E. Shepherd, 'An Econometric Approach to the Demand for Urban Passenger Travel', *Australian Road Research Board Proceedings* (1972), 214–45.

22 Ben-Akiva (1973), 165 n. 3.

23 C. R. Fleet and S. R. Robertson, 'Trip Generation in the Transportation Planning Process', *Highway Research Record No. 240* (1968).

24 P. L. Watson 'A Comparison of the Model Structure and Predictive Power of Aggregate and Disaggregate Models of Inter-City Mode Choice', Paper presented at 53rd Annual meeting of the Transportation Research Board (Washington DC, January 1974).

25 Watson (1974), 8.

26 The importance of relative travel time has only been completely ascertained for journeys to and from work. The evidence for non-work trips is not conclusive either way.

27 A. J. Harrison and D. A. Quarmby, 'The Value of Time in Transport Planning – A Review', *Cost–Benefit Analysis* (ed. R. A. Layard) (Penguin, London, 1972); and D. A. Hensher, 'Review of Studies Leading to Existing Values of Travel Time' *Valuation of*

Travel Time, Transportation Research Board Special Report (Washington DC, January 1976).

28 Two important references on the allocation of time as a scarce resource are Linder (1971); and Alan W. Evans, 'On the Theory of Valuation and Allocation of Time', *Scottish Journal of Political Economy* (February 1972).

29 P. B. Goodwin has recently suggested that the generalised cost of travel should also include 'effort' to represent those effects experienced over time which should not be identified with time, such as the use of an irregular and uncertain service and the penalties associated with transfer from one vehicle to another. Physiological units of measurement such as pulse rate are suggested as possible dimensions for quantification. P. B. Goodwin, 'Time Effort and Money: Three Components of the Generalised Cost of Travel', *Journal of Transport Economies and Policy* (1976);

30 N. A. Bruzelius, *Economic Theories of the Allocation of Time–A Survey*, unpublished MSocSc thesis, Department of Industrial Economies and Business Studies, University of Birmingham (October 1972).

31 Hansen has pointed out that Bruzelius's model is special in the sense that simultaneous consumption of several goods such as reading the newspaper on the train at least need special definition of goods and activities, in order to be covered by Bruzelius's model: Hansen (1974); and Richard Muth, 'Household Production and Consumer Demand Functions', *Econometrica* (1966).

32 The developments in the theory of time allocation can be traced through: G. M. Becker, 'A Theory of the Allocation of Time', *Economic Journal* (1965); DeDonnea (1971), ch. 2; A. C. DeSerpa, 'A Theory of the Economics of Time', *Economic Journal* (1971); Evans, (1972); C. J. Oort, 'The Evaluation of Travelling Time', *Journal of Transport Economics and Policy* (1969); C. J. Phillips, 'Valuing Travel Time: Some Implications of Recent Theories', *Time Research Note No. 10*, Department of the Environment (London, 1969).

33 An alternative interpretation is – associated with each level of t, there is a maximum amount of x_i, but the consumer may choose a lower level.

34 The Lagrangeian function is:

$$L = U(x_1, \ldots, x_n, t_1, \ldots, t_n, t_w)$$
$$-\lambda(\Sigma p_i x_i - wt_w - y_{ex}) - \mu(\Sigma t_i + t_w - T) - \Sigma k_i g_i(x_i, t_i)$$

λ is the marginal utility of income, k_i is the marginal loss in utility per unit of x_i from increasing the minimum required time per unit of good *i* in an activity *i*. μ is the marginal utility of time as a resource.

35 DeSerpa (1971), 834.

36 D. G. Tipping, 'Time Savings in Transport Studies', *Economic Journal* (1968).

37 A. C. DeSerpa (1971), 833.

38 For example, D. A. Quarmby, 'Choice of Travel Mode for the Journey to Work: Some Findings', *Journal of Transport Economics and Policy* (1967).

39 For example, T. C. Thomas, *The Value of Time for Passenger Cars: An Experimental Approach*, Final Report, vol. II, Stanford Research Institute (May 1967).

40 A number of studies have found that estimates of the value of travel time savings based on the sample as a whole differ significantly from those attained when the analysis is confined to a sample consisting exclusively of traders. See D. A. Hensher, *The Consumer's Choice Function: A Study of Traveller Behaviour and Values*, unpublished PhD thesis, School of Economics, University of New South Wales (October 1972).

41 This assumption was either implicitly or explicitly adopted in the studies by M. E. Beesley (UK), Local Government Operation Research Unit (UK) and D. A. Hensher, (Australia): M. E. Beesley 'The Value of Time Spent Travelling: Some New Evidence', *Economica* (May 1965); Hensher (1972); Local Government Operational Research Unit, *Modal Choice and the Value of Time*, Report No. C. 143 Reading (1973).

42 With suitable specification, both time-dependent (e.g. in-vehicle) and non-time-dependant (e.g. boarding a bus) components of effort can be incorporated.

43 The details of the empirical study are given in Charles River Associates (1972), ch. 6.

44 The socio-economic variables are standard transportation study data: number of residents in a household, number of residents in household 5 years and older, cars per household, family gross income, race, number of workers per household, number of licensed drivers per household, occupation of head of the household and of the tripmaker, sex and age of head of the household and of the tripmaker, employment by industry by traffic zone of the tripmaker. Four dummy variables were constructed out of the basic variables:
1. $D_1 = 0$ if no car; otherwise $D_1 = 1$.
2. $D_2 = 0$ if number of cars is less than number of workers; otherwise $D_2 = 1$.
3. $D_3 = 0$ if number of cars is less than number of licensed drivers; otherwise $D_3 = 1$.
4. $D_4 = D_2D_3$.

45 The various procedures are documented and tested in A. Talvitie, 'Comparison of Probabilistic Modal-Choice Models: Estimation Methods and System Inputs', *Highway Research Record No. 392* (1972); P. R. Stopher and J. O. Lavender, 'Disaggregate, Behavioral Travel Demand Models: Empirical Tests of Three Hypothesis', *USA Transportation Research Forum Proceedings* (1972); and D. A. Hensher, 'A Probabilistic Disaggregate Model of Mode Choice', in D. A. Hensher (ed.), *Urban Travel Choice and Demand Models*, Australian Road Research Board, Special Report no. 12 (Melbourne, August 1974).

46 For example Hensher (1972); C. A. Lave 'A Behavioral Approach to Modal Split Forecasting', *Transportation Research* (December 1969); and P. R. Stopher and A. H. Meyburg, 'The Role of Socioeconomic Variables in Studies of Mode Choice', *Transportation and Traffic Theory* (ed. D. J. Buckley), Proceedings of 6th International Symposium on Transportation and Traffic Theory (Sydney, August 1974).

47 D. McFadden, 'Conditional Logit Analysis of Qualitative Choice Behavior', *Frontiers in Econometrics* (Academic Press, New York, 1973), 105–42.

48 Charles River Associates (1972), chs. 7, 39.

49 Ben-Akiva (1973), 183–4.

50 L. E. Shepherd, 'A Probabilistic Aggregate Travel Demand Model' in D. A. Hensher (ed.), *Urban Travel Choice and Demand Models*, Australian Road Research Board (Melbourne, August 1974).

Notes to chapter 7

1 OECD, *Future Directions for Research in Urban Transportation* (Paris, 1969), 14.

2 Department of Transportation, US, *National Transportation Report* (Washington DC, 1972), 244.

3 S. L. Edwards, 'Transport Cost in British Industry', *Journal of Transport Economics and Policy* (1970); Department of Transportation, US (1972), 71.

4 R. S. Wallace, *A Domestic Multi-Modal Goods Distribution Model with Emphasis on Air Cargo*, PhD dissertation, Department of Civil Engineering, University of Waterloo, Ontario (1971), cited in B. G. Hutchinson, 'Estimating Urban Goods Movement Demands, *Paper to 53rd Annual Meeting, Highway Research Board* (Washington DC, 1974).

5 Bayliss cites a British study which showed that 'only in a small percentage of cases was the operator on own account aware of his transport costs'. Knowledge of costs by holders of 'C' licences for ancillary carriage (abolished by the 1968 Transport Act) was:

No accurate information on costs	31%
Knowledge only of overall costs from accounts	47%
Knowledge of overall ton/mile costs	12%
Knowledge of particular tone/mile costs on certain journeys	4%
Operating costs of each vehicle related to items carried	6%
	100%

See B. T. Bayliss, *European Transport* (Kenneth Mason, London, 1965), 31–2.

6 K. W. Ogden, 'Issues in Urban Goods Movement Planning', *Proceedings of the Seventh Australian Road Research Board Conference* (Adelaide, 1974). The data are derived from the 1964 Melbourne Transportation Survey. The daily route distance travelled is here given as the straight-line distance between points of origin and destination.

7 J. H. Marino, 'Urban Goods Movement: The Key to Improved Transportation Productivity', *Transportation Research Forum, Proceedings, Fourteenth Annual Meeting* (1973), 275.

8 See, for example: Ministry of Transport, Great Britain, *Road Track Costs: A report by the Ministry of Transport*, HMSO (London, 1968); J. C. Oehmann and S. F. Bielak, *Allocation of Cost Responsibility and Tax Payments, 1969*, Bureau of Public Roads, US Department of Transportation; *Report of the Board of Inquiry into the Victorian Land Transport System* (Melbourne, 1972); and Z. Haritos, *Rational Road Pricing Policies in Canada*, Canadian Transport Commission (Ottawa, 1973).

9 A semitrailer 14.5 metres by 2.5 metres, when making a 90° turn, sweeps a path more than 6 metres wide. See National Association of Australian State Road Authorities, 'A Study of the Economics of Road Vehicle Limits: Report on Concepts and Procedures', *NAASRA Study Team Report R-1* (Melbourne, 1974), 60.

10 Charles River Associates, *Competition between Rail and Truck in Intercity Freight Transportation*, Study Prepared for the US Department of Transportation (Cambridge, Mass., 1969), 69.

11 See G. Sharp, *Living with the Lorry: A Study of Goods Vehicles in the Environment*, Feight Transport Association (London, 1973).

12 This suggestion was made by Dr A. Hitchcock of the Transport and Road Research Laboratory, UK whose perceptive discussion with the author on this topic is gratefully acknowledged.

13 P. Hallstrom, 'A New System for Solid Waste Disposal', in OECD, *The Urban Movement of Goods*, Proceedings of the Third Technology Assessment Review (Paris, 1970).

14 See C. B. Lewis, 'Applications of New Technology to the Transport of Urban Goods'; and A. E. J. Morris, 'Automated Household Goods Distribution System as Proposed for the New Town of Etarea, Czechoslovakia', in OECD (1970).

15 E. J. Mishan, *The Costs of Economic Growth* (Penguin, London, 1969), 129.

16 Marino (1973).

17 The scheme is described in J. D. C. Churchill, 'Operation Moondrop': An Experiment in Out of Hours Goods Delivery', OECD (1970).

18 Ibid., 138.

19 The Heavy Commercial Vehicles (Controls and Regulations) Act of 1973, usually referred to as the 'Dykes Act' in deference to the Member of Parliament who sponsored it as a Private Member's Bill.

20 See, for example, A. A. Walters, 'The Theory and Measurement of Private and Social Cost of Highway Congestion', *Econometrica* (1961), reprinted in D. Munby (ed.), *Transport: Selected Readings* (Penguin, London, 1968).

21 On the customary assumption that the relevant ranges of the demand and supply (cost) curves are not vertically sloped.

22 The CRISTAL planning model for London assumes the average travelling time cost per person-hour for car occupants to be 20p and for crew members of goods vehicles to be 75p. See J. C. Tanner, L. Gyenes, D. A. Lynam, S. V. Magee and A. H. Tulpule, 'Development and Calibration of the CRISTAL Transport Planning Model', *TRRL Report LR 574*, Crowthorne, Transport and Road Research Laboratory (1973).

23 The CRISTAL model assumes an elasticity of demand of −1.5 for cars and −0.6 for trucks. See Tanner *et al.* (1973).

24 S. N. Jacobi, 'The Use of Economic Incentives to Relieve Urban Traffic Congestion', *Paper to 45th ANZAAS Congress* (Perth, 1973).

25 The more expensive 'luxury' items, such as televisions and diamond rings, usually have

only a small proportion of their price made up by transport costs. Road levies on the transport of these items would thus make only a relatively small difference in their price.

26 L. E. Keefer, 'Trucks at Rest', in 'Origin and Destination Techniques and Evaluations', *Highway Research Record No. 41* (Washington DC, 1963); and J. D. Decker, 'Truck Movement in Urban Areas', in OECD (1970). Generally, the heavier the truck the more likely it is to be in operation at any time of the day: Wilbur Smith and Associates, *Motor Trucks in the Metropolis* (New Haven, Conn, 1969), 56.

27 Wilbur Smith and Associates (1969), 54.

28 Decker in OECD (1970), 144.

29 Transportation Branch, Greater London Council, *Goods Vehicles in Town Centres*, a digest of Metra Consulting Group's report 'Study of Generation of Goods Vehicles in Selected Town Centres' prepared for the Greater London Council (London, 1971), 2.

30 Barnstead, 'Truck Activities in the City Centre', in OECD (1970), 108.

31 D. S. Berry, G. W. Bloome, P. W. Shuldiner and J. H. Jones, *The Technology of Urban Transportation*, Transportation Centre, Northwestern University (1963), 133n.

32 The findings of an ongoing study at Ohio University. For a report see 'Ohio University Study Urges Consolidation of City Terminals', *Transport Topics* (23 December 1973), 6.

33 M. H. Vandenberge, *Consolidation of Urban Shipments*, MS dissertation, Northwestern University (August 1973).

34 For an insider's description of the highly sophisticated operation of UPS see C.W.L. Foreman, 'Problems Associated with Urban Goods Movement at the Local Level: A Nationwide Trucking Company', in 'Urban Commodity Flow', *Highway Research Board Special Report 120*, Highway Research Board (Washington DC, 1971).

35 R. de Neufville and N. H. M. Wilson, *Analysis of Consolidation Terminals for Urban Truck Movements*, report of a feasibility study for the Transportation Administration, City of New York (1973).

36 E. M. Horwood, 'Center City Goods Movement: An Aspect of Congestion' in 'Travel Characteristics in Urban Areas', *Highway Research Board Bulletin No. 203* (Washington DC, 1958).

37 See S. K. Hicks, 'Urban Goods Movement: A Political Economists's Viewpoint', in K. W. Ogden and S. K. Hicks (eds.), *Goods Movement and Goods Vehicles in Urban Areas*, Commonwealth Bureau of Roads (Melbourne, 1975).

38 C. A. Hedges, 'Demand Forecasting and Development of a Framework for Analysis of Urban Commodity Flow: Statement of the Problem', in *Highway Research Board Special Report 120* (1971), 145.

39 See, for example: C. W. Chappell and M. T. Smith, 'Review of Urban Goods Movement Studies', *Highway Research Board Special Report 120* (1971).

40 A. H. Meyburg and P. R. Stopher, 'A Framework for the Analysis of Demand for Urban Goods Movements', *Paper to 52nd Annual Meeting, Highway Research Board*, Highway Research Board (Washington DC, 1973).

41 Source of estimate: K. T. Solomon, 'Roads and Road Use in Australia, Statistical Summary 1971', *Australian Road Research* (June 1974), 29.

42 M. Chisholm and P. O'Sullivan, *Freight Flows and Spatial Aspects of the British Economy* (Cambridge University Press, Cambridge 1973), 37.

43 B. T. Bayliss, *Methodische Probleme von Verkehrsprognosen* (Vanderhoek and Ruprecht, 1972), cited in B. T. Bayliss, book review of 'Freight Flows and Spatial Aspects of the British Economy' by M. Chisholm and P. O'Sullivan, *Journal of Transport Economics and Policy* (1974), 313. About 85–90 per cent of total British inland freight tonnage is generated by seven industrial groupings. These are: Building and construction materials; Food, drink and tobacco; Solid fuel; Metals (including iron and steel); Petroleum and petroleum products; Chemicals (including fertilizers); Machinery. A. H. Brown and A. S.

Maultby, 'Methods of Fonecasting the Quantities of Freight in Great Britain', *Statistical News*, Central Statistical Office, Great Britain (May 1974), 15.

44 W. L. Schneider, 'Studies (Notably from the Econometric Approach) of Factors Determining the Demand for Freight Transport' in Economic Research Centre, *Report of the Sixteenth Round Table on Transport Economics* (European Conference of Ministers of Transport (Paris, 1972), 36.

45 Janet Barber, *Appraisal of Existing Freight Traffic Models*, Department of the Environment, Great Britain, MAU Note 204 (1971).

46 For a description of input–output analysis in the urban context see W. Z. Hirsch, *Urban Economic Analysis*, (McGraw-Hill, New York, 1973), ch. 7 and 8.

47 M. M. Stein and E. J. Mosbaeck, 'Evaluation of Alternative Transportation Investment Decisions: Modification and Use of a Multiregional Input–Output Model', *Highway Research Record No. 348* (1971).

48 Brown and Maultby (1974).

49 M. J. Demetsky, 'The Measurement of Urban Commody Movements', *Proceedings of the 53rd Annual Meeting, Highway Research Board* (Washington DC, 1974).

50 W. I. Morrison and P. Smith, 'Non-survey Input–Output Techniques at the Small Area Level: An Evaluation', *Journal of Regional Science* (1974).

51 D. N. M. Starkie, *Traffic and Industry: A Study of Traffic Generation and Spacial Interaction*, LSE Geographical Papers No. 3 (London, 1967). See also the pioneering study, of freight traffic generation (in p.c.u.'s) by factories on industrial estates in the north-east of England, by T. E. H. Williams and J. C. R. Latchford: 'Prediction of Traffic in Industrial Areas – 2: Traffic Generation', *Traffic Engineering and Control* (January 1966).

52 Ibid., 33.

53 D. Maltby, 'Traffic at Manufacturing Plants', *Traffic Engineering and Control* (June 1970).

54 B. G. Redding, 'Traffic Generated by Industrial Premises in London', *Traffic Engineering and Control* (August, 1972).

55 S. Gaudio and E. Meko, *A Study of Plant Characteristics and Factors which Lend Themselves to an Explanation of Goods Movements at Industrial Sites*, MS thesis, Transportation Center, Northwestern University (1973).

56 A. H. Meyburg and P. R. Stopher, 'Towards Trip Attraction Models for Freight Vehicle Trips to Shopping Plazas', *Transportation Research Forum Proceedings* (1973).

57 M. Kolifrath and P. Shuldiner, 'Covariance Analysis of Manufacturing Trip Generation', *Highway Research Record No. 165* (1967).

58 Reported in Hutchinson (1974).

59 See, for example, the reports of the Transport and Road Research Laboratory's investigations of the main street in Putney, Newbury and Camberley: A. W. Christie, J. Prudhoe and M. A. Cundill, 'Urban Freight Distribution: A Study of Operations in High Street, Putney', *TRRL Report 556*, Crowthorne (1973); A. W. Christie, R. S. Bartlett, M. A. Cundhill and J. Prudhoe, 'Urban Freight Distribution: Studies of Operations in Shopping Streets at Newbury and Camberley', *TRRL Report 603*, Crowthorne (1973).

60 See T. J. Grigg, 'Modelling Land Use Activity and Urban Spatial Structure', *Proceedings of the Seventh Australian Road Research Board Conference* (Adelaide, 1974).

Notes to chapter 8

1 G. Ribrandt, 'Stordriftsfordelar Inom Industriproduktionen' (economies of scale in industrial production), SOU Stockholm, 1970.

2 L. Wingo, *Transportation and Urban Land* (Washington DC, 1961).

3 R. Muth, *Cities and Housing* (University of Chicago, 1969).

4 W. Alonso, *Location and Land Use* (Harvard Cambridge Mass., 1964).

5 E. Mills, 'An Aggregative Model of Resource Allocation in a Metropolitan Area', *American Economic Review* (1967).

6 E. Mills, *Studies in The Structure of the Urban Economy* (Johns Hopkins, Baltimore, 1972).
7 Ibid.
8 M. E. Beesley and M. Q. Dalvi, 'Spatial Equilibrium and the Journey to Work', *Journal of Transport Economics and Policy* (1974).
9 L. Lefeber, *Allocation in Space; Production, Transport and Industrial Location* (North-Holland, Amsterdam, 1958).
10 M. Beckmann and T. Koopmans, 'Assignment Problems and the Location of Economic Activities', *Econometrica* (January 1957).
11 L. Moses, 'Location and the Theory of Production', *Quarterly Journal of Economics* (1958).
12 A. E. Anderson and B. Marksjø, 'General Equilibrium Models for Allocation in Space under Interdependency and Increasing Returns to Scale', *Regional and Urban Economics* (1972).
13 Ibid., 153.
14 Other studies worthy of investigation are: J. R. Beck, and J. B. Schneider, *Reducing the Travel Requirements of the American City: An Investigation of Alternative Urban Spatial Structures.* Research Report No. 73–1 (UMTA-URT-3-73-1). Dept. of Urban Planning and Civil Engineering, University of Washington (Seattle, 1973), and R. Sharpe, and J. Brotchie, 'An Urban Systems Study', *Royal Australian Planning Institute Journal* (1972).
15 S. H. Putman, 'Preliminary Results from an Integrated Transportation and Land Use Model Package', *Transportation* (1974).
16 F. Snickars (ed.), *Dynamic Allocation in Urban Space* (Lexington, 1974).
17 A. E. Andersson, 'Towards an Integrated Theory of Inter-Sectoral and Interregional Growth', in Snickars (ed.) (1974).
18 L. Lundquist, 'Integrated Location–Transportation Analysis, a Decomposition Approach', *Regional and Urban Economics* (1973).
19 L. Lundquist, 'Transportation Analysis and Activity–Location in Land Use Planning – with Applications to the Stockholm Region', in Snickars (ed.) (1974).
20 Further details of the theoretical and empirical results regarding distributional issues ning – with Applications to the Stockholm Region', in Snickars (ed.) (1974).
21 See Lundquist (1974).
22 R. Shorpe and J. Brotchie (1972).
23 A mathematical exposition is presented in Lundquist (1973).

Notes to chapter 9

1 L. Wingo, *Transportation and Urban Land*, Resources for the Future (Washington DC, 1961).
2 W. Alonso, *Location and Land Use* (Harvard University Press, Cambridge, Mass., 1964).
3 R. Muth, *Cities and Housing* (Chicago University Press, Chicago, 1969).
4 E. S. Mills, *Studies in the Structure of the Urban Economy*, Resources for the Future (Johns Hopkins, Baltimore 1972).
5 Ibid.
6 S. Angel and Geoffrey Hyman, 'Urban Transport Expenditures', *Papers of the Regional Science Association* (1972), 105–24.
7 H. W. Richardson, Joan Vipond and Robert A. Furby, 'Determinants of Urban House Prices', *Urban Studies* (June 1974), 189–200.
8 I. S. Lowry, *Seven Models of Urban Development: A Structural Comparison*, RAND corporation (Santa Monica, September 1967), 3673.
9 Mills (1972).
10 J. Lansing, Robert W. Marans and Robert B. Zehner, *Planned Residential Environments*, Survey Research Centre (Ann Arbor, 1970).

11 See, for example, Jones, F. Lancaster, *Dimensions of Urban Social Structure – the Social Areas of Melbourne, Australia* (Australian National University Press, Canberra, 1969).
12 H. Richardson *et al.* (1974).
13 R. Muth (1969), 313.
14 W. Alonso (1964).
15 A. M. Voorhees, Salvatore J. Bellomo, Joseph L. Schofer and Donald E. Cleveland, 'Factors in Work Trip Lengths', *Highway Research Record* (1966), 24–39.
16 E. M. Hoover and Raymond Vernon, *Anatomy of a Metropolis* (Harvard University Press, Cambridge, Mass., 1959).
17 Paterson J. P., *Programming Urban Development and the Incremental Costs of Public Services, Melbourne, 1953–54 to 1965–66*, unpublished PhD thesis, Urban Research Unit, Australian National University.

Notes to chapter 10

1 This paper is a revised excerpt from Peter J. Rimmer, 'Transport Decision-Making and Its Spatial Repercussions: Shooting an Arrow at a Moving Target', *Monash Publications in Geography No. 11*, Department of Geography, Monash University, (Melbourne, 1974). Permission to republish this paper has been given by the Department of Geography, Monash University. The Department of Geography at Monash University is thanked for providing a forum for discussing these ideas. Eric Woolmington, Chris Kissling, Herb Weinand, Roger Munro, Don Seiler, Barry Johnston, Jeff Best, Ihian MacKenzie and Bill Faulkner have proved valuable sounding boards. All the figures have been drawn by Manlio Pancino, Cartographic Section, Department of Human Geography, RSPacS, The Australian National University, Canberra.
2 W. L. Garrison, 'Coupling Knowledge and Decisions', in D. R. Miller (ed.), *Urban Transportation Policy: New Perspectives*, (D.C. Heath and Company, Lexington, 1972), 37–49.
3 D. Boswell, 'Conceptions of Social Role', Open University (ed.) in *Social Interaction* (Walton Hall, 1972), 57.
4 A. H. McCarty, and J. B. Lindbergh, *A Preface to Economic Geography* (Prentice-Hall, Englewood Cliffs, 1972), 163.
5 H. A. Simon, 'Theories of Decision Making in Economics and Behavioral Science' in F. G. Castles, D. J. Murray and D. C. Potter (eds.), *Decisions, Organizations and Society* (Penguin, London, 1971), 49.
6 Sir G. Vickers, *The Art of Judgement: A Study of Policy Making* (Chapman and Hall, London 1965).
7 T. Parsons and E. A. Shils (eds.), *Toward a General Theory of Action* (Harvard University Press, Cambridge, Mass., 1951), 26.
8 H. F. Andrews, 'Consumer Behaviour and the Tertiary Activity System', in A. G. Wilson (ed.), *Urban and Regional Planning: London Papers in Regional Science* 2, 2nd edn, (Pion, London, 1972), 1–20.
9 G. M. Vernon, *Human Interaction: An Introduction to Sociology*, 2nd edn (Ronald Press, New York, 1972), 134.
10 Compare with M. L. Manheim, 'Principles of Transport Systems Analysis', *Highway Research Record No. 180* (1967), 11–20; M. L. Manheim, 'Search and Choice in Transport Systems Analysis', *Highway Research Record No. 293* (1969), 54–82.
11 H. M. Kolsen, *The Economics and Control of Road–Rail Competition: A Critical Study of Theory and Practice in the United States of America, Great Britain, and Australia* (Sydney University Press, Sydney, 1968), 62.
12 Note that the demand for transport can exist in the absence of supply. The transport of goods is, in essence, a derived demand which rests on the demand for the goods and is independent of the supply of transport.

13 Ibid., 55.
14 Vickers (1965), 23–5.
15 Ann F. Friedlaender, *The Dilemma of Freight Transport Regulation* (Brookings Institution Washington DC, 1969); K. M. Studnicki-Gizbert, 'Regulatory Policy Options in Transport', *Transportation Research Forum Proceedings*, (1971), 1–30.
16 A. G. Wilson, *et al.*, 'New Directions in Strategic Transportation Planning', in OECD, *The Urban Transportation Planning Process* (OECD, 1971), 242–8.
17 D. Harvey, *Social Justice and the City* (Edward Arnold, London, 1973), 96–118.
18 G. J. Fielding, 'Locating Urban Freeways: A Method for Resolving Conflict', in F. Horton (ed.), *Geographic Studies of Urban Transportation and Network Analysis*, Department of Geography, Northwestern University (Evanston, 1968), 76–101; M. R. Levin and N. A. Abend, *Bureaucrats in Collision: Case Studies in Area Transportation Planning*, (MIT, Cambridge, Mass., 1971).
19 N. Wengert, 'Political and Administrative Realities of Regional Transportation Planning', in J. S. DeSalvo (ed.), *Perspectives on Regional Transportation Planning* (D.C. Heath and Company, Lexington, 1973), 379–430; R. E. Kasperson and M. Breitbart, 'Participation, Decentralisation, and Advocacy Planning', *Association of American Geographers – Commission on College Geography: Resource Paper No. 25* (Washington DC, 1974).
20 M. E. Eliot Hurst, *A Geography of Economic Behaviour: An Introduction* (Duxbury Press, North Scituate, 1972), 40–67.
21 P. Healey, 'Social Impact Analysis in the Planning Process', Paper No. A95, *Australian Road Research Board Seventh Conference* (Adelaide, 1974).
22 D. Harvey, 'Social Processes, Spatial Form and the Redistribution of Real Income in an Urban System', in M. Chisholm, A. E. Frey and P. Haggett (eds.), *Regional Forecasting* (Butterworths, London, 1971), 267–300; A. J. Mumphrey and J. Wolpert, 'Equity Considerations and Concessions in the Siting of Public Facilities', *Economic Geography* (1973), 109–21.
23 G. F. White, 'Human Adjustment to Floods: A Geographical Approach to the Flood Problem in the United States', *Department of Geography, University of Chicago Research Paper No. 29* (University of Chicago, Chicago, 1945).
24 G. F. White, 'Choice of Adjustment to Floods, *Department of Geography, University of Chicago Research Paper No. 93* (University of Chicago, Chicago, 1964), 1.
25 Manheim (1969), 62.
26 Simon (1971), 51.
27 Andrews (1972), 2–3.
28 P. J. Runkel and J. E. McGrath, *Research on Human Behavior: A Systematic Guide to Method* (Holt, Rinehart and Winston, New York, 1972).
29 P. J. Rimmer, 'Government Influence on Transport Decision-Making in Thailand', in G. J. R. Linge and P. J. Rimmer (eds.), *Government Influence and the Location of Economic Activity*, Department of Human Geography Publication HG/5, RSPacS (The Australian National University, Canberra, 1971), 325–57.
30 M. E. Eliot Hurst, 'Transportation and the Societal Framework', *Economic Geography* (1973), 171.
31 D. A. Hensher and P. B. McLeod, 'Approaches to Modelling Consumer Preferences and Demand in Transportation', *Australian Transportation Research Forum* (Sydney, April 1974).
32 Compare with A. J. Blackburn, 'A Non-Linear Model of the Demand for Travel', in R. E. Quandt (ed.), *The Demand for Travel: Theory and Estimation* (D.C. Heath and Company, Lexington, 1970), 163–80; A. J. Blackburn, 'An Alternative Approach to Aggregation and Estimation in the Non-Linear Model', in Quandt (ed.) (1970), 181–96.
33 E. K. Morlok, *An Analysis of Transport Technology and Network Structure*, The Transportation Center (Northwestern University, Evanston, 1970). 21.

34 See Morlok (1970), 13–21; M. Wohl and B. V. Martin, *Traffic Systems Analysis for Engineers and Planners* (McGraw-Hill, New York, 1967), 374–95.
35 G. Kraft, J. R. Meyer and J. P. Valette, *The Role of Transportation in Regional Economic Development* (D.C. Heath and Company, Lexington. 1971).
36 Harvey (1973), 96–118.
37 W. Isard, *General Theory: Social, Political, Economic and Regional with Particular Reference to Decision Making Analysis* (MIT, Cambridge, Mass., 1969); M. J. Webber, *Impact of Uncertainty on Location* (Australian National University, Canberra, 1972); R. H. Ballou, *Business Logistics Management* (Prentice-Hall, Englewood Cliffs, 1973).
38 J. W. Forrester, *Principles of Systems: Text and Workbook* (Wright-Allen Press, Cambridge, Mass., 1968).
39 Webber (1972).
40 J. W. Forrester, *Industrial Dynamics* (MIT, Cambridge, Mass., 1961), 102–3.
41 Ibid., 61–3; C. McMillan and R. F. Gonzalez, *Systems Analysis: A Computer Approach to Decision Models*, revised edn (Richard D. Irwin, Homewood, 1968), 265–89.
42 G. Chadwick, *A Systems View of Planning: Towards a Theory of the Urban and Regional Planning Process* (Pergamon, Oxford, 1971), 171–8.
43 Forrester (1961), 15–16.
44 Andrews (1972), 4.
45 Andrews (1972).
46 R. J. Chorley and Barbara A. Kennedy, *Physical Geography: A Systems Approach* (Prentice-Hall International, London, 1971), 251–4.
47 R. G. Golledge, L. A. Brown and F. Williamson, 'Behavioural Approaches in Geography: An Overview', *The Australian Geographer* (1972), 59–79.
48 Chadwick (1971), 8.
49 D. L. Meadows, *Dynamics of Commodity Production Cycles* (Wright-Allen Press, Cambridge, Mass., 1970), 4–9.
50 R. L. Meek, *Figuring Out Society* (Fontana/Collins, 1971), 74–82; P. A. Samuelson *et al.*, *Economics*, Australian Edition (McGraw-Hill, Sydney, 1970), 442–4.
51 Meadows (1970), 11.
52 Personal communication from Don Seiler.
53 Meadows (1970), 19–35.
54 Forrester (1961), 50–1.
55 R. E. Johnson, F. E. Kast and J. E. Rosenweing, *The Theory and Management of Systems*, 2nd edn (McGraw-Hill, New York, 1967).
56 W. Alonso, 'Markets and Planning Regions for Transportation', in DeSalvo (ed.) (1973), 177–93.
57 D. M. Smith, *The Geography of Well-Being in the United States: An Introduction to Territorial Social Indicators* (McGraw-Hill, New York, 1973); I. D. Illich, *Energy and Equality* (Calder and Boyars, London, 1974).
58 DeSalvo (ed.) (1973), 17.
59 H. C. Kellman, 'Societal, Attitudinal and Structural Factors in International Relations', *Journal of Social Issues* (1955), 42–56.
60 Chorley and Kennedy (1971), 116.
61 G. H. Orcutt *et al.*, *Microanalysis of Socioeconomic systems: A Simulation Study* (Harper and Brothers, New York, 1961).
62 Chadwick (1971), 364–73.
63 A. J. Catanese and A. W. Steiss, *Systemic Planning: Theory and Application* (D.C. Heath and Company, Lexington, 1973), 302–19.
64 R. L., Ackoff, *A Concept of Corporate Planning* (Wiley Interscience, New York, 1970), 1–21.
65 E. Jantsch, *Technological Planning and Social Futures* (Associated Business Programmes, London, 1972), 27–61.

66 A. Etzioni. *The Active Society: A Theory of Societal and Political Processes* (Collier-Macmillan, New York 1968).
67 Chadwick (1971), 301–19.
68 Wilson, *et al.* (1971).
69 A. G. Wilson, 'Models in Urban Planning: A Synoptic Review of Recent Literature', *Urban Studies* (1968), 250–5.
70 Manheim (1969).
71 W. L. Garrison, 'Fragments on Future Transportation Policy and Programs', *Economic Geography* (1973), 95–102.
72 Ackoff (1970), 128–38.
73 W. J. Murin, *Mass Transit Policy Planning: An Incremental Approach* (D. C. Heath and Company, Lexington, 1971).
74 Garrison (1973).
75 J. W. Drake, *The Administration of Transportation Modelling Projects* (D. C. Heath and Company, Lexington, 1973).
76 F. E. Emery, 'The Next Thirty Years: Concepts, Methods and Anticipations', *Human Relations* (1967), 202.
77 Isard (1969); Wengert (1973).
78 Wilson, *et al.* (1971).

Notes to chapter 11

1 *Acknowledgement.* Many people have helped me in the formulation of my ideas on the subject of this chapter. Particular debts are owed to John Stanley and David Hensher, of the Australian Commonwealth Bureau of Roads, and Ross King of the Centre for Environmental Studies, Melbourne University.
2 Donald A. Schon, *Beyond the Stable State: Public and Private Learning in a Changing Society* (Temple Smith, London, 1971).
3 R. Pahl. Review of *Citizens in Conflict*, by J. M. Simmie (Hutchinson, London, 1971), in *The Planner* (December 1974), 968.
4 K. Mannheim, *Ideology and Utopia* (Routledge and Kegan Paul, London, 1968).
5 This definition excludes psychology as a *social* science, except in so far as it relates the study of individual behaviour to the social context within which it is manifested.
6 System is here a heuristic device, and has no other connotation. It may refer to minimal interaction sets, social institutions as complexes of role relations organised around common goals or purposes, larger and more aggregate sub-system (agglomerates of institutions) or total national or international social systems. It indicates no more than the interconnectedness of elements of the social universe.
7 This is, of course, not the same as saying that social relationships or social systems are solely the product of the intentions of social actors.
8 M. Weber, *The Theory of Social and Economic Organization* (Free Press, US, 1947). Excerpted in L. A. Coser and B. Rosenberg, *Sociological Theory: A Book of Readings* 2nd edn (Macmillan, New York, 1964), 66–71.
9 K. Mannheim (1968), preface by Louis Wirth, xxiii.
10 Despite its problematic nature, the concept of a paradigm remains a challenging analytical construct. For a discussion of the concept see: T. S. Kuhn, *The Structure of Scientific Revolutions*, 2nd edn (University of Chicago Press, Chicago, 1970).
11 K. Mannheim (1968), preface by Louis Wirth, xxiv.
12 For a discussion of these models and their conservative implication, see D. Martindale, *The Nature and Types of Sociological Theory* (Routledge and Kegan Paul, 1970), part two and part six.
13 J. Rex, *Key Problems of Sociological Theory* (Routledge and Kegan Paul, London 1970). Rex details the organic analogy in the following way (p. 63):

	Biological Organism	*Social Organism*
Units	Cell	Individual Human Being
Structure	Relations between cells	Relations between human beings
Activities	Observed behaviour of cells	Observed behaviour of human beings and groups
Functions	Activities role in maintaining the structure or correspondence between the effects of the activity and the needs of the structure	Activities role in maintaining the social structure or correspondence between the effects of the activity and the needs of the social structure.

14 Lewis A. Coser, *The Functions of Social Conflict* (Free Press, US, 1956).

15 T. Parsons, *Societies: Evolutionary and Comparative Perspectives* (Prentice-Hall, Englewood Cliffs, 1966), 10.

16 Rex (1970), 129–31.

17 The phases are adopted in broad outline from the work of W. Hansen of A. M. Voorhees and Associates Inc. reported in J. R. Evans, *Report on the U.S. Multi-Regional Project on Urban Transportation*, Australian Department of Transportation (mimeo) (1974).

18 A contemporary example of this is Australia, where the overall development lags behind the USA, but where, internally, Federal agencies lead state organisations.

19 D. W. Pearce, *Cost Benefit Analysis* (Macmillan, London, 1971), 18.

20 For a discussion of aspects of this issue, see Maruyama, 'Hierarchists, and Mutualists: Three Paradigms Among Planners', *Futures* (April 1974), 103–13.

21 The classic statement of this view is that of D. Bell, *The End of Ideology: On The Exhaustion of political Ideas in the Fifties*, revised edn (New York, 1961).

22 S. J. Bellomo, S. C. Lockwood and M. S. Goldberg, *Metropolitan Transportation and Land Use Planning*, p. 5–10, in Transport and Environment Conference Proceedings, Southampton University, England (1972).

23 These issues are indicated in: S. C. Lockwood, *Participation: Its Influence on Planning Methodology*, in Citizen Participation in Transportation Planning, Special Report 142, Highway Research Board (Washington DC, 1973), 116–20. The other papers in this Special Report are also highly relevant to these questions.

24 This rejection is based in part on the realisation that market forces do not represent free preferences by consumers which will be coordinated by an invisible hand into maximum and *general* social welfare, but rather are the consequence of manipulation of consumption by powerful sectional interests. 'The initiative in deciding what is to be produced comes not from the sovereign consumer who, through the market, issues the instructions that bend the productive mechanism to his ultimate will. Rather it comes from the great producing organizations which reach forward to control the markets that it is to serve.' J. K. Galbraith, *The New Industrial Estate* (Penguin, London, 1970), 18.

25 A. Voorhees and Associates Inc., *A Study Design for Planning and Programming of Transportation in Cities*. Report prepared for the Australian Commonwealth Bureau of Roads (1974).

26 D. W. Pearce (1971), 18.

27 J. Plamenatz, *Man and Society* (Longmans, London, 1963) vol. two, 11–12.

28 Ibid., 12, 13.

29 M. Maruyama (1974).

30 P. Weiner *et al.*, *Non User Factors in Highway Planning* (University of Connecticut, USA, 1970).

31 These are clumsy terms, but the ideas they represent are of considerable interest to transport planning. For a discussion of them, see M. Maruyama, 'Endogenous Research vs "Experts" From Outside', *Futures* (October 1974), 389–94.

32 Questions of ethics in sociological research are considered in I. L. Horowitz (ed.),

The Use and Abuse of Social Science (Transaction Books, New Brunswick, 1971); and I. L. Horowitz, ed., *The Rise and Fall of Project Camelot* (MIT, Cambridge, Mass., 1970).

33 C. Bell and H. Newby, *Community Studies* (Allen and Unwin, London, 1971).

34 M. Stacey, 'The Myth of Community Studies', *British Journal of Sociology*, 20 (1969), 134–47. 137.

35 MSJ Keys Young Planners Pty Ltd, *Social Impact Analysis*, Australian Commonwealth Bureau of Roads (1974).

36 S. Encel, *Equality and Authority: A Study of Class, Status and Power in Australia* (Cheshire, Melbourne; 1970), 6.

37 T. B. Bottomore, *Sociology* (Allen and Unwin, London, 1962), 179.

38 E. J. Mishan, *What is Wrong with Roskill?* in R. Layard ed., *Cost Benefit Analysis* (Penguin, London, 1972), 452–72, 462.

39 Ibid., 471.

40 D. W. Pearce, 'An Incompatability in Planning for a Steady State and Planning for Maximum Welfare', *Environment and Planning* (1973), 267–71. 267.

41 Ibid., 268.

42 Ibid., 270.

43 This model has emerged in the USA where transport planning, unlike the UK, has not been dominated by cost–benefit analysis.

44 US Department of Transportation, Federal Highway Administration, *Guide for Highway Impact Studies* (Washington DC, 1972), I–2.

45 Ibid., II–I.

46 Ibid., III–A–I.

47 L. A. Coser (1956) excerpted in Coser and Rosenberg (1964), 205–9. p. 205.

48 M. Stacey (1969), 137.

49 R. Frankenberg, *Communities in Britain: Social Life in Town and Country* (Penguin, London, 1969).

50 M. Stacey (1969), 139.

51 Ibid., 139.

52 J. M. Thomson, 'Halfway to a Motorized Society,' in J. B. Cullingworth, ed., *Problems of an Urban Society*, vol. 3 (Allen and Unwin, London, 1973), 142–61. 146.

53 Highway Research Board, *Costs and Benefits of Transportation Planning*, Report No. 314 (Washington DC, 1970), foreword.

54 M. Maruyama (1974).

55 H. Gans, *People and Plans* (Penguin, London, 1972) 1.

56 For an examination of the Sociological concern with these issues see: R. E. Pahl, 'Urban Social Theory and Research, *Environment and Planning*, vol. 1, 143–53 (1969); and R. E. Pahl, *Whose City*? (Longman, London, 1970).

57 A. Voorhees *et al.* (1974).

58 I. Illich, *Energy and Equity* (Calder and Boyars, London, 1974).

59 J. W. Drake, *The Administration of Transportation Modelling Projects* (Lexington, 1973), 39.

60 I. Illich (1974), 24.

61 J. W. Drake (1973), 1.

62 E. J. Mishan (1972), 454.

63 M. Rein 'Social Planning: the Search for Legitimacy', *Journal of the American Institute of Planners* (1969), 233–44, reprinted in M. Stewart (ed.), *The City* (Penguin, London, 1973), 425–52.

64 H. Gans (1972), 104.

65 B. Russell, *History of Western Philosophy* (Unwin University Books, London, 1971), 117.

66 F. Engels, *Socialism, Utopian and Scientific*, in Marx and Engels', Selected Works (Lawrence and Wishart, 1970), 375–428.

67 M. Stewart, ed. (1973), intro., 24.

68 A. Powell, 'National Urban Strategy', *Royal Australian Planning Institute Journal* (January 1974), 8–10. 10.

Notes to chapter 12

1 The research for and writing of this paper was undertaken while John Beggs was on leave from the Main Roads Department, Queensland, Australia.

2 Some problems relating to the adequacy of such underlying data for the case of the Australian capital cities are discussed in Appendix B of 'A Study of Trends in Employment and Land Use in Australian Capital Cities', a report submitted to the Commonwealth Bureau of Roads (October 1971), by G. Dowcra, K. Davidson, A. Duhs and M. Philpott, Department of Economics, University of Queensland.

3 For example, six or eight income group – car ownership categories might be distinguished and a specific trip production and modal split pattern established for each.

4 Including parking fees, public transport fares, frequency of service, comfort and speed.

5 Thus public transport fares could be set at zero in the future if desired, or all-day parking charges at many times their present level.

6 What is the aggregate social cost of a scheme which resumes houses from little old ladies who say they would not voluntarily shift at *any* price?

7 W. M. Rahmann, 'Cities, Freeways, and the Something for Nothing Syndrome', paper presented to Section 24, *Australian and New Zealand Association for the Advancement of Science Conference* (August 1973).

8 For an excellent survey on this topic see G. Weinschenck, W. Henrichsmeyer and F. Aldinger, 'The Theory of Spatial Equilibrium and Optimal Location in Agriculture: A Survey', *Review of Marketing and Agricultural Economics* (March 1969).

9 *Perth Regional Transportation Study (PERTS)*, prepared for West Australian Department of Transport (1970); and, *Perth Regional Transport Study, 1972.*

10 This view has also been offered very forcefully by J. Paterson, 'Predictive Errors Arising from Transportation Study Techniques with Special Reference to Melbourne', *Proceedings of the 5th Australian Road Research Board Conference* (1970).

11 Recent work in the examination of appropriate transformations for travel demand analysis is found in L. E. Shepherd, 'An Econometric Approach to the Demand for Urban Travel', *Proceedings of the 6th Australian Road Research Board Conference* (1972), Paper No. 913; and L. E. Shepherd, 'A Probabilistic Aggregate Travel Demand Model', in D. A. Hensher (ed.), *Urban Travel Choice and Demand Modelling*, Australian Road Research Board Special Report. No. 12 (August 1974), 1–24. Another useful approach to determining the shape of response surfaces is found in W. J. White, 'The Use of Multi-Dimensional Cubic Spline Functions for Regression and Smoothing', *The Australian Computer Journal* (May 1971), 81–8.

12 With a few minor exceptions in the Study.

13 H. J. Wootton, and G. W. Pick, 'A Model for Trips Generated by Households', *Journal of Transport Economics and Policy* (1967), 137–53; A. A. Douglas and R. J. Lewis, 'Trip Generation Techniques: Category Analysis', *Traffic Engineering and Control* (February 1971), 532–5; S. Golding, 'A Category Analysis Approach to Trip Generation', *Proceedings of the 6th Australian Road Research Board Conference* (1972), A. K. Kafani, 'An Aggregative Model of Trip Making', *Transportation Research* (1972), 119–24.

14 Y. W. Oi and P. W. Shuldiner, *An Analysis of Urban Travel Demands* (Northwestern University Press, 1962), 51–7. Growth factor methods were employed in major transportation studies for the cities of Detroit and Cleveland, Ohio.

15 S. Eilon, R. P. R. Tilley, and T. R. Fowkes, 'Analysis of a Gravity Demand Model', *Regional Studies* (1969), 115.

16 J. Q. Stewart, 'Empirical Mathematical Rules Concerning the Distribution and Equilibrium of Population', *Geographic Review* (1947), cited from W. Isard, 'Distance Inputs in the Space Economy', *Quarterly Journal of Economics* (1951), 183.

17 See W. Isard, 'Distance Inputs in a Space Economy' (1951), 182. For some further discussion of empirical distributions see Y. Zahavi, 'Introducing the Idea of the *K* Distribu-

tion to Transportation Patterns', *Highway Research Record No. 322*, Washington DC, Highway Research Board (1970).

18 A. G. Wilson, *Entropy in Urban and Regional Modelling* (Pion, 1971). The relationship between the traditional utility concept and the entropy concept is shown by S. Hansen, 'Utility, Accessibility and Entropy in Spatial Modelling', *Swedish Journal of Economics* (1972).

19 P. M. Fisher and J. Paterson, 'Evaluating the Wilson Derived Gravity Model', *Proceedings of the 6th Australian Road Research Board Conference*, Paper no. 840 (1972).

20 N. Georgescu-Roegen, *The Entropy Law and the Economic Process* (Harvard University Press, Cambridge, Mass., 1971), ch. 4.

21 This was developed for the Chicago Area Transportation Study (1960), vol. 2.

22 *Hobart Area Transportation Study* (Wilbur Smith & Associates, 1964). *Brisbane Transportation Study* (Wilbur-Smith and Associates, 1965).

23 See A. Duhs, H. Kolsen and G. Docwra, 'A Critique of Brisbane's Transportation Studies', *Economic Analysis and Policy* (March 1971).

24 By 1970/71 Brisbane bus patronage had already fallen below the level predicted by BTS for 1981. BTS forecast a 9% decline between 1964 and 1981.

25 The Brisbane Transportation Study simply accepts that public transport has been accounting for a declining proportion of overall trips, and that this decline will continue inexorably from 45% in 1960 and 30% in 1964 to 15% in 1981.

26 L. A. Duhs and M. J. Gibbings, 'An Enquiry Into Modal Choice in Brisbane Passenger Transport', University of Queensland (January 1973). Other Studies have used direct survey methods: T. F. Golob, E. T. Canty and R. G. Gustafson, 'An Analysis of Consumer Preferences for Public Transport System', *Transportation Research* (1971), 81–102; S. J. Hille and T. K. Martin, 'Consumer Preferences in Transportation', *Highway Research Record No. 197*, Washington DC, Highway Research Board (1967), 36.

27 D. A. Quarmby and P. T. McIntosh, 'Generalized Costs and the Estimation of Movement Benefits and Costs in Transport Planning', *Highway Research Record No. 383*, Washington DC, Highway Research Board (1972), 12.

28 See for example K. E. Cook and P. A. Rush, 'Consumer Awareness of Motor Fuel Tax Rates and Prices', *Highway Research Record No. 138*, Washington DC, Highway Research Board (1963); M. Wohl, 'Users of Urban Transportation Services and their Incomes', *Traffic Quarterly*, vol. 24 (1970); A. Lansing and J. Hendricks, 'How People Perceive the Cost of the Journey to Work', *Highway Research Record No. 197*, Washington DC, Highway Research Board (1967), 55.

29 If this (hypothetical) approximation to consumer sovereignty is rejected here, it is not clear what implicit value judgements can be substantiated in the subsequent cost–benefit type evaluation of the welfare effects of the alternative plans under consideration.

30 See D. A. Hensher, 'Review of Studies Leading to Existing Values of Travel Time', *Valuation of Travel Time*, Transportation Research Board Special Report, Washington DC, Transportation Research Board (1977).

31 D. G. Tipping, 'Time Savings in Transport Studies', *Economic Journal* (1968).

32 Average work trip length by car is given as just under fifteen minutes, and a high proportion of total time-savings may be expected to accrue in (relatively valueless) individual lumps of 0–5 minutes. See also table one in D. A. Hensher and W. E. Hotchkiss, 'Choice of Mode and the Value of Travel Time Savings for the Journey to Work', *Economic Record* (March 1974).

33 Including capitalisation to a terminal value of different benefit streams at STP and SOP respectively. The 'normalisation procedure' reveals deficiencies in the non-normalised criteria that have been in standard use, but may not itself be definitive. Procedural problems exist when the common time period 'beyond which no further reversal of ranking' can occur in so far distant in time as to conflict with common sense.

This problem cannot be expounded here, but see Mishan's *Cost-Benefit Analysis* (Allen and Unwin, London, 1971), chs. 34–6.

34 The necessary number of trials will vary, being dictated by costs of simulation trials and by the need to obtain statistically meaningful results.

35 Note the endless array of products that can be offered via varying the quality of 'the product', e.g. buses do not have to be of the present shape and size, and the introduction of mini-buses, different road regulations, headway times, and distance between stops etc. would all influence the overall cost–benefit picture. The *Merseyside Area Land Use Transportation Study* (Traffic Research Corporation Ltd. 1969, Technical Report No. 15) offers more than most studies in the way of evaluation of particular system components; three rail links were deleted from one option in order to increase the overall rate of return of that option.

36 Note that the *Hong Kong Mass Transport Study* (Freeman, Fox, Wilbur Smith & Associates, 1967) argues that a rail rapid transit system is necessary for Hong Kong on the ground that a surface road transport system would be more expensive (and more land consuming) while to do nothing would be to allow the city to run to a halt. A capital intensive, forty-mile-long rail transit system is accordingly recommended, and 'validated' by certain calculations of the internal rate of return to be attributed to the system. Although it is stated that several alternative plans were tested, no details of such plans are offered and there are certainly no comparative economic evaluations of such alternatives. The implication is that Hong Kong *has* to have a rail transit system and there is no remaining scope for choice between rail systems of various shapes, sizes and qualities. Indeed the 4.2% internal rate of return might have been given as – 196%, these being the two real roots of the 36th order polynomial in question.

37 Note that only 50% of p.m. peak car trips in Perth are work journeys.

38 The 1970 recommended plan advocated the use of the existing suburban rail right-of-way for a new bitumen right-of-way for bus rapid transit.

39 *Perth Regional Transport Study*, 1972.

40 The selection of the bus way scheme in the first place was without any comprehensive sensitivity analysis.

41 See A. Duhs, H. Kolsen and G. Docwra (1971).

42 *Adelaide Transportation 1970 Report*, Social Technology Systems Inc., Massachusetts.

43 For example, there is no appraisal of a bus rapid-transit system on the 1965 freeway system.

44 Pollution cost would further increase this 12.8¢ figure.

45 Or a fear of political difficulties of course.

46 These sensitivity results should not be construed as a complete evaluation of the whole Brisbane freeway plan. A more comprehensive empirical illustration of such sensitivity analysis may be found in Cassidy, Rodgers, and McCarthy 'A Simulation Approach to Rish Assessment in Investment Analysis', *Journal of Marketing and Agricultural Economics* (March 1970). See also McCarthy, Ferguson and Cassidy 'Sensitivity of Plant Location Solutions to Changes in Raw Product Supplies' *Journal of Marketing and Agricultural Economics* (September 1971); and, Shlomo Reutlinger, *Techniques for Project Appraisal Under Uncertainty*, World Bank Staff Occasional Papers, no. 10 (Johns Hopkins Press, 1970).

47 See W. M. Rahmann (1973), for comments on the technology of freeway interchanges, 'overloaded' moderate speed freeways, etc.

Index